The Limits of
Coercive Diplomacy

D1715352

SECOND EDITION

The Limits of
Coercive Diplomacy

EDITED BY
Alexander L. George and
William E. Simons

WITH CONTRIBUTIONS BY

David K. Hall	Richard Herrmann
Bruce W. Jentleson	Paul Gordon Lauren
Scott D. Sagan	Tim Zimmermann

Westview Press
BOULDER • SAN FRANCISCO • OXFORD

Copyright © 1994 by Westview Press, Inc.

Published in 1994 in the United States of America by Westview Press, Inc., 5500 Central Avenue, Boulder, Colorado 80301-2877, and in the United Kingdom by Westview Press, 36 Lonsdale Road, Summertown, Oxford OX2 7EW

First edition published in 1971 by Little, Brown & Co.

Library of Congress Cataloging-in-Publication Data
The Limits of coercive diplomacy / edited by Alexander L. George and
    William E. Simons ; with contributions by David K. Hall ... [et
    al.] — 2nd ed.
        p.   cm.
    Rev. ed. of: The limits of coercive diplomacy / by Alexander L.
George, David K. Hall, William E. Simons. 1971.
    Includes bibliographical references and index.
    ISBN 0-8133-1786-X. — ISBN 0-8133-1787-8 (pbk.)
    1. United States—Foreign relations—1945–1989.   I. George,
Alexander L.   II. Simons, William E.   III. George, Alexander L.
Limits of coercive diplomacy.
JX1417.G45   1994
327.2'0973—dc20   93-26472
                                                                        CIP

Printed and bound in the United States of America

The paper used in this publication meets the requirements
of the American National Standard for Permanence of Paper
for Printed Library Materials Z39.48-1984.

10   9   8   7   6   5   4   3   2

For Mary and John
—*A.L.G.*

For Mike, Eric, and Kendall
—*W.E.S.*

Contents

Preface

This book updates and considerably expands *The Limits of Coercive Diplomacy* (Boston: Little, Brown, 1971), coauthored by Alexander L. George, David K. Hall, and William E. Simons, which has been out of print since the late 1970s. The framework and analysis of coercive diplomacy developed in that book have held up rather well, and the book continues to be widely cited in related research studies. But it has been clear for some time that a major expansion and reworking of the text was needed.

The 1971 book contained studies of only three cases in which the strategy of coercive diplomacy was employed by the United States—in the Laos crisis of 1961, in the Cuban Missile Crisis of 1962, and against North Vietnam in early 1965. All three of these earlier case studies have been updated and revised on the basis of new primary source data and secondary accounts. In addition, four new case studies have been prepared for this volume: the effort to use coercive diplomacy against Japan in 1941, which boomeranged; the Reagan administration's attempt to coerce the Sandinista regime in Nicaragua; that same administration's coercive pressure against Libya, which culminated in the air strikes of 1986; and the U.N.-supported use of coercive diplomacy against Iraq in the Persian Gulf crisis of 1990–1991.

The opening chapter of the first edition, "The Development of Strategy," which provided a timely context for the newly developing interest in coercive diplomacy in the 1960s, seems no longer necessary in the 1990s and has been eliminated from the present edition. The theoretical framework of coercive diplomacy has been much improved and is the major focus of Part One. The addition of a new chapter by Paul Gordon Lauren analyzing the experience with ultimata during the nineteenth and early twentieth centuries provides a historical context for the study that was lacking in the 1971 edition. Finally, the statement of findings regarding the context-dependent nature of the strategy of coercive diplomacy, the various constraints and obstacles it encounters, and the conditions that favor its success has been considerably elaborated for Part Three of the present study. A short essay giving a preview of some aspects of the present study was published in 1991 by the United States Institute of Peace under the title *Forceful Persuasion: Coercive Diplomacy as an Alternative to War.*

I would like to express appreciation to the Carnegie Corporation of New York for a grant that made this study possible and to the United States Institute of Peace for the award of a Distinguished Fellowship (1990–1992) and for the provision of a stimulating and congenial atmosphere in which to work. I would like to thank the contributors to this volume for essays that I believe notably enrich our understanding of coercive diplomacy. In particular, I express my deep appreciation to William Simons for assuming responsibility as coeditor when, as the project neared completion, I was sidelined for several months by surgery. He reviewed and improved drafts of Parts One and Two of the study and made a valuable contribution as coauthor of Part Three.

We are indebted to Rachelle Marshall for her careful editing of the entire manuscript, to Arlee Ellis for expediting administrative services with her customary skill and good cheer, and to David Joel for preparation of the index. Finally, I would like to thank Jennifer Knerr and her colleagues at Westview Press for making publication of the study so pleasant an experience.

Alexander L. George
Stanford, California

Introduction: The Limits of Coercive Diplomacy

ALEXANDER L. GEORGE

In February 1993, when the Clinton administration decided to take a more assertive role in the Bosnian crisis, it embarked implicitly on a variant of coercive diplomacy. The problems the administration encountered in directing its initiative at the opponent and in mobilizing Western allies behind its strategy are illustrative of the kinds of complexities and constraints affecting the implementation of coercive diplomacy that we explore in this book. By demanding that the Bosnian combatants guarantee humanitarian access to the beleaguered villagers and accept the territorial settlement outlined in the United Nations/European Community (U.N./EC) peace plan, and backing these demands with allusions to a possible punitive use of airpower and calls for tougher economic sanctions, the United States undertook what we call a "try-and-see" variant of the strategy. Early in April, a modest escalation of the coercive pressure came via U.S. success in getting the U.N. Security Council to authorize military enforcement of the "no-fly zone" it had first declared in October 1992.

As of early summer 1993, however, it appeared unlikely that a stronger coercive strategy would be adopted. The Clinton administration felt politically constrained to act only as a member of a Western coalition, and the European partners objected to proposed actions to increase military pressure on the Serbs. To further complicate an already complex situation, the proper focus for harsher coercive measures became murky as the Bosnian Croats resumed their version of "ethnic cleansing" against Muslim villages in an effort, like that of the Bosnian Serbs, to take control of more territory than provided for in the U.N./EC plan. Moreover, whereas the prospect of direct military action against one or more of the aggressors appeared likely to fan the flames of ethnic nationalism in the region, stiffer economic sanctions imposed against

1

Serbia seemed to influence the leadership of that country to come out in support of the U.N. solution and, for awhile, to press the Bosnian Serbs to agree. However, the Western governments' follow-on strategy remained in a state of flux, and it appeared increasingly likely that the Serbs and Croats would retain much of the Bosnian territory that their forces had seized.

As this example shows, coercive diplomacy, or coercive persuasion as some prefer to call it, is not an esoteric concept. The use of intimidation of one kind or another in order to get others to comply with one's wishes is an everyday occurrence in human affairs. What we refer to here as coercive diplomacy has often been employed in the long history of international conflict, sometimes successfully and sometimes not. The general intent of coercive diplomacy is to back a demand on an adversary with a threat of punishment for noncompliance that will be credible and potent enough to persuade him that it is in his interest to comply with the demand.

The essentials of coercive diplomacy have long been known, although the use of diplomacy in the European balance-of-power era was evidently not systematically articulated or evaluated. Rather, it was part of the conventional wisdom and accumulated experience of statesmen and diplomats of that era. Properly analyzed and compared, however, earlier historical cases of efforts at coercive diplomacy can contribute to a more refined understanding of the uses and limitations of this strategy as an instrument of foreign policy.

Coercive diplomacy bears a close resemblance to the ultimatum, which was often employed in the conduct of European diplomacy. A full-blown ultimatum has three components: a specific demand on the opponent, a time limit for compliance, and a threat of punishment for noncompliance. Not all of these components are always present in efforts at coercive diplomacy, however. In consequence, as discussed in Chapter 2, there are several variants of the strategy; each is illustrated in the case studies presented in Part Two.

In Chapter 1 I provide the conceptual groundwork for the study. Coercive diplomacy is defined as a defensive strategy and is distinguished from other nonmilitary strategies for preventing opponents from altering status quo situations in their own favor. In this chapter I also distinguish coercive diplomacy from exclusive reliance on military force to deal with opponents' actions and, in this connection, indicate why policy makers often regard it as an attractive alternative to war. It should be kept in mind that coercive diplomacy is essentially a diplomatic strategy, one that relies on the threat of force rather than the use of force to achieve the objective. If force must be used to strengthen diplomatic efforts at persuasion, it is employed in an exemplary manner, in the form of a quite limited military action, to demonstrate resolution and willingness to escalate to high levels of military action if necessary.

Chapter 2 takes up the complex, murky question of the relationship between the theory and practice of coercive diplomacy. This discussion is based on the fundamental proposition that theory, in any of its forms and even in its most developed stage, cannot serve as a substitute for the judgment that a decision maker must make in deciding whether and how to employ coercive diplomacy in any particular situation. Theory can aid in making such judgments, but the decision maker is nonetheless left with the need to understand the specific configuration of a particular situation well enough to judge whether coercive diplomacy is likely to be a viable strategy and to formulate a workable, specific version of the strategy.

In brief, good theory can help to bridge the gap between theory and practice, but it cannot eliminate that gap. A moment's reflection should serve to underline the accuracy of this observation. After all, as is so often stressed, theory must necessarily simplify the reality it addresses. Theory can seldom—and indeed it does not attempt to—encapsulate all the variables and conditions that can influence the outcomes of interaction between states. In addition, as theorists of international conflict relations have noted, the outcomes of that interaction are generally indeterminate. Events and relevant variables outside the direct influence of the actors can significantly affect the consequences of their interaction.

All this does not imply that theory is irrelevant to policy making. Theory can make a useful contribution to the analysis of a specific situation that policy makers must undertake in order to identify and diagnose its special configuration—how it is similar to and different from other cases. In addition to contributing to the diagnostic function of policy making, theory may also help policy makers judge whether the general model of coercive diplomacy can be adapted and tailored to fit the characteristics of the case at hand.

Accordingly, Chapter 2 starts with a description of the abstract, general model of coercive diplomacy and discusses its uses and limitations for policy making. Viewed as a deductive theory, this abstract model is not developed fully enough to allow reliable predictions to be made regarding the success of coercive diplomacy in each situation in which its use might be considered. Nor is the abstract model by itself capable of providing explanations for actual cases in which coercive diplomacy succeeded or failed. Nonetheless, the abstract model does identify the key variables of coercive diplomacy and the general "logic" associated with its efficacy. As a result, the abstract model has a number of important potential uses for policy making (as well as limitations that must be recognized); these uses are discussed in Chapter 2. Chapter 2 also emphasizes another fundamental point—namely, that the abstract model is not itself a strategy of coercive diplomacy—and discusses four tasks that the policy maker must accomplish in order to convert the abstract model into a specific strategy of coercive diplomacy.

Finally, in Chapter 2 I discuss the need for an empirical theory of coercive diplomacy that provides generic knowledge of the conditions under which the strategy is likely to succeed or to fail. Empirical knowledge of this kind can be derived from a systematic analysis of historical experience; it is informed in part by the framework of the abstract model and in part by the addition of other variables not encompassed by that model. To this end, we have included in Part Two seven historical cases in which the United States attempted some variant of coercive diplomacy. The contributions of these cases to empirical theory and generic knowledge are presented in Part Three.

Like our earlier edition, the present study focuses entirely on post–World War II cases in which the United States attempted to employ coercive diplomacy against a state perceived to be a threat to its interests. A much broader set of historical cases, some going back to the nineteenth century and involving actors other than the United States, is discussed by Paul Gordon Lauren in Chapter 3. This chapter provides perspective on the origins and varieties of international political behavior that is closely akin to coercive diplomacy—particularly as practiced by European statesmen in the decades between the Napoleonic Wars and World War II.

PART ONE

1

Coercive Diplomacy: Definition and Characteristics

ALEXANDER L. GEORGE

THE CONCEPT OF COERCIVE DIPLOMACY

First we need to clarify how we are using the concept of coercive diplomacy in this study and to differentiate it from other ways in which threats are used as an instrument of policy.[1] In this study, we restrict the definition of the term *coercive diplomacy* to defensive uses of the strategy—that is, efforts to persuade an opponent to stop or reverse an action. Defensive uses are quite distinct from offensive ones, wherein coercive threats can be employed aggressively to persuade a victim to give up something of value without putting up resistance. Such offensive uses of coercive threats are better designated by the term *blackmail strategy.*

Coercive diplomacy also needs to be distinguished from deterrence, a strategy that employs threats to dissuade an adversary from undertaking a damaging action not yet initiated. In contrast, coercive diplomacy is a response to an action already undertaken.

The term *compellance,* which Thomas Schelling introduced into the literature almost thirty years ago, is often employed to encompass both coercive diplomacy and blackmail and sometimes deterrence as well. I prefer not to use this term for two reasons. First, it is useful to distinguish between defensive and offensive uses of coercive threats; compellance does not. Second, the concept of compellence implies exclusive or heavy reliance on coercive threats, whereas I wish to emphasize the possibility of a more flexible diplomacy that can employ rational persuasion and accommodation as well as coercive threats to encourage the adversary either to comply with the demands or to work out an acceptable compromise.

As defined here, then, coercive diplomacy is a defensive strategy that is employed to deal with the efforts of an adversary to change a status quo situation in his own favor. We have found it useful also to distinguish among three quite different defensive objectives coercive diplomacy can pursue. The aim may be limited to merely stopping the action. A more ambitious aim is the reversal of what has already been accomplished. An even more ambitious aim, as Bruce Jentleson notes in his case study, is a cessation of the opponent's hostile behavior through a demand for change in the composition of the adversary's government or in the nature of the regime. This type of demand stretches coercive diplomacy to its outer limits since it may blur the distinction between defensive and offensive uses of threats. And, quite obviously, the more ambitious the demand on the opponent, the more difficult the task of coercive diplomacy becomes. Table 1 differentiates among these three types of defensive coercive diplomacy and illustrates their primary distinction from the strategy of deterrence.

OTHER NONMILITARY STRATEGIES

Coercive diplomacy is only one of several nonmilitary strategies that may be resorted to by the "defender" when confronted by an adversary's attempt to change an existing situation to his own advantage. Some other strategies the defender can employ are listed below.[2]

1. *"Drawing a line."* When confronted by an adversary's efforts to alter an existing situation in his own favor, the defender may respond by drawing a line to indicate that further action would provoke a strong response.

2. *Buying time to explore a negotiated settlement.* This defensive strategy may be resorted to when the defender (1) is operating under political, diplomatic, or military disadvantages; (2) recognizes that the adversary's dissatisfaction with the status quo has some merit; or (3) believes that the most important of his own interests might first be safeguarded through negotiation before contemplating more forceful strategies.

3. *Retaliation and reprisals.* In some situations this strategy may be preferable to weaker or stronger responses to the adversary's provocation. Carefully measured reprisals, chosen to match but not exceed the adversary's actions, may be necessary to communicate clearly an intention to resist and, hence, offer the possibility that the opponent will desist or that the crisis may then enter a stage of negotiations. Retaliation or reprisals, however, may have to be accompanied by deterrent threats to dissuade the opponent from escalating to stronger action.

4. *Engaging in a "test of capabilities."* When the defender is confronted by a relatively low-level, controlled challenge to the status quo—a blockade, for example—he may forego coercive diplomacy or military action and instead

TABLE 1   Three Types of Defensive Coercive Diplomacy

Deterrence	Coercive Diplomacy		
	Type A	*Type B*	*Type C*
Persuade opponent not to initiate an action	Persuade opponent to stop short of the goal	Persuade opponent to undo the action	Persuade opponent to make changes in government

attempt to meet the challenge within the framework of the ground rules associated with the opponent's challenge. Even though at that early stage the ground rules seem to favor the opponent's eventual success, the defender may hope that the expected outcome can be reversed through hard work, skill, improvisation, and efficient use of available resources, thereby forcing the adversary to decide whether to engage in a risky escalation of the crisis or to accept the failure of his initiative. The defender may also have to undertake measures to deter the opponent from escalation. Two examples of this strategy, both successful, were the response of the West to the Berlin Blockade of 1948 by using an airlift and the U.S. response to the Chinese artillery blockade of Quemoy and Matsu in 1958.

Thus, coercive diplomacy is not the only nonmilitary option available to the defender when confronted by an action that encroaches on his interests. Any of these four strategies may be preferable to an immediate resort to coercive diplomacy. And coercive diplomacy may be tried (as in the Persian Gulf crisis) before resorting to war.

THE APPEAL OF COERCIVE DIPLOMACY

Coercive diplomacy is an attractive strategy because it offers the defender a chance to achieve reasonable objectives in a crisis with less cost, with much less—if any—bloodshed, with fewer political and psychological costs, and often with less risk of unwanted escalation than is true with traditional military strategy. A crisis resolved by means of coercive diplomacy is also less likely to contaminate future relations between the two sides than is a war.

However, precisely because of these attractions, coercive diplomacy can also be a beguiling strategy. Leaders of militarily powerful states may be tempted at times to believe that they can, with little risk, intimidate weaker opponents into giving up their challenge to a status quo situation. But the militarily weaker state may be strongly motivated by what it has at stake and refuse to back down, in effect calling the bluff of the coercing power. The latter, then, must decide whether to back off or to escalate the crisis into a military confrontation.

Moreover, as illustrated in the case studies, militarily powerful states may encounter other constraints, risks, and uncertainties in attempting to employ a coercive strategy. Finally, it should be noted that coercive diplomacy is sometimes chosen by the defender not because of its attractions but rather (as in the Bush administration's response to Saddam Hussein's invasion of Kuwait) because at the inception of the crisis, political-diplomatic support, or military readiness, for a resort to force is lacking.

COERCIVE DIPLOMACY: AN ALTERNATIVE TO MILITARY STRATEGY

Coercive diplomacy, then, offers an alternative to reliance on military action. It seeks to persuade an opponent to cease aggression rather than to bludgeon him into stopping. In contrast to the blunt use of force to repel an adversary, coercive diplomacy emphasizes the use of threats of punishment if the adversary does not comply with what is demanded. If force is used in coercive diplomacy, it takes the form of an exemplary or symbolic use of limited military action to help persuade the opponent to back down. By "exemplary" I mean just enough force of an appropriate kind to demonstrate resolution and to give credibility to the threat that greater force will be used if necessary.[3] Even a relatively small exemplary action (as, for example, President Kennedy's ordering U.S. "civilian advisers" in Laos in April 1961 to put on their uniforms) can have a disproportionately large coercive impact if it is coupled with a credible threat of additional action. The strategy of coercive diplomacy, however, does not require use of exemplary actions. The crisis may be satisfactorily resolved without an exemplary use of force; or the strategy of coercive diplomacy may be abandoned in favor of full-scale military operations without a preliminary use of exemplary force. Hence, in coercive diplomacy, if force is used at all it is not part of conventional military strategy but rather a component of a more complex political-diplomatic strategy for resolving a conflict of interests, which is why *coercive diplomacy* is an appropriate description.

Coercive diplomacy, then, calls for using just enough force of an appropriate kind—if force is used at all—to demonstrate one's resolve to protect well-defined interests as well as the credibility of one's determination to use more force if necessary. To this end, both the threat and employment of force should be coupled with (that is, preceded, accompanied, or followed by) appropriate communications to the opponent. The coercive strategy necessarily includes the signaling, bargaining, and negotiating that are built into the conceptualization and conduct of any military alerts, deployments, or actions—features that are not found or are of secondary interest in traditional military strategy.

Coercive diplomacy seeks to make force a much more flexible, refined psychological instrument of policy in contrast to the "quick, decisive" military strategy, which uses force as a blunt instrument. In coercive diplomacy, the goal is to persuade the opponent to stop or to undo encroachment instead of bludgeoning him into doing so or physically preventing him from continuing.

NOTES

1. I remind the reader that the definitions offered here—as is true of most definitions of complex phenomena—tend to oversimplify reality and are best regarded as a starting point for empirical analysis of a particular phenomenon that should go beyond the confines of the definition.

2. These alternative defensive strategies, their uses and limitations, and examples of each are discussed in A. L. George, ed., *Avoiding War: Problems of Crisis Management* (Boulder, Colo.: Westview Press, 1991), pp. 383–392.

3. The concept of exemplary use of force presented here as a possible component of coercive diplomacy is not always easily distinguishable in historical situations from the practice of retaliation and reprisals. Strictly speaking, the term *reprisal* should be reserved for an action that is limited in purpose to punishing an opponent for a transgression in some appropriate way. Retaliation and reprisal may also constitute what some writers refer to as *active deterrence.* In contrast, the purpose of an exemplary use of force in coercive diplomacy is to convey a willingness to do more, if necessary, to persuade the opponent to stop or to undo his transgression. When the offended state does not make clear whether its action is merely a reprisal or an exemplary component of coercive diplomacy, the historian will have difficulty determining the purpose of that action.

2

Theory and Practice

ALEXANDER L. GEORGE

THE ABSTRACT MODEL OF COERCIVE
DIPLOMACY: ITS USES AND LIMITATIONS

The abstract model identifies the general characteristics of coercive diplomacy and the basic "logic" on which its presumed efficacy rests. The logic of coercive diplomacy postulates that such diplomacy will be successful if demands on an adversary are backed with a threat of punishment for noncompliance that will be considered credible and potent enough to encourage compliance. It should be evident that the logic of coercive diplomacy rests upon the assumption of a "rational" opponent; that is, it assumes that the adversary will be receptive to and will correctly evaluate information that is critical to the question of whether the costs and risks of not complying will outweigh the gains to be expected from pursuing the course of action.

I discuss under "Task 3" in this chapter the various limitations of this assumption of rationality and here address three other characteristics and limitations of the abstract model. First, it gives the policy maker only limited help in devising an effective version of coercive diplomacy for any specific situation; second, it cannot be used to predict whether coercive diplomacy will be successful in a specific situation; and third, it is not a *strategy* of coercive diplomacy.

The first of these three limitations means, quite simply, that the abstract model identifies only the general logic of successful coercive diplomacy and does not include what must be done to inject that logic into the adversary's calculations and lead him to comply with the demand made. To achieve that result, the policy maker must tailor the abstract model to the specific configuration of each situation in which coercive diplomacy is attempted, a task discussed more fully under "Task 4" in this chapter.

Second, to achieve the possibility of predicting outcomes of coercive diplomacy, a specification of the conditions under which its general logic can be achieved in a variety of situations would have to be added to the abstract model. Only if such specificity is added to the model—thereby making it a fully developed, robust deductive theory—could individual situations be analyzed to predict the success of coercive diplomacy. To achieve this predictive capability, the abstract model would have to be operationalized, which requires specification of ways of measuring or assessing the value of the key variables that enter into the particular interaction between the coercer and his opponent and also of the relationships that must exist among these variables in that specific situation for coercive diplomacy to be successful. These key variables are the magnitude of the demand(s) made on the opponent, the magnitude of the opponent's motivation not to comply, and the factor of whether the opponent will feel the threatened punishment is sufficiently credible and potent to cause him to comply. Operationalizing the model by means of such specifications is such an extremely complex task that it is difficult, if not impossible, to achieve.[1] It has not been done, for example, for the abstract rational model of deterrence,[2] and it would be equally, if not more, difficult to perform for the abstract rational model of coercive diplomacy.

The abstract model of coercive diplomacy that exists at present is at best only a quasi, incomplete deductive theory. The logic of the model indicates in a general way what must be achieved in any particular situation for coercive diplomacy to be effective, which is indeed useful. This logic at least identifies what some "necessary" conditions may be for successful coercive diplomacy, albeit under the questionable assumption of pure rationality on the part of the adversary. But the abstract model does not provide either a basis for judging whether in any particular situation the conditions for success already exist or, as already noted, for judging whether and how they can be created by the coercing power in implementing the strategy.

The third limiting characteristic of the abstract model is that it is not in and of itself a strategy. Rather, the abstract model is only a starting point—to be sure, a useful and relevant one—to assist policy makers in considering whether a particular version of coercive diplomacy can be designed that might be effective in a specific situation. In other words, for policy makers to make use of the abstract model, they must transform it into a specific strategy.

Notwithstanding these limitations, this logic of coercive diplomacy has several general implications that are relevant in various aspects of policy making: first, in the process of judging whether coercive diplomacy may be a viable strategy in a particular situation and, second, in the attempt to design and implement an effective version of the strategy for that situation. These implications become self-evident once we look more closely at the central task of coercive diplomacy, which is to cause the adversary to expect sufficient costs and risks to cause him to stop what he is doing.[3] To have this impact we may ask how much of a threat, or of a combination of threat and positive inducement, will be necessary to persuade the adversary to comply with the demand made. The logic that underlies the abstract model tells us, by implication, that the answer will depend on two variables and on the relationship between them: first, what the coercing power demands of the opponent and, second, how strongly disinclined the opponent is to comply with that demand. From the logic of the model we also discern that these two variables are not independent of each other. That is, the strength of the adversary's disinclination to comply is highly sensitive to the magnitude of the demand made by the coercing power. Thus, asking relatively little of the opponent should make it easier for him to be coerced. Conversely, demanding a great deal of an opponent will strengthen his resistance and make the task of coercive persuasion more difficult.

Another important implication of the model's basic logic is that the coercer's choice of a demand will influence not only the strength of the opponent's motivation to resist but also the strength of the coercer's own motivation and, hence, the relative motivation of the two sides. *Motivation* in this context refers to each side's conception of what it has at stake in the dispute, the importance each side attaches to the interests engaged by the crisis, and what level of costs and risks each is willing to incur on behalf of those interests. If the coercing power demands something that is more important to it than to the adversary, then the coercer should benefit from what may be called an *asymmetry of interests.* Conversely, if the coercing power pursues ambitious objectives that go beyond its own vital or important interests, and if its demands infringe on vital or important interests of the adversary, then the asymmetry of interests and balance of motivation will favor the adversary and make successful application of coercive diplomacy much more difficult.

The way in which asymmetry of interests and relative motivation will be perceived by the two sides and what influence this will have on the outcome in real-life cases is more complicated than is suggested by the general logic of the abstract model, as our case studies demonstrate. Nonetheless, the logic of the model is important because it demonstrates that there is an important strategic dimension to the choice of the demand the coercing power makes on its adversary. Quite simply, strategic interests affect the motivation of both sides and the balance of motivation between them, variables that will likely influence both the interaction between them and the efficacy of the attempt at coercive diplomacy.

We see in the case studies in Part Two that these implications of the model's logic do indeed manifest themselves in practice and that they can play an extremely important role in determining the ease or difficulty of conducting coercive diplomacy. But we also see that various impediments to information processing, and political and psychological variables not encompassed by the abstract model's assumption of rationality, can have an important impact on the way the model's logic actually operates in the real world, often making it more difficult for the coercing power to use the strategy effectively.

Another characteristic of coercive diplomacy is the possibility that the coercing power may couple its threat of punishment for noncompliance with positive inducements to encourage the adversary to comply with the demand. When this is done, the resulting variant of coercive diplomacy is often referred to as an example of the "carrot-and-stick" approach. As with threats of punishment, positive inducements and reassurances must also be credible. When both negative sanctions and positive inducements are employed, the adversary must make a more complex calculation of the utility of complying with the demand, although the logic of the model operates in the same way.

CONVERTING THE ABSTRACT MODEL
INTO A STRATEGY: FOUR TASKS

I have noted that the abstract model of coercive diplomacy is not in and of itself a strategy. The model is only a starting point for designing a particular strategy of coercive diplomacy for a specific situation and also for helping to assess whether that strategy or variant of it would likely be successful in that situation.

How, then, is the abstract model transformed by the policy maker into a specific strategy? To achieve this, four tasks must be accomplished.

Task 1: Fill in the Four "Empty Boxes"
(Variables) of the Model

To design a specific strategy of coercive diplomacy, the policy maker must make decisions regarding the four variables, or empty boxes, of the abstract model:

1. what to demand of the opponent
2. whether and how to create a sense of urgency for compliance with the demand
3. what punishment to threaten for noncompliance, and how to make it sufficiently potent and credible
4. whether also to offer positive inducements and, if so, what "carrot" to offer together with the "stick" to induce acceptance of the demand

I have indicated that what is demanded of the opponent is of critical importance in determining the balance of interests and motivation that will create ease or difficulty in carrying out coercive diplomacy. The case histories illustrate the importance of this variable in determining the success or failure of the strategy on different occasions.

The strategy one chooses in any particular situation may include an effort to convey to the adversary a sense of urgency for compliance with one's demand. It is generally presumed that a sense of urgency generally adds to the coercive impact the strategy has on the adversary. But, as is noted in Chapter 3 and in Part Three, risks are sometimes associated with creating urgency, and other reasons may exist for not placing the adversary under undue time pressure. There are different ways of transmitting a sense of urgency, most notably by setting an explicit and relatively brief time limit for compliance with the demand. However, a sense of urgency may also be conveyed by actions such as alerts and deployments of military forces, which may be coupled with verbal communications indicating that time is short.

The fact that coercive diplomacy functions on two levels of communication—both words and actions—is also evident in addressing the third variable in the model. The threat of punishment in the event of noncompliance may be signaled through military actions or political-diplomatic moves as well as by explicit verbal warnings. As is seen in the cases in Part Two, however, the defender's actions in any given situation can either strengthen or detract from the credibility of verbal threats. Hence, actions intended to convey a specific threat must be chosen carefully, in sensitive accord with the structure and evolution of the particular situation.

Another important decision to be made in designing and implementing a specific strategy of coercive diplomacy is whether to rely solely on a threat of punishment or also to offer positive inducements, concessions on behalf of a compromise settlement, or reassurances in order to secure the adversary's acceptance of the demand. The "carrot" in such a strategy can be any of a variety of things the adversary values. The magnitude and significance of the carrot can range from a seemingly trivial face-saving concession to substantial concessions and side payments that bring about a stable settlement of the crisis. Such a settlement may take shape either as a genuine, balanced quid pro quo or in the form of concessions that favor the opponent and do little more than permit the coercing power to save face and avoid an outright defeat.

Whether coercive diplomacy will work in a particular case may depend on whether reliance is placed solely on negative sanctions or on whether threats are coupled with positive inducements. This point has considerable practical as well as theoretical significance. What the threatened stick cannot achieve by itself, unless it is formidable, can possibly be achieved by combining it with a carrot. Indeed, in some cases the hard-pressed defender may rely more on offering a substantial carrot than on making a strong threat to achieve a minimal success.

Finally, the decisions made in specifying these four ingredients of a strategy at the outset are subject to change during the course of the crisis. The coercive power may stiffen or dilute its demands, enhance or relax the sense of urgency initially conveyed, strengthen or soften the threat of punishment and its credibility, and move from reliance only on threats to a carrot-and-stick variant of the strategy.

Task 2: Identify the Preferred Variant of the Strategy of Coercive Diplomacy

Depending on what choices the policy maker makes with regard to the four variables of the model, the resulting combinations will define significantly different variants of the strategy. For analytical purposes, I have identified four such variants: the classic ultimatum, the tacit ultimatum, the "gradual turning of the screw," and the "try-and-see" approach.

The starkest variant of the strategy includes all three ingredients of a full-fledged classic ultimatum: (1) a demand on the opponent; (2) a time limit or sense of urgency for compliance with the demand; and (3) a threat of punishment for noncompliance that is credible and sufficiently potent to convince the opponent that compliance is preferable to other courses of action. An ultimatum, although the starkest variant of coercive diplomacy, is not necessarily the most effective. Moreover, as is seen in Chapter 3, ultimata may take a variety of forms. An ultimatum may be inappropriate, infeasible, or even highly risky in a particular situation. (We return to this in some of the case studies and in Part Three.)

When a time limit is not set forth explicitly but a sense of urgency is nonetheless conveyed by other means, this variant of the strategy is referred to as a *tacit* ultimatum. Similarly, when the threat of punishment is not specifically set forth but is nonetheless credibly conveyed by actions, this variant may also be referred to as a tacit ultimatum. If a strategy incorporates an implicit rather than an explicit form of one of the three components of a classic ultimatum, however, it is not necessarily less potent. Before delivering an explicit ultimatum, a state may find it preferable—as John F. Kennedy did in the Cuban Missile Crisis—to convey the gist of that ultimatum through some combination of military preparations and stern warnings.

Other variants of coercive diplomacy exist in which one or another of these components of an ultimatum is diluted or absent. One is the try-and-see approach. In this version of the strategy, only the first element of an ultimatum—a demand—is made; the coercing power does not announce a time limit or convey a strong sense of urgency for compliance. Instead, it employs one limited coercive threat or action and waits to see whether it will persuade the opponent before making another threat or taking another step. There are several versions of the try-and-see approach, as is evident in some of the case studies in Part Two.

Stronger in coercive potential, though still falling well short of the ultimatum, is the variant of coercive diplomacy that relies on a gradual turning of the screw. This differs from the try-and-see approach in that a threat to gradually step up pressure is conveyed at the outset and is carried out incrementally. At the same time, the gradual turning of the screw differs from the ultimatum in that it lacks a sense of time urgency for compliance and relies on the threat of a step-by-step increase in coercive pressure rather than of escalation to strong, decisive military action if the opponent does not comply. In practice, the analytical distinction I have just made between the try-and-see approach and the gradual turning of the screw may be blurred if the policy maker wavers or behaves inconsistently.

Several observations about these variants of coercive diplomacy are made in the next section, "Needed: An Empirical Theory and Generic Knowledge." It is sufficient to note here that when an ultimatum or a tacit ultimatum is not appropriate or feasible or is considered premature or too risky, a try-and-see or gradual turning of the screw approach may better fit the political-diplomatic-military configuration of the conflict. It is also true that, as happened in some of our historical cases, policy makers may shift from one of these variants to another. Sometimes, in fact, such strategy shifts may be inadvertent—especially if the policy makers do not maintain a consistent sense of operational purpose.

Indeed, helping to maintain a clarity of purpose is the main reason we distinguish among these four different forms the strategy of coercive diplomacy may take. These brief characterizations help sharpen the focus on the combination of policy choices made in Task 1. Still, although such a distinction is useful, it would be misleading to imply that the form of the strategy alone determines the likelihood of its success. Certainly from a formalistic standpoint, the ultimatum is a stronger, or starker, variant of the strategy than are the gradual turning of the screw and the try-and-see approaches. But the coercive impact of any particular form of the strategy and whether it will be effective depend on other factors to be discussed under "Needed: An Empirical Theory and Generic Knowledge."

Task 3: Replace the General Assumption of a "Rational" Opponent with an Empirically Derived Behavioral Model

The abstract model of coercive diplomacy, as noted earlier, assumes pure rationality on the part of an opponent. But in real life decision makers are not attentive to and do not correctly perceive all incoming information; various external and internal psychological factors influence their receptivity to new information and its assessment, and these factors also affect their identification and evaluation of options.

It is clear, therefore, that a specific behavioral model of the adversary is needed that will characterize in a more discriminating way how that opponent tends to approach the task of rational calculation—for example, how his values and beliefs influence his processing of information and evaluation of options, and how political factors and organizational variables enter into his policy making.[4] In sum, policy makers making use of a strategy of coercive diplomacy must replace the assumption of pure rationality with sensitivity to the psychological, cultural, and political variables that may influence the adversary's behavior when he is subjected to one or another variant of the strategy.

Task 4: Take into Account Contextual Variables

The abstract model of coercive diplomacy spins out its general logic without reference to the characteristics of any particular situation. In this sense, the abstract model is context-free. But in transforming the model into a variant of the strategy to be used in an actual situation, the policy maker must pay close attention to whether and how the logic associated with successful coercive diplomacy can be achieved in that particular set of circumstances. Many different situational-contextual factors vary from one crisis to another. The policy maker faces the difficult but necessary task of adapting the strategy of coercive diplomacy to the special configuration of the situation.

That this task is an important one quickly becomes evident when we study and compare different historical cases in which some type of coercive diplomacy was attempted. A number of the important contextual variables that were identified in the case studies are reported and discussed in Part Three. It will suffice here to emphasize that coercive diplomacy is a highly context-dependent strategy.

NEEDED: AN EMPIRICAL THEORY
AND GENERIC KNOWLEDGE

Why does coercive diplomacy succeed on some occasions and fail on others? The abstract model provides only limited help in answering this question. It does offer a useful, though incomplete, framework that can serve as a starting point for such an inquiry. The model helps to identify some, though not all, of the variables that may account for success or failure of the strategy. Familiarity with the abstract model and its logic can also help investigators to raise some relevant questions and to formulate hypotheses as to why coercive diplomacy succeeded or failed. But the model itself cannot identify all possible explanations or assess explanatory hypotheses.

The abstract model lacks not only the ability to predict the outcome of efforts at coercive diplomacy but also adequate explanatory power. True, *after* the outcome of any attempt at coercive diplomacy is known, the model can be invoked to explain it. For example, one might be tempted to say that coercive diplomacy failed in a particular case because the threatened punishment was not credible or potent enough. Such pseudo-explanations lack relevant supporting data and have a circular character. Post-facto "explanations" of this kind violate methodological canons and are not acceptable. A satisfactory explanation is possible—and then only possible—if adequate data are available on the decision-making processes of the two sides and the interaction between them that led to the success or failure of the coercive diplomacy. But even then, such data must be adequately analyzed and interpreted before valid conclusions can be drawn.

To understand why the strategy succeeds on some occasions and fails on others, we need to develop an empirical theory of coercive diplomacy by studying and comparing in a systematic way actual historical cases of success and failure. *Theory* in this context refers to the cumulation of generic knowledge about the conditions under which different variants of the strategy have succeeded or failed.

The policy maker who knows from the abstract logic of coercive diplomacy what must be accomplished in general terms can turn to generic knowledge of the strategy's past applications to diagnose its potential in a current situation. Judging from past cases, what kinds of circumstances favor the use of specific variants of coercive diplomacy? What possible obstacles and constraints to its success are likely to be encountered? How have specific opponents reacted to its use in different kinds of situations?

In sum, the abstract theory does not provide the policy maker with a basis for judging whether coercive diplomacy is likely to be effective in a particular situation. Rather, policy makers must turn to the generic knowledge derived from study of a variety of past cases for help in making such judgments.

NOTES

1. The difficulty or virtual impossibility of fully operationalizing the model stems from the fact that the outcomes of strategic interaction in a conflict situation are indeterminate.

2. For a discussion of the lack of a fully developed, "rational" deductive theory of deterrence and the difficulty in achieving it, see A. L. George and R. Smoke, "Deterrence and Foreign Policy," *World Politics* 41, no. 2 (January 1989): 170–182.

3. These implications of the abstract model emerged as analytical conclusions from the empirical case studies reported in the 1971 study by A. L. George, David K. Hall, and William E. Simons, *The Limits of Coercive Diplomacy* (Boston: Little, Brown, 1971). It is now possible, as I have done, to identify them as logical implications of a more fully stated abstract model.

4. For a more detailed discussion, see A. L. George, *Presidential Decisionmaking in Foreign Policy: The Effective Use of Information and Advice* (Boulder, Colo.: Westview Press, 1980), pp. 66–72. Also see George's *Bridging the Gap: Theory and Practice of Foreign Policy* (Washington, D.C.: United States Institute of Peace, 1993).

3

Coercive Diplomacy and Ultimata: Theory and Practice in History

PAUL GORDON LAUREN

The essentials of coercive diplomacy are as old as the arts of diplomacy and warfare themselves and have been known for centuries. Thoughtful practitioners and observers throughout history have recognized that in an uncertain and precarious world in which military power, violence, and ambition were seemingly always present, intimidation occurred frequently. Moreover, they learned long ago that although such tactics are dangerous and subject to serious limitations, attempts to gain objectives by threatening—rather than actually using—punishment might be accomplished with fewer costs and less bloodshed than is the case with war. For this reason, the history of international conflict has been characterized by the recurrence of bargaining accompanied by threats designed to induce fear sufficient to change behavior through coercive diplomacy.[1]

THE HISTORICAL EVOLUTION OF COERCIVE DIPLOMACY

Sun Tzu, who wrote his famous *The Art of War* in China twenty-three hundred years ago, for example, observed the importance of threatening punishment to influence an adversary's will but actually using it "only when there is no alternative."[2] Thucydides, who wrote his *The Peloponnesian War* at approximately the same time, described how the Greek city-states frequently used threats to make others "think twice" and thereby secured their objectives through intimidation.[3] He recounted how in one of the classic cases of coercive diplomacy, the powerful Athenians issued demands to the much weaker Melians and threatened that failure to comply would result in complete devastation, declaring:

> You, by giving in, would save yourself from disaster … your actual resources
> are too scanty to give you a chance of survival against the forces that are op-
> posed to you at this moment. You will therefore be showing an extraordinary
> lack of common sense if … you still fail to reach a conclusion wiser than any-
> thing you have mentioned so far. … Think it over again … and let this be a
> point that constantly recurs to your minds—that you are discussing the fate of
> your country, that you have only one country, and its future for good or ill de-
> pends on this one single decision which you are going to make.[4]

In his *Art of War* (1521) and *The Prince* (1532), the gifted Italian Niccolo
Machiavelli deliberately laid down guidelines for manipulation in statecraft.[5]
The English philosopher Thomas Hobbes, in his masterpiece *Leviathan*
(1651), emphasized the importance of power in creating "a Feare of the consequences" and in providing "some coercive Power to compel men equally
to the performance of their Covenants by the terror of some punishment
greater than the benefit they expect by breach of their Covenant."[6] Even the
refined and restrained French diplomat François de Callières, who insisted
that diplomats should be Christian men of peace rather than of war, maintained in *De la manière de négocier avec les Souverains* (1716) that every negotiator must understand the significance of pressure to be effective in persuasion and bargaining.[7] Finally, in his classic book *Vom Krieg* (1832), the
Prussian officer and insightful observer of international conflict Carl von
Clausewitz contributed still further to an understanding of coercive diplomacy by describing how the threat or the actual use of armed force as a means
"can never be considered in isolation from [its] purpose."[8]

As they entered the period of European balance-of-power diplomacy in
the nineteenth century, those engaged in statecraft possessed a knowledge of
a number of these important writings and, through time, increasingly made
coercive diplomacy an integral part of their conventional wisdom and practice. They never systematically articulated a theory of the strategy, however,
or explicitly identified its various characteristics. Instead, they simply observed through their own successes and failures that it was a political-diplomatic strategy of crisis bargaining that provided a valuable alternative to an
exclusive reliance upon military action by attempting to persuade opponents
to stop or undo encroachments through the use of threats. By threatening,
for example, they learned that an opponent might be persuaded to call off an
invasion or to give up occupied territory. By conveying a determined will
and a credible ability to enforce their threats to inflict damage, they learned
that adversaries might be more willing to comply with their demands. In
sharp contrast, they also learned through time that coercive diplomacy could

be a beguiling and seductive strategy that held hidden dangers and limitations. If a government failed to take into sufficient account its opponent's disinclination to yield to demands and motivation to resist if pushed too far, for example, coercion could backfire and quickly escalate to dangerous levels or even to unanticipated war.

Those practicing and refining coercive diplomacy also learned through historical experience that their strategy could take a variety of forms along a continuum, as identified and discussed by Alexander George in Chapter 2. On the weaker end of this spectrum was the "try-and-see" approach, in which coercing powers in the past had attempted to persuade opponents by taking only one threatening step at a time. Using this variant of the strategy, and particularly during those times in the nineteenth century when the Concert of Europe operated with some measure of mutual restraint and collective decision making,[9] these powers deliberately avoided creating a sense of urgency and postponed making additional threats or taking further action until they could see whether the steps already taken possessed a sufficiently coercive impact upon opponents. At the other end of the spectrum was the most distinctive, urgent, dangerous, and extreme variant of coercive diplomacy: the ultimatum.

THE ULTIMATUM

During critical international crises and watersheds of history in the nineteenth and twentieth centuries, statesmen used ultimata with alarming frequency.[10] They believed that despite its inherent dangers, this extreme variant of coercive diplomacy could convey resolve and urgency better than, say, an ambiguously worded diplomatic protest or the limited deployment of troops along a border. When the general context and structure of the situation alone appeared far too equivocal, weak, or unfavorable, those practicing coercion sought reinforcement through more precise, direct, explicit, and urgent bargaining in the extreme. In fact, in looking back on earlier historical experiences, we can see that it is precisely in these extremities of an ultimatum that some of the distinctive components, features, uses, and limitations of coercive diplomacy can be understood most clearly.

The use of ultimata, for example, revealed the common intent of all those practicing coercive diplomacy, regardless of time or place, to communicate certain demands upon an opponent, and to convey a sense of urgency by means of a time limit for compliance and a threat of punishment for noncompliance. The ultimative character of these elements could be conveyed not only by written or spoken words but also by the surrounding circumstances, such as troops poised along a border, naval demonstrations, or the reputation of the coercing power, which gave the message meaning, credibility, and potency. Regardless of the particular combination employed, however, all classical or full-fledged ultimata possessed common components, and a brief analysis of each reveals much about the nature of coercive diplomacy itself.

Specific Demands or Terms of Compliance

Historically, states issuing ultimata insisted upon unconditional compliance with certain specified demands requiring that an adversary either stop what he was doing or undo what had been accomplished. In the 1914 British ultimatum to Germany, for example, the British demanded that German ground forces stop their forward progress short of an invasion of Belgian territory and thus refrain from violating guaranteed neutrality. At the outset of World War II, Britain and France issued an ultimatum to Adolf Hitler in which they demanded that he stop all aggressive action against Poland, undo the territorial occupation, and withdraw all German forces from Polish territory. A demand that required that an opponent stop obviously asked appreciably less than one that insisted upon his undoing whatever had been already achieved.

As a rule, states coupled their ultimata with the demand for a prompt, clear, categorical reply that expressed acceptance of all of the terms of compliance. At times, states explicitly expressed such conditions, as in the case of South Africa's 1899 ultimatum to Britain demanding an "affirmative answer," the Austrian demands on Serbia in 1914 for "an unconditional and favorable response," and the 1938 Polish ultimatum to Czechoslovakia over disputed territory and Polish political prisoners that required *"une reponse non-equivoque."* Although a response might be a formal, written answer or an oral answer in the form of a *note verbale* provided within the specific time limit, the mere existence of a reply did not constitute compliance, for efforts were sometimes made to be deliberately ambiguous and to bargain over accepting only part of the demands. For example, to foreclose this possibility, in its 1909 ultimatum to Russia, Germany demanded "an answer—yes or no" and declared that it would regard "any evasive, conditional, or unclear answer as a refusal."[11] The Serbian reply to the 1914 Austrian ultimatum provides a masterful example of just such an equivocal answer to a barrage of demands. One must carefully read the reply word by word to discover what the Serbs accepted and what remained as areas of disagreement with the original demands. In the end, the Austrians, who did not expect and probably did not want their ultimatum to be accepted, considered the Serbian reply to be "inadequate" and promptly declared war.

Regardless of specific demands for action and replies, however, the sine qua non of ultimata was the desire of those practicing coercive diplomacy to convey the message that the conditions presented were *final* and that noncompliance would result in punishment. In the recent U.N. Security Council ultimatum issued to Iraq because of Saddam Hussein's invasion of Kuwait, for example, the text explicitly stated that Iraq was being given "one final opportunity" to avoid war by complying with the demands of the international community.[12] Iraq's refusal to comply with these demands prior to the January 15, 1991, deadline led to an immediate and devastating military invasion.

Time Limit

Historical experience has also taught states that the intimidating impact of this extreme variant of coercive diplomacy can be further facilitated by the presence of a time limit, an element that came to be frequently associated with ultimata. Although surrounding circumstances may lend equal urgency, a time limit for a reply to demands was a critical component in creating the urgent and tense atmosphere that accompanied an ultimatum. Such limits have traditionally ranged from several days to only a few hours. In their ultimatum to the Soviet Union in 1923, for example, the British demanded compliance within ten days; the Italian deadline in the 1911 ultimatum to Turkey was twenty-four hours; the Anglo-French time limit imposed upon Egypt and Israel in 1956 was twelve hours; the British in their ultimatum to Hitler in 1939 demanded a reply within two hours; and in the ultimatum to Germany in 1916, the United States demanded compliance "immediately."

The time limit and the deliberate use of an ultimatum to convey urgency, of course, created obvious and serious tensions with the requirements of crisis management. Managing crises, particularly as practiced in the context of classical diplomacy, required the slowing down of momentum in order to provide enough time for careful decision making and communication between the two sides. An ultimatum, however, deliberately attempted to speed up the pace of bargaining; to convey the sense that time was running out, that "a countdown had started" or "the clock was ticking toward a showdown"; and to push an opponent quickly into compliance with demands.[13]

Threats of Punishment

The final element of the ultimatum was the threat, which gave notice that rejection and noncompliance with the demands would lead to coercive measures. As we will see by examining a number of historical cases, these threats could take a wide variety of forms. To make such threats credible and more intimidating, coercing powers attempted to create the impression that they were definitely willing and able to enforce punishment (not that they might, for this would only invite speculation) and that their threats were sufficiently potent to overcome the natural reluctance of opponents to comply.

Introduction and Conclusion

Prior to, or following, the three essential components of an ultimatum, powers practicing coercive diplomacy at the extreme sometimes presented either an oral or a written statement. Although the critical context and the urgency of time required that ultimata texts be short, terse, and expressed in *termes peremptoires,* states occasionally attempted to say something more: to raise an issue to the fore, express a lengthy complaint, provide a justification for action, or explain intentions and purpose.

In the 1921 London Ultimatum to Germany, for example, the former Allied powers noted their innumerable past concessions and complained that "in spite of the warnings and sanctions agreed upon ... the German Government is still in default in the fulfillment of the obligations incumbent upon it" regarding disarmament, reparation payments, and the trial of war criminals.[14] The 1958 Soviet ultimatum to the Western powers regarding Berlin similarly presented both an introduction and a conclusion. The Kremlin recounted what it described as the treacherous policies of Winston Churchill and the rise of militarism in West Germany, accused the West of subversive activity and of hampering the reunification of Germany, declared that it would no longer consider itself bound by earlier agreements on the division of Berlin, and cautioned that "only madmen can go the length of unleashing another world war."[15]

Incentives

Some past statesmen, especially during the classical system of diplomacy, understood that even when using the extreme variant of the ultimatum, they could create features that provided for at least some measure of conflict resolution and cooperation rather than simply intimidation and winning at the expense of others. That is, within the strategy of coercive diplomacy itself, they could couple the "sticks" of negative threats with the "carrots" of positive incentives. Credible incentives were seen as components that might reduce an opponent's disinclination to comply with demands, encourage a quid pro quo, avoid the mutually unpleasant consequences of enforced punishment, and thus play something of the same role in deescalation that threats play in escalation. As de Callières advised: "Every Christian prince must take as his chief maxim not to employ arms to support or vindicate his rights until he has employed and exhausted the way of reason and persuasion. It is to his interest also to add to reason and persuasion the influence of benefits conferred."[16]

A mixture of incentives with threats occurred in the 1840 ultimatum issued by Austria, Prussia, Russia, and England to Mehemet Ali of Egypt. They demanded that he return to the Ottoman Empire all of the gains acquired by means of military conquest, including the Turkish fleet. The four powers then coupled this demand with rather ingeniously graduated incentives designed to encourage quick compliance. If Mehemet Ali complied by the deadline, he would receive hereditary rule of Egypt and lifetime control over southern Syria. If he failed to comply within ten days, he would lose all claims in Syria. Finally, if the demands were not accepted within twenty days, he would lose all of Egypt as well.[17] Similarly, in its 1899 ultimatum to Britain, the Republic of South Africa offered incentives for compliance with its demands regarding the buildup of British troops along its borders. An acceptable response, it promised, would result in "a mutual assurance and guarantee on the part of this government that no attack upon or hostilities against any portion of the British Government shall be made ... and on compliance therewith, [South Africa would] be prepared to withdraw the armed burghers of this Republic from the borders."[18]

THREATS IN ULTIMATA:
FLEXIBILITY EVEN AT THE EXTREMES

Statesmen engaging in coercive diplomacy gradually learned that even within the extreme variant of the ultimatum, they could threaten to use a wide variety of instruments of intimidation or persuasion. That is, coercion did not necessarily or automatically involve armed force or violence. Diplomatic, economic, and psychological measures also existed as valuable possibilities that could be specifically tailored to fit the unique configuration of each situation, and threats could be made in varying combinations and sequences with differing degrees of intensity to achieve the desired level of coercion.

Today discrete and flexible selections of coercive measures in an ultimatum are often thought to be inappropriate at best or impossible at worst. In fact, with the breakdown of the European balance-of-power system during World War I and the emergence of a global, less homogeneous international system, the ultimatum has come to be associated almost exclusively with the most extreme and crude form of coercion—namely, the threat of war—and with assertions that ultimata "are, of course, the antithesis of flexibility" and "a preliminary step in going to war."[19] The increased danger of escalation and of crisis mismanagement inherent in such attitudes makes it imperative, therefore, to learn from earlier historical experience and to recognize that even with the extreme variant of the ultimatum, numerous options for threats short of war have traditionally been available in coercive diplomacy.

Perhaps the flexibility and range of possible alternatives for ultimata can best be depicted on a continuum of threats involving coercive measures, extending from the mildest (such as breaking off negotiations or breaching existing agreements) through an ascending scale of intensity to the most severe (such as declaring war or even escalating a war in progress). An analysis of these threats may provide a greater appreciation of the sophistication and nuances of the statecraft of nations in the past and thereby assist in refining both the theory and practice of coercive diplomacy. In the process, it may also suggest the value of gradual and highly differentiated levels of coercive threats that might otherwise remain unexplored.

Threats of a Nonviolent Break in Negotiations

It is essential to recognize that even within the strongest variant of a strategy of coercive diplomacy that employed ultimata, many possibilities of intimidation short of war existed. Perhaps the least amount of pressure that could be threatened in an ultimatum was to break off discussions in progress. Certainly from early eighteenth-century European diplomacy to contemporary collective bargaining, negotiators have recognized that ultimata can be used to express the maximum amount of concession possible.[20] Thus, an ultimatum could convey the "final offer" or "last word": that unless one's own proposed, irreducible minimum proposal was accepted, discussions would automatically cease.

Evidence of such threats is provided by the Austrian ultimatum to Russia at the conclusion of the Crimean War. Upon discovering the existence of secret negotiations between Russia and France, Count Karl von Buol of Austria offered to act as mediator and demanded that his terms of mediation be accepted. He transmitted the conditions to Russia *"sous forme d'ultimatum."* Emperor Alexander then proposed several modifications, which Buol refused, demanding a "yes or no" answer. After consulting his principal advisers, the tsar complied and expressed his willingness to "accept the Austrian ultimatum" as a basis for further negotiations.[21]

The ultimatum threatening the temporary withdrawal of diplomatic representatives may also be considered a threat to break off negotiations. During the famous *Trent* Affair in 1861, for example, Great Britain issued an ultimatum to the United States in which it demanded the release of two Confederate emissaries and their secretaries who had been seized from a British ship. If President Abraham Lincoln did not comply within seven days, the British threatened to withdraw their legation from Washington.[22] In 1915 Russia issued a similar ultimatum to Bulgaria. Decrying Bulgarian subordination to Germany, Russia demanded that the government openly break with the Central Powers and remove enemy officers within twenty-four hours. If Bulgaria did not comply, Russia threatened that its minister would "leave Bulgaria with all staffs of legations and consulates." Russia did withdraw, yet neither side considered such a measure to be as serious as a formal break in diplomatic relations, which occurred later.[23] Britain issued a similar ultimatum to Portugal in 1898, as did Serbia to Turkey in 1912. Similarly, when the Soviets withdrew their ambassador to Israel in 1956, they were careful to note that a difference existed between withdrawing a diplomatic representative and the more drastic breaking of relations.[24]

Threats of the Nonviolent Breach of Existing Agreements

Ascending the scale of coercive pressure, we find threats that entailed the provocative breach or termination of formal agreements already in force. Threats to rupture commercial, communication, and transportation agreements or to break off diplomatic and consular relations, for example, provided traditional and standard indicators that normal relations were strained to such an extent that armed conflict could result. Measures of armed force did not necessarily follow, however, for differences could still be flexibly adjusted within a nonviolent context, even with the extreme variant of an ultimatum.

The threat to terminate a commercial agreement, for instance, appeared in the 1923 British ultimatum to the Soviet Union. Lord George Curzon demanded the cessation of certain Communist propaganda, the acceptance of British terms on several disputed issues, and a reply within ten days. Both of the disputants, however, realized that the ultimatum threatened only the termination of a 1921 trade agreement and not physical violence.[25] Similarly, the Soviet Union, in a 1929 ultimatum to China, threatened to terminate previous agreements through a break in diplomatic relations. The Soviets dispatched a demand for a reply within a specific time limit that unconditionally accepted the restoration of the management of the Eastern Chinese Railway to its former status. When the Chinese response proved unacceptable, the Kremlin severed formal relations. Each government recognized, however, that the threat involved no demonstration or use of armed force.[26] Many additional examples of ultimata that threatened a rupture of diplomatic relations between nations during periods of international crises also exist, including those from Spain to Chile in 1865, Turkey to Greece in 1868, Russia to Turkey in 1876, Austria to Serbia in 1914, and the United States to Germany in 1916.

This type of historical practice provided a model for the Soviet Union when it issued an ultimatum to Lithuania in April 1990. Angered and frustrated by a growing Lithuanian independence movement that might spread to other Soviet republics, President Mikhail Gorbachev announced that the situation could "no longer be tolerated" and demanded that the leaders of Lithuania withdraw their declaration of independence and repeal their newly passed laws within two days. Failure to comply would result in the termination of existing agreements on trade and the imposition of an economic embargo on vital oil and natural gas shipments on which the small republic totally depended.[27]

Threats Involving the Demonstration of Force

Although substantial levels of coercion could be achieved through diplomatic and economic threats, more intense coercion sometimes required mili-

tary threats. For example, attempts to give credibility to previously disre-
garded, misunderstood, or misconstrued demands were facilitated by the
threat value of weapons: namely, a nonviolent demonstration of military potential. Military exercises in sensitive areas, maneuvers of naval forces, and
mobilization of reserves were all intended to bring pressure upon an opponent without resorting to actual violence. Such demonstrations were token in
character, in the hope that the appearance of a fraction of the power available
would create the perception that more force would follow if necessary. Thus,
the coercive effect of what little was actually done could be magnified substantially by linking it to a credible threat of additional action.[28]

States practicing coercive diplomacy and using ultimata learned that in
demonstrating force, naval rather than other military means were more effective for purposes of display, controllability, and crisis management. Mobilization of troops, for instance, proved to be relatively dangerous and expen-
sive and was apt to arouse hostility that was not easily terminated or revoked.
Navies, however, could be moved about more easily than land-based forces,
could remain nearby but still be out of sight, and could be used in flexible and
incremental ways during diplomatic crises. For these reasons, British and
U.S. naval demonstrations were often selected for coercive diplomatic tasks
to create a "presence," to "show the flag," and to engage in "gunboat diplomacy." In the words of one contemporary analyst, navies could "best unite
force with persuasion" and thus be used to create an exemplary show of force
as punishment for noncompliance with an ultimatum.[29] For example, during
the years preceding the Young Turk Revolution, the Ottoman Empire was
frequently confronted with displays of force. Great Britain issued an ultimatum to the empire in 1906 accompanied with charges of "trifling" with His
Majesty's government and demands for the evacuation of Taba by Turkish
troops and the acceptance of the Sinai boundary with Egypt within ten days.
The threat for noncompliance was "the immediate dispatch of a British ship
of war" to the locality in question. Significant for our analysis, the British
representative, in an internal document, directed that British forces were not
to interfere with foreign troops and that the ship was sent "as a precautionary
measure, and *without hostile intention.*"[30]

Threats of Compulsive Settlement by Force
Short of Limited Invasion

Nineteenth-century statesmen also realized that at times mere displays or
demonstrations of force might be ineffective. It did not follow, however, that
the next level of intimidation would be war. Instead, they understood that it
was both possible and desirable to avoid the disruption, embarrassment, and
danger of invasion or war while at the same time employing the "desired
amount of coercion." The recourse by states to restricted uses of force for

limited objectives gradually gave rise to the French phrase *persuasion en rade* and an accompanying body of legal doctrine for compulsive settlement by re-tortion, reprisals, and pacific blockade—all features generally classified as "measures short of war."[31] Threats of a hostile embargo, for example, sug-gested the sequestration or temporary seizure of property, and those of a pa-cific blockade suggested the closing of one or more ports of a country by force. As with all threats of force in coercive diplomacy, these measures were directed primarily at an opponent's will and calculations of interest rather than at his military capabilities. Their purpose was not to destroy but rather to frighten, demoralize, and persuade and thereby influence behavior.

In 1850, for example, Lord Henry Palmerston ordered the British minister at Athens to present the Greek government with an ultimatum that threat-ened "coercive measures" short of invasion or war in the form of a pacific blockade. Britain demanded settlement of the damage claims for property be-longing to a British subject living in Athens within twenty-four hours. The threat for noncompliance stated that "the Commander-in-Chief of Her Maj-esty's Naval Forces in the Mediterranean will have no other alternative (how-ever painful the necessity may be to him) than to act at once" in the establish-ment of a blockade on the coasts of Greece. The intention behind this ultimatum was clearly indicated by the British minister, who stated that "the adoption of some *mild measure,* such as that of preventing any Greek Gov-ernment vessel leaving the Piraeus, might have the effect of convincing the Greek Government that his orders to resort to *active* measures are posi-tive."[32] The French government issued a similar ultimatum in 1893 to intimi-date Siam with threats of compulsive settlement.

Threats of Limited Armed Invasion

In historical international bargaining situations, states issuing ultimata also knew that a greater application of force was possible than that required for embargoes or blockades but less than that needed for actual war. Such forc-ible measures traditionally involved the threat of limited armed invasion of noncontiguous or nonnational, or even the opponent's own, territory. De-pending upon the degree and credibility of its commitment, a state threaten-ing this action (with its costs in terms of destruction, casualties, and humilia-tion) not surprisingly risked the recipient's perceiving the ultimatum as a casus belli, even though it may not have been so intended. The original inten-tion of a forcible entry into an opponent's territorial domain, for example, could be limited to the seizure of certain ports, control of police and commu-nication centers, or the temporary and partial "belligerent occupation" of territory.[33]

This important distinction between limited armed invasion and war was recognized by Russia in its ultimatum to Turkey in 1853, by the United States in its ultimatum to Nicaragua in the following year, by Italy in its dispute with Turkey over Tripoli and Cyrene in 1911, and by Mussolini's Italy in its controversy with Greece over the island of Corfu in 1923. In their 1921 ultimatum to Germany, the former Allied powers demanded fulfillment of treaty provisions regarding reparations payments, disarmament, and a trial of war criminals. They threatened that noncompliance within twenty-four hours would lead to a limited armed "occupation of the Valley of the Ruhr and ... military and naval measures that may be required."[34] Several years later, Poland issued a similar ultimatum to Czechoslovakia. In 1938, impressed by the success of Hitler's foreign policy and the weakness of the Czechs, Poland demanded the evacuation of certain disputed territory around Teschen and the release of Polish political prisoners. Failure to comply within the specified time limit, the Poles threatened, would lead to an armed invasion and occupation of only the territory in question.[35]

These historical cases of ultimata threatening limited armed invasion rather than war foreshadowed more recent efforts of coercive diplomacy. One of these occurred with the Israeli ultimatum to Lebanon in March 1970. Here the Israelis demanded that the government in Beirut stop Arab guerrillas from launching attacks across the Lebanese border. If compliance was not immediately forthcoming, Israel threatened to turn a six-mile stretch of southern Lebanon into a "scorched-earth desert."[36] Both parties recognized that the use of force would be restricted to a particular border territory and would not involve a full-scale war.

Threats of War

A theoretical distinction between the "state of peace" and the "state of war" is as ancient as Cicero's dictum that "there is no middle ground between war and peace." Coercion within the complexities of international politics, however, can seldom be accurately defined in terms of this simplistic dichotomy. Indeed, the inherent ambiguity is reflected in a highly regarded book about the struggle for power in the post–World War II period suggestively entitled *Neither War nor Peace.*[37] Thus, in the absence of any universally accepted criteria for determining precisely at what point conflict becomes war, it is perhaps more realistic to regard war as approaching the upper extremity of coercive measures in our scale of ascending intensity.[38]

This conception of the relative location of war within levels of coercion was recognized in the past when ultimata were issued that implicitly threatened war if demands were not met. If no commitment to localize the area of coercion or to limit the degree of violence appeared, states generally came to understand from the context and surrounding circumstances that the ultimatum presented an implicit threat of war. Previous statements and commitments, the tension of the occasion, reputations of decision makers, and the capabilities and intentions of the disputants were all factors that determined whether the measures threatened would be perceived as acts of war.

Immediately before the outbreak of World War I, the British became alarmed by German troop mobilizations and threats against Belgian neutrality. Considering such action to be in serious opposition to its traditional policies and vital interests, Britain issued an ultimatum to Germany demanding that satisfactory assurances respecting Belgium be provided by midnight that same day, August 4. The threat stated that in the event of noncompliance, His Majesty's government would "feel bound to take all steps in [its] power to uphold the neutrality of Belgium."[39] A similar ultimatum was used at the time of the Suez Crisis in 1956. Following Colonel Gamel Nasser's seizure of the Suez Canal, Britain, France, and Israel colluded to engage in military action to topple him from power in Egypt. After the Israeli invasion of the Sinai, the British and French issued an ultimatum to Egypt with the demands to "stop all warlike action on land, sea, and air," to withdraw forces within ten miles of the canal, and to accept temporary occupation of key positions at Port Said, Ismailia, and Suez. A reply was demanded within twelve hours. Failure to meet these demands would result in the intervention of Anglo-French forces "in whatever strength may be necessary to secure compliance."[40] In both these cases, the efforts at coercive diplomacy through ultimata failed, and the antagonists found themselves at war.

States sometimes found that implicit threats, however, could be overly subject to various interpretations and misperceptions. In these cases, they chose to issue an ultimatum explicitly stating that unless compliance with demands was forthcoming within a fixed period of time, war would follow immediately. They formalized this procedure as early as 1907 in the Third Hague Convention. Intending to give prior notice to adversaries and thus prevent "surprise" and "equivocation" in beginning war, Article I provided: "the Contracting Powers recognize that hostilities between them are not to commence without a previous unequivocal warning, which shall take the form either of a declaration of war, giving reasons, or of an ultimatum with a conditional declaration of war."[41] Such a conditional declaration of war needed no subsequent announcement, for states understood that a status of war would be the consequence ipso facto of the expiration of the time limit or the rejection of the demands.

An example of this type of conditional declaration of war is provided by the ultimatum issued to Great Britain by President Paulus Kruger of the Transvaal in 1899. After expressing fear concerning the concentration of British forces near its borders, the South African Republic demanded that all points of difference be resolved by amicable means and that troops on its borders be withdrawn. The ultimatum pressed for an affirmative reply within three days. In the event of noncompliance, the ultimatum threatened that the republic would "with great regret be compelled to regard the action of Her

Majesty's Government as a formal declaration of war" and would not hold itself responsible for the consequences.[42] Noncompliance in this case resulted in the outbreak of the Boer War. The British and French ultimata in 1939 likewise threatened a conditional declaration of war, and Hitler's refusal to comply resulted in the subsequent outbreak of World War II.

Today and at first glance, formal declarations of war may appear as only ceremonial baggage or legalistic trivia carried over from an earlier era. The complexities of international politics and the speed of contemporary weapons delivery systems may seem to make such declarations much more difficult to issue and receive. The experience of the past, however, does have considerable relevance for the theory and practice of coercive diplomacy. The difference between an implicit threat of war and an explicit declaration of war in an ultimatum is not solely a matter of what is verbalized or left unstated. The failure of one side to comply with demands coupled with an implicit threat of war by the other does not automatically produce war (as does a conditional declaration) but is followed by another procedural step: a formal declaration of war. Thus, when Germany failed to comply with the demands in its 1914 ultimatum, Britain then issued a formal declaration of war on the following day: "Owing to the summary rejection by the German Government ... His Majesty's Government [has] declared ... that a state of war exists."[43] This deliberate, additional procedure of declaring war should not be considered a mere legal formality but rather a built-in delay factor that at least carried the possibility of giving adversaries invaluable time for further utility calculations and considerations of prudent crisis management.

Threats of Escalating a War

At the extreme end of the scale of intensifying violence are those threats in an ultimatum that involve escalating a war already in progress. This increase in coercive pressure can be accomplished by widening the geographical area of conflict, compounding the escalation, or increasing its intensity. Escalation, for example, could result by invading additional territory, attacking new targets or an ally or client of the opponent, or quantitatively increasing the intensity of the conflict by using more equipment or even new types of weapons.[44]

One of the most critical escalations of war in our own time is that involving crossing the threshold from conventional to nuclear weapons. In fact, the coercive potential of nuclear weapons was first communicated by means of an ultimatum. In a joint communication issued in 1945 during the last few days of World War II, the United States, Britain, and China sent the Potsdam Declaration to Japan, demanding the unconditional surrender of Japanese armed forces, the removal of "irresponsible" and "militaristic" leaders, and the destruction of Japanese war-making potential. The time limit was ambiguously phrased in the statement that the Allies "shall brook no delay." The threat, made increasingly credible by air and sea attacks on the Japanese mainland and the dropping of thousands of leaflets over major cities, contained no explicit reference to the use of atomic weapons but did refer to the employment of "immeasurably greater" might than that ever used against Nazi Germany. Noncompliance, the ultimatum threatened, would be met by the "complete destruction of the Japanese armed forces" and the "utter devastation of the Japanese homeland."[45] The failure of Japan to comply with these demands resulted in the unleashing of atomic bombs on Hiroshima and Nagasaki.

Interestingly, all of the ultimata discussed thus far that threatened war or the escalation of an existing war failed to coerce those threatened. That is, they failed for one reason or another to persuade opponents to change their behavior in a positive direction. Every one of the ultimata issued in 1899 before the Boer War, in 1914 prior to World War I, in 1939 before World War II, in 1945 during that war, and in 1956 during the Suez Crisis, among others, resulted not in compliance with the accompanying demands but rather in increased armed conflict and war.

VARIABLE PURPOSES OF ULTIMATA

Thus far we have seen from historical practice that even in the extreme variant of coercive diplomacy—the ultimatum—threats of punishment for noncompliance may range from nonviolent measures through limited degrees of coercion to the escalation of war itself. Similarly, demands may vary in their expansiveness, and even time limits may extend from a few hours to several weeks in duration. The particular degree of violence, extensiveness, or urgency in each requisite element of an ultimatum, it is important to observe, is highly dependent not only upon the contextual variables deemed relevant by the coercing power but also upon the purposes for which these extreme variants are employed. Ultimata are the means, von Clausewitz would argue, designed to achieve particular ends and for this reason cannot be considered apart from their purposes. And, like other features of ultimata, even at the extremes purposes can also vary.

The varieties and interdependence of intentions, motivations, and objectives for which any power will resort to an ultimatum may be impossible to determine fully. At times, for instance, there may be significant differences between the actual purpose of an ultimatum and the one that might be announced publicly. On other occasions a coercing power might issue an ultimatum as a part of a plan for aggression or, in sharp contrast, for a defense of peace and protection of the status quo. Yet an examination of several recurring characteristics in historical cases might help us to identify, clarify, and distinguish at least several types of purposes for which ultimata are used.

In the past, states generally employed ultimata as the most extreme variant of coercive diplomacy in order to impart a sense of tension, urgency, and finality to the "final" statement or "last word" given. Within this general framework of a common purpose for which they were used, however, ultimata also may or may not have been primarily, or even necessarily, intended for the immediate intimidation of an opponent. Ultimata, as we will see, were sometimes employed to mobilize domestic opinion, to demonstrate bravado and posture at home in order to improve one's bargaining position, to set a war into motion, to bring an issue to the fore, or to indicate the maximum amount of concession one would make, among other purposes.

To Bring an Issue to the Fore for Resolution

States practicing coercive diplomacy sometimes used an ultimatum to resolve a dispute by bringing an issue dramatically to the fore. To do so effectively, they reasoned, might focus an opponent's attention on a particular neglected and serious problem by saying, in effect, "*This* is the issue that we want resolved, and we want it settled *now.*" Thus, an ultimatum could be used to deliberately create a diplomatic crisis and actually increase tension in order to induce an opponent to address a serious complaint or demand.

Frustrated by the failure to resolve a number of long-standing disputes with its neighbor, the Polish government, for example, issued an ultimatum to Lithuania in March 1938. It observed that the two countries had not maintained normal diplomatic relations for nearly twenty years and thus had been unable to settle festering problems such as explosive frontier incidents along their common border and retaliatory actions taken against their respective national minorities. If this situation continued any longer, the Poles argued, it would become intolerable. One of the possible results of a quarrel between states, as we have seen, is the breaking off of diplomatic relations. Ironically, in this case (and because the purpose was different), the Poles demanded in their forty-eight hour ultimatum that diplomatic relations between the two countries actually be established in order that disputes might be brought to the fore and thereby resolved.[46]

The Soviets used their 1958 ultimatum to the West over Berlin for the same purpose. In his lengthy introduction to the ultimatum, Soviet Premier Nikita Khrushchev recalled the history of Germany since World War II, the Potsdam Agreements, and the abnormal situation of a divided Berlin. The text described West Berlin as "a slow-burning fuse leading to a barrel of gunpowder" and expressed the desire to see the German Democratic Republic after so many years finally recognized "like any other independent state." The extraordinarily long six-month time limit for compliance indicated a desire not to launch a war but to begin discussions. The Soviet government, Khrushchev stated, "regards this period as quite adequate for finding a sound basis for a solution to the problems connected with the change in the position of Berlin and for preventing the possibility of any complications. ... During this period the sides will have the possibility of proving, by settling the Berlin issue, their desire for a relaxation of international tension."[47] This ultimatum appeared designed not to terminate negotiations but rather to open them.[48]

To State the Maximum Amount of Concession

Ultimata were also used to indicate the maximum amount of concession the coercing state would make in order to reach a settlement. Ultimata could be employed to convey the irreducible minimum that would be accepted, a plan or scheme of arrangement to be imposed, or the maximum amount that would be conceded.[49]

The case of the Austrian ultimatum to Russia near the end of the Crimean War in 1856, as noted earlier, provides ample evidence of such a purpose. Frustrated by a war that seemingly could not be favorably concluded and by the discovery of secret negotiations among other belligerents, Count Buol of Austria issued an ultimatum to Russia demanding that his terms of mediation be accepted as the basis for settlement. His demands included a "yes or no" answer, and he steadfastly refused to accept any modifications to his "maximum concessions."[50] Likewise, nearly one century later at the end of another war, the chief negotiator for the United Nations Command received instructions to issue the "last offer" to his counterparts during the Korean War. In May 1953, the Chinese from the People's Republic of China and the North Koreans were given a tacit ultimatum stating a time limit of one week for them to accept the U.N. "final position" and "last conditions" of settlement. This conveyed the maximum amount of concession that the Allies would grant and represented, in the words of one authority, a "take-it-or-leave-it" proposal.[51]

To Issue Obligatory Warnings
or Follow Customary Procedure

In the past, ultimata were used frequently to fulfill either customary or legal obligations for warning opponents prior to the outbreak of hostilities and thus set into motion a certain sequence of events. The idea that war should not commence without notification or a declaration, of course, was ritualistically accepted practice among the ancients and was insisted upon by Hugo Grotius and other early writers on international law. Although the issuance of such warnings partially lapsed into disuse, the Institute de Droit International located in Switzerland recognized the advantages of issuing a warning and of pacing events for the sake of crisis management and thus recommended that these practices be continued. The Hague Conference of 1907 adopted this recommendation, agreeing that hostilities between the contending parties "must not commence without previous and explicit warning." This warning was to be provided by either a separate declaration of war or an ultimatum containing a conditional declaration of war.[52]

For this reason, all of the ultimata issued just prior to the tragic outbreak of World War I contained conditional warnings of war. To illustrate, as a signatory to the Hague Convention, Germany issued an ultimatum to Belgium in 1914 threatening that unless compliance with demands was forthcoming, Germany would be "compelled to consider Belgium as an enemy" and be forced to adjust relations by "the decision of arms."[53] In accordance with customarily expected behavior, this warning was followed by a formal declaration of war. When the world eliminated this norm of behavior from the classical system of diplomacy, the comfort of past predictability was replaced by the twentieth-century terror of surprise attacks.

To Humiliate an Opponent

The humiliation or embarrassment of an opponent was occasionally the purpose of ultimata.[54] During some international crises, a power deliberately wanted to embarrass another leader or country before domestic or foreign observers. By such means the coercing power sought to increase its bargaining position or simply bolster its own self-esteem.

Historically, the British appear to have used ultimata for this purpose and with a certain arrogance on numerous occasions, particularly when dealing with significantly weaker states. The ultimatum issued from Britain to Greece in 1850 over the Don Pacifico Affair provided one notable example. Although the initial provocation had occurred against a British subject three years earlier, Lord Palmerston calculated that even a late ultimatum would humiliate the Greeks before the authority of Pax Britannica and also might appeal to British national pride and chauvinism. The man who would soon reject the argument that ethics should prevent intimidation in international relations[55] announced with a flourish that it had to be determined "whether, as the Roman, in days of old, held himself free from indignity when he could say *Civis Romanus sum;* so also a British subject, in whatever land he may be, shall feel confident that the watchful eye and the strong arm of England will protect him against injustice and wrong."[56] Nearly a century later, the British issued a similar ultimatum to King Faruq of Egypt. In an effort to humiliate the king and to embarrass him before his own people and his political opposition, British Ambassador Miles Lampson delivered an ultimatum in February 1942 described as a "gross insult" and as "Faruq's humiliation." "Lampson," wrote one observer, placing the episode in very personal terms, "regarded the twenty-two-year-old Faruq, some forty years his junior, as a youth who had to be brought to heel."[57]

To Prepare for Offensive Action or Aggression

Historically, one of the most frequently recurring purposes for which states employed ultimata was that of preparing for offensive action or carrying out aggressive designs. A power issuing an ultimatum, for example, did so in an attempt to manipulate public opinion, mobilize resources, or provide justification for its own aggression. Perhaps this is why one observer of international politics wrote that there is a "deeply ingrained" view that employing ultimata "shows one to the world as wicked and reckless."[58] An opponent's failure to comply with the demands of an ultimatum in these cases could be used as an indication of the cause of a conflict or as an excuse for waging war. Such attempted justifications could manipulate perceptions for bargaining purposes; influence allies, neutrals, and opinion within the opponent's territory; or mobilize elite and public opinion in one's own country. Convincingly placing blame on the opponent might provide authority for legislative or executive acts that depended upon the existence of emergencies to remove some inhibitions against the use of force and coercion and to arouse support and favor at home and abroad. Policy, in these cases, faced inward as well as outward.[59]

Italy issued an ultimatum to Turkey in 1911, for example, as a means of declaring that the imperial government "has shown constant hostility toward all Italian activity in Tripoli and Cyrene" and of rejecting any proposals for new negotiations—"the uselessness of which has been demonstrated by past experience and which ... would be themselves permanent causes of disagreement and conflict." It asserted that "the events which will follow can only be regarded as the necessary consequences of the conduct followed for so long by the Turkish authorities."[60] Austria's 1914 ultimatum likewise accused Serbia of being a "perpetual menace to tranquility" and drew attention to "the painful events" of the recent past involving "acts of terrorism and a series of outrages and murders"[61] in order to justify a military attack.

In like manner, even after the Nanking government had accepted an emergency form of settlement following the Japanese ultimatum to China in 1937, the leading Japanese general justified his offensive measures on the basis "that every means to reach a peaceful settlement has been exhausted, and that the peace of North China, which is of vital importance to both Japan and Manchukuo, has been disrupted with consequent imminent danger to the lives and property of Japanese citizens."[62] Several years later, Joseph Stalin issued his 1940 ultimatum to Lithuania just prior to occupying and absorbing the Baltic states into the Soviet Union. He accused the Lithuanians of scheming to form an anti-Soviet military pact and of being "directly guilty of acts of provocation committed against the garrisons of the Soviet Union in Lithuania."[63] Certainly, to foreign audiences, the excuses and justifications in these offensive ultimata were far from convincing and were seen instead as fabrications and provocations designed to justify aggression.

To Prepare Prudently for Defense Against Aggression

In sharp contrast to the use of ultimata for aggressive intent, states practicing coercive diplomacy even at the extreme also issued ultimata for purposes of genuine self-defense, that is, to protect important objectives, values, or interests. These nations intended to stop or undo the aggression of others, to prevent something worse from happening, to demonstrate resolve in order to deter additional aggressive action by an opponent, or to prepare prudently for likely escalation by the other side.

Faced with the German invasion of Poland in September 1939, for example, Britain and France sought to halt Hitler's offensive designs and prevent the outbreak of yet another major world war in the first half of the twentieth century. Their ultimatum therefore threatened that unless the Germans suspended "all aggressive action in Poland" and "promptly withdrew their forces from Polish territory," a state of war would result.[64] This joint Anglo-French effort at coercive diplomacy was undertaken far too late, however, and following a consistent pattern of appeasement lacked sufficient potency if not also credibility. Hitler refused to comply, and when the time limit expired, World War II began, quickly engulfing Europe and then much of the rest of the world. Members of the U.N. Security Council likewise intended for their November 1990 ultimatum to Saddam Hussein to undo his aggression against Kuwait. They wanted to defend Kuwait by persuading Iraq to withdraw from the occupied territory, preferably without armed conflict. Like the British and French before them, however, they failed in this effort to avert hostilities, and the Persian Gulf War started in January 1991.

CONCLUSIONS FROM HISTORY
AND FROM THE EXTREMES OF COERCION

These many historical examples of ultimata and of the extreme uses of coercion suggest several conclusions or "lessons" as we think about the theory and practice of coercive diplomacy.[65]

Flexibility in Components

Even when states employ the extreme variant of coercive diplomacy, an ultimatum can allow many possibilities for discrete measures, paced events, carefully tailored conditions, and general flexibility. As we have seen, in making demands, states need not insist upon the total capitulation of a regime or upon undoing whatever has been accomplished at great expense but can make less ambitious demands, such as requiring that an opponent stop what he is doing. Nor do demands need to stand alone, for they may be accompanied by positive incentives or inducements that can assist in reaching accommodation and conflict resolution. In setting time limits, states do not need to resort to hours but can use days, weeks, or even months to convey a sense of urgency and yet still slow the pace of a crisis. Similarly, states need not resort to war or violence as punishment but can threaten a wide range of diplomatic, economic, or psychological measures to exert different levels and types of coercion. The distinctions employed in the past may become increasingly important, for as the threat of actual force becomes increasingly less usable in bargaining during the international crises of our own age, more flexible and measured sanctions may become essential.

Variety in Purposes

States use ultimata for a wide variety of purposes. One may be to intimidate an opponent, but others may be designed to bring an issue to the fore, to stake out a "take-it-or-leave-it" position, to carry out customary procedure, to humiliate an opponent, to prepare for defense, or to initiate offensive action. Recognition of these varied purposes from the past is as important as awareness of the various gradations of threats, for during tense international crises actions are not always perceived as they are intended. A state unaware of the potential dangers and risks, for instance, might present an ultimatum merely to raise an issue as a means of resolving a conflict; but an opponent who is genuinely unaware of the variety of possible motives might read this message as a signal for war and therefore be tempted to launch a preemptive strike. For this reason, interpretative skill and cognizance of these variable purposes may save a recipient of an ultimatum from disastrous consequences.

Apparent Attractiveness

The number, frequency, and wide geographical scope of historical cases from the past suggest, as noted in Chapter 1, that when compared with traditional military strategies, coercive diplomacy and ultimata are apparently attractive to statesmen during international crises. They offer at least the possibility of achieving policy objectives with much greater economy, less bloodshed, and fewer risks than do strategies that rely more directly and exclusively on the actual use of force and on only implicit communications. The direct and serious nature of ultimata can be very effective in enabling the power employing coercive diplomacy to convey the impression of urgency and resolve. Coercing powers may also regard the explicit quality of ultimata as useful for direct communication that conveys greater precision not only to what is demanded, but equally important, to what is *not* demanded of an opponent. This process may reduce the likelihood of dangerous misperception or serious miscalculation.

Ethical Limitations

The beguiling character of coercive diplomacy and ultimata, however, should not detract from their inherent ethical and practical dangers and limitations. For as long as some have known the basic principles of coercion, other thoughtful men and women have attempted to find ways of constraining the use of intimidation and possible violence through the creation of ethical norms. They learned long ago that without some measure of caution and distrust, states can fall victim to exploitation and assault; they also know that without some measure of trust established through limitations and norms, states cannot cooperate on the basis of shared values or common goals.[66] This should not surprise us, for although the world of international politics and diplomacy frequently resembles that described by Machiavelli and Hobbes, as Stanley Hoffmann observes in *Duties Beyond Borders,* "We must remember that states are led by human beings whose actions affect human beings within and outside: considerations of good and evil, right or wrong, are therefore both inevitable and legitimate."[67]

Evidence from the past suggests that those features of coercive diplomacy characterized as manipulation, intimidation, blackmail, hostility, preparations to inflict punishment, breaches of faith, and lawlessness can easily clash with the normative values of honesty, mutual respect, reciprocity, self-restraint, equality, justice, sovereignty, peace, and the principles of international law. Defensive uses of coercive diplomacy and ultimata, as we have seen, in certain circumstances may actually foster and protect these norms; this is recognized by the provisions of the U.N. Charter and several subsequent declarations that make coercive threats of force, as well as the use of force, against the territorial integrity or political independence of any state legal if it is applied in defense of the purposes of the United Nations.[68] Offensive uses of coercion for aggression and conquest, however, and as history amply demonstrates, violate any such norms that seek to create limits or restraints on unbridled behavior.

Practical Dangers and Limitations

Historical experience also indicates that by its very nature an ultimatum is potentially escalatory. It insists upon compliance with heretofore unknown demands, imposes an urgent time limit upon a less-pressured pace of events, and, of particular importance, threatens that more coercion than was previously employed will result as punishment if compliance with the demands is not forthcoming. This urgent and final character of ultimata, as noted in Chapter 2, often flagrantly contradicts prudent crisis management, which requires that measures be slowed up and spaced out and that time be provided for reflection and ample communication between the contesting states. Consequently, coercion tends to beget coercion in a dangerously escalating cycle.[69] As one observer correctly notes, "Diplomatic history is littered with conflicts that escalated far beyond the goals either party initially perceived to be in conflict as a result of needlessly severe coercive tactics adopted by one or both parties."[70] (A more detailed discussion of the risks of ultimata is presented in Part Three.)

In addition, an ultimatum aimed at blatant intimidation by its very nature readily excites rather than inhibits tensions and thereby increases the possibilities for miscalculation. Historically, ultimata have often appeared without warning and have been perceived by the recipients as needless provocation, capricious manipulation, unwarranted interference, vindictive bullying, or dangerous blackmail.[71] As such, they carry the danger of being seriously dysfunctional if they increase the probability of exceeding an opponent's threshold of tolerance, provoking a spasmodic outrage, strengthening the initial resistance to comply, or producing an imprudent and unfavorable response, thereby precipitating a crisis into eruption through emotional miscalculation.

✻   ✻   ✻

Examining coercive diplomacy from both the perspective of history and the perspective of the extremes of coercion offers two advantages. The first is that the richness of the past and the experiences of others in different times and places establish a historical context that can provide invaluable insights and perspectives on our contemporary concerns. The second is that an analysis of the extremes of any phenomenon often magnifies and illumines characteristics that might otherwise go unnoticed or unexplored. Consequently, experiences from the nineteenth and twentieth centuries involving the extreme variability of coercion may help us to better understand the cases that follow and thus lead to a more refined development of the theory and a greater appreciation for the practice—and the limitations—of coercive diplomacy in general, and of ultimata in particular, as instruments of foreign policy.

NOTES

1. See Alexander L. George, David K. Hall, and William E. Simons, *The Limits of Coercive Diplomacy* (Boston: Little, Brown, 1971); Paul Gordon Lauren, ed., *Diplomacy: New Approaches in History, Theory, and Policy* (New York: Free Press, 1979), pp. 183ff.; Glenn Snyder and Paul Diesing, *Conflict Among Nations* (Princeton: Princeton University Press, 1977); Charles Lockhart, *Bargaining in International Conflicts* (New York: Columbia University Press, 1979); Oran Young, *The Politics of Force: Bargaining During International Crises* (Princeton: Princeton University Press 1968); Thomas Schelling, *Arms and Influence* (New Haven: Yale University Press, 1966); R. J. Leng, "When Will They Ever Learn? Coercive Bargaining in Recurrent Crises," *Journal of Conflict Resolution* 27 (September 1983): 379–419; and William Butler, ed., *The Non-Use of Force in International Law* (Dordrecht: Martinus Nijhoff, 1989).

2. Sun Tzu, *The Art of War,* translated with an Introduction by Samuel Griffith (Oxford: Oxford University Press, 1971), p. 40.

3. Thucydides, *The Peloponnesian War,* Introduction by M. I. Finley (New York: Penguin Books, 1972), p. 57.

4. Ibid., Book V, pp. 402, 406–407.

5. Niccolo Machiavelli, *Art of War,* Introduction by Neal Wood (New York: Bobbs-Merrill, 1965), Book I, p. 30, Book VII, pp. 210–212; and *The Prince,* Introduction by Christian Gauss (New York: New American Library, 1952), Ch. 13, p. 80; Ch. 14, p. 81; and Ch. 24, p. 118.

6. Thomas Hobbes, *Leviathan,* Introduction by Francis B. Randall (New York: Washington Square Press, 1964), Ch. 14, p. 96; and Ch. 15, p. 98.

7. François de Callières, in translation, by A. F. Whyte, under the title *On the Manner of Negotiating with Princes* (Notre Dame: University of Notre Dame Press, 1963), p. 117. Also see pp. 7, 41, and 55.

8. Carl von Clausewitz, *On War,* edited and translated by Michael Howard and Peter Paret (Princeton: Princeton University Press, 1976), Book I, Ch. 1, p. 87. Also see the interesting discussion in Sissela Bok, *A Strategy for Peace: Human Values and the Threat of War* (New York: Vintage, 1990), especially pp. 55–78, "Clausewitz, War, and Strategy."

9. See Paul Gordon Lauren, "Crisis Prevention in Nineteenth-Century Diplomacy," in Alexander L. George, ed., *Managing U.S.-Soviet Rivalry* (Boulder, Colo.: Westview Press, 1983), pp. 31–64.

10. For earlier discussions of ultimata and the problem of definitions, see Paul Gordon Lauren, "Ultimata and Coercive Diplomacy," *International Studies Quarterly* (June 1972): 131–165; Donald M. Snow, *National Security: Enduring Problems in a Changing Defense Environment* (New York: St. Martin's Press, 1991), pp. 4ff.; Herman Kahn, *On Escalation: Metaphors and Scenarios* (Baltimore: Penguin Books, 1968); Ian Brownlie, *International Law and the Use of Force by States* (Oxford: Clarendon Press, 1963); J. Philipp Rosenberg, "The Cheshire Ultimatum," *The Journal of Politics* (August 1979): 933–940; Melquiades Gamboa, *A Dictionary of International Law and Diplomacy* (New York: Oceana, 1973), pp. 260–261; Fred Charles Iklé, *How Nations Negotiate* (New York: Praeger, 1963), p. 104; Brownlie, *International Law and the Use of Force by States,* p. 123; *Oxford English Dictionary,* vol. 11, "U" (Oxford: Clarendon, 1961), p. 12; H. Lauterpacht, ed., *Oppenheim's International Law: A Treatise* (London: Longmans Green, 1952), "Disputes, War, and Neutrality"; Academie Diplomatique Internationale, *Dictionnaire Diplomatique* (Paris: Academie Diplomatique, 1933); Hans Asbeck, *Das Ultimatum in Modernen Volkerrecht* (Berlin: Rothschild, 1933); Jack C. Plano and Roy Olton, *The International Relations Dictionary* (New York: Holt, Rinehart & Winston, 1969), p. 223; Melquiades Gamboa, *Elements of Diplomatic and Consular Practice: A Glossary* (Quezon City, Phillipines: Phoenix Press, 1966), p. 393; and T. E. Holland, *Lectures in International Law* (London: Sweet and Maxwell, 1933).

11. As cited in Raymond Sontag, *European Diplomatic History, 1871–1932* (New York: Century, 1933), p. 123.

12. Security Council Resolution 678 (1990), text in news release SC/5237, November 29, 1990, and as reproduced in many newspapers. The press in both the United States and abroad correctly referred to the Security Council communication

as an ultimatum. Among many examples, see "U.S. and Allies Discuss How to Use 45 Days," *Los Angeles Times,* November 30, 1990; and "Treffen mit Bush abgesagt," *Frankfurter Allgemeine,* December 16, 1990.

13. See, for example, Eduard Shevardnadze, as cited in "UN Vote Marks Turning Point," *Washington Post,* November 30, 1990; "UN Security Council Clears Use of Force," *Wall Street Journal,* November 30, 1990; and "Logistics in the Desert," *International Herald Tribune,* December 14, 1990.

14. Great Britain Foreign Office, *Documents on British Foreign Policy, 1919–1939,* First Series (London: Her Majesty's Stationery Office, 1967) 15: 579.

15. U.S. Department of State, *American Foreign Policy: Current Documents 1958* (Washington, D.C.: Government Printing Office, 1962), pp. 691–696. Also see Wichard Woyke, ed., *Handworterbuch Internationale Politik* (Opladen: Leske und Budrich, 1980), pp. 5, 43–44.

16. De Callières, *On the Manner of Negotiating with Princes,* p. 7.

17. See Gordon A. Craig and Alexander L. George, *Force and Statecraft* (New York: Oxford University Press, 1983), pp. 193–195.

18. U.S. Naval War College, *International Law Topics and Discussions, 1913* (Washington, D.C.: Government Printing Office, 1914), p. 61.

19. Iklé, *How Nations Negotiate,* p. 104. Also see J. B. Scott, ed., *Proceedings of the Hague Peace Conference of 1907,* vol. 3 (New York: Oxford University Press, 1921), p. 43; *Oxford English Dictionary,* vol. 11, p. 12; Brownlie, *International Law and the Use of Force,* p. 123; and Gamboa, *Elements of Diplomatic and Consular Practice,* p. 393.

20. An early example is provided in "Foreign Advices," *Gentleman's Magazine* (January 1731): "There are privately handed about here Coppies of the Ultimatum (or last Proposals) of the Allies of Seville, as transmitted hither from Paris." For additional discussions of this type of ultimatum, see Harold Nicolson, *Diplomacy* (New York: Oxford University Press, 1963), p. 135; *Dictionnaire de la Terminologie du Droit International* (Paris: Sirey, 1960), p. 624; Ernest Satow, *A Guide to Diplomatic Practice* (London: Longman's Green, 1922), pp. 162–168; Ernest Satow, *A Guide to Diplomatic Practice* (London: Longman's Green, 1957), p. 107; and C. M. Stevens, *Strategy and Collective Bargaining Negotiation* (New York: McGraw-Hill, 1963).

21. Satow, *A Guide to Diplomatic Practice (1922),* p. 167.

22. Norman Ferris, "Abraham Lincoln and the *Trent* Affair," *Lincoln Herald* 69 (Fall 1967): 131–135.

23. U.S. Naval War College, *International Law Documents* (Washington, D.C.: Government Printing Office 1922), p. 208.

24. Hans Speier, "Soviet Atomic Blackmail and the North Atlantic Alliance," *World Politics* 9 (1957): 318.

25. Great Britain, Parliament, House of Commons, Command Paper 1858, *Sessional Papers, 1923,* vol. 25 (London: His Majesty's Stationery Office, 1923), pp. 5–13.

26. H.G.W. Woodhead, ed., *The China Year Book, 1929–1930* (Tientsin: Tientsin Press, 1930), p. 1225; and N. Hill, "Was There an Ultimatum Before Pearl Harbor?" *American Journal of International Law* 42 (1948): 356.

27. Michael Binyon and Peter Stothard, "Lithuanians Given 48-Hour Ultimatum," *The Times* (London), April 14, 1990.

28. See George in Chapter 1 of this volume; Kahn, *On Escalation,* p. 67; Speier, "Soviet Atomic Blackmail," p. 307; and Alfred Vagts, *Defense and Diplomacy: The Soldier and the Conduct of Foreign Relations* (New York: King's Crown Press, 1956), p. 231.

29. C. O. Paullin, *Diplomatic Negotiations of American Naval Officers* (Baltimore: Johns Hopkins University Press, 1912), p. 9. For more recent examples of the use of armed force as a political instrument of demonstration, see Barry Blechman and Stephen Kaplan, *Force Without War: U.S. Armed Forces as a Political Instrument* (Washington, D.C.: Brookings Institute, 1978), pp. 23, 38. Also see the interesting discussion in Robert Mandel, "The Effectiveness of Gunboat Diplomacy," *International Studies Quarterly* 30 (1986): 59–76.

30. Great Britain, Parliament, House of Commons, Command Paper 3006, *Sessional Papers, 1906,* vol. 137 (London: His Majesty's Stationery Office, 1906), Egypt no. 2, p. 8 [emphasis added].

31. See Brownlie, *International Law and the Use of Force;* M. McDougal and F. Feliciano, *Law and Minimum World Public Order: Legal Regulations of International Coercion* (New Haven: Yale University Press, 1961); and A. Hindmarsh, *Force in Peace: Force Short of War in International Relations* (Cambridge: Harvard University Press, 1933).

32. Great Britain, Parliament, House of Commons, "Further Correspondence Respecting the Demands Made upon the Greek Government," *Sessional Papers,* 1850, vol. 56 (London: Her Majesty's Stationery Office, 1850), pp. 3, 6, and 9 [emphasis added].

33. McDougal and Feliciano, *Law and Minimum World Public Order;* Lauterpacht, *Oppenheim's International Law;* and F. Jones, "Military Occupation of Alien Territory in Time of Peace," *Transactions of the Grotius Society* 9 (1924): 131–163.

34. Great Britain, Foreign Office, *Documents on British Foreign Policy, 1919–1939,* First Series, vol. 15 (London: Her Majesty's Stationery Office, 1967), p. 579.

35. Great Britain, Foreign Office, *Documents on British Foreign Policy, 1919–1939,* Third Series, vol. 3 (London: His Majesty's Stationery Office, 1950), p. 70.

36. "Threat to Beirut Reported," *New York Times,* March 7, 1970. The U.S. ultimatum to the Soviet Union during the Cuban Missile Crisis of 1962, in which the United States threatened to attack the missile bases, provides another example of this type.

37. Hugh Seton-Watson, *Neither War nor Peace* (New York: Praeger, 1966).

38. Myers McDougal et al., *Studies in World Public Order* (New Haven: Yale University Press, 1960); and Robert Osgood, *Limited War: The Challenge to American Strategy* (Chicago: University of Chicago Press, 1957).

39. U.S. Naval War College, *International Law Documents,* p. 116.

40. D. C. Watt, ed., *Documents on the Suez Crisis* (London: Royal Institute of International Affairs, 1957), p. 86. Technically speaking, and for the purpose of appearances, the ultimatum was issued to both Israel and Egypt. The Israeli government accepted the terms because they enabled Israel to retain military conquests. Egypt, just as naturally, refused them.

41. Scott, *Proceedings of the Hague Peace Conference,* 3: 43.

42. U.S. Naval War College, *International Law Topics and Discussions,* pp. 60–61.

43. U.S. Naval War College, *International Law Documents,* p. 117.

44. See Richard Smoke, *War: Controlling Escalation* (Cambridge: Harvard University Press 1977); Kahn, *On Escalation;* Bernard Brodie, *Escalation and the Nuclear Option* (Princeton: Princeton University Press, 1966); Stanley Hoffmann, *The State of War* (New York: Praeger, 1965); and Morton Halperin, *Limited War* (Cambridge: Center for International Affairs, 1962).

45. U.S. Department of State, *Foreign Relations of the United States: The Conference of Berlin, 1945* (Washington, D.C.: Government Printing Office, 1960), pp. 1474–1476. A more recent example of this type of ultimatum threatening escalation occurred during the 1991 Persian Gulf War, as documented in "U.S. Statements," and "A Defiant Baghdad Says Ultimatum Issued by U.S. is Shameful," *New York Times,* February 23, 1991.

46. Alfred Senn, "The Polish Ultimatum to Lithuania," *Journal of Baltic Studies* (Summer 1982): 144–156; and George Sakwa, "The Polish Ultimatum to Lithuania in March 1938," *Slavonic and East European Review* 55 (April 1977): 204–226.

47. U.S. Department of State, *American Foreign Policy: Current Documents, 1958* (Washington, D.C.: Government Printing Office, 1962), pp. 591–596.

48. See J. Herbert Altschull, "Khrushchev and the Berlin 'Ultimatum,'" *Journalism Quarterly* (Autumn 1977): 545–551, 565; J. Smith, *The Defense of Berlin* (Baltimore: Johns Hopkins Press, 1963), p. 194; and Peter Winters, "Vor 30 Jahren: Chruschtschows Berlin-Ultimatum," *Deutschland Archiv: Zeitschrift für Fragen der Deutschen Demokratischen Republik und der Deutschlandpolitik* 21 (1988): 1058–1067.

49. In collective bargaining this is known as *Boulwareism,* after the chief proponent of the technique, Lemuel Boulware, at one time the management negotiator for the General Electric Company. See Stevens, *Strategy and Collective Bargaining Negotiation,* pp. 34–37; and Iklé, *How Nations Negotiate,* p. 212.

50. See Satow, *A Guide to Diplomatic Practice* (1957), p. 107; and Paul W. Schroeder, *Austria, Great Britain, and the Crimean War* (Ithaca: Cornell University Press, 1972), especially "Austria's Ultimatum," pp. 311–346.

51. Rosemary Foot, "Nuclear Coercion and the Ending of the Korean Conflict," *International Security* (Winter 1988–1989): 111.

52. Scott, *Proceedings of the Hague Peace Conference,* 3: 43.

53. U.S. Naval War College, *International Law Documents,* p. 102.

54. I am grateful to Robert Jervis for drawing this to my attention.

55. See Schroeder, *Austria, Britain, and the Crimean War,* p. 317.

56. Lord Palmerston, as cited in J. Ridley, *Lord Palmerston* (London: Constable, 1970), p. 387. For similar nineteenth-century examples, see Andor Klay, *Daring Diplomacy: The Case of the First American Ultimatum* (Minneapolis: University of Minnesota Press, 1957), discussing the ultimatum from the United States to Austria in 1853; and George Paulsen, "The Szechwan Riots of 1895 and American 'Missionary Diplomacy,'" *Journal of Asian Studies* 28 (February 1969): 285–298, discussing the U.S. ultimatum to China in 1895.

57. Gabriel Warburg, "Lampson's Ultimatum to Faruq, 4 February 1942," *Middle Eastern Studies* (January 1975): 24, 29.

58. Iklé, *How Nations Negotiate,* p. 104.

59. See Roger Hilsman, *To Move a Nation* (New York: Dell, 1968), p. 13.

60. U.S. Naval War College, *International Law Topics and Discussions,* p. 64.

61. U.S. Naval War College, *International Law Documents,* p. 38.

62. Foreign Affairs Association of Japan, *Japan Year Book, 1937* (Tokyo: Keukyusha Press, 1938), p. 181.

63. See Thomas Remeikis, "The Decision of the Lithuanian Government to Accept the Soviet Ultimatum of June 14, 1940," *Lituanus* 21 (Winter 1975): 19–44.

64. Great Britain, Parliament, House of Commons, Command Paper 6106, *Sessional Papers,* 1938–39, vol. 27 (London: His Majesty's Stationery Office, 1939), p. 175.

65. For a fascinating discussion of the subject of learning "lessons" from history, see Richard E. Neustadt and Ernest R. May, *Thinking in Time: The Use of History for Decision Makers* (New York: Free Press, 1986). Also see Paul Gordon Lauren, "Diplomacy: History, Theory, and Policy," in Lauren, *Diplomacy,* pp. 3–18.

66. See Bok, *A Strategy for Peace,* p. 148; Kenneth W. Thompson, *Ethics, Functionalism, and Power in International Politics* (Baton Rouge: Louisiana State University Press, 1979); and David Gauthier, *Moral Dealing: Contract, Ethics, and Reason* (Ithaca: Cornell University Press, 1990), especially pp. 337, 341 and 351.

67. Stanley Hoffmann, *Duties Beyond Borders: On the Limits and Possibilities of Ethical International Politics* (Syracuse: Syracuse University Press, 1981), p. xii.

68. The key provisions are found in Article 2(4) of the U.N. Charter, signed in 1945, and the Declaration on Enhancing the Effectiveness of the Principle of the Non-Use of Force, adopted in 1987. For more discussion, see Butler, *The Non-Use of Force in International Law;* and F. S. Northedge, ed., *The Use of Force in International Relations* (New York: Free Press, 1974), especially Chapter 7, "Internal Restraints on the Use of Force," and Chapter 8, "Force and International Law."

69. Leng, "When Will They Ever Learn?" pp. 412–417.

70. Lockhart, *Bargaining in International Conflicts,* p. 146.

71. The role and importance of perceptions are discussed at length in Robert Jervis, *Perception and Misperception in International Politics* (Princeton: Princeton University Press 1976). Also see Paul S. Holbo, "Perilous Obscurity: Public Diplomacy and the Press in the Venezuelan Crisis, 1902–1903," *The Historian* 32 (May 1970): 428–448.

PART TWO

Introduction: The Practice of Coercive Diplomacy— Case Studies

ALEXANDER L. GEORGE

The abstract model of coercive diplomacy presented in Part One can enlighten and guide policy makers only to a limited extent. What is needed, in addition, is generic knowledge of how and why variants of coercive diplomacy work or fail in practice, what challenges and obstacles the strategy can encounter, and under what conditions it is likely to be successful or to fail. Therefore, one must study historical experience with coercive persuasion to understand what the general model has omitted or oversimplified and what policy makers ignore at their own peril. Past efforts to employ coercive diplomacy need to be studied analytically and systematically in order to provide a better understanding of the task that confronts policy makers when they consider using this strategy and attempt to adapt the general concept of coercive diplomacy to the specific configuration of a particular situation.

Part Two provides case materials for the formulation of generic knowledge of coercive diplomacy. Seven case studies are presented of instances in which the United States employed some variant of coercive diplomacy in the post–World War II era. It should be understood that, as in the writing of history in general, the reconstruction of events and the interpretations offered in these case studies are provisional; new data and alternative interpretations that may emerge in future scholarship would require us to reconsider these case studies.

The seven cases differ strikingly in the following respects: the magnitude of the objective the United States pursued by means of this strategy; the contexts in which the cases occurred; the variant of the strategy that was employed; and the success or failure of coercive diplomacy. The diversity of the cases serves the purposes of the study by enabling us better to understand the problems policy makers face in attempting to operationalize the general model of coercive diplomacy and adapt it to different circumstances. The cases examined also provide a basis for understanding why policy makers employ different variants of the strategy in different circumstances, the constraints and obstacles they encounter, and the reasons the strategy sometimes succeeds and at other times fails to achieve its objective. Each case provides information that is useful for developing generic knowledge. In the research strategy being employed in this study, similar questions are asked about each case, and the results serve as building blocks for the construction of generic knowledge.[1]

In no sense do these seven cases constitute a representative sample of the many historical instances in which the strategy has been attempted;[2] therefore, one cannot extrapolate from them the probability of success or failure of future attempts at coercive diplomacy. The seven cases do, however, provide a basis for understanding the context-dependent nature of the strategy, the conditions that favor success, the obstacles that may be encountered, and, more generally, the uses and limitations of the strategy. These findings, drawn from the case studies, are presented in Part Three.

The work as a whole should be an aid in the future judgment policy makers must exercise in determining whether to employ this strategy in dealing with different kinds of encroachments that arise. As noted earlier, coercive diplomacy is not the only nonmilitary option for dealing with encroachments on one's interests. In many cases U.S. policy makers decided not to resort to this strategy, evidently sensing that it would have been inappropriate, ineffectual, or too risky in the existing circumstances. Examples include the Iran crisis of 1946, the Berlin Blockade crisis of 1948–1949, the Taiwan Strait crisis of 1954–1955, the Quemoy crisis of 1958, and the Pueblo and Mayaguez incidents of 1968 and 1975, respectively.

NOTES

1. For discussion of this methodology, see Alexander L. George, "Case Studies and Theory Development: The Method of Structured, Focused Comparison," in Paul G. Lauren, ed., *Diplomatic History: New Approaches in History, Theory, and Policy* (New York: Free Press, 1979), pp. 43–68; and Alexander L. George and Timothy J. McKeown, "Case Studies and Theories of Organizational Decision Making," in *Advances in Information Processing in Organizations*, vol. 2 (Greenwich, Conn.: JAI Press, 1985), pp. 21–58.

2. The United States attempted variants of coercive diplomacy in a number of other crises; for example in the early phase of its response to the North Korean attack on South Korea in June 1950; in President Eisenhower's threat of financial pressure to induce England to call off its war against Egypt in 1956; in President Nixon's effort to

induce a withdrawal of Syrian tanks that invaded Jordan in 1970; in President Reagan's effort to deal with Syrian involvement in Lebanon in 1982; and perhaps at an early stage in the Iran hostage crisis of 1979–1981. Other cases in which the United States attempted the strategy of coercive diplomacy can probably be found if history were combed more thoroughly.

Of course, other states have also at least occasionally used this strategy. Joseph Stalin blockaded Allied ground access to West Berlin in 1948 in order to pressure the Western powers to give up their new policy toward the western zones of occupied Germany. In the prolonged Sino-Soviet border crisis of 1969, Nikita Khrushchev finally threatened to destroy China's nuclear facilities in order to induce Mao Tse-tung to cease his provocations. In the Falkland Islands case, the British use of coercive diplomacy failed to induce a withdrawal of Argentine forces, and war followed.

4

From Deterrence to Coercion to War: The Road to Pearl Harbor

SCOTT D. SAGAN

"Everything in war is very simple, but even the simplest thing is very difficult," Karl von Clausewitz once noted. The same thing could be said about strategies of deterrence and coercive diplomacy. The abstract logic of both strategies is simple: A statesman must make threats that are sufficiently potent and credible so as to persuade an adversary not to initiate an undesired action (deterrence) or to undo steps that have already been taken (coercion or compellence). Designing and implementing such strategies in the real world, however, is very difficult.

First, consider the issue of intelligence assessment. Statesmen using such strategies should attempt to make accurate evaluations of an adversary's motives, perceptions, and values. Yet considerable uncertainty usually exists because an adversary's motives, perceptions, and values are often unclear to the actors themselves, are sometimes inconsistent, and are always subject to change, deception, and manipulation. Second, consider the political constraints on effective bargaining behavior. Although statesmen may want to choose actions that maximize the likelihood of diplomatic success, domestic political concerns and alliance considerations can constrain the range of their practical choices. Third, consider the problems of implementation. Statesmen using tools of deterrence or coercive diplomacy should attempt to calibrate and control their threats and inducements to another state. Yet bureaucratic politics and organizational routines can greatly reduce their ability to manage the use of diplomatic and military tools with precision.

These are not, of course, novel insights. Although some scholars of international politics ignore these complicating problems for the sake of analytic clarity or theoretical parsimony, important research on deterrence and coercive diplomacy has shown that leaders' misperceptions, domestic and alliance constraints on behavior, and organizational impediments to centralized control often determine whether such strategies succeed or fail.[1] Studying history can remind political scientists what statesmen more intuitively know: The threat to use military force is an inherently difficult tool of diplomacy and is often subject to failure due to factors beyond the direct control of the leaders involved.

In the following case study of the origins of the Pacific War, I examine how such factors can influence decision makers during an international crisis.[2] At an abstract level, the history is a rather simple story: The United States successfully used the threat of an oil embargo and military intervention to deter a Japanese attack on Allied colonial possessions in Southeast Asia until the summer of 1941; but when the United States attempted to compel or coerce the Tokyo government into withdrawing its forces from China, the plan backfired, resulting in a Japanese decision for war. At a deeper level, however, the way in which these choices were made is precisely what needs to be explained. Why were these strategies chosen, and how did each side assess the power and credibility of the other's threats? Why did the United States place an oil embargo on Japan in 1941 and attempt to coerce all Japanese troops to withdraw from China? How did the Japanese government perceive the costs of an oil embargo and the withdrawal of its forces from China? How did the government think Japan could win a war against a vastly stronger military power? One must examine the decision-making processes in Tokyo and Washington and the strategic interaction between the two governments in considerable detail in order to answer these critical questions.

DETERRENCE AND THE ORIGINS
OF THE PACIFIC WAR

In the summer of 1940, after Germany's blitzkrieg through France and the British withdrawal at Dunkirk, the Japanese government faced unprecedented opportunities in Southeast Asia. The Dutch government went into exile, the new Vichy regime controlled French Indochina, and the British—who had always been hard-pressed to provide capabilities to support their forward position at Singapore—were fighting for their lives in the Battle of Britain. On July 5, 1940, junior officers in the Imperial Army attempted to assassinate Prime Minister Yonai Mitsumasa, who they considered too cautious and prone to appeasing U.S. and British interests. Within days, Army Minister Hata Shunroku resigned, bringing down the Yonai government.[3]

By the end of the month, Japan had a new prime minister—Prince Konoe Fumimaro—a new cabinet, and a new policy for the strategic possibilities created by the war in Europe. On July 27, the new Liaison Conference, composed of the senior civilian and military leadership, met and approved a historic document, "The Main Principles for Coping with the Changing World Situation." Its first sentence stated that "Japan shall expedite the settlement of the China Incident by taking measures to cope with the changing international situation and ... shall solve the Southern Area problem when a favorable opportunity is presented."[4]

Japanese Calculations

How did the Japanese military and civilian leaders assess the costs and benefits of expanding to the south? How did they evaluate whether the U.S. government would intervene if Tokyo's forces invaded the Asian colonies of Holland, France, and Great Britain? The origins of the Liaison Conference's "Main Principles" agreement can be directly traced to an earlier Imperial Army document, which called for an attempt to "settle the China Incident as quickly as possible" and stated that "preparations for war should be completed generally by the target date of the end of August [1940]." Article 2 of the document dealt specifically with contingencies in which the army wanted to go to war:

> In regard to the use of military force in the south, Japan will decide its time, scope and method upon consideration of various conditions at home and abroad, especially the state of the China Incident, the European situation, and our war preparedness. It will attack Hong Kong and the Malay peninsula, restricting insofar as possible its operations to Britain alone. It will endeavor insofar as possible to avoid war with the United States; however, anticipating that in the end it will resort to force against the United States if the situation requires, Japan will make the necessary military preparations.[5]

The closing sentence, threatening a war with the United States "if the situation requires," is less revealing than it appears because army leaders did not believe U.S. intervention was at all likely if Japan attacked Hong Kong and Singapore. In June 1940, army officers began to discuss a surprise attack aimed at Singapore alone, but when the Army General Staff approached the Navy General Staff in order to coordinate operational planning, officers in the Navy Operations Division refused to cooperate.[6] The Imperial Navy's position was that it would be highly imprudent to assume that the United States would remain uninvolved if Japan attacked the British and Dutch colonies.

Why did the navy believe this? The Imperial Navy based its position purely on U.S. military *capabilities* to intervene; it made no serious effort to study the probability of American intervention. The navy's position appears to have been crystallized by its reading of the large-scale strategic map exercises conducted in May 1940 in which the Imperial Navy attempted a surprise attack on the Borneo oil fields. This hypothetical attack succeeded in its preliminary stages, but the U.S. fleet at Pearl Harbor counterattacked, and what had been designed as a "quick grab" of the resource-rich islands became a prolonged war with the most feared enemy.[7] The navy's official report reached a devastating conclusion. The navy depended on U.S. and Dutch oil for the running of the fleet, and thus a total war against the United States would be a disaster:

1. If the US exports of petroleum are totally banned, it will be impossible to continue the war unless within four months we are able to secure oil in the Dutch East Indies and acquire the capacity to transport it to Japan.
2. Even then, Japan would be able to continue the war for a year at most. Should the war continue beyond a year, our chances of winning would be nil.[8]

Following these exercises, the navy insisted that it would be unwise to plan an attack against the British alone. Although it hoped to avoid using military force altogether, the navy insisted that all war plans include the United States as well as the European colonial powers. This requirement, it argued, meant that the Imperial Navy must receive a larger proportion of defense resources if the army insisted on planning for a Southern Advance.

The differences between the military services were not resolved at higher levels of the Japanese government. Instead, the Liaison Conference of July 26, 1940, approved a cautious compromise position: An "utmost effort shall be made to employ force of arms against Britain only" and yet, "since involvement in a war with the United States may become unavoidable in such an event, all possible preparations shall be made."[9] In short, the Japanese government had decided to prepare for an expansion into Southeast Asia but had not decided whether military force would be necessary or against what countries force would have to be used. As long as it appeared that Japan might achieve its ends through threats of force, the Liaison Conference was not forced to decide what it would do if such coercive threats failed.

U.S. Deterrence Policy in 1940

How accurate was the Imperial Navy's assessment that the United States would intervene if Japan expanded into Southeast Asia? Was the Imperial Army's position—that the United States would not become involved in a Japanese war against the British and Dutch colonies—more valid? The available evidence suggests that the army's position was more accurate. For example, in May 1940, General George Marshall presented a memorandum that implicitly called for defending no American possessions west of Hawaii to President Franklin Roosevelt, Admiral Harold Stark, and Under Secretary of State

Sumner Welles. Each agreed with the strategic assessment: "They all felt [Marshall's notes of the meeting read] that we must not become involved with Japan, that we must not concern ourselves beyond the 180th meridian, and that we must concentrate on the South American situation."[10] U.S. leaders knew, however, that the Japanese government had expansionist desires, and they sought to thwart them. The U.S. goal was to take actions that were strong enough to deter Japanese aggression in Southeast Asia but not so strong as to provoke Tokyo into a war. The United States possessed two tools of coercion with which it could influence Tokyo's decisions: U.S. military strength and Japanese dependence on American oil.

The first tool was wielded in May 1940, when Admiral James O. Richardson, commander in chief of the U.S. Fleet, received orders to maintain his forces at Pearl Harbor instead of at their regular bases on the U.S. West Coast. Admiral Stark explained the rationale behind the naval redeployment:

Why are you in the Hawaiian area? Answer: You are there because of the deterrent effect which it is thought your presence may have on the Japs going into the East Indies. Suppose the Japs do go into the East Indies? What are we going to do about it? My answer to that is, I don't know, and I think there is nobody on God's green earth who can tell you. ... I would point out one thing, and that is even if the decision here were for the U.S. to take no decisive action if the Japs should decide to go into the Dutch East Indies, we must not breathe it to a soul, as by so doing we would completely nullify the reason for your presence in the Hawaiian area. Just remember that the Japs don't know what we are going to do, and so long as they don't know, they may hesitate or be deterred.[11]

Many U.S. officials were not comfortable relying on a deterrent threat as vague as stationing the U.S. Fleet at Pearl Harbor. One reason for their concern was the growing need for American naval forces in the Atlantic: If U.S. forces had to be moved to the Atlantic, would Japan quickly move south? The other reason for their concern was that the threat might be perceived in Tokyo as merely a bluff. Given Roosevelt's domestic concerns in an election year, however, pandering to isolationist sentiment was politically expedient even if it was diplomatically unwise. On September 11 in Washington, D.C., Roosevelt announced that "we will not participate in foreign wars, and we will not send our Army, naval or air forces to fight in foreign lands outside of the Americas, except in case of attack."[12] In response, U.S. Ambassador Joseph Grew in Tokyo cabled home a prescient message: "It is clear that Japan has been deterred from taking greater liberties with American interests only out of respect for our potential power; it is equally [clear] that she has trampled upon our rights in precise ratio to the strength of her conviction that the American people would not permit that power to be used."[13]

Mutual Deterrent Policies

In September 1940, the leadership in Tokyo took two major steps that eventually led to the Pacific War. The decision to move into northern Indochina
and the decision to join Germany and Italy in the Tripartite Pact were both
made with an eye on the U.S. domestic scene. The Japanese government
hoped to reduce the risk of American reactions to its Southern Advance by
expanding the empire in incremental steps and presenting Washington with
the prospect of a war with Japan's new allies in Europe if the United States in-
tervened in Asia.

After the July 26 Liaison Conference agreement to push for the Southern
Advance, Japanese pressures on the French authorities in Indochina increased.[14] The army strongly favored using military force, if necessary, since
it wanted to secure control of the Tonkin region in order to stop supplies
from reaching Chiang Kai-shek's forces in the southern provinces of China.
The Imperial Navy, however, was greatly concerned as usual about the U.S.
reaction, especially fearing the prospect of an oil embargo. On August 5, the
navy staff prepared a study on whether force should be used against Indochina if the French authorities could not be intimidated by threats and ulti-
matums. The report concluded that U.S. reactions would depend upon a
number of political conditions:

> In case our troops advance on French Indochina, the attitude America must
> take depends on our pretext of advancing, cue, method, skill of propaganda,
> etc. ... If we choose a means to send troops to a part of Tonkin Province and
> leave them there, we must use as cues the uprising based on Chinese artifice,
> Chinese troops invading French Indochina, etc., and the underlying pretext
> must be the exercise of the right of self-defense, incident settlement, etc. ...
> Coupled with the appropriate propaganda, it will provide little stimulus for
> America. Consequently the probability that America will embargo all aspects
> of shipments is not necessarily large. ... However if we ... invade the whole of
> French Indochina, the probability of a strengthened embargo on Japanese ship-
> ments [of oil] increases compared with above.[15]

The navy thus believed that if Japan used proper strategy, the Americans
would not react harshly. This prediction turned out to be accurate. After a
long series of negotiations and threats of intervention, the French colonial
authorities backed down and granted Japan permission to use airfields in
Tonkin Province and to station six thousand troops there. The United States
retaliated by placing an embargo on scrap metal only.

Japan's second method of influencing U.S. opinion was employed on September 7, when German General Heinrich Stahmer arrived in Tokyo to negotiate the Tripartite Pact. Stahmer presented Japanese Foreign Minister
Matsuoka Yosuke with a preliminary proposal for an alliance and explained
its primary purpose: "A strong and determined attitude, unequivocal and un-

mistakable, on the part of the three nations, Japan, Germany and Italy, and the knowledge of it by the U.S. and the world at large at this juncture, that alone can only be a powerful and effective deterrent on the U.S. A weak, lukewarm attitude or declaration at this juncture will only invite derision and danger."[16]

Matsuoka agreed, but both the army and the navy were opposed to a firm Japanese commitment to Nazi Germany and made the rejection of any "automatic involvement" in a war a prerequisite for agreeing to sign the Tripartite Pact. The navy was especially worried that Germany and the United States might soon come to blows in the Atlantic before Japanese naval power was sufficiently prepared for any major conflict.[17] With the Japanese navy so strongly opposed, Matsuoka agreed to the join the Tripartite Pact only after a secret agreement was accepted according to which Japan would be allowed to determine independently whether to go to war.[18] The public statements on the pact, however, were firm, for reasons outlined by Stahmer: "In our opinion an explicit emphasis on the obligation to declare war would have a specially strong neutralizing effect on the United States."[19]

Despite this prediction, the attitude of the United States did stiffen when it learned of the Tripartite Pact. On October 4, the cabinet met and displayed, according to Secretary of the Interior Harold Ickes's diary, "no disposition ... to do anything except stand up firmly" to Japan. Secretary of War Henry Stimson declared that "the Japanese were notorious bluffers," and the group agreed "that none of us would say anything to Japan or about Japan but would simply go ahead and let our actions speak for us."[20]

Three types of deterrence tools—military movements, trade embargoes, and verbal threats—were discussed in Washington, D.C., in late 1940 and early 1941. The problem for U.S. policy makers, however, was one of how to signal to Japan a commitment to deterrence without either provoking the Tokyo government or arousing isolationist protests in the United States. On the military front, a decision was made in November 1940, when Roosevelt agreed to a navy proposal to send five submarines to reinforce the U.S. base in Manila. Secretary of State Cordell Hull convinced Roosevelt to keep the Japanese "guessing" without making a "formal announcement," thereby avoiding "misconstruction both in Japan and in some quarters here":

> The Japanese higher authorities, I pointed out, would obtain knowledge of our moves by their own methods. By letting the public obtain information piecemeal and gradually, there would be public knowledge of the moves we made, but several possible varieties of agitation might be avoided. Doing it quietly would facilitate the present movement of forces and possible similar operations in the future. ... This was in line with my theory that, in dealing with lawless governments, it was important to lead them to do a bit of guessing, without making any threats.[21]

In addition to these military activities, economic sanctions were actively considered in Washington. Immediately after the Tripartite Pact was signed, Stimson, Ickes, and Secretary of the Treasury Henry Morgenthau began to push for economic sanctions—especially an oil embargo—against Japan. With Hull, Marshall, and Stark all arguing that strong economic sanctions would provoke, not deter, Japan, however, the president took a cautious position. On October 10, Roosevelt presented his views in a cabinet meeting:

> The President's position was that we were not to shut off oil from Japan or machine tools from Japan and thereby force her into a military expedition against the Dutch East Indies but that we were to withhold from Japan only such things as high test gas and certain machine tools and certain machinery which we now absolutely needed ourselves; that there was to be no prodding of Japan and that we were not going to get into any war by forcing Japan into a position where she was going to fight for some reason or another.[22]

The third tool of deterrence, verbal warnings, predominated during the next major crisis in the Far East. In early January 1941, Washington was made aware that a Japanese move south might be imminent. On February 8, the new British ambassador to Washington, Lord Halifax, met with the president to hear what the United States would do if Japan attempted such a fait accompli. Roosevelt reported that he was "through with bluffing" Japan and promised to hint to Japanese Ambassador Nomura Kichisaburo that attacks in the south might lead to war with the United States. Still, Halifax's account of the conversation suggests that Roosevelt's policy of bluff had not entirely ended:

> There were three directions in which the Japanese might take action: against the Netherlands East Indies, against Thailand or directly against Singapore. He had been anxiously considering what action the United States Government would take in any of these eventualities. While the United States Government would declare war on Japan if the latter were to attack American possessions, he did not think that the country would approve of this action if the Japanese only attacked the Netherlands East Indies or British possessions.[23]

On February 14, Ambassador Nomura, accompanied by Secretary Hull, met with Roosevelt and offered the president the opportunity to prove he was done bluffing. According to Hull's account of the meeting, the president did repeatedly stress that the "American people" were "thoroughly and seriously concerned" about possible Japanese expansion. Roosevelt later described his performance as "really emotional. ... Interspersing it with [mock] sobs ... he hoped Admiral Nomura would make it plain to his government that ... everybody here was doing their best to keep things quiet. ... Should the dikes ever break [three sobs], civilization would end."[24]

This speech was reinforced by other verbal warnings in Tokyo. On February 14—on his own authority—Eugene H. Dooman, the consul of the American embassy, was explaining the U.S. position in the Far East to Japanese Vice-Foreign Minister Ohashi Chuichi when Ohashi suddenly asked, "Do you mean to say that if Japan were to attack Singapore there would be war with the United States?" Dooman answered, "The logic of the situation would inevitably raise that question." Ambassador Grew reinforced the warning by telling Matsuoka that he fully approved of Dooman's comments.[25]

Spring 1941: "Secret" Talks and Naval Visits

Tokyo received two more explicit signals of American-British ties in the spring of 1941. The first came at a military planners' conference, held in Singapore in April, in which U.S., British, and Dutch officers met to discuss possible combined operations in the event of war. Their report acknowledged that no political commitment was to be implied by the conference but explicitly recommended that "active military counter-action" should be taken against Japan under any one of the following circumstances:

1. A "direct act of war" by Japanese armed forces against American, British or Dutch territory.
2. A movement of Japanese forces into Thailand west of the meridian of Bangkok or south of the Kra Isthmus.
3. The occupation of Portuguese Timor or the Loyalty Islands of New Caladonia.
4. The movement of "a large number of Japanese warships" toward Malaya or the Kra Isthmus.[26]

Although senior officials in Washington correctly viewed the final report as mere contingency planning, the conference had another purpose: to signal Tokyo. Indeed, the British proposed making the talks public in order to enhance this deterrent effect. The Americans disagreed. Publicity might be provocative and, as Sumner Welles explained to the British, it was not necessary: "I said it seemed to me that through their intelligence organization the highest ranking officers of the Japanese Army and Navy would know in any event that these staff conferences were going to take place, and that if the holding of these conferences was going to have any deterrent effect upon them, that effect would be created without publicity."[27] Japanese intelligence did soon learn of the Singapore conference, and its meaning was discussed in Tokyo.[28] In short, Washington officials had discovered a form of diplomatic signal to Japan that was believable to Tokyo and that would still not be picked up by the U.S. public: "secret" talks among British, Dutch, and American military officers.

The second signal was sent to Tokyo by way of a U.S. naval visit to Australia and New Zealand. In March, after refusing to send ships to Singapore, Roosevelt approved a State Department recommendation—over the initial objection of the United States Navy—to send a small detachment of the Pacific Fleet on a "goodwill tour." Franklin Roosevelt was enthusiastic about the idea, telling Admiral Stark that "just as soon as those ships come back from Australia and New Zealand, or perhaps a little before, I want to send some more out. I just want to keep them popping up here and there, and keep the Japs guessing."[29]

The Summer of 1941: North or South?

The Japanese government was surprised when Hitler attacked the Soviet Union on June 22, 1941, and the Japanese leaders vigorously debated the appropriate response. Their final decision, reached on July 2, was to prepare for war against Russia but not to attack immediately and to prepare for war in the south while advancing into southern Indochina. The Imperial Army was told to prepare plans for an attack on the Soviet Union but not to launch hostilities until a German victory appeared imminent. The army high command called this policy "the principle of the ripe persimmon": They would pick the fruit when it was the easiest to do so. The navy agreed with the plan as long as it did not jeopardize naval preparations for any southern contingency. The army agreed to attack only if the Soviet Union moved two-thirds of its eastern air force and one-half of its ground forces to the west to fight the Germans.[30] Japanese forces were mobilized throughout the summer, but the Soviet force movement to the west failed to materialize.[31] Only in late autumn did the Soviets begin to move troops from the Manchurian border, but by then Japan's actions in the south had precipitated a crisis with the Americans.

As early as January 1941, the Japanese army and navy had agreed that it was desirable to extend Japanese control into southern Indochina and Thailand, but they had not agreed on the advisability of using military force to do so. The army was particularly interested in stopping trade into China; the navy hoped to increase the ability of Japan to pressure the Dutch authorities in the Netherlands East Indies to make a deal on oil.[32] The two military services continued to differ, however, in their estimates of U.S. reactions. On April 17 they finally reached an agreement on the Southern Advance, when the army accepted the navy's position that Thailand and French Indochina should be brought into Japan's sphere of influence through "diplomatic means" but that military force would be considered if either of the following developments occurred:

    a. If the empire's self-existence is threatened by embargoes imposed by the United States, the Netherlands and others.

b. If the United States, alone or in cooperation with Britain, the Netherlands, and China, gradually increases its pressures to contain the empire, making it impossible for the empire any longer to bear those pressures in the light of its self-defense.[33]

The Japanese leadership did not, however, believe either of these conditions was likely to develop if Japan moved into southern Indochina. The head of navy intelligence reported to Konoe on June 5 that "the navy deems it quite safe to move into southern Indochina." The navy stressed that a U.S. oil embargo was extremely unlikely if the Japanese moved south: The navy believed that the policy makers in Washington "knew well enough" that such an embargo would force Japan to attack the Dutch East Indies. Since the United States wanted to avoid a two-ocean war, it could not afford to compel Japan to strike.[34] The Imperial Conference granted official approval to this policy on July 2, *1941*, after Matsuoka told the emperor that "a war against Great Britain and the United States is unlikely to occur if we proceed with great caution."[35]

FROM DETERRENCE TO COERCION

On July 2, 1941, when the Japanese Foreign Office informed its ambassadors that "preparations decided upon with reference to French Indo-China and Thailand shall be executed," U.S. "Magic" cryptographers were listening. By July 8 these Magic messages were available at the highest levels of the U.S. government, and by July 15 the details of the Japanese plan for the occupation of the rest of Indochina were known.[36] The dilemma the United States now faced was one of how to respond to this forthcoming aggression in a way that would reinforce deterrence without provoking Japan into an attack on the British and Dutch colonies or even on the United States itself.

July 1941: The U.S. Embargo "Decision"

For the past year President Roosevelt had insisted that a full oil embargo against Japan would merely force Tokyo to launch an attack against the Dutch East Indies; on July 5, Ambassador Nomura hinted that such an attack would be the result of an embargo, saying that "if Japan should thus be shut off from American sources of oil, Japan must obtain them elsewhere and that under the circumstances, it was necessary for Japan to take appropriate preparatory measures."[37] The record clearly demonstrates that Roosevelt took this threat seriously. As Morgenthau stated in his diary, the president feared that an embargo "would simply drive the Japanese down to the Dutch East Indies."[38]

This cautionary attitude does not mean that Roosevelt was unwilling to *threaten* economic sanctions in order to prevent Japan from moving south.

On July 22, Ambassador Grew suggested that it was critical to inform the
Japanese of any retaliatory plans "privately and without any publicity" and
"before rather than after a Japanese occupation of bases in Indochina." The
logic of his argument was simple: "A clear, unambiguous statement of such
intentions might conceivably exert a deterrent effect, but, once an occupation
were effected, Japanese prestige would render subsequent withdrawal out of
the question."[39] Roosevelt followed Grew's advice, although his method was
neither entirely "without any publicity" nor entirely "unambiguous." The
president, as usual, sought to keep his options open by explaining to the U.S.
public that an embargo would be unwise while still threatening the Japanese
with one. On July 24, he gave a speech to the Volunteer Participation Committee, a group of civilian defense activists, in which he sought to explain his
"no-embargo" policy—a difficult task given that Americans on the Atlantic
Coast were facing a gasoline shortage:

> Why am I asked to curtail my consumption of gasoline when I read in the pa-
> pers that thousands of tons of gasoline are going out from Los Angeles—West
> Coast—to Japan; and we are helping Japan in what looks like aggression? All
> right. Now the answer is simple. ... It was essential from our own selfish point
> of view of defense to prevent a war from starting in the South Pacific. So our
> foreign policy was—trying to stop a war from breaking out down there. ...
> Now if we cut the oil off, they [the Japanese] probably would have gone down
> to the Dutch East Indies a year ago, and you would have had war. Therefore,
> there was—you might call—a method in letting this oil go to Japan.[40]

That afternoon, Roosevelt met with Nomura and issued the most direct
warning yet about American involvement if Tokyo continued the Southward
Advance. According to Welles's memorandum:

> The President said that if Japan attempted to seize the oil supplies by force in
> the Netherlands East Indies, the Dutch would, without a shadow of a doubt,
> resist, the British would immediately come to their assistance and, in view of
> our own policy of assisting Great Britain, *an exceedingly serious situation
> would immediately result.* It was with all of these facts in mind, the President
> said, that notwithstanding the bitter criticism that had been leveled against the
> Administration and against the Department of State, the President *up to now*
> had permitted oil to be shipped by Japan from the United States.[41]

The implicit threat was easily understood by Nomura, who wired home
that Roosevelt "hinted that an embargo on oil might be imminent."[42] Yet
again the president was bluffing, and Roosevelt's genuine concerns were
made clear earlier that same afternoon in a cabinet meeting when a decision
was made to freeze Japanese assets in the United States in retaliation for Japan's military occupation of southern Indochina. When asked whether an order freezing Japanese assets in the United States "might not force [Japan] to

take action in the Far East which we had tried to forestall during the past year," Roosevelt replied that he did not think this was the case; the freezing order simply meant that all Japanese imports of U.S. oil would require a license issued by the Treasury Department, and "he was inclined to go ahead with the order in a regular way and grant licenses for the shipment of petroleum as the applications are presented to the Treasury." He further added that the policy had the advantage of flexibility: It could change whenever the president wanted it to change.[43] Secretary Ickes, who supported a complete embargo, recorded the president's decision with some bitterness, but with considerable insight: "Notwithstanding that Japan was boldly making this hostile move, the President on Thursday was still unwilling to draw the noose tight. He thought that it might be better to slip the noose around Japan's neck and give it a jerk now and then. ... The effect of the freezing order is an export license before any goods can be shipped to Japan but the President indicated that we would still continue to ship oil and gasoline."[44]

From the Freeze to the Embargo

Despite Roosevelt's statement on July 24, and despite the fact that on August 1 the U.S. government publicly announced that the Japanese could resubmit applications for petroleum licenses as long as the total did not exceed previous levels, no American oil was shipped to Japan after its assets were frozen on July 26, 1941. What caused the change in U.S. policy? Why did the United States place a total embargo of oil on Japan?

Some detail is necessary for us to understand why this happened. In August 1941, Franklin Roosevelt's effort to give himself a flexible instrument for controlling future oil export policy backfired. His essential mistake was, in the words of historian Irvine Anderson, Jr., giving control of approval for releasing funds to "an unguided bureaucracy biased at the working level against liberality toward Japan."[45] Although Roosevelt had approved plans for the automatic granting of oil import licenses, he had not focused on the mechanics of the release of funds as he left on August 3 for his secret meeting with British Prime Minister Winston Churchill. While he was gone, the noose he put around Japan's neck was pulled so tightly that he could not loosen it when he returned. The authority to release, or not release, funds was given to Dean Acheson, the assistant secretary of state and head of the Foreign Funds Committee (FFC). Acheson was a self-proclaimed "hawk" who was battling the "doves" in the State Department who opposed economic sanctions against Japan. His memoirs candidly set forth his views on the embargo question. He understood the arguments for prudence but felt that Japan would simply never attack the United States:

> The issue was over the embargo or drastic reduction of petroleum exports other than the already embargoed aviation gasoline. The aim was to limit Japanese

military action in East and Southeast Asia; the danger, provoking Japan to seize or intimidate the Dutch East Indies—a great source of petroleum—or move against us. ... The argument for it was that no rational Japanese could believe that an attack on us could result in anything but disaster for his country.[46]

Acheson later claimed that Welles had suggested in late July that the FCC "take no action" on Japanese applications and that when he refused to release funds, "to our surprise and pleasure, these proposals met with unanimous support for the first time within our government."[47] These statements, however, do not accord with the record. Welles supported the policy of allowing *limited* exports of petroleum to Japan as approved on July 31, and the State Department's Far Eastern Division pushed Acheson "to let the oil be exported" and argued that he "had no authority to hold it up."[48] Indeed, the evidence suggests that Acheson simply refused to go along with the interpretations others had of the ambiguous U.S. policy. As he later put it, "Whether or not we had a policy, we had a state of affairs." Acheson's motives were later presented in his memoirs: "[If] President Roosevelt lacked decisiveness in the degree his successor possessed it, he had a sense of direction in which he constantly advanced. It seemed to those in government that our most useful function was to increase in so far as we could the rate of that advance."[49]

It appears that Acheson, acting on the belief that he was "increasing the rate of advance" toward a full embargo and only helping to compensate for the president's indecision, purposely created a de facto embargo in August 1941. Hull clearly did not believe a complete embargo was in place on August 2.[50] Indeed, both Roosevelt and Hull may have been unaware that no licenses had been approved as late as August 27 and 28: Roosevelt told Nomura that Japan could still purchase oil, and Hull admitted that he "had not checked fully on the details of this matter."[51]

It is not known when Roosevelt and Hull first became aware of the de facto embargo, although eventually they clearly approved the policy. Why did Roosevelt agree to this major change? The record does not provide a clear answer, but one can speculate on two factors that probably contributed. First, once a provocative action is taken, it may appear more dangerous to reverse course than to maintain it. Give that both the Japanese government and the U.S. public incorrectly believed that a complete embargo of petroleum had been ordered, it would have been very difficult for Roosevelt to soften his position against Japan. Second, a simple disinclination to believe that the Japanese would ever attack a far more powerful nation may also have played a role in Roosevelt's agreeing to the embargo. Roosevelt, like other Americans, still found it difficult to believe that rational Japanese leaders would choose to go to war with the much stronger United States. Warnings that an oil embargo would lead to war may therefore have been discounted once the action was taken.

Reactions in Tokyo

The U.S. oil embargo, de facto or not, changed the calculus in Tokyo, making the alternatives appear in stark outlines and pushing the government toward painful decisions. The Japanese leadership understood that without supplies of oil, the Japanese Empire would become powerless militarily. As U.S. military strength increased while Japanese power declined, it was believed, in the words of an Imperial Conference document, that Japan "will finally be forced to surrender to the United States and Great Britain without a fight."[52] And Japanese leaders were almost unanimous in their pessimism about the likelihood of victory in a total war against the United States. Three questions plagued the Japanese government: Could oil imports be obtained through a negotiated settlement of Japanese-American disagreements? If this were not possible, should Japan go to war, and against whom? If Japan did go to war, how could it win?

This pessimistic assessment of Japan's oil dilemma was not exaggerated. Japan produced less than 10 percent of its fuel requirements; the rest was imported from the United States (80 percent) and the Netherlands East Indies (10 percent), neither of which provided supplies after August 1. A navy study reported that the Dutch oil fields would have to be secured quickly or the fleet would run out of fuel early in any war against the United States.[53] This fear was described most graphically by Admiral Schimada Shigetaro after the war: "If there were no supply of oil, battleships and any other warships would be nothing more than scarecrows."[54]

During the first week of August, the Japanese government was still uncertain about U.S. intentions but suspected that a complete embargo was imminent. The top leadership of the Imperial Navy had only faint hopes of victory in any war against the United States but became increasingly convinced that this thin margin of chance was the only possibility for Japan's survival. Admiral Nagano Osami met the emperor and explained his fears by comparing the nation to a critically ill man: A desperate operation offered the only hope of saving his life.[55] There were only two alternatives to the risky operation that was being considered: the possibility that diplomatic negotiations could produce the "life blood" the patient needed—in other words, a resumption of U.S. oil exports; or Japan's acceptance of the risk of "gradual exhaustion"—in other words, living with the military danger Nagano so hoped to avoid. Few of Japan's leaders thought that the latter option promised security in the long run. An air of deep despair shrouded the important meetings during September 1941: The dangerous operation might be necessary, but no one felt it was likely to succeed.[56]

The preferred alternative to the desperate war was clearly a diplomatic settlement allowing a renewal of petroleum imports. Under what conditions would the United States end its embargo? Nagano argued forcefully for continuing negotiations with the United States but warned that a false peace such as that which followed the legendary "Winter Battle at Osaka Castle" (the Japanese equivalent of the Munich settlement) would not ensure the "long-term prosperity of our Empire."[57] There was a growing belief that with the oil embargo, the United States had demonstrated its hostile intent to Japan. As the Liaison Conference concluded, "If they do not accede to the conditions we propose, we must regard it as disclosing their true intention, which is to bring Japan to her knees."[58] Indeed, even if an agreement were reached, there was no guarantee that the United States would abide by its terms in the future. The consensus opinion of the Liaison Conference was expressed in the notes prepared for the September 6 Imperial Conference:

> It need not be repeated that unless the United States changes its policy toward Japan, our Empire is placed in a desperate situation, where it must resort to the ultimate step—namely, war—to defend itself and to assure its preservation. Even if we should make concessions to the United States by giving up part of our national policy for the sake of a temporary peace, the United States, its military position strengthened, is sure to demand more and more concessions on our part; and ultimately our Empire will have to lie prostrate at the feet of the United States.[59]

On September 6, the Imperial Conference approved a final list of minimum demands and maximum concessions for negotiations with the United States. The Empire's minimum demands were (1) an agreement by the United States and Great Britain to end interference in the "China Incident" by ceasing to assist Chiang Kai-shek, (2) a promise by these two countries to not build up military strength in the Far East, and (3) the immediate restoration of oil exports. Tokyo's position on the China Incident was especially important. The government stated that it was "in principle prepared to withdraw our troops following the settlement of the Incident" and was willing to pledge that "the economic activities of the United States and Great Britain in China will not be restricted."[60] But to the entire Japanese leadership, "settling" the China Incident did not mean simply giving up after four years of fighting; they wanted a settlement that would protect Japanese interests on the mainland. In return the Japanese were willing to make the following concessions:

1. Our Empire will not advance militarily from the bases in French Indochina to the neighboring areas other than China.
2. Our Empire is prepared to withdraw its forces from French Indochina after a just peace has been established in the Far East.
3. Our Empire is prepared to guarantee the neutrality of the Philippine Islands.[61]

The final important point of discussion at the September 6 Imperial Conference was the conduct of the war itself, if war could not be avoided. War plans were only at a preliminary stage of development, yet the basic idea behind the strategy was simple. Japan might win a limited war through attacking first, achieving a strong defensive position, and then waiting for a decline in U.S. willingness to fight.

> What is the outlook in a war with Great Britain and the United States; particularly, how shall we end the war?
>
> A war with the United States and Great Britain will be long and will become a war of endurance. It is very difficult to predict the termination of war and it would be well-nigh impossible to expect the surrender of the United States. However, we cannot exclude the possibility that the war may end because of a great change in American public opinion, which may result from such factors as the remarkable success of our military operations in the South or the surrender of Great Britain.[62]

These decisions represented a watershed. The U.S. policy had succeeded in one sense: The Japanese were now clearly deterred from immediately attacking the British and Dutch colonies. Yet the policy was failing in another sense: The Tokyo leadership was clearly preparing for a desperate war that it had hoped to avoid. Prime Minister Konoe therefore issued an urgent proposal that he and Roosevelt meet personally to resolve the difficulties in Japanese-American relations. He had the support of the "responsible chiefs of the Army and Navy" for now, he told Grew, but "time is of the essence."[63]

Roosevelt's Refusal to Meet with Konoe

Negotiations between Secretary Hull and Ambassador Nomura had been under way since April 1941, and the initial U.S. position on the settlement of the China Incident—that Japanese troops there would eventually have to withdraw to Manchuria and the Japanese homeland—had remained firm. What the oil embargo did accomplish was to force a decision in Tokyo. The secret Magic decrypts revealed that Japanese leaders saw the proposed Konoe-Roosevelt meeting as essential to avoiding war. Foreign Minister Togo Shigenori cabled to the Japanese embassy in Washington: "Now the international situation as well as our internal situation is strained in the extreme and we have reached the point where we will pin our last hopes on an interview between the Premier and the President."[64] Yet despite this warning, despite the fact that the U.S. military was pleading for time to continue military preparations, and despite Roosevelt's early position favoring the meeting, the Japanese were informed on October 2 that no such conference would take place in the foreseeable future. How was this decision made? Why was this effort to pursue a peaceful settlement in the Pacific turned aside?

Throughout September, Hull insisted that the outlines of a basic agreement had to be worked out prior to any top-level meeting. U.S. decision makers strongly suspected that Konoe was merely seeking a joint statement, as Hull later put it, of "vague generalities that would all be to Japan's advantage." Such a meeting would therefore represent appeasement: "As for me, I was thoroughly satisfied that a meeting with Konoye, without an advance agreement, could only result in another Munich or in nothing at all. I was opposed to the first Munich and still more opposed to a second Munich."[65] It was not possible, however, to get Konoe to give advance assurances of a complete end to Japanese military involvement in China. Ambassador Nomura only agreed that a troop withdrawal could occur once the China affair was settled and peace was brought to the region.

Was Konoe sincere, and could he have persuaded the Japanese military to accept any settlement terms he would have agreed to with Roosevelt? Unfortunately, no conclusive answer can be given to either question. Konoe later claimed that he would have been willing to accept a rapid withdrawal of Japanese troops from China. The record is clear that he personally favored such a concession, and Konoe claimed he would have asked the emperor to intervene in order to ensure that the army would have accepted the settlement.[66] It is not clear, however, that such a scheme would have succeeded. Yet if Konoe's freedom of action were limited by the Japanese army's desire to stay in China, then Hull wanted the unattainable. He would settle for nothing less than "unequivocal evidence" that Japan would "abandon her course of aggression."[67] When Hull informed Nomura that a Konoe-Roosevelt meeting could not occur unless Japan more clearly defined its policy, he understood that this was likely to mean the end of the Konoe government and the emergence of a less accommodating one. He still proceeded with the refusal.[68]

The Fall of the Konoe Cabinet

By the end of September 1941, Konoe understood that the most critical question remaining involved the withdrawal of troops from China, and he sought support from the navy in order to persuade the army that a concession was necessary. On October 1, he met with Navy Minister Oikawa Koshiro, who agreed that Japan should accept all U.S. demands in order to be able to import oil and avoid war. Five days later, the top leadership of the navy met and agreed that the government should accept gradual withdrawal of all troops in China "in principle." Oikawa knew, however, that this would cause enormous domestic turmoil, possibly even an army coup attempt; therefore he asked Nagano whether "if worst comes to worst, the navy is prepared to come to blows with the army." Nagano would only reply, "I cannot definitely say yes."[69]

On October 12, 1941, Konoe called the five key cabinet ministers to his villa to make a final decision. The navy's position was presented by Oikawa. Prior to the conference Konoe had received a message from the chief of the Bureau of Naval Affairs warning him that, although the navy wanted the American-Japanese negotiations to continue in order to "avoid war as much as circumstances permit ... the Navy cannot say it openly." Instead, the navy would entrust the issue to the prime minister. Three reasons contributed to Oikawa's refusal to state his desire to avoid war more forcefully. First, Oikawa appears to have been reluctant to state publicly that the Imperial Navy lacked sufficient strength to take on the United States Navy, stating after the war that "if we were to say that we were not able to carry out operations against the United States, it would have meant that we had been lying to the Emperor" when discussing war plans in the past. Second, Oikawa believed that it was Konoe's responsibility, not the navy's, to make the difficult decision against army wishes. Last, Oikawa was probably concerned that open opposition to war would create turmoil inside the navy because some officers were siding with the army in preferring war to compromise.[70]

The army's position, as expressed by War Minister Tojo Hideki, was firm. The army believed Japan must *not* completely withdraw from China under pressure from Washington: "If we yield to the United States at this time, the latter will become more arrogant and more overbearing"; such a withdrawal "would not be in keeping with the dignity of the Army."[71] Faced with the army's refusal to pull out of China, Konoe could only express his belief that continuing negotiations indefinitely still seemed to hold fewer risks than starting a war. But Tojo insisted that no compromise was possible because the United States wanted immediate and unconditional troop withdrawals. The two men could clearly reach no agreement on October 12. The meeting ended when the prime minister declared that he simply could not take responsibility for an Imperial Army decision for war.[72]

The conflict between Konoe and Tojo had become so intense that the two men were barely on speaking terms. Tojo fully understood that the risks of war were enormous, but he believed that failure to act quickly and decisively would doom Japan. Tojo maintained that a war against the United States in 1941, however dangerous, was a less risky option than going to war at a later date. A bold act of determination was needed to save Japan from certain defeat. As he told Konoe, it was sometimes necessary for a man to jump from the Kiyomizu Temple into the ravine below.[73]

The impasse between Konoe and Tojo continued in the Liaison Conferences until October 15. On October 16 Konoe resigned. Both he and Tojo recommended that Prince Higashikuni become prime minister, believing that only a member of the imperial family could restrain the army if a decision was made to continue negotiations. The emperor, however, feared that if a member of the imperial household was forced to lead Japan into a war of desperation, the long-term stability of the emperor's position might be compromised. After a series of discussions among the senior statesmen and the emperor's political advisers, it was decided that only the leading member of the army, Tojo, could exert sufficient influence on the army. The emperor, again acting without precedent, suggested that Tojo accept the premier position *without* being bound to the September 6 decision to make a determination by October. Instead "a clean-slate debate" was to be held in Tokyo: All future policy was to be decided anew.[74]

The "Clean-Slate Debate"

When the Tojo cabinet held its first Liaison Conference on October 23, 1941, it may have had a clean slate for discussing Japanese policy options, but the time pressure was relentless. For each day that passed without petroleum imports, Japan consumed twelve thousand tons of oil; for each month that passed, an estimated four thousand Allied soldiers reinforced U.S. and British garrisons in the Far East.[75] It was believed that if Japan were to have even the slightest hope of victory in a war, the initial attack must come in early December at the latest.

Under this severe time pressure, the Tojo government analyzed, debated, and finally, on November 1, reached conclusions on the two major questions of national policy. First, what should Japan's negotiating position be, especially on the issue of troop withdrawals from China? A heated debate ensued over this issue. The navy, according to notes taken at the November 1 meeting, "was not enthusiastic about stationing troops" in China, and Foreign Minister Togo vigorously argued that Japan should accept all the U.S. demands. Everyone else who was present, however, felt this was unacceptable.

There is considerable disagreement in the literature about why the Japanese leadership would not accept a total troop withdrawal from China and an end to the China Incident. Some historians emphasize Japan's psychological "defensiveness": The Japanese military officers were trained to behave in accord with a strict code of honor, and to back down under pressure was a fate worse than death. Others have been less charitable, arguing that the Japanese military was expansionist by nature and only used its "old jargon" of defensiveness to cover its aggressive intentions.[76]

Both schools of thought contain an element of truth, for the Japanese army was undoubtedly imbued with the samurai spirit and clearly did have offensive ambitions in Asia. Yet we should emphasize that most Japanese military and civilian leaders did not see the troop withdrawal issue in isolation. Instead, they feared that giving in on this issue would not only endanger Japanese security in the short term but would encourage the United States to make even more demands in the future. The army and navy leadership thus agreed that "even if we reach an agreement with the United States, she may not give us materials. ... We would be subject to American obstruction at any time."[77] How could Tokyo be certain that the United States would keep its promises? When Liaison Conference members were specifically asked "what would happen to Japan if the American proposals were accepted in their entirety," according to the records, "all except the Foreign Minister judged that the Empire would become a third-rate country."[78]

Eventually, under Tojo's threat of resignation, the army agreed to a concession. Japanese troops in North China, in Inner Mongolia, and on Hainan Island would remain for approximately twenty-five years after "the establishment of peace" in China; all troops throughout the rest of China would be withdrawn within two years. Japanese troops in Indochina would be withdrawn immediately after a settlement in China. After the meeting, Foreign Minister Togo reportedly received Tojo's word that he would support further softening of Japan's position on troop withdrawals if it later appeared that such withdrawal was all that prevented a negotiated settlement.[79]

An answer to the second question—Could a war be limited to the Dutch and British?—was also critically important. If the pressures Japan felt to go to war were due largely to the dwindling oil supply, then the key target for Japanese expansion was the Dutch East Indies. But how would the United States respond? Could the United States be split from its allies? Japanese leaders finally reached an agreement. Both the Foreign Ministry and the Imperial General Headquarters studied U.S. commitments to Britain and the Netherlands and concluded that such a limited war would be "impossible." In the spring and summer of 1941, the Foreign Ministry had conducted studies of the ties between the United States and the Far Eastern colonial powers. These studies reported that agents had learned "from American sources" that the Allies had decided "to declare war against the aggressor" in the event of an attack against the Dutch East Indies or Burma.[80] Based on this false information, the Foreign Office agreed that "undoubtedly, an understanding exists" among the powers "to stand united in the event of an armed invasion of the southern area by Japan."[81]

The navy's similar conclusion was based on military operational requirements rather than on political judgments. It presented three reasons that a limited war against the Dutch and British was "impossible" for the navy "from the standpoint of operations":

   a. Any attempt to carryout operations against the Netherlands East Indies alone or against the Netherlands and Great Britain without taking into consideration the attitude of the United States would result in a situation whereby we would expose our flank to attack from Singapore, Hong Kong and the Philippines.

b. Under the present circumstances, it would be extremely difficult to carry out operations against Great Britain and the United States if Japan did not have the initiative. If war against Great Britain and the United States was launched after the commencement of hostilities against the Netherlands, it would be impossible for Japan to retain the initiative in view of the present ratio of military strength between the United States, Great Britain and Japan. The necessity to launch the initial attacks becomes even more urgent when the rapid increase in the military strength of Great Britain and the United States is taken into consideration.

c. It would be impossible to establish a strong strategical position without securing Malaya and the Philippines.[82]

Interviews with military officers after the war indicate that the effect of the ongoing buildup of U.S. air and sea power in the area was decisive. Even Admiral Shinichi Kondo, who had questioned the strategy of attacking the United States, later argued that "it was imperative that these [Philippine] islands be captured at the outset of war, not only because they constituted a direct threat to Japan … but also because the sea lanes between the homeland and the South could not be secured otherwise."[83] Hattori Takushiro, chief of the 2nd section at General Staff Headquarters, later stressed that the Philippines were included "not for political and economic reasons, but from following purely strategic considerations, especially those of the Navy."[84]

In the concluding session of the clean-slate debate, Prime Minister Tojo accepted the navy's arguments, even though he had personally raised the argument that any attack on the South could exclude U.S. territory.[85] Why? The evidence suggests that the army leadership, which had consistently argued that the United States would not enter a war over an attack on European colonies, accepted the navy's position as a necessary compromise to avoid further paralysis. At the October 28 Liaison Conference, the army thus argued that "from the point of view of strategy it is not impossible to separate them [the United States from the British and the Dutch]; but if it is impossible from the point of view of naval strategy, then it would be the same for the Army."[86]

The Decision for War

On October 30, Tojo announced that time was running out; at the next Liaison Conference the government would have to come to a decision. The November 1 meeting lasted seventeen hours, and angry arguments frequently erupted. The meeting began with the finance and foreign ministers challenging the "theory of gradual exhaustion," which the navy had so often presented. In contradiction, the navy continued to insist that a war in the near future was Japan's only hope:

Foreign Minister Togo: I, too, cannot believe that the American fleet would come and attack us. I don't believe there is any need to go to war now.

Navy Chief of Staff Nagano: There is a saying, "Don't rely on what won't come." The future is uncertain; we can't take anything for granted. In three years enemy defenses in the South will be strong and the number of enemy warships will also increase.

Finance Minister Kaya: Well, then, when can we go to war and win?

Nagano: Now! The time for war will not come later![87]

The option to end negotiations and go to war immediately was strongly supported by Army Chief of Staff Sugiyama Gen. He argued that further negotiations were useless, although he suggested that they could continue in order to mislead the United States about Japan's intent. Togo and Tojo vigorously opposed this idea, demanding that military leaders "must give your word that if diplomacy is successful we will give up going to war."[88] The military insisted, however, that operational considerations necessitated that if war were unavoidable, Japan should attack in early December at the latest. After extensive debate, a negotiations deadline of November 30 was agreed upon.

The meeting came to a close early in the morning of November 2. No one was optimistic concerning the prospects for success in the final negotiation effort. Indeed, the leaders of the Imperial Army warned against trusting that the United States would keep its promises: "Even if we reach an agreement with the United States, she may not give us materials."[89]

Last-Minute Diplomacy

In the fall of 1941, what created fear in Tokyo enhanced hope in Washington. For the Japanese, the Allied military buildup in the Far East created significant pressure to push south quickly before Allied strength grew. For the U.S. leadership, the growth of air strength in the Philippines created a new sense of confidence that Japan would not risk going to war. The emergence of the B-17 flying fortress and the B-24 "super-flying fortress" especially altered U.S. thinking because these weapons placed Japan's homeland under threat of immediate retaliation if a war began. On October 21, 1941, Stimson wrote a memorandum to Roosevelt in which he spelled out the new hopes for deterrence through air power:

A strategic opportunity of the utmost importance has suddenly arisen in the southwestern Pacific. Our whole strategic possibilities of the past twenty years have been revolutionized by the events in the world in the past six months. From being impotent to influence events in that area, we suddenly find ourselves vested with the possibility of great effective power. ... We are rushing planes and other preparations to the Philippines from a base in the United

States which has not yet in existence the number of planes necessary for our immediate minimum requirements in that southwestern Pacific Theater. ... Yet even this imperfect threat, if not promptly called by the Japanese, bids fair to stop Japan's march to the south and secure the safety of Singapore, with all the revolutionary consequences of such actions.[90]

Stimson's enthusiasm was tempered, however, by the fact that at the time, the U.S. bomber force was so small that it could be "promptly called" by a Japanese first strike. American planners expected to have four squadrons of heavy bombers, a total of 165 planes, in the Philippines by March 1942. The Joint Board of the Army and Navy strongly recommended to Roosevelt on November 5 that conflict in the Far East be avoided until the reinforcements in the Philippines reached their projected strength in February or March 1942. Until that time, the Joint Board recommended that no ultimatum be delivered to Japan.[91]

Roosevelt appears to have immediately grasped the importance of the board's recommendation. On November 5, Winston Churchill urged Roosevelt to make a direct warning to Japan, but in reply, Roosevelt counseled caution to avoid provoking the Japanese: "[Continuing] efforts to strengthen defenses in the Philippine Islands, paralleled by similar efforts by you in the Singapore area, will tend to increase Japan's hesitation, whereas in Japan's present mood, new formalized verbal warning or remonstrance might have, with at least an even chance, an opposite effect."[92]

In Tokyo, the Imperial Conference gave formal approval to the final negotiating positions on November 5. Two alternative positions were to be offered successively to the U.S. secretary of state. Proposal A, a comprehensive settlement of the major issues between the United States and Japan, included Tokyo's "concession" on troop withdrawal from China and stated that the Japanese would "act independently" in interpreting the Tripartite Pact. Proposal B was more limited in scope: a modus vivendi, a resumption of oil shipments in exchange for a Japanese pledge not to "make an armed advance" further into Southeast Asia. Togo was given until midnight November 30 to reach an agreement.[93]

Only an outline of the complex details of the month-long negotiations between Hull and Nomura need be presented here. The United States quickly rejected the comprehensive proposal, believing it would result in China's being left permanently at the mercy of Japanese aggression. But the plan was considered essential for gaining the time needed to finalize the Philippine defense force. Roosevelt informed Hull in a handwritten note of what he was willing to accept as a modus vivendi if war could be held off for the coming months:

President Roosevelt to the Secretary of State
6 months

1. U.S. to resume economic relations—some oil and rice now—more later.
2. Japan to send no more troops to Indochina or Manchurian border or any place South—(Dutch, Brit. or Siam).
3. Japan to agree not to invoke tripartite pact even if U.S. gets into European war.
4. U.S. to introduce Japs to Chinese to talk things over but U.S. to take no part in their conversations.[94]

On November 25, Roosevelt met with Hull, Stimson, Secretary of the Navy Frank Knox, Stark, and Marshall to go over the negotiations proposal. Everyone was becoming pessimistic, but they agreed that an offer of a modus vivendi would be made. Some time that night, however, without consulting the U.S. military, Secretary Hull decided (in his phrase) to "kick the whole thing over," to abandon the effort to reach a temporary agreement and instead simply to restate the basic U.S. goals in Asia when he next met with the Japanese negotiators.

Four factors apparently contributed to this critical decision. First, as Hull told Roosevelt, there was "the opposition of the Chinese government," which had strongly objected to any movement toward a settlement that did not include a complete Japanese withdrawal. Second, there was the opposition of the British, the Dutch, and the Australian governments. Third, domestic politics argued against anything that seemed like appeasement. As Hull told Roosevelt, notwithstanding "the vast importance and value otherwise of the *modus vivendi*," the publicity involved would create "additional opposition," presumably in the United States. (Rumors about the modus vivendi had already created talk of "appeasement" in Washington.[95])

One final factor not mentioned by Hull likely also influenced the decision. In the tense atmosphere of late November, U.S. leaders had begun to fear that Japan was using the negotiations as a tactic to delay war until it was prepared. Indeed, on November 26, before Roosevelt approved Hull's decision not to seek a modus vivendi, Stimson informed the president that Japanese naval forces were moving south: "He fairly blew up [Stimson recorded in his diary], jumped in the air so to speak, and said … that changed the whole situation because it was evidence of bad faith on the part of the Japanese that while they were negotiating for an entire truce—an entire withdrawal—they should be sending this expedition down there to Indochina."[96] The information turned out to be false, but the resulting sense of betrayal may have tipped the balance against the modus vivendi effort in Roosevelt's calculations.[97]

On November 26, with Roosevelt's approval, Hull therefore handed the Japanese negotiators not the modus vivendi proposal but rather a general

statement of "fundamental principles of peace." He also presented ten specific proposals, including an agreement to remove the freeze on Japanese assets, mutual promises to support no government in China except that headed
by Chiang Kai-shek, mutual relinquishment of extraterritorial rights in
China, and a Japanese commitment to withdraw all armed forces from China
and Indochina. Ambassador Nomura's report back to Tokyo noted that Hull
explicitly stated that the United States was "not necessarily asking that it
[complete troop withdrawals] be effected immediately" and stressed that he
would still continue to meet with the president to discuss Japanese-American
relations.[98]

In Tokyo, however, the news was alarming. Hull's message, a sign that
Washington had abandoned what Tokyo considered the last hope for peace,
was interpreted to mean that the United States had decided that war was inevitable. It was widely believed that basic hostile intentions of the United States
toward Japan had now been revealed. Some Japanese officials claimed that
Hull's message was the equivalent of an ultimatum; others argued that the
United States would likely demand a Japanese withdrawal from Manchukuo
if Tokyo accepted the current proposal.[99] Indeed, Tojo later stated that he was
so convinced Hull's actions signaled that the United States now wanted a war
that he feared an American first strike.[100]

The depth of this feeling that war was inevitable was demonstrated in numerous meetings in the final days before Pearl Harbor. On November 29, the
emperor and a group of Japanese senior statesmen met with Tojo and leading
members of the government. They all agreed that the issue no longer consisted of just the China Incident but rather involved actual Japanese survival.
No one questioned Baron Watatsuki Reijiro's view: "If this war was for self-
existence, then we must be prepared to wage it, even if we foresaw eventual
defeat, but it might prove dangerous if we resorted to war simply to uphold
the Great East Asia Co-prosperity Plan."[101]

On December 1, the Imperial Conference met to formally approve Japan's
decision to go to war. Tojo began by stressing that the United States had
hardened its negotiating position, thereby threatening Japan's security:

> The United States not only refused to make even one concession with respect to
> the position she had maintained in the past, but also stipulated new conditions.
> ... The United States demanded complete and unconditional withdrawal of
> troops from China, withdrawal of our recognition of the Nanking Govern-
> ment, and the reduction of the Tripartite Pact to a dead letter. This not only be-
> littled the dignity of our Empire and made it impossible to harvest the fruits of
> the China Incident, but also threatened the very existence of our Empire. ...
> Under the circumstances, our Empire has no alternative but to begin war
> against the United States, Great Britain, and the Netherlands in order to resolve
> the present crisis and assure survival.[102]

During the two hours of the Imperial Conference meeting, no one questioned whether war was now inevitable. Togo, who had previously held out against war, reviewed the diplomatic negotiations conducted over the preceding six months and concluded that "if we were to accept their present proposal, the international position of our Empire would be reduced to a status lower than it was prior to the Manchurian Incident, and our very survival would inevitably be threatened."[103] At the meeting's conclusion, the president of the Privy Council Hara Yoshimichi, speaking for the emperor, argued that Japan had no choice but to gamble on war:

> The United States is being utterly conceited, obstinate, and disrespectful. ... If we were to give in, we would give up in one stroke not only our gains in the Sino-Japanese and Russo-Japanese wars, but also the benefits of the Manchurian Incident. This we cannot do. We are loath to compel our people to suffer even greater hardships, on top of what they have endured during the four years since the China Incident. But it is clear that the great achievements of the Emperor Meiji would all come to nought, and that there is nothing else we can do.[104]

The emperor remained silent throughout the conference. The prime minister, in calling the meeting to a close, stated that "our Empire stands at the threshold of glory or oblivion."[105] The Imperial Conference of December 1, 1941, was adjourned. Japan's painful choice had been made.

CONCLUSIONS:
WHY COERCIVE DIPLOMACY FAILED IN 1941

The origins of the Pacific War present an apparent puzzle for many deterrence theorists: Why did the Japanese government decide to attack a nation that was, by Tokyo's own calculations, so superior in military strength that the likelihood of victory was exceedingly remote? A common response has been to question the rationality of Japanese decision makers. This irrationality theme permeates numerous analyses of the Pacific War that focus on the army's militarism, the Japanese samurai culture, or the Tokyo leadership's psychological distortions and wishful thinking.[106] In contrast, I suggest here that the Japanese government did behave rationally in the sense that it made reasonable calculations to maximize Japan's national interests based on a set of consistent values.

The focus of this study has been on the interaction of U.S. and Japanese strategies in 1941 and on how the U.S. effort to coerce a total Japanese military withdrawal from China backfired, leading to war. The history does not provide reassuring lessons for the practice of coercive diplomacy. The U.S. policy of deterrence succeeded in 1941 in the limited sense that Washington

persuaded Tokyo that it would likely intervene in any Japanese attack on
British or Dutch colonies in Asia. The Japanese government therefore did decide that the benefits of the Southern Advance were not worth the risks of
war. It was Washington's coercive strategy that failed in 1941: The oil embargo, coupled with the demand for a complete withdrawal from China, led
Tokyo officials to believe Japanese security was so threatened by the United
States that even a desperate war was a better alternative than what was seen as
abject appeasement or an even more dangerous war in the future.

There are three major lessons here for theorists of coercive diplomacy.
First, it is widely believed that practicing coercion is comparatively more difficult than employing deterrence because of the effects of what Thomas
Schelling called the "last clear chance" phenomenon.[107] A state making a
commitment to deterrence places the burden of choice on a potential aggressor, who has the last clear chance to avoid conflict by choosing to refrain
from an attack. "Compellence, in contrast, usually involves *initiating* an action ... the overt act, the first step, is up to the side that makes the compellent
threat."[108] This may often be true, but the 1941 case constitutes a very important exception. Under extreme conditions, embargoes or other kinds of trade
sanctions need not fit Schelling's model. The U.S. oil embargo was a "passive," but extremely powerful, tool of coercion. Washington did not have to
make the first military move after July 1941; it simply had to wait for Japanese stockpiles to dwindle. Japan's domestic economy and its naval power—
and hence its national security—were so dependent upon oil imports that Tokyo agreed to abandon the Southern Advance and made important concessions with regard to a troop withdrawal from China. The Japanese would
not, however, agree to a total withdrawal under the conditions that existed in
November 1941.

This leads us to a second lesson. Robert Art has argued that compellence
tends to be relatively more difficult than deterrence because "it demands
more humiliation from the compelled state."[109] A state that is deterred can
deny that it ever had the intention of attacking another; a state that is coerced
into changing its behavior, however, often faces the loss of prestige that
comes from having publicly succumbed to pressure from another power. The
1941 case supports this argument. The Japanese government was clearly capable of reversing its intention to attack the British and Dutch colonies when
confronted with the possibility of war with the United States. The complete
withdrawal from China, however, was another matter. Even Togo, who had
initially favored compromises on the troop issue, believed after learning of
the Hull note that "the prestige of our Empire would fall to the ground" if
U.S. demands had been accepted.[110]

The third lesson, however, points to what appears to have been an even
more important factor in the Japanese calculation: the belief that the U.S. oil
embargo and its unrelenting demands for troop withdrawals from China

were signs of a deep-seated hostility toward Japan. Under such conditions, it was widely believed in Tokyo that the United States would simply make more demands if concessions were made. In addition, as has been demonstrated, the Tokyo decision makers also noted that there was no guarantee that the United States would keep its commitment to sell oil to Japan in the future. The lesson is simple, though often ignored: Successful coercive diplomacy requires that the compelling state appear committed not only to executing its threats if necessary but also to keeping its promises if a political settlement is reached.

In conclusion, one final, tragic irony must be noted. Although I have tried to demonstrate that the governments in both Tokyo and Washington made the decision to go to war through a process of reasonable calculation and debate in 1941, this does *not* mean that either government was fully in control of the forces that caused that decision to be made. In retrospect, the immediate cause of the Pacific War was a conflict over the future of China: The government in Washington wanted Japan to withdraw its troops and end the China Incident; the government in Tokyo refused to do so. How did the two governments end up in this conflict? In both cases, unauthorized activities of lower-level officials caused senior leaders to face unexpected problems. The Japanese government began to head toward the Pacific War in 1931, when senior Kwantung Army officers—on their own authority and against orders from Tokyo—initiated the Manchurian Incident, which led to the conquest of Manchukuo.[111] Ten years later, U.S. policy suffered a similar fate when Roosevelt's freeze on Japanese assets was transformed—again by lower-ranking officials acting on their own authority—into a total embargo on oil exports. It is ironic that the U.S. government, which for over ten years had been unwilling to initiate a war with Japan over the China Incident, forced such a choice on Tokyo in late 1941. The senior leaderships of both countries made their own histories, but they did not make them exactly as they had wanted.

NOTES

1. For seminal works emphasizing these constraints on purely rational behavior, see Graham T. Allison, *Essence of Decision* (Boston: Little, Brown, 1971); Alexander L. George and Richard Smoke, *Deterrence in American Foreign Policy* (New York: Columbia University Press, 1974); and Robert Jervis, *Perception and Misperception in International Politics* (Princeton: Princeton University Press, 1976).

2. This chapter is an updated version of the Pearl Harbor case study in my doctoral dissertation. For further details see "Deterrence and Decision: An Historical Critique of Modern Deterrence Theory," unpublished Ph.D. diss., Harvard University, Department of Government, 1983. I would like to thank Roger Dingman, Hosoya Chihiro, and Akira Iriye for helpful comments on earlier versions of the case study.

3. International Military Tribunal Far East (hereinafter IMTFE), National Archives, Washington, D.C., exhibit 532. The Japanese cabinet could not function without an army or a navy minister. If either service disagreed with a policy, it could bring down the government because any replacement for the position of minister had to be approved by the service itself.

4. Colonel Hattori Takushiro, *The Complete History of the Greater East Asia War*, vol. 1, (1953), pp. 33–38. A 1953 English translation of this valuable study is available at the Center of Military History, Washington, D.C.

5. Hosoya Chihiro, "The Tripartite Pact 1939–1940," in James W. Morely, ed., *Deterrent Diplomacy: Japan, Germany and the USSR 1935–40* (New York: Columbia University Press, 1976), pp. 208–209.

6. Arthur J. Marder, *Old Friends, New Enemies: The Royal Navy and the Imperial Japanese Navy: Strategic Illusions 1936–1941* (New York: Oxford University Press, 1981), p. 154.

7. Tsunoda Jun, "The Navy's Role in the Southern Strategy," in James W. Morley, ed., *The Fateful Choice: Japan's Advance into Southeast Asia, 1939–1941* (New York: Columbia University Press, 1980), p. 245.

8. Ibid., p. 246. Also see Rogers Spotswood, "Japan's Southward Advance as an Issue in Japanese-American Relations, 1940–1941," unpublished Ph.D. diss., University of Washington, Department of History, 1974, pp. 68–69.

9. Ibid., p. 34.

10. The document is quoted in Mark S. Watson, *Chief of Staff: Prewar Plans and Preparations* (Washington, D.C.: U.S. Government Printing Office, 1974), p. 105.

11. *Pearl Harbor Attack Hearings*, vol. 1, p. 259 (hereinafter *PHAH*). As quoted in Robert J. Quinlan, "The United States Fleet," in Harold Stein, ed., *American Civil Military Relations* (Birmingham: University of Alabama Press, 1963), p. 158.

12. Quoted in Herbert Feis, *The Road to Pearl Harbor* (Princeton: Princeton University Press, 1950), p. 102.

13. *Foreign Relations of the United States*, 1940, vol. 4, *The Far East*, pp. 602–603 (hereinafter *FRUS* followed by year and volume.)

14. See Hata Ikohiko, "The Army's Move into Northern Indochina," in Morley, *Fateful Choice*, pp. 155–209.

15. "Study Concerning Policy for Indochina," in *Gendai Shi Shiryo*, vol. 10, *Nicchu Senso*, part 3 (Tokyo: Misuzu Shobo, 1964), pp. 369–371. I would like to thank Howard Stern for the translation.

16. IMTFE exhibit 549, reprinted in *Documents in German Foreign Policy* (Washington, D.C.: U.S. Government Printing Office, 1949), series D, xi, p. 57 (hereinafter *DGFP*).

17. See Marder, *Old Friends, New Enemies*, pp. 105–135; and Hosoya Chihiro, "The Japanese-Soviet Neutrality Pact," in Morley, *Fateful Choice*, p. 50.

18. Hosoya, "The Tripartite Pact," pp. 243–244. The German ambassador signed the secret protocol on his own authority against orders from Berlin. See Morley, "Introduction" to ibid., p. 189.

19. Ibid., p. 251.

20. Harold L. Ickes, *The Secret Diary of Harold L. Ickes*, vol. III, *The Lowering Clouds* 1939–1941 (New York: Simon and Schuster, 1954), p. 346.

21. Cordell Hull, *The Memoirs of Cordell Hull,* vol. 1 (New York: Macmillan, 1948), p. 915.

22. Breckenridge Long diary entry, as quoted in Spotswood, "Japan's Southern Advance," p. 218.

23. Halifax is quoted in Joseph P. Lash, *Roosevelt and Churchill* (New York: W. W. Norton, 1976), p. 293.

24. As quoted in Robert Dallek, *Franklin D. Roosevelt and American Foreign Policy* (New York: Oxford University Press, 1979), p. 272.

25. *FRUS Japan, 1931–1941,* vol. 2, pp. 137–138.

26. See Marder, *Old Friends, New Enemies,* pp. 206–207.

27. As quoted in Feis, *The Road to Pearl Harbor,* p. 190.

28. See Spotswood, "Japan's Southern Advance," p. 343, note 10.

29. Stark to Kimmel, 4/19/41. *PHAH,* part 16, p. 2163.

30. For details see Hosoya, "The Neutrality Pact," pp. 92–102.

31. This was probably no coincidence because Stalin received secret intelligence about the Japanese calculations from his spy in Tokyo, Richard Sorge. See Chalmers Johnson, *An Instance of Treason: Ozaki Hotsumi and the Sorge Spy Ring* (Stanford: Stanford University Press, 1964), p. 159.

32. Marder, *Old Friends, New Enemies,* p. 165.

33. Tsunoda, "The Navy's Role," p. 292 and appendix 2, p. 303.

34. Asada Sadao, "The Japanese Navy and the United States," in Dorothy Borg and Shumpei Okawoto, *Pearl Harbor as History: U.S.-Japanese Relations, 1931–1941* (New York: Columbia University Press, 1973), p. 254; and Hattori, *Complete History,* p. 131.

35. Nobutaka Ike, *Japan's Decision for War: Records of the 1941 Policy Conferences* (Stanford: Stanford University Press, 1967), p. 87.

36. See Feis, *The Road to Pearl Harbor,* pp. 219, 227–229; and *The "Magic" Background of Pearl Harbor* (Washington, D.C.: U.S. Government Printing Office, 1979), vol. 2, appendix, p. A-56.

37. *FRUS Japan,* 1931–1941, vol. 2, p. 501.

38. John M. Blum, *From the Morgenthau Diaries,* vol. 2 (Boston: Houghton Mifflin, 1959–1967), p. 377.

39. *FRUS The Far East,* 1941, vol. 5, p. 223.

40. Excerpt in *FRUS Japan,* 1931–1941, vol. 2, pp. 264–265.

41. Ibid., pp. 527–528 [emphasis added].

42. *The "Magic" Background,* vol. 2, p. A-97.

43. Blum, *Morgenthau Diaries,* vol. 2, pp. 378–379.

44. Ickes, *Secret Diary,* Vol. III, p. 588.

45. Irvine H. Anderson, Jr., *The Standard Vacuum Oil Company and United States East Asian Policy, 1933–1941* (Princeton: Princeton University Press, 1975), p. 178. Also see Michael A. Barnhart, *Japan Prepares for Total War* (Ithaca, N.Y.: Cornell University Press, 1987), pp. 227–232. For an opposing interpretation, see Waldo Heinrichs, *Threshold of War: Franklin D. Roosevelt and American Entry into World War II* (New York: Oxford University Press, 1988), pp. 246–247.

46. Dean Acheson, *Present at the Creation* (New York: New American Library Paperback, 1970), pp. 43–44.

47. Ibid., pp. 51–52.

48. Jonathan G. Utley, "Upstairs, Downstairs at Foggy Bottom," *Prologue* 8 (Spring 1988): 26–28. See especially note 36, p. 26.

49. Acheson, *Present at the Creation*, pp. 52, 46.

50. See *FRUS The Far East*, 1941, vol. 4, p. 359.

51. *FRUS Japan*, 1931–1941, vol. 2, pp. 567, 572.

52. Ike, *Japan's Decision for War*, p. 152.

53. The contemporary Japanese estimates of fuel consumption and imports are described in Marder, *Old Friends, New Enemies*, p. 167, and Barnhart, *Japan Prepares for Total War*, p. 146.

54. Marder, ibid., p. 167.

55. See *PHAH*, part 20, p. 4005.

56. The best discussion is in Robert J. Butow, *Tojo and the Coming of the War* (Stanford: Stanford University Press, 1961), pp. 237–245.

57. Ike, *Japan's Decision for War*, p. 140.

58. Ibid., pp. 160–161.

59. Ibid., p. 152.

60. Ibid., pp. 135–136.

61. Ibid., p. 136.

62. Ibid., p. 153.

63. *FRUS Japan*, 1931–1941, vol. 2, p. 605.

64. *The "Magic" Background*, appendix, vol. 3, p. A-45.

65. Hull, *Memoirs*, vol. 2, pp. 1024, 1025. Stimson also feared the "appeasement syndrome" and had an entire file of anti-appeasement editorials. See Stimson, Safe File, Record Group 107, Box 4, National Archives, Washington, D.C.

66. See William L. Langer and S. Everett Gleason, *The Undeclared War, 1940–1941* (New York: Harper, 1953), p. 707.

67. Hull, *Memoirs*, vol. 2, p. 1035.

68. Ibid., p. 1025, and *FRUS Japan*, 1931–1941, vol. 2, p. 652.

69. Marder, *Old Friends, New Enemies*, p. 175.

70. See ibid., pp. 177–178.

71. The first quote is from Tojo's October 14 meeting with Konoe as quoted in Marder, *Old Friends, New Enemies*, p. 179; the second is from the October 12 conference, Butow, *Tojo*, pp. 273–274.

72. *War in Asia and the Pacific* (New York: Garland Publishing, 1980), monograph 147, p. 59, and appendix no. 6.

73. See Butow, *Tojo*, p. 267, and "Konoe's Memoirs," *PHAH*, part 20, p. 4013. This was not, however, an espousal of national suicide. Tojo was borrowing a metaphor from an eighteenth-century Buddhist "miracle tale" to emphasize the need for decisive, even risky, action. See Saburo Hayashi, *Kogun: The Japanese Army in the Pacific War* (Quantico, Va.: Marine Corps Association, 1959), note 41, p. 199.

74. See Butow, *Tojo*, pp. 289–309.

75. Ibid., p. 243, and *War in Asia*, vol. 2, monograph 150, appendix 2, p. 89.

76. For contrasting views, see Hosoya Chihiro, "Twenty-five Years After Pearl Harbor: A New Look at Japan's Decision for War," in Grant Goodman (compiler), *Imperial Japan and Asia: A Reassessment* (Occasional paper of the East Asian Institute, Columbia University, New York, 1967), p. 58; Paul W. Schroeder, *The Axis Alli-*

ance and Japanese-American Relations 1941 (Ithaca, N.Y.: Cornell University Press, 1958), pp. 175–176; and Butow, *Tojo*, p. 326.

77. Ike, *Japan's Decision*, p. 205.

78. Ibid., p. 198.

79. Ibid., pp. 209–210, and Shigenori Togo, *The Cause of Japan* (New York: Simon & Schuster, 1956), p. 144.

80. IMTFE exhibit no. 3566. Also see IMTFE exhibit no. 3567, and Togo, ibid., p. 215.

81. *War in Asia*, vol. 2, monograph 150, appendix no. 2, p. 85.

82. Ibid.

83. Statements of Japanese officials in World War II, General Headquarters, Far East Command, Military Intelligence Section Historical Division, Office of the Chief of Military History, Historical Manuscript AD4, vol. 2, p. 298.

84. Ibid., vol. 1, document no. 62013.

85. *War in Asia*, vol. 2, part 6.

86. Ike, *Japan's Decision*, p. 193.

87. Ibid., p. 202.

88. Ibid., p. 203.

89. Ibid., p. 205.

90. Stimson memorandum to FDR, 10/21/41, Stimson Safe File, Philippines Folder, Record Group 107, National Archives.

91. Langer and Gleason, *The Undeclared War*, pp. 845–846.

92. Ibid., p. 847.

93. See Ike, *Japan's Decision*, pp. 209–211.

94. Undated memorandum, *FRUS The Far East*, 1941, vol. 4, p. 626. The best discussion is in Jonathan T. Utley, *Going to War With Japan* (Knoxville: University of Tennessee Press, 1985), pp. 165–175.

95. *FRUS Japan*, 1941, vol. 4, pp. 665–666. Also see Hull, *Memoirs*, vol. 2, pp. 1081–1082. For talk of appeasement, see Ickes, *The Secret Diary*, vol. 3, pp. 654–655.

96. Stimson Diary, November 26, 1941, entry. Appendix to statement of Henry Stimson, Pearl Harbor Liaison Office, Record Group 80, General Record of Navy Department, Box 30, National Archives, Washington, D.C.

97. The timing suggested here disagrees with that proposed by Langer and Gleason, *The Undeclared War*, pp. 893–894. There is no conclusive evidence on whether Stimson's telephone message warning of Japanese military movements came before or after Hull met with the president to receive approval to abandon the modus vivendi. There is some circumstantial evidence, which Langer and Gleason missed. The Stimson diary states that Hull told him on November 26 that he was "*about* to kick the whole thing over" (emphasis added). This suggests, contrary to Langer and Gleason's view, that Roosevelt's approval had not yet been given.

98. *The "Magic" Background*, pp. A-104–105.

99. Even a relative "moderate" such as Togo held this view. He reported to the Imperial Conference on December 1 that although Hull's proposal would not require an immediate withdrawal from Manchukuo, "if we look at this in light of the fact that there has been a change in their position, that they look upon Chungking as the one and only legitimate regime, and that they want to destroy the Nanking regime, they may retract what they have said previously." Ike, *Japan's Decision*, p. 279.

100. Tojo testimony, IMTFE exhibit 3655, p. 185.

101. Ibid., appendix 4. Also see Butow, *Tojo,* pp. 345–348.

102. Ike, *Japan's Decision,* p. 263.

103. Ibid., p. 270.

104. Ibid., p. 282.

105. Ibid., p. 283.

106. See Richard Ned Lebow, *Between Peace and War* (Baltimore: Johns Hopkins University Press, 1981), p. 274; Glenn H. Snyder and Paul Diesing, *Conflict Among Nations* (Princeton: Princeton University Press, 1977), p. 301; Jack Snyder, *Myths of Empire: Domestic Politics and International Ambition* (Ithaca, N.Y.: Cornell University Press, 1981), pp. 130–133; and Robert Jervis, "Deterrence and Perception," *International Security* 7, no. 3 (Winter 1982–1983): 30.

107. See Thomas C. Schelling, *Arms and Influence* (New Haven: Yale University Press, 1966), pp. 69–91.

108. Ibid., p. 72.

109. Robert J. Art, "To What Ends Military Power," *International Security* 4, no. 4 (Spring 1980): 10.

110. Ike, *Japan's Decision,* p. 271.

111. See Seki Hiroharu, "The Manchurian Incident," in James W. Morley, ed., *Japan Erupts: The London Naval Conference and the Manchurian Incident, 1928–1932* (New York: Columbia University Press, 1984).

5

The Laos Crisis of 1961–1962: Coercive Diplomacy for Minimal Objectives

DAVID K. HALL

When President John F. Kennedy took office in January 1961, he found the U.S. government embroiled in a dangerous international crisis that threatened to drag the nation into a direct military confrontation with the Soviet Union. During the next eighteen months, President Kennedy ordered a series of diplomatic and military actions that enabled him to achieve his minimal political and military objectives in Laos while preventing the armed conflict with the Soviet Union he was determined to avoid.

THE HISTORICAL SETTING

The Laos crisis facing John Kennedy in January 1961 was one facet of the prolonged struggle between the Communist and non-Communist states in Southeast Asia, which had been halted only briefly by the 1954 Geneva Conference ending the first Indochina War. Laos emerged from this 1954 international conference as a sparsely populated nation of mountains and jungle bordered by the Communist states of China and North Vietnam on the north and the non-Communist countries of Thailand, South Vietnam, and Cambodia on the south. The Geneva Accords required that the Vietminh (the Vietnamese Communist army) withdraw from Laos to North Vietnam and directed the Pathet Lao (the Laotian Communist army) to regroup in Laos's two northern provinces pending the Pathet Lao's integration into the Royal Lao Army and the formation of a national unity government. All nations except France were barred from establishing military bases and training missions in Laos. External economic and military aid programs, such as those begun by the United States in 1950, were permitted to continue. An International Commission for Supervision and Control in Laos (ICC)—composed of members from India (the representative of which served as chairperson), Canada, and Poland—was created to police these agreements and report any violations to the permanent cochairs of the Geneva Conference, the United Kingdom and the Soviet Union.[1]

When French colonial rule in Southeast Asia collapsed in 1954, the Eisenhower administration rushed to block any further expansion of communism in the region. To deter a Korean-style invasion of Laos and the other nations in the area, the administration organized the Southeast Asia Treaty Organization (SEATO), a mutual security pact consisting of the United States, the United Kingdom, France, Thailand, Australia, New Zealand, the Philippines, and Pakistan. With the consent of the Laotian, Cambodian, and South Vietnamese governments, a protocol attached to the security pact extended its military and economic provisions to these three nations as well. To counter the threat of Communist internal subversion, Washington provided economic and military assistance programs throughout Southeast Asia. In 1955, the United States began direct military assistance to Laos to augment the declining French program. To avoid open violation of the Geneva Accords prohibiting such a U.S. mission, American military personnel in Laos were given civilian status and clothing.

U.S. violations of the Geneva Agreement were easily justified by the fact that comparable violations were committed by Communist forces in Laos. The Pathet Lao showed little interest in completing the negotiations leading to its integration into the political and military institutions of the country. Throughout 1955 and 1956 the group devoted its efforts to recruiting peasants in northern Laos and harassing elements of the Royal Lao Army garrisoned there. The Pathet Lao's political and military efforts were covertly assisted by cadres of the Vietminh left behind in Laos in violation of the Geneva Accords.

Despite the recalcitrance of the Pathet Lao, Prince Souvanna Phouma—the first Laotian prime minister—patiently pursued his long-term goals of reuniting his nation and establishing its neutrality in international affairs. The Eisenhower administration considered Souvanna's negotiations toward integration of the Pathet Lao into the national parliament, army, and bureaucracy to be politically naive and dangerous. The Pathet Lao's leaders, it felt, were far more organized and disciplined than their Royal government counterparts and therefore were fully capable of taking control of the political and military institutions of Laos if they were granted an official role within the government.

In early 1958, the Eisenhower administration's worse fears materialized, as the Pathet Lao's leaders finally agreed to terms for their reintegration into the Royal government and the Royal Lao Army. Souvanna Phouma viewed this agreement as Laos's fulfillment of its obligations under the Geneva Accords and officially requested that the ICC discontinue its peace-keeping activities in Laos. The U.S. government reacted to these developments by suspending its large economic assistance program in Laos and helping its Laotian clients, led by General Phoumi Nosavan, foment a parliamentary crisis that ousted Souvanna Phouma from the prime ministership. A new pro-American government was formed that forced the Pathet Lao ministers from the cabinet. One of the Pathet Lao battalions in the Lao national army mutinied, and with the assistance of its Vietminh cadres, it began to drive Royal Lao soldiers and officials out of Laos's northern provinces.

Growing fear of civil war moderated the Laotian government's treatment of the Pathet Lao, but rigid anticommunism recommenced in December 1959 after a military coup led by General Phoumi Nosavan. Lao policy reversed course yet again in August 1960 when General Phoumi was overthrown by Captain Kong Le, a respected paratroop battalion commander who viewed the Lao government's departure from international neutrality to be the cause of the nation's growing bloodshed and corruption. Kong Le and his soldiers arranged for the Laotian king to reappoint Souvanna Phouma as prime minister.

After briefly joining Souvanna in a national unity cabinet, General Phoumi broke away to establish his own government and army headquarters in southern Laos. General Phoumi's cousin, Thai Premier Sarit Thanarat, imposed a crippling blockade on all food and fuel shipped to Laos through Thailand. When the Eisenhower administration refused to assist Souvanna Phouma in breaking Thailand's economic blockade, the Laotian prime minister tried to pressure Washington by establishing diplomatic relations with the Soviet Union and reopening national unification talks with the Pathet Lao. In response to General Phoumi's massing of his troops for an attack on the Lao capital of Vientiane, Souvanna requested an emergency airlift of food and fuel from the Soviet Union, which commenced between Hanoi and Vientiane on December 3, 1960.

General Phoumi's troops attacked Vientiane, and Souvanna Phouma abandoned the capital to Captain Kong Le's neutralist troops and fled to Cambodia. Meanwhile, Souvanna's information minister struck a deal with Hanoi: In exchange for military supplies to be delivered to Kong Le's soldiers, Souvanna Phouma's government agreed to a formal alliance between Kong Le and the Pathet Lao. On December 15, the first Soviet arms and ammunition arrived for the neutralist army. Kong Le's forces were driven out of the capital by Phoumi's army, but they marched northward to the all-weather landing field at the strategic Plain of Jars. In combined attack with the Pathet Lao, Kong Le's troops seized the airfield and surrounding villages from the Royal Lao Army and French advisers guarding the plain. Forty-five tons of Soviet supplies from Hanoi started landing daily at this airfield as part of what Soviet Deputy Foreign Minister N. G. Kuznetsov later described as the Soviet Union's highest-priority supply operation since the Russian Revolution. The Eisenhower administration reacted to this escalation by transferring six heavily armed AT-6 aircraft to Laos and secretly replacing the three hundred U.S. infantry trainers of the Royal Lao Army with four hundred Special Forces personnel.

A provisional government under Souvanna Phouma was established at Kong Le's headquarters at Khang Khay. In Vientiane, a new Laotian government headed by Prince Boun Oum as prime minister and General Phoumi as deputy prime minister was approved by the Lao National Assembly. Although the United States, Britain, France, and Thailand quickly extended official recognition to the new government, the Soviet Union, China, India, and other nations continued to recognize Souvanna Phouma as the legal ruler. Eisenhower confided to Kennedy that the escalating war in Laos was the most difficult and dangerous situation he was passing on to the new administration.

THE QUIET-DIPLOMACY PHASE

As John Kennedy assumed control of U.S. foreign policy, several proposals already existed for dampening the growing crisis. In September 1960, the Soviet Union had proposed reconvening the Geneva Conference to work out new settlement terms in Laos, and China officially endorsed this recommendation on December 28. On December 15, India, as the former chair of the ICC, had called on Great Britain and the Soviet Union to exercise their authority as cochairs of the 1954 Geneva Conference and reconvene the peacekeeping work of the ICC in Laos. Both proposals had been rejected by the Eisenhower administration. The outgoing U.S. leadership felt that Washington was still in a position to control events in Laos without entering into a series of frustrating negotiations with the Communists, and no one had been satisfied with the effectiveness of the ICC's peace-keeping operations during the period 1954–1958.

Based on the advice of his appointees, State Department specialists, and several longtime congressional colleagues, John Kennedy soon signaled that he was launching a new policy on Laos and scaling back the Eisenhower administration's political objectives there. On January 22, 1961, the new administration encouraged the British government to hand the Soviet Union a proposal calling for resumption of the ICC's activities in Laos to supervise a cease-fire.[2] At his first press conference as president on January 25, Kennedy stated that he favored an "independent, peaceful, uncommitted" Laos.[3] And on February 5, the administration's Laos Task Force gave Kennedy a "concept telegram," drafted jointly by the State Department, the Defense Department, National Security Council (NSC) staff, the Central Intelligence

Agency (CIA), and the U.S. ambassador to Laos, which was subsequently sent to key embassies and allies. The telegram stated that:

> US wishes leave no stone unturned find peaceful solution and has therefore joined in attempt find conditions under which ICC might function. ...
>
> We are acting in conformance with the guidance in the President's inaugural address that, while we do not fear to negotiate for genuine peace and understanding, we will not abandon our friends. ...
>
> Having taken positive step toward peaceful solution [by requesting resumption of ICC] onus passes to the USSR for recalcitrance. ...
>
> We conceive of Laos as a neutral state, unaligned in her international relations but determined to preserve her national integrity. In order to exist in this special status, enjoy independence and territorial integrity, some temporary international machinery to guard this neutrality will have to be devised. Neutralized state would permit, except as provided by previous agreements, no foreign military bases, no foreign troops and no military alliances. State of Austria may serve as precedent. An underlying assumption is that it is in best interest of US and USSR avoid widespread hostilities in Laos.[4]

The Kennedy administration's new goals for Laos did not end the crisis, however. With General Phoumi's army slow to advance on the combined Neutralist–Pathet Lao–Vietminh forces in northern Laos, there was little reason for the Soviet Union, China, and North Vietnam to alter their course. Moscow rejected the U.S. call for reactivation of the ICC and instead reiterated its earlier proposal to convene an enlarged Geneva Conference on Indochina to settle the conflict. Kennedy's initiatives up to this point were generally regarded by diplomats as constituting a sign of weakness, an interpretation that was reflected in the U.S. press. The *New York Times* characterized U.S. policy as "amounting to a decision not to be drawn into a Laotian jungle war" based, in part, on British and French reluctance to support a harder line.[5]

Meanwhile supplies continued to pour into northern Laos on Soviet planes and trucks originating in North Vietnam. American intelligence detected independent Vietminh combat units crossing the border into Laos. Then in mid-March, the combined 35,000-man Neutralist–Pathet Lao–Vietminh army launched a major offensive that quickly sent the 50,000-man Royal Lao Army into disorderly retreat throughout northern and eastern Laos.

Suddenly and unexpectedly, the U.S. government faced the possibility of a complete and humiliating military defeat in Laos. Kennedy quickly concluded that this outcome was unacceptable. The SEATO treaty's promise of military protection for Laos as well as for its common borders with Thailand, South Vietnam, and Cambodia gave Laos considerable strategic, political, and psychological importance. The Thai government in particular was committed to the political independence of Laos and felt that its northeast neighbor must serve as Thailand's buffer against Communist power in Asia. Thailand had long provided covert military assistance and advisers for the anti-Communist forces in Laos.[6]

The growing violence in South Vietnam also heightened Laos's importance to the United States. Kennedy had been briefed in late January on North Vietnam's increasing efforts to establish control over Laotian territory bordering on South Vietnam, on Hanoi's road improvement program running through Laos into South Vietnam, and on the growing terrorist disruption of South Vietnam's economy and government by the Viet Cong. And although it was Eisenhower and not Kennedy who had coined the phrase "row of dominoes" to emphasize the adverse consequences of a setback in one locale on other neighboring countries, the new president was sensitive to the same considerations. At a March 23 press conference, Kennedy asserted that "the security of all Southeast Asia will be endangered if Laos loses its neutral independence."[7]

At the same time, there were powerful reasons why Kennedy remained extremely reluctant to resort to U.S. military force in Laos. The new president did not want to begin his White House tenure with a military confrontation with the Soviet Union. Kennedy was committed to improving the quality of Soviet-American relations through a resumption of the high-level negotiations that had broken down after the May 1960 U-2 incident. As early as December 1960, the president-elect had authorized two of his new White House assistants to discuss strategic arms control and the German problem with Soviet officials in Moscow. At a White House meeting on February 11, Kennedy and his top Russian experts agreed that he should meet with Soviet Premier Nikita Khrushchev as soon as possible so that each leader could increase his understanding of the other's interests, concerns, and reactions; Kennedy had communicated this desire to Khrushchev through the U.S. ambassador to the Soviet Union. Kennedy worried throughout his entire administration that some unnecessary or unintended superpower clash, arising from "miscalculation," would spiral out of control and result in a superpower nuclear exchange.[8]

A further constraint on U.S. policy was the lack of unanimity within the Southeast Asia Treaty Organization. Only Thailand, Pakistan, and the Philippines favored military intervention; of these Thailand, the member nation most directly threatened, was the only other member that could be counted on to provide substantial military support. The true strength of the organization lay with its North Atlantic members, but France and Great Britain privately refused to offer assistance. France was resolutely unwilling to embark upon another Indochina War; Great Britain, although somewhat more sympathetic, had just emerged from a costly ten-year jungle campaign against Communist guerrillas in Malaya. Instead of intervention, these nations urged the United States to support a neutralist Laos with a coalition government that included the Pathet Lao. With France and Great Britain not eager for intervention, the deterrent value of possible SEATO intervention was unquestionably diluted, and any U.S. attempt to glorify its intrusion as a multinational police action would be awkward at best.

For these reasons, despite the Neutralist–Pathet Lao–Vietminh offensive in Laos, Kennedy made several more efforts to end the crisis through diplomatic means. He directed U.S. Ambassador Llewellyn Thompson in Moscow to remind Khrushchev of Kennedy's desire to neutralize Laos but also of the new president's determination to prevent a complete Communist takeover of Laos. His assurances on neutralization included willingness by the United States to withdraw completely its military mission in Laos and to channel all aid through an international body acceptable to both sides. Kennedy also informed Khrushchev that any future progress on other common international concerns depended on satisfactory resolution of the crisis in Laos. Similar messages were sent to China and North Vietnam through U.S. ambassadors. As the Communist offensive rolled on in Laos, Kennedy ordered Secretary of State Dean Rusk to meet with Soviet Foreign Minister Andrei Gromyko, who was then visiting the United Nations in New York, so that Rusk could repeat the current U.S. position.[9]

THE TACIT-ULTIMATUM PHASE

None of these U.S. diplomatic approaches elicited the hoped-for response from the Communist governments or slowed their Laotian clients' steady march through northern and eastern Laos. Kennedy now realized that although the Soviet Union, China, and North Vietnam might still be willing to settle for neutralization of Laos, threats being made for noncompliance with U.S. demands were lacking in sufficient credibility, potency, and urgency. To prevent a total loss of the U.S. position in Laos, Kennedy felt compelled to confront the Communists with a more systematic package of military and political threats, even if this risked deeper U.S. involvement in Laos and undesired provocation of the opposition.

On March 21, Kennedy placed U.S. forces in Okinawa and Japan on in-place alert, dispatched a five-hundred-man helicopter unit to the Thai air base nearest to Laos, sent stockpiles of U.S. supplies and equipment in Thailand to bases near Laos, and ordered the three aircraft carriers of the Seventh Fleet into the Gulf of Siam.[10] Two days later, the president appeared on prime-time U.S. television to describe the mounting crisis in Laos and to demand "a cessation of the present armed attacks by externally supported Communists."[11] Although Kennedy did not place a specific time limit on compliance with his demand, he did say in response to a question that "I think the matter, of course, becomes increasingly serious as the days go by."[12] Meanwhile, from

Bangkok, Thailand, word came from the SEATO foreign ministers conference that "appropriate retaliatory action" would be taken "if diplomatic actions fail to restore peace."[13]

Kennedy also increased the diplomatic stakes at risk for the Soviet Union by drawing India more deeply into the crisis. As self-appointed leader of the neutralist movement and chair of the International Commission for Supervision and Control in Laos, India had a particular interest in the peace and international neutrality of Laos. On March 24, U.S. Special Ambassador Averell Harriman handed Indian Prime Minister Jawaharal Nehru a personal letter from Kennedy that called on the Indian leader to assume a leading role in arranging a cease-fire in Laos. Kennedy's note emphasized the U.S. intention of withdrawing completely from Laos provided neutrality was restored, but it warned that SEATO would be forced to intervene if this did not develop. Pleased with the U.S. support for neutrality, and concerned that Washington might be provoked into escalating the war, Nehru sent an urgent note to Khrushchev that same day asking the Soviet premier to end the fighting. He also instructed the Indian ambassador to inform the Soviets of the urgency of a truce and of the reactivation of the ICC.[14]

Although bringing to bear greater military and diplomatic pressure, Kennedy also increased the attractiveness of the neutralization "carrot" he had been holding out to the Soviets, Chinese, and North Vietnamese. On the same day as his national press conference, a British-American proposal was presented to the Soviet Union that called for an immediate cease-fire and the reconvening of an enlarged Geneva Conference to work out a permanent political settlement in Laos. The U.S. government had accepted for the first time the long-standing Communist demand for a fourteen-nation conference on the future of Laos, provided that an effective military cease-fire was established first.[15]

As Kennedy increased the credibility and potency of U.S. threats and concessions, he soon discovered the complication of applying coercive diplomacy against a coalition of opponents. Khrushchev quickly signaled that given the Soviet Union's limited strategic and political interests in Laos, he did not want a military conflict with the United States. *Pravda*'s lead editorial on March 27 complained that Kennedy's recent action "actually means presenting an ultimatum to the Laotian people," but it acknowledged that "the realistic way to the solution of the Laos problem lies not in aggravating the situation in the area of Laos, not in preparing military intervention, but in peace talks and in the calling of an international conference and the renewal of the work of the ICC."[16]

The sticking point, however, was Khrushchev's growing competition with Communist China for influence in North Vietnam. This competition within the Communist world made it impossible for the Soviet premier to negotiate an end to the Laotian crisis without taking into account the reactions of

China and North Vietnam, and these latter two Communist governments opposed any cease-fire in Laos prior to a renewed Geneva Conference so long as the Communist forces were advancing on the battlefield and the military risks from the United States appeared manageable. As Chinese Premier Chou En-Lai had said in February, "The Chinese Government is, in general, not against reactivating the International Commission for Supervision and Control in Laos, but … it is necessary first to convene an international conference of the countries concerned, which will make new provisions on the tasks and functions of the Commission in light of the new situation."[17]

With the United States and China demanding diametrically opposite phasing of the cease-fire and the international conference, Khrushchev's actions began to reflect his desire to anger neither party. On April 1, he suggested that the Soviet Union and the United Kingdom should issue an appeal for a cease-fire in Laos *simultaneously* with the commencement of a new international conference. Then on April 3, the Soviets agreed in private talks with the British that an end to the fighting in Laos must precede negotiations on that nation, but they failed to consent to ICC *verification* of the cease-fire prior to the international conference. Then the following day, Moscow began to circumvent Peking through Vietnamese-language broadcasts direct to North Vietnam and Laos, calling for a cease-fire to "help to create a favorable atmosphere for negotiations."[18] Prospects for a negotiated settlement were improving, but Kennedy remained adamant as to his terms of compliance.

By mid-April the Soviet Union had yet to persuade China and North Vietnam to accept the U.S.-demanded cease-fire, and the Neutralist–Pathet Lao–Vietminh troops were still expanding their territorial control. Suddenly, the U.S. failure at the Bay of Pigs was injected into this troubling situation. Kennedy became alarmed that his decision not to back the Cuban exile force with military action might be construed as a sign of U.S. unwillingness to fight in Laos as well. To counteract this possibility, he ordered the four hundred "civilian" Special Forces personnel in Laos to put on their military uniforms and join the Royal Lao Army units at the front lines. The U.S. State Department announced this change in policy. By accepting the increased risk of U.S. casualties in Laos, Kennedy hoped to make his threat of military intervention more potent and credible.[19]

Ordering U.S. military advisers to put on their uniforms and move to the front lines was a small step, but it was an "exemplary action" that was clearly perceived and strongly condemned by China and North Vietnam. Hanoi immediately called on the Soviet Union and Great Britain to stop the United States from sending its advisers into combat, and Chou En-Lai called it a "serious step taken by the United States in preparation for direct participation in the civil war in Laos."[20] The move helped persuade Hanoi and Peking to accept the U.S. terms for stopping the fighting. On April 24, Great Britain and the Soviet Union announced that as the original cochairs of the Geneva Conference, they were reactivating the ICC and dispatching it to Laos to verify a cease-fire. They also announced that invitations were being sent to fourteen nations to convene at Geneva on May 12 to consider the Laos problem. Peking and Hanoi quickly accepted the plan.[21]

Despite formal agreement among the concerned governments, the Pathet Lao–Vietminh troops continued their attacks throughout the countryside, as if to gain as much territory as possible before the cease-fire took hold. The continuing Communist advances again brought the U.S. government to the brink of military intervention, and Kennedy once again received from his advisers recommendations ranging from the movement of U.S. combat troops into Thailand's portion of the Mekong Valley all the way to the massive intervention of one hundred thousand U.S. soldiers in southern Laos, Thailand, and South Vietnam.[22]

Instead, Kennedy again rejected these military recommendations and again placed a Marine division in Okinawa on alert for possible intervention in case the opposing army advanced dangerously close to the capital of Vientiane. It was clear that the ineffectiveness of the Royal Lao Army, its particular fear of the Vietminh cadres and units, and the hazards of fighting a ground war in a nation of mountains and rain forests that lacked transportation and communication infrastructure were enough to make Kennedy elect not to take his stand against communism in Laos but in Thailand and South Vietnam.[23] (The only Laotians consistently effective in resisting the Pathet Lao and Vietminh were the aggressive Meo tribespeople living in villages between Communist lines, and Washington was only beginning to appreciate their utility in the spring of 1961.)

Fortunately, the Pathet Lao, the Neutralists, and the Royal Lao government soon reached an agreement on cease-fire terms, and the fighting declined to sporadic clashes and shellings along the cease-fire line, clearing the way for the Geneva Conference on May 16. At their summit meeting in Vienna in early June, Kennedy and Khrushchev "reaffirmed their support of a neutral and independent Laos under a government chosen by the Laotians themselves, and of international agreements for insuring that neutrality and independence, and in this connection they have recognized the importance of an effective cease-fire."[24] Privately, Kennedy and Khrushchev agreed to withdraw their military advisers from Lao after completion of new international accords to reduce the chance of an unwanted confrontation.[25]

OVERCOMING OBSTACLES TO COOPERATION

Even after the Geneva negotiations began, the United States had to rely on diplomatic and military pressures to keep the cease-fire from collapsing. The Pathet Lao and North Vietnamese did not want to give away at the conference table what could be won without significant risk on the battlefield. As early as June 6, chief U.S. delegate Averell Harriman temporarily suspended U.S. participation in the Geneva Conference because of continuing attacks on U.S.-supported Meo tribesmen living in northern Laos. As the Geneva Conference recessed in August 1961, Harriman and chief British delegate Malcolm MacDonald obtained from their Soviet counterpart Georgi Pushkin the reluctant agreement that each conference cochair would ensure adherence to the cease-fire by those parties in its political camp until the conference resumed. (This private promise came to be referred to as "the Pushkin agreement.") Meanwhile, Kennedy rejected Khrushchev's request for a summit meeting on Berlin until the Soviet Union exhibited better faith in controlling its clients in Laos.[26]

In addition to policing the cease-fire, the most taxing problem in Laos was forcing the three political factions into a power-sharing agreement that would permanently end the civil war that had pulled the United States and the Soviet Union into Laos's internal affairs. Agreement on such a power-sharing agreement proved far more difficult to achieve than anyone expected. In October 1961, the Laotian Rightists, Neutralists, and Communists finally agreed to create a new coalition government with Souvanna Phouma serving as prime minister, and in December the envoys from the fourteen nations at the Geneva Conference completed a draft agreement guaranteeing the international neutrality of Laos. However, final approval of the new Geneva Accords awaited actual formation of a Laotian coalition government that could initial the agreement, and such a unity government could not be arranged.

The insurmountable problem became General Phoumi Nosavan, the commander in chief of the Royal Lao Army and the true leader of the Boun Oum government. The Kennedy administration's continuing assistance to Phoumi was critical to the pro-American forces' capability to prevent the Pathet Lao–Neutralist forces from rapidly occupying all of Laos. This assistance, however, reinforced Phoumi's long-standing belief that the United States was dependent on his political and military survival. Under these circumstances, General Phoumi stubbornly demanded that the Rightists in the proposed coalition government be assigned the cabinet portfolios of Defense (which controlled the army) and Interior (which controlled the police and the courts). This unrealistic position was apparently fueled by the belief that Souvanna would eventually resign in frustration or that the U.S. military would be compelled to intervene when the Communists next launched an offensive. In fact, the Laotian cease-fire was seriously strained in December 1961 and again in February 1962 because of military probes and counterpoises by the Pathet Lao and General Phoumi's troops.[27]

Finally, the Kennedy administration had to resort to coercive diplomacy against its own client to obtain a political settlement of the civil war. By February 1962 the White House was so frustrated by Phoumi's refusal to accept Souvanna Phouma's coalition terms that it suspended its $3 million in payroll assistance to the Lao government and hinted that it might terminate the delivery of military equipment as well. In late March, at a meeting in Vientiane with Phoumi and his cabinet, Averell Harriman was extraordinarily blunt. The only alternative to a neutral Laos was a Communist one, Harriman said, and if the current cabinet members would not accept Souvanna's terms, then they would soon have to swim the Mekong River to Thailand because the United States would no longer protect them. In April, as another element of the coercion of Phoumi, Kennedy gave Harriman approval to withdraw the Special Forces training teams operating with the Royal Lao Army in forward field positions. In early May, before this step could be implemented, however, five thousand of Phoumi's best troops were overrun at Nam Tha by Pathet Lao and Vietminh troops.[28]

Some U.S. officials suspected that Phoumi had intentionally provoked this battle with the Pathet Lao–Vietminh by placing his troops in this northern outpost only fifteen miles from China's border, so as to force Kennedy into resuming full support for the Rightists. Instead, Harriman told the Lao ambassador in Washington that Phoumi's political career was finished. The U.S. government refused to replace the military equipment lost at Nam Tha and actively discouraged Thailand, South Vietnam, South Korea, Japan, Taiwan, Malaya, and the Philippines from extending any of the economic or political support immediately sought by Phoumi and Boun Oum.[29]

At the same time, this military defeat of some of the Royal Lao Army's best troops raised the prospect that the Communists no longer had any incentive for peacefully settling the civil war. Kennedy ordered the U.S. Seventh Fleet back into the Gulf of Siam and landed five thousand U.S. troops in neighboring Thailand. Of all the military options available to Kennedy, this one seemed best suited to signaling to the Communists, without actually lending direct assistance to Phoumi or reinforcing his obstinacy, that the United States might intervene if the civil war resumed. Meanwhile, word was sent to the Soviet Union through multiple channels, including meetings between Khrushchev and the U.S. ambassador and between Secretary of State Rusk and the Soviet ambassador, that the U.S. political objective remained a neutralized Laos but that Moscow must dissuade the Communist forces from further military action.[30]

Although Khrushchev was carefully informed of the limited goals of the American troop movement into Thailand, he publicly described the risks and consequences of this U.S. action in dramatic terms, apparently to dissuade his Vietnamese, Chinese, and Laotian comrades from taking any future military action. He predicted that the U.S. forces would become involved in a shooting war: "They arrived with their weapons. They did not come to play golf. They will shoot, and those they shoot will shoot back."[31] *Pravda* condemned the United States for "preparing for intervention in Laos," which "would certainly widen the military conflict and enhance the danger of war not only on the borders of Laos but also in the whole of Southeast Asia," and concluded that failure to peacefully resolve the Laos problem was the worst possible outcome for all parties, including the Communist bloc.[32]

On May 15, Phoumi and Boun Oum cracked under the weight of intense U.S. pressure and military humiliation. They indicated their willingness to accept a coalition government in which the Interior and Defense ministries were led by Neutralists, provided that Souvanna Phouma could "prove he is not working for the communists." On June 8, in the first full exchange of views among the three Lao factions in several months, Phoumi agreed to cede the Foreign Affairs, Defense, and Interior portfolios to Souvanna. The last major obstacle had been cleared for the signing of the coalition agreement on June 12, and the Declaration on the Neutrality of Laos was signed on July 23, 1962, by the fourteen foreign ministers assembled at the Geneva Conference.[33]

The Declaration on the Neutrality of Laos specifically required its signatories to:

1. Do nothing to impair the sovereignty, independence, neutrality, unity, or territorial integrity of the Kingdom of Laos
2. Refrain from direct or indirect interference in Laotian internal affairs
3. Refrain from attaching political conditions to any assistance which they might offer or which Laos might seek
4. Refrain from bringing Laos into a military alliance
5. Respect Laotian wishes not to recognize the protection of any military alliance, including SEATO
6. Refrain from introducing any military personnel into Laos
7. Refrain from establishing in Laos any foreign military bases or strong points
8. Refrain from using the territory of Laos for interference in the internal affairs of other countries[34]

Given the long history of both Western and Communist violation of the 1954 accords, it is not surprising that both political camps would seek some additional guarantees that the 1962 Geneva Agreements would be more faithfully implemented. To this end, the terms of the declaration were reinforced by a continuation of the private 1961 agreement among Harriman, British delegate MacDonald, and Soviet delegate Pushkin that each Geneva cochair would ensure that the members of its political bloc would comply with the accords. In other words, Great Britain promised to keep the United States, Thailand, and others from meddling in Laos's internal affairs, and the Soviet Union promised to hold China, North Vietnam, and the Pathet Lao in check.[35]

The Geneva Agreements required that all foreign military personnel leave Laos within 75 days. Kennedy concluded that only through full compliance with this provision—even if it were violated by North Vietnam—would the United States defuse the threat to Soviet-American relations, maintain a cooperative relationship with Prime Minister Souvanna Phouma, and be able to bring effective political pressure on Khrushchev to restrain the North Vietnamese and the Pathet Lao. Therefore, 666 U.S. military advisory personnel were withdrawn from Laos through designated checkpoints and under the supervision of the ICC prior to the October 7, 1962 deadline. In addition, 403 Filipino technicians maintaining Lao equipment under contract to the United States departed under ICC supervision.[36]

The Soviet Union also adhered very carefully to the withdrawal terms of the 1962 Geneva Agreement. By October 7, Moscow had withdrawn all of the five hundred military technicians and pilots it had sent to Laos during 1960 and 1961. It turned over to the Pathet Lao the Soviet road-building machinery and six hundred trucks, which had constituted the overland supply train originating in North Vietnam. And, despite strong protests from both Hanoi and Peking, it terminated its airlift of supplies between Hanoi and northern Laos for the Pathet Lao and Neutralist forces. Ten Soviet cargo planes involved in this airlift were turned over to North Vietnam, with the understanding that the USSR would assist in training Vietnamese air crews.[37]

The private explanation the Soviets gave to their Communist allies for their careful adherence to the Geneva Agreements revealed the secondary importance Khrushchev had come to assign to the Laos problem. The departing Soviet ambassador to Laos explained to Poland's ICC representative in August 1962 that "Moscow hoped that the Laotian success would pave the way for reopening of the Berlin negotiations, which Soviet Deputy Foreign Minister Kuznetsov was instructed to take up in Geneva with U.S. representatives. Moscow attached importance to the correct implementation of the Laotian experiment: the general aim was to turn the Laotian settlement into profit in European affairs."[38]

North Vietnam's interests were quite different from Moscow's, and it quickly became apparent that it had no intention of adhering to the Geneva Agreement's required departure of foreign military personnel. In particular, North Vietnam would insist on retaining control and use of the infiltration routes entering South Vietnam through eastern Laos. Only forty North Vietnamese technicians withdrew from Laos through ICC checkpoints. American intelligence acquired through Meo trail watchers and overhead reconnaissance flights indicated that Hanoi withdrew about fifteen hundred of its approximately nine thousand ground troops by the October 7 deadline and regrouped some of its battalions within Laos closer to North Vietnam's border. When ICC representatives attempted to investigate North Vietnamese violations of Laos's sovereignty, the Pathet Lao denied them access to certain zones within the country.[39]

North Vietnam's continued use of Laos in violation of the 1962 Geneva Accords did not surprise the Kennedy administration. It was widely predicted within U.S. government circles that it would be many years, if ever, before the three existing military forces and separate civil administrations in Laos could be integrated into a cohesive governmental and administrative structure that could exercise effective control over its territory. Yet Kennedy and his chief advisers were prepared to accept their failure to fully neutralize Laos provided the Mekong River valley separating Laos and Thailand did not fall to the Pathet Lao–North Vietnamese. American intelligence estimated that two thousand North Vietnamese personnel would infiltrate South Vietnam by way of the Ho Chi Minh trails in 1962, and this was considered to be a threat that could be neutralized within South Vietnam itself. So long as neither Kennedy nor Khrushchev was visibly humiliated by events in Laos, both could withdraw their military personnel and eliminate the potential for a dangerous superpower clash.[40]

CONCLUSIONS AND LESSONS

A week after he took office, John Kennedy lowered the U.S. objectives in Laos to the establishment of a cease-fire and the creation of a neutral Laos. In doing so, he implicitly acknowledged the principle of coercive diplomacy that states that the opposition's as well as one's own level of motivation is highly dependent upon the nature of the objectives sought. Kennedy's decision amounted to a substantial modification of the Eisenhower administration's stated desire to make Laos a "bastion for freedom," but it was in fact consistent with the limited military means the Eisenhower administration had been willing to employ during its last days in office.

By reducing the U.S. military objective in Laos to denial of the Mekong basin—or perhaps only Vientiane—to the Pathet Lao–Vietminh, Kennedy eroded the Communist forces' motivation to resist his demand, enhanced his own initially low level of motivation, and thus established a goal that avoided a motivational asymmetry favoring the opposition. Of course, this reduced military objective was compatible with Hanoi's immediate aim of communizing South Vietnam because it left Laos in the hands of the Vietminh, but it represented a far less satisfactory outcome for the Pathet Lao given that group's ambition to control all of Laos.

As I have noted, however, Kennedy's decision to reduce the U.S. military objective in Laos did not bring about the cease-fire he requested. Prior to his shift toward a "tacit-ultimatum" approach in March 1961, only his commitment to a neutralization of Laos gave the Communists incentive to comply, and this incentive proved insufficient. During January 1961, however, the

Eisenhower administration had attempted to intimidate the Communists with many of the same military preparations Kennedy would eventually employ but without any firm offer of diplomatic benefits. It was not until late March, then, that the United States offered the Communists both substantial diplomatic inducements and a strong variant of coercive diplomacy simultaneously. That this combination proved reasonably effective where Eisenhower's and Kennedy's previous efforts had failed suggests the truth of the proposition that what neither the "carrot" nor the "stick" can achieve alone may be obtainable by combining the two.

The case illustrates some of the complexities associated with coercing a multinational opposition. Kennedy's initial threat of punishment as expressed through military movements and international consultation proved sufficiently potent and credible to erode the Soviet Union's motivation, but it failed to influence significantly the Pathet Lao, the North Vietnamese, and the Chinese. Only when he assigned U.S. advisers to the combat zones does it appear that Kennedy's threat became sufficiently convincing to these targets. This crisis illustrates, therefore, that when an attempt is made to coerce a multinational opposition, a threat sufficiently strong and credible for one member of the opposition may be insufficient for the other.

U.S. military action during spring of 1961 also illustrates the importance of context in strengthening the credibility and impact of coercive threats. Within the context of the tacit ultimatum Kennedy had already communicated to the Communist governments involved in the Laotian crisis, the president's "exemplary action" of ordering U.S. military advisers to put on their uniforms and move into the combat zones had an effect on the opposition quite disproportionate to the military importance of the action. Within the context of the diplomatic and military actions already in motion, placing U.S. advisers in harm's way was an escalatory step that signaled the American government's new-found willingness to visibly risk the lives of its soldiers in the defense of Laos. The potential political and psychological importance of this step was not lost on the Communist leadership, and it contributed greatly to the credibility of the other military actions off the battlefield.

The case also illustrates some of the dilemmas of doing business with uncooperative clients. Resolving international disputes short of war may depend as much on controlling the behavior of one's allies as it does on influencing the behavior of one's opponents. And although military threats are unlikely to be employed against one's allies as a part of some tacit or explicit ultimatum, lesser versions of diplomatic or economic coercion may be necessary to obtain needed compliance. This was true in the case of Laos, where General Phoumi Nosavan's obstinate refusal to accept the power-sharing compromise that was acceptable to the United States ultimately forced the Kennedy administration to employ a form of coercive diplomacy against Phoumi himself. The task of applying such coercive tactics against one's own allies is made all the more delicate by the requirement that one try to avoid undermining the client's long-term effectiveness while attempting to change his near-term behavior.

Many aspects of Kennedy's behavior showed a very keen awareness of the trade-off between the requirements of crisis management and those of effecting maximum coercive impact. Kennedy's difference of opinion with the Joint Chiefs of Staff centered around this problem. Whereas the military suggested the deployment of tens of thousands of U.S. troops on Laotian territory to achieve maximum intimidation of the Pathet Lao, the Vietminh, and the Chinese, the president feared that such a large troop movement might be interpreted by the Communists as a prelude to reversing, rather than stopping, the Pathet Lao drive and thus as contradictory to his offer of neutralization.

Kennedy's use of diplomatic redundancy was another way of reducing the odds that military pressure would provoke an escalatory response by the intended target. In the president's news conferences; in each British-American proposal; in consultations with Khrushchev, Gromyko, Pushkin, and Nehru; in ambassadorial communications to Hanoi and Peking, one point was consistently and repetitiously driven home: The United States seeks only the neutralization of Laos. It was this type of redundancy that was useful in precluding Communist misinterpretation of and overreaction to Kennedy's increasing military pressure. This is not to say, however, that U.S. diplomatic action served only in a crisis management capacity for, in fact, it was instrumental in creating the sense of urgency necessary to gain compliance from the Communists. This very ability to carry out the crisis management objective of specifying the limited demand for which pressure was being increased while at the same time enhancing that coercive pressure made the Kennedy administration's diplomatic campaign an effective but unprovocative instrument for coercive diplomacy.

Finally, despite Kennedy's apparent success at coercive diplomacy, we must be cautious in interpreting the results. First, Kennedy's success was modest at best. In a most difficult political and military situation, his administration had been forced to salvage what it could. It had avoided the superpower collision that haunted Kennedy's thoughts, but he had to accept Communist control over much of Laos and North Vietnam's use of Lao territory in pursuit of its war aims against South Vietnam. Only a president willing to tolerate partial success and public criticism can exercise coercive diplomacy at these prices.

Second, only a special set of conditions surrounding the crisis made even Kennedy's moderate success possible. Although he was able to alter the balance between the opposition's and his own level of motivation by reducing and clarifying the U.S. objective in Laos, this change had the desired impact on the motivation level of the opposing Communist governments only be-

cause they assigned a low priority to the immediate communization of all of
Laos. Moreover, the Communists were generally fearful of military escalation in Laos. Given North Vietnam's greater involvement and interest in
South Vietnam, it was unwilling to risk war with the United States in Laos.
The Soviet Union had no interests in Southeast Asia that were worth a direct
military confrontation with the United States, and China refrained from any
action other than vague and highly conditional threats of intervention. Also,
fortunately for Kennedy, the Soviet Union, China, North Vietnam, and the
Pathet Lao all had reasons to favor some form of neutralization over previous
U.S. objectives. The clarity with which the United States was able to communicate its new political objective and its specific terms of compliance—an effective and verified cease-fire—was clearly influential in achieving a negotiated settlement of the crisis.

Third, the existence of both international and Laotian structures put in
place by the prior 1954 Geneva Accords greatly facilitated communication,
coordination, and final settlement among the multiple actors party to the
1961–1962 Laotian crisis. As the crisis began to escalate, all of the plans proposed for ending it made use of the diplomatic machinery established in 1954,
including the prior terms of the settlement, the United Kingdom's and Soviet
Union's permanent chairing of the conference, the modalities of the International Commission for Supervision and Control in Laos, and the possibility
of reconvening the conference itself. In a similar fashion, the eventual success
of the second Geneva Conference and the ability of the involved nations to
reach a political agreement were greatly facilitated by Prince Souvanna
Phouma, a longtime leader of Laos whom both Kennedy and Khrushchev
could trust to steer Laos toward international neutrality. In the absence of
such a respected and experienced statesperson, an internationally and domes-
tically acceptable power-sharing arrangement for Laos may have proved impossible.

Although the domestic elements of the 1962 Geneva Accords on Laos
failed to function after 1963 when the coalition government envisioned for
that country dissolved into pro-American and pro-Vietnamese factions occupying a partitioned country, the international terms of the accords on Laos
were an influence until 1973. For Moscow, the 1962 Laos neutralization
agreement was a convenient rationale for its permanent extrication from a
messy civil war in which it had minimal strategic interests and that, to its surprise, had brought it close to armed conflict with the United States. For suc-
ceeding U.S. administrations, the 1962 Geneva Accords provided an international mechanism for preventing Soviet-American friction over the status of
Laos, for constraining North Vietnam's military operations in Laos, and for
acknowledging Souvanna Phouma's dream of returning his country to a unified neutral status. As the war in Southeast Asia escalated, both North Vietnam and the United States increasingly violated Laos's territorial integrity.

Nonetheless, until final U.S. withdrawal from Southeast Asia, the political bargains struck at Geneva in 1962 remained a restraining force on the visible military actions the signatories were willing to undertake in Laos.

NOTES

1. Unless otherwise indicated, the following historical information is drawn from Charles A. Stevenson, *The End of Nowhere* (Boston: Beacon Press, 1973); Arthur J. Dommen, *Laos: Keystone of Indochina* (Boulder: Westview Press, 1985); and David K. Hall, "The Laos Neutralization Agreement, 1962," in Alexander L. George et al., *U.S.-Soviet Security Cooperation* (New York: Oxford University Press 1988), pp. 435–465.

2. *New York Times,* January 22, 1961, p. 1.

3. Press Conference, January 25, 1961, *Public Papers of the Presidents of the United States: John F. Kennedy, 1961* (Washington, D.C.: U.S. Government Printing Office, 1962), p. 16.

4. Dean Rusk to John F. Kennedy, Draft circular telegram on Laos, February 5, 1961. National Security Files. Boxes 131–139. Laos. John F. Kennedy Library, Boston, Mass.

5. Roger Hilsman, *To Move a Nation* (New York: Dell Publishing Co., 1964), p. 127; *New York Times,* January 24, 1961, p. 12; February 20, 1961, p. 13.

6. Hall, "The Laos Neutralization Agreement, 1962," pp. 447–448.

7. "The Situation in Laos," *Department of State Bulletin,* April 17, 1961, p. 544.

8. Hall, "The Laos Neutralization Agreement, 1962," p. 440.

9. Theodore Sorensen, *Kennedy* (New York: Harper & Row, 1965), pp. 642–643; Hugh Sidey, *John F. Kennedy, President* (New York: Atheneum, 1963), p. 77; Dommen, *Laos,* pp. 191–192.

10. Hilsman, *To Move a Nation,* p. 131.

11. Press Conference, March 23, 1961, *Public Papers of the Presidents of the United States, John F. Kennedy, 1961,* p. 215.

12. Ibid.

13. *New York Times,* March 30, 1961, p. 1; Frank Darling, *Thailand and the United States* (Washington, D.C.: Public Affairs Press, 1965), p. 205.

14. *New York Times,* March 25, 1961, p. 1; *New York Times,* March 26, 1961, p. 1; *New York Times,* March 27, 1961, p. 2.

15. *New York Times,* March 24, 1961, p. 1.

16. *New York Times,* March 28, 1961, p. 1.

17. *Peking Review,* February 19, 1961, p. 18.

18. *New York Times,* April 2, 1961, p. 1; *New York Herald Tribune,* April 4, 1961, p. 11.

19. Arthur Schlesinger, Jr., *A Thousand Days* (New York: Fawcett World Library, 1965), pp. 257–258.

20. U.S. Consulate General Hong Kong, *Survey of China Mainland Press,* no. 2485 (April 28, 1961), p. 37.

21. *New York Times,* April 25, 1961, p. 1.

22. Schlesinger, *A Thousand Days*, pp. 315–316; Sorensen, *Kennedy*, pp. 727, 736; Hilsman, *To Move a Nation*, pp. 133–134.

23. Hall, "The Laos Neutralization Agreement, 1962," pp. 441–442.

24. *Department of State Bulletin*, June 26, 1961, p. 999.

25. Michael V. Forrestal, recorded interview by David K. Hall, January 2, 1987.

26. Hall, "The Laos Neutralization Agreement, 1962," p. 447.

27. Ibid., p. 449.

28. Ibid., p. 448.

29. Ibid.

30. Ibid., p. 447.

31. Quoted in *New York Times*, May 19, 1962, p. 1.

32. Quoted in *New York Times*, May 21, 1962, p. 1.

33. Hall, "The Laos Neutralization Agreement, 1962," pp. 449–450.

34. Marek Thee, *Notes of a Witness* (New York: Vintage Books, 1973), pp. 417–418.

35. Hall, "The Laos Neutralization Agreement, 1962," pp. 449–450.

36. Ibid., p. 455.

37. Ibid., p. 456.

38. Thee, *Notes of a Witness*, p. 326.

39. Hall, "The Laos Neutralization Agreement, 1962," p. 457.

40. Michael V. Forrestal, recorded interview by Joseph Kraft, August 14, 1964, p. 131, John F. Kennedy Oral History Program, John F. Kennedy Library, Columbia Point, Boston, Mass.

6

The Cuban Missile Crisis: Peaceful Resolution Through Coercive Diplomacy

ALEXANDER L. GEORGE

The Soviet attempt to deploy forty-two medium-range and twenty-four to thirty-two intermediate-range ballistic missiles into Cuba during the late summer and early fall of 1962 triggered the most dangerous crisis of the cold war. This war-threatening confrontation, unforeseen and unwanted by either side, was eventually resolved peacefully. Such an outcome was possible because instead of resorting to military action to destroy the missiles, President John F. Kennedy attempted the strategy of coercive diplomacy in an effort to induce Nikita Khrushchev to remove them.

Although coercive diplomacy was ultimately successful, careful crisis management was required by both Washington and Moscow to give diplomatic efforts a chance to develop a mutually acceptable compromise settlement of the crisis. There was no assurance at the outset that the coercive pressure Kennedy brought to bear would succeed. The naval blockade of Cuba put into effect by the United States could prevent additional missiles and military equipment from reaching Cuba, but obviously the blockade alone could not remove the substantial number of missiles already there or prevent them from becoming operational. Nonetheless, the president hoped that the blockade and the substantial preparations he ordered for a possible air strike or invasion of Cuba would demonstrate his resolution and exert enough pressure on Khrushchev to induce the latter to remove the missiles.

But was the Soviet leader, having gone so far and invested so much in the missile deployment, capable of an ignominious retreat? Would he not feel it necessary to test Kennedy's resolve by challenging in some way the naval blockade, which he quickly denounced as "an act of war"? Would Soviet vessels and submarines attempt to pass through the blockade line, and if so, might this lead to a shooting war on the high seas or to Soviet retaliation elsewhere that could set into motion uncontrollable escalation to a major war—perhaps even a nuclear war—between the superpowers? Or, conversely, could Soviet agreement to withdraw the missiles be made part of a mutually acceptable quid pro quo?

There was, in brief, no assurance that coercive diplomacy was a viable strategy for achieving a peaceful outcome acceptable to the United States. How and why, then, did the strategy succeed? What analytical "lessons" and conclusions can be drawn from the case?

KENNEDY'S TASK: DEMONSTRATE RESOLUTION WITHOUT TRIGGERING WAR

Kennedy has been criticized for imposing the blockade and creating a war-threatening confrontation without first taking up the matter of the missile deployment with Khrushchev in private diplomatic channels, as several of the president's advisers recommended.[1] A diplomatic approach confined to strong words without action was briefly considered after the missiles were discovered, but this was rejected as not only ineffectual but highly risky. If approached in this way, Khrushchev might have seized the diplomatic initiative and tried to capitalize on the bargaining advantages gained by the missiles already in Cuba. Moreover, a purely diplomatic U.S. response might have been interpreted by the Soviet leader as demonstrating irresolution on Kennedy's part and encouraged Khrushchev to regard subsequent threats by the president as mere bluffs.[2]

To Kennedy, this was a particularly important consideration. From the beginning of the missile crisis the president believed Khrushchev's bold missile gambit could be understood only in terms of a long-standing problem he had sensed in his relationship with the Soviet leader. Almost from his first day in office, the president had wrestled with the problem of how to convey his determination to the Soviet leader in order to discourage Khrushchev from attempting dangerous encroachments on the U.S. world position, in particular with respect to the still unresolved crisis of Berlin. The Bay of Pigs disaster and Khrushchev's assertive behavior at their summit meeting in Vienna exacerbated Kennedy's concern that Khrushchev regarded him as weak and irresolute and that this could lead the Soviet leader to miscalculate and take actions that could lead to war. Just such a miscalculation, the president now believed, had led Khrushchev to think he could get away with the missile deployment despite Kennedy's explicit warnings that he would take strong action in that event.[3]

There is in fact reason to believe that Khrushchev's image of Kennedy as an inexperienced, weak opponent may have played a role in his calculation that the missile deployment was an acceptable risk. Some Soviet officials who have given their recollections on the origins of the missile crisis have acknowledged this possibility, adding that Khrushchev also believed Kennedy was too rational and prudent to risk war in order to get the missiles removed.

One would like to believe that fateful questions of war or peace are not influenced by such subjective, psychological variables. However, each leader's image of the other unquestionably played an important role in both the inception and the resolution of the missile crisis. Just as Khrushchev's *defective* image of Kennedy influenced his decision to deploy the missiles into Cuba, so too did Kennedy's *correct* image of Khrushchev as a rational, intelligent man who would retreat if given sufficient time and shown determination play a critical role in the president's decision to respond with coercive diplomacy rather than military action and to give that diplomacy a chance to succeed.[4]

It should be recognized that the issue confronting Kennedy was not merely one of whether he could persuade Khrushchev to remove the missiles but also of what price the Soviet leader would try to extract in return for doing so. After all, Khrushchev—as was true of earlier Soviet leaders—had a well-deserved reputation for being a tough bargainer. There was no basis for assuming the Soviet leader would back off in the event that Kennedy confined his response to discovery of the missiles to a stern diplomatic demarche. Had Kennedy chosen this option, the crisis would have entered its bargaining phase under conditions highly favorable to the Soviet leader and severely disadvantageous for Kennedy. The presence of a large number of medium-range missiles already in Cuba provided an important bargaining asset for Khrushchev, and his negotiating leverage would increase each day as preparations for making the missiles operational continued apace. And additional missiles, including the longer-range intermediate missiles and possibly nuclear warheads, were being carried in the large number of Soviet vessels en route to Cuba.

In such a disadvantageous bargaining position, the president—foregoing even a blockade—might conceivably have bought his way out of the crisis. But in that event, Khrushchev's price tag for removing the missiles, if indeed he had agreed to remove them all, would in all likelihood have been extremely high and might have included a demand for a substantial change in the status of West Berlin. In short, in this hypothetical scenario of diplomatic bargaining over the price for removal of the missiles, Khrushchev would have had Kennedy at his mercy. Almost intuitively, the president saw that his only chance of getting the missiles out without resorting to military action and at an acceptable diplomatic price lay in finding a way to impress the Soviet leader, as never before, with his determination. Kennedy perceived that if he tried to bargain with Khrushchev *before* correcting the Soviet leader's mistaken view of his resoluteness, Khrushchev's appetite for and expectation of gains to be extracted would remain excessive. In that event either Kennedy would have to pay an exorbitant price to secure voluntary removal of the missiles—which could have devastating political consequences at home and for the U.S. world position—or the negotiations would break down and the president would have to resort to military force.

This hypothetical scenario of the crisis—negotiation without a military buildup and blockade—could have led to a rapidly deteriorating, possibly prolonged bargaining situation for Kennedy in which eventually he could have found himself pressed to resort to air strikes against the missile sites or to an invasion of Cuba. The possibility that the risk of war might have become much greater had Kennedy pursued the purely diplomatic option has been ignored by those who have criticized him for not trying that track first.[5]

It is not surprising, therefore, that given his commitment to have the missiles withdrawn from Cuba, the president should quickly conclude that he desperately needed to take concrete action to counteract Khrushchev's bargaining advantages and obtain the enhanced leverage Washington would need to enable it to negotiate an acceptable deal for withdrawal. A blockade would not only prevent additional missiles and warheads from reaching Cuba, which would have further enhanced Khrushchev's bargaining leverage, but it should also impress the Soviet leader with Kennedy's resoluteness, convince Khrushchev that he had grossly miscalculated, and give him an opportunity to resolve the crisis peacefully by agreeing to remove the missiles. And coupled with the buildup of U.S. military forces in the Caribbean, a blockade might generate sufficient pressure and bargaining leverage to induce Khrushchev to agree to a formula for withdrawing the missiles on terms acceptable to Kennedy.

These, then, were the beliefs and calculations that led Kennedy to conclude that he would have to combine coercion with bargaining over the terms of a settlement if an acceptable diplomatic solution to the crisis were to be possible. At the same time, however, the president did not intend to rely exclusively on coercion to persuade Khrushchev to withdraw the missiles. It may come as a surprise even to those who have closely followed the voluminous literature on the missile crisis to learn that from an early stage, the president believed he would probably have to pay a price to get the missiles withdrawn.

Although he envisaged a bargaining process in which he would eventually offer concessions to Khrushchev as part of an as yet undefined quid pro quo, Kennedy believed that all talk of concessions and accommodation should be postponed until he had impressed upon Khrushchev—by deeds as well as words—his determination and resolve.[6] Accordingly, in the initial phase of the confrontation—from Monday, October 22, to Saturday, October 27—the president emphasized the coercive dimension of his bargaining strategy and gave no intimation of a willingness to compromise or to make concessions. Kennedy thus hoped to improve his own bargaining leverage at Khrushchev's expense and thereby to reduce substantially the price he would eventually have to pay to induce Khrushchev to remove the missiles.[7]

Thus, although Kennedy began with a variant of the strategy that emphasized coercive threats, he contemplated eventually shifting to the "carrot-and-stick" variant of coercive diplomacy. In fact, for almost four days—from late Monday to late Friday of that week—both leaders gave priority to the coercive component of their bargaining strategies and at the same time tried to persuade each other and world opinion of the legitimacy of the positions they were taking in the dispute. Although neither Kennedy nor Khrushchev initiated a reckless "competition in risk-taking" during this period, their crisis-bargaining tactics during these tense days occasionally threatened to assume some of the chilling and dangerous features of the game of "chicken." However, in order to control and reduce the risks, both sides adhered to essential principles of careful crisis management, a critically important aspect of the confrontation to which we now turn.

COOPERATION IN CRISIS MANAGEMENT

A study of the missile crisis reveals an unexpected, striking tension between some of the features of the strongest form of coercive diplomacy and some important principles of managing a crisis in order to avoid triggering unwanted escalation to a shooting war. This was likely part of the reason Kennedy chose to employ the relatively weak "try-and-see" variant of coercive diplomacy at the outset. During the first five days of the confrontation, the president deliberately avoided giving Khrushchev a time limit for compliance with his demand for removal of the missiles and backing it with an explicit threat of punishment for noncompliance by way of an air strike or invasion. Had Kennedy issued such a threat and set a time limit, he would have confronted the Soviets with a full-fledged ultimatum. In contrast, the blockade was part of a weaker try-and-see approach to coercive diplomacy. Although the blockade was accompanied by an ominous buildup of U.S. military forces, the president did not establish a deadline for Khrushchev's agreement to remove the missiles; nor did he indicate what actions the United States would take if the blockade did not persuade the Soviet Union to back down. These two important elements of an ultimatum were missing during this phase of the crisis.

There is little evidence to indicate that during these five days Kennedy even thought of shifting to an ultimatum. In fact, as late as Friday, October 26, when it seemed increasingly clear that the blockade and the military buildup would not put sufficient pressure on Khrushchev, the president began to move from the try-and-see approach to the somewhat stronger "gradual turning of the screw" variant of coercive diplomacy.[8] I consider later the unexpected developments of Saturday, October 27, that pushed Kennedy to

ALEXANDER L. GEORGE

hastily improvise and transmit the equivalent of an ultimatum to Khrushchev. I first look more closely at how during the first five days Kennedy gave priority to crisis management considerations over the requirements for the strongest ultimatum type of coercive diplomacy and how, in turn, Khrushchev operated with restraint in the interest of crisis management.

In applying coercive threats in his bargaining strategy during this phase of the crisis, the president gave careful attention and, indeed, priority to crisis management, hoping that Khrushchev would do the same so that together they could try to end the confrontation before it escalated to a shooting war. To this end, Kennedy observed a number of crisis management principles.[9] When a crisis entails, as this one did, the risk of unacceptable escalation, policy makers are well advised to consider two "political" principles of prudent crisis management—limitation of objectives and limitation of means employed on their behalf. Kennedy adhered to both of these principles. He limited his objective to removal of the missiles, rejecting advice that he use the crisis to get rid of Fidel Castro or, at least, eliminate Soviet influence in Cuba. Kennedy realized that if he pursued these more ambitious goals, he would greatly strengthen Soviet motivation, make coercive persuasion much more difficult, and increase the likelihood of war. In addition to limiting his objective, the president limited the means he employed. The blockade option appealed to Kennedy because it enabled him to initiate a showdown with Khrushchev without immediate resort to force and, most important, it offered time for an effort to persuade the Soviet leader to remove the missiles voluntarily.

The president also adhered to important "operational" principles of crisis management, which contribute to controlling the risk of escalation, reduce the likelihood of dangerous misperceptions and miscalculations, and improve the possibility of good communication and judgment on both sides in the interest of securing a mutually acceptable settlement. Adherence to operational crisis management principles facilitates the role diplomacy can play in settling crises of this kind. To this end, Kennedy maintained informed presidential-level control over the movements of U.S. military forces, slowed the momentum of the crisis to enable both sides to carefully consider their policy options and to give time for diplomatic communications, coordinated military and political actions to ensure clear and consistent signaling, accompanied a firm demand for removal of the missiles and conduct of the blockade with a clear signal of his preference for a peaceful resolution of the crisis, and finally, avoided boxing Khrushchev into a corner where he might be desperate enough to escalate the crisis in the hope of avoiding a humiliating defeat.

As for Khrushchev, even though at first he issued coercive threats of his own in an effort to undermine Kennedy's resolve, the Soviet leader nonetheless went to great lengths to avoid a clash at sea. Within hours after Kennedy announced the blockade on Monday evening, October 22, Khrushchev directed all Soviet vessels carrying missiles and other military equipment to Cuba to immediately turn back.[10] Other Soviet vessels carrying nonmilitary cargo temporarily halted and later resumed movement toward the blockade line to test and weaken if possible Kennedy's resolution to implement it. In addition, the Soviet leader attempted, to no avail, to persuade the president and world opinion of the legitimacy of his military assistance to Cuba and his claim that the missiles were "defensive"—that is, had no offensive purpose.

Thus, both Khrushchev and Kennedy behaved with sober prudence and reasonable skill to extricate themselves from the war-threatening crisis. The danger of escalation to war did cast an ominous pall over crisis developments. But although both leaders attempted to gain advantage through crisis bargaining, and although their behavior evoked concern that they might be about to embark on the dangerous game of chicken on the high seas, in fact neither Kennedy nor Khrushchev engaged in a reckless competition in risk-taking but acted cautiously and with restraint to avoid escalation.

IMPLEMENTATION OF THE BLOCKADE
AND THE U.S. NAVY'S
ANTISUBMARINE OPERATIONS

I pass quickly over many of the interesting details of the implementation of the blockade.[11] Since Soviet ships carrying missiles and other military equipment quickly turned back and were returning to the Soviet Union, President Kennedy found it judicious to allow several other Soviet vessels with *non*military cargo to pass through the blockade line without being stopped and searched. However, he had yet to demonstrate willingness to enforce the blockade. Finally, on Friday morning, October 26, the president authorized the navy to apply its stop-and-board procedures to the *Marcula*, which he carefully selected to avoid a direct affront to Moscow. (The *Marcula* was not a Soviet vessel but was a Panamanian-owned, Lebanese-registered vessel under charter to the Soviet Union.) But by Friday morning it had become less urgent to demonstrate willingness to enforce the blockade; Khrushchev had apparently already become sufficiently impressed with Kennedy's determination and was seeking to find a way to stabilize the crisis by cooperating with U.N. Secretary-General U Thant's proposals.[12]

If the boarding of the *Marcula* on Friday morning was not the decisive turning point of the confrontation—indeed, there may not have been any clearly identifiable turning point—let us consider whether earlier developments may have convinced Khrushchev that Kennedy would not weaken his demand that the missiles be removed and that Moscow should not further test the president's determination to get them out by whatever means. It is possible—although speculative in the absence of confirmation from more authoritative Soviet sources—that the U.S. Navy's actions against Soviet sub-

marines in the Caribbean and in the Atlantic had already convinced Khrushchev of Kennedy's resolve to use force if necessary to remove the missiles.

It should be noted that the rules of engagement given the U.S. Navy on
Tuesday, October 23, included permission to initiate military action against
Soviet submarines in self-defense if they acted in a manner that could be reasonably interpreted as hostile. Concern over the role Soviet submarines
might play in the crisis had developed some days earlier when the president
and his advisers noted the possibility that submarines might be used to bring
nuclear warheads into Cuba. Accordingly, submarines had been included in
the general order for quarantine operations against Soviet vessels approaching Cuba; they too could be stopped and searched if they attempted to proceed beyond the blockade line. Washington's concern was heightened on
Tuesday evening, October 23, when intelligence reported that Soviet submarines were moving from the Atlantic into the Caribbean. A special set of signals was quickly devised to be used to signal Soviet submarines to surface; the
signals were broadcast publicly and perhaps were conveyed to Moscow
through private channels as well to ensure that Soviet leaders had advance
notice and could inform their submarine commanders of what to expect and,
it was hoped, direct them to comply.

The rules of engagement authorized U.S. naval forces to signal Soviet submarines to surface with sonar and, if necessary, to employ nonlethal depth
charges. (If a submarine commander continued to refuse to cooperate, warning shots and minimal use of force could be employed to reinforce the demand to surface.) Sonar signals and nonlethal charges were employed several
times, apparently on at least two of the five confirmed Soviet submarines.
(Two of these submarines were already in the Caribbean when the president
announced the quarantine, and the other three were detected moving toward
the Caribbean from the Atlantic before the blockade went into effect.)

The results of the navy's antisubmarine warfare (ASW) operations were
mixed. As Joseph F. Bouchard reports in his detailed study of the U.S.
Navy's activities during the crisis, "Submerged Soviet submarines essentially
ignored the sonar and explosive charge signals." Bouchard found "no reported instances of a Soviet submarine immediately surfacing" in response to
signals to do so: "The Soviet submarines did not react to the signals with
other than their normal efforts at evasion." Thus, the U.S. Navy did not liter-
ally force any of the submarines to surface. However, the U.S. Navy's ASW
forces pursued and continued to harass them until they did eventually surface, perhaps either to replenish air and batteries or because of some mechan-
ical problem that had to be repaired on the surface.[13]

Moscow's directives to its submarines as to how they should respond to
the U.S. Navy's ASW operations can only be inferred from what did and did
not take place. Particularly noteworthy, and contrary to the impression conveyed in previous accounts, the data obtained by Bouchard from U.S. Navy

sources indicate that the three Soviet submarines that were headed toward the Caribbean from the Atlantic "had all reversed their course and were headed home by the time U.S. Navy ASW forces were able to locate them and prosecute them."[14] It appears, therefore, that the Soviet government decided to recall these three submarines on October 24, and possibly as early as October 23—the same day Moscow ordered merchant ships carrying missiles and other military equipment to turn back.

Thus, it should be noted that the U.S. Navy gave a very broad interpretation to its authorization to conduct ASW operations to protect ships engaged in implementing the blockade. The Soviet submarines that had been moving from the Atlantic toward the Caribbean were aggressively pursued and pressured to surface after they had turned back and were moving even further away from the designated blockade line. Not only did Soviet submarine commanders limit their response to normal efforts at evasion, they were also evidently careful—perhaps under explicit instructions from Moscow—not to maneuver in any way that might be interpreted as posing a threat to the safety of the U.S. naval forces that were harassing them, exhibiting behavior that might have led U.S. commanders to initiate hostile action in self-defense. Moscow's directives to its submarine commanders may have contained cautions not only to avoid actions that might provoke the U.S. Navy to initiate a military response but may have also advised them that at some point they should cease evasive actions and obey the U.S. Navy's signals to come to the surface. Normally, these Soviet Foxtrot submarines need only expose their snorkels in order to recharge batteries and replenish air. Therefore it was unusual, Bouchard reports, that the Soviet submarines "fully surfaced sometimes repeatedly, rather than just snorkeling. This led some Navy officers to conclude that the submarines were ordered [by Moscow] to surface and identify themselves if challenged by the U.S. Navy."[15] As it turned out, with the exception of one of the Soviet submarines possibly being crippled by the navy's nonlethal depth charges, there were no significant incidents and no near collisions.[16]

I have reviewed the directives and modalities of the navy's ASW operations in some detail in order to pose the question of whether these actions contributed significantly to the coercive pressure on Khrushchev. Two questions need to be addressed: First, were the assertiveness and vigor of the ASW operations intended by the president to be a means of enhancing his coercive diplomatic pressure? Second, did the navy's assertive harassment of Soviet submarines contribute importantly, if not decisively, to Khrushchev's decision to forego further efforts to exert counterpressure on Kennedy during the course of their crisis bargaining?

Neither of these questions can be answered with certainty. It is possible, as Scott Sagan has suggested and as Bouchard acknowledges, that the president and the secretary of defense may not have fully understood and anticipated how the navy would implement the general authorization to conduct ASW operations.[17]

Concerning the impact of the ASW operations on Khrushchev, in the absence of authoritative Soviet accounts we have only Sergei Mikoyan's conjecture that the operations decisively demonstrated Kennedy's resolve.[18] Other than that there is only circumstantial evidence that at best supports only a speculative answer to this question. Although Moscow was undoubtedly impressed by the U.S. willingness to employ its naval superiority in the Caribbean to institute a blockade, we cannot determine how important—if they were at all—the ASW operations were in persuading Khrushchev to alter his bargaining strategy and his crisis objectives. Whatever Khrushchev's reasons for doing so, during the course of Friday, October 26, he initiated several probes suggesting a possible offer to remove the missiles in return for a U.S. pledge not to invade Cuba.

CRISIS MANAGEMENT
BEGINS TO BREAK DOWN

On the morning of Saturday, October 27, which was to become the last day of the confrontation, Kennedy and Khrushchev suddenly experienced disturbing new challenges to their ability to control the escalation potential of the crisis.[19] A startling lack of synchronization in the interaction between the two sides emerged. The context and meaning of possibly critical moves and communications became confusing; deciphering the intentions of and calculations behind specific moves of the opponent became difficult. Kennedy experienced this problem acutely, and his adversary felt the same unsettling phenomenon in Moscow. There was real danger in this; the disturbing sensation that things were getting out of control and the mounting fear that one side or the other might miscalculate strongly motivated the two leaders to find a mutually acceptable formula for ending the crisis early Sunday morning.[20]

Policy makers in Washington puzzled over the discrepancy between Khrushchev's more personal and emotional private letter of Friday evening, in which he suggested a deal of some kind that would call for a U.S. pledge not to invade Cuba but without explicitly linking that pledge to an offer to withdraw the missiles, and his more formal letter of Saturday morning, in which he did offer to withdraw the missiles but added a demand for removal of U.S. Jupiter missiles from Turkey as well as a noninvasion-of-Cuba pledge. Other disturbing events occurred on Saturday. A U-2 was shot down over Cuba; two other U.S. reconnaissance aircraft were fired at by Cuban air defense forces as they swooped low over the missile sites; a U.S. reconnaissance plane wandered over Siberia; and an FBI report raised the possibility that Soviet consulate personnel in New York were preparing to burn classified papers. Confronted and confused by these developments, U.S. policy makers anxiously speculated that perhaps the Kremlin was taking a harder line and was determined to test U.S. resolve, that perhaps Khrushchev was no longer in charge, or that perhaps Moscow was trying to extract a higher price for removal of the missiles.

The president and his advisers worried in particular that the shooting down of the U-2 portended a major escalation of the crisis. Kennedy momentarily withstood pressures to retaliate with an air strike against a Soviet surface-to-air missile (SAM) site in Cuba. But U-2 reconnaissance flights over Cuba would clearly have to continue in order to monitor activity at the missile sites, and if another U-2 were shot down—a development that had to be expected—the president could not continue to hold off reprisal. What would happen thereafter, he feared, could lead to uncontrollable military escalation.[21] Since it appeared to be only a matter of days before another U-2 would be shot down, a new sense of urgency to end the crisis emerged. The White House deemed it necessary to end the crisis before it went out of control. To this end, the president was finally ready—indeed, now felt compelled—to exert much stronger pressure on Khrushchev. But at the same time, Kennedy believed it was necessary to couple the additional pressure with concessions to make it easier for the Soviet leader to agree to remove the missiles.

FROM TURNING OF THE SCREW
TO ULTIMATUM AND CARROT AND STICK

Two important changes in the president's strategy of coercive diplomacy now took place. He finally converted his turning of the screw approach into a virtual ultimatum. But at the same time he incorporated the ultimatum into a carrot-and-stick variant of the strategy, adding concessions he had earlier refused to discuss. I consider first the coercive component of the shift in the president's approach.

Kennedy accepted his advisers' suggestion that he reply to the two contradictory letters from Khrushchev by ignoring the Saturday morning demand for the exchange of missile bases and accepting the suggestion contained in Khrushchev's first letter for a quid pro quo linking removal of the missiles from Cuba with a U.S. pledge not to invade Cuba. (As we will see, the president decided to deal with the issue of the Jupiters through private discussions his brother would have with Anatoly Dobrynin, Soviet ambassador to the United States.) Kennedy's formal reply to Khrushchev did not hint at an ultimatum, although it did convey a sense of urgency. The equivalent of an ultimatum in the form of a warning seems to have been conveyed by Robert Kennedy in a private meeting with Dobrynin in the early evening of October 27.

According to Robert Kennedy's posthumous account in *Thirteen Days*, he told Dobrynin:

> We had to have a commitment by tomorrow that those bases [missiles in Cuba] would be removed. I was not giving them an ultimatum but a statement of fact. He should understand that if they did not remove those bases, we would remove them. ... Time was running out. We had only a few more hours—we needed an answer immediately from the Soviet Union. I said we must have it the next day.[22]

If Robert Kennedy's account can be taken substantially at face value, as I believe, this meant that President Kennedy had finally decided to add to his long-standing demand that the missiles be removed the two missing elements of a full-blown ultimatum—a time limit for compliance with the demand and a credible threat of punishment for noncompliance—although, as Robert Kennedy puts it, this was conveyed not as an explicit ultimatum but as "a statement of fact."

An ultimatum may also possibly have been conveyed by an American news reporter, John Scali, who was serving both sides as an informal intermediary. Aleksandr Fomin, a KGB official assigned to the Soviet embassy who was Scali's contact in these exchanges, recalls that in a meeting on Saturday, October 27, the U.S. journalist angrily threatened that if the missiles were not removed within hours, the United States would mount an attack.[23]

Finally, it should be recognized that the substance of an ultimatum can sometimes be effectively conveyed to an adversary without being fully transmitted verbally. The sense of urgency for compliance and the threat of punishment for noncompliance particularly may be effectively transmitted by actions that convey time-urgent pressure or suggest that the threatener may not be able to maintain control over his side's actions for much longer. In this connection it should be noted that before the end of the day on Saturday, October 27, preparations for an invasion of Cuba had reached an advanced stage, and Soviet and Cuban intelligence services appear to have reported to Moscow the possibility of imminent U.S. military action.[24] It is possible, therefore, that regardless of whether something like an ultimatum was conveyed by Robert Kennedy, Khrushchev concluded for other reasons that time was running out and that he should terminate the crisis immediately.

The inclusion of the removal of Jupiter missiles from Turkish bases in the quid pro quo was a delicate political and diplomatic matter for the president. However, disclosure of new information in recent years establishes that Kennedy felt strongly that incurring the disapproval of the U.S. North Atlantic Treaty Organization (NATO) allies was an acceptable price to pay if it became necessary to remove the Jupiters in order to achieve a quick settlement of the crisis. The president's attitude emerged most clearly in his meeting with his advisory group on Saturday, October 27, when he stated and pressed this view. He was finally persuaded by his Soviet expert Llewellyn Thompson to try to resolve the crisis first without including the Jupiters in the quid pro quo.[25] And, as noted earlier, the president did not refer to Khrushchev's demand for removal of the Jupiters in his formal reply to the Soviet leader. But then, as few members of the advisory circle were to know, the president authorized his brother to make a secret deal that explicitly included an agreement to remove the Jupiters when he had a private conversation with Dobrynin later that day.

The account in *Thirteen Days* of Robert Kennedy's discussion of the Jupiters with Dobrynin on this occasion is incorrect. At the Moscow conference on the missile crisis in January 1989, Theodore Sorensen disclosed that in editing the manuscript of the book, which was based on Robert Kennedy's diaries, he had altered the sensitive facts of the secret missile deal to convey that Robert Kennedy had told Dobrynin that although the Jupiters were in any case to be removed from Turkey, their removal could not be made a part of the formal settlement terms.[26]

However, this recent disclosure does not challenge the fact that an understanding was reached with the Soviets to keep the missile swap secret. More recently too we have been told that the president's determination not to let the matter of the Jupiters prevent a quick settlement of the crisis went further than his authorization of the secret deal for a missile swap. Dean Rusk disclosed at the Hawks Cay Conference in March 1987 that the president quickly followed up the concession on the Jupiters his brother made secretly on Saturday evening by creating a fallback option that would make this concession public. If the secret deal on the missiles did not suffice, the U.N. secretary-general might then be asked to propose an open missile swap as part of the terms for settling the crisis.[27]

I noted earlier that crisis management began to break down on Saturday, October 27, and that the disturbing sensation that the situation was getting out of control had a significant impact on Kennedy's policy. These developments had an unsettling effect in Moscow as well. As a result, Khrushchev was motivated to accept within a matter of hours the formula for settling the crisis the president proposed toward the end of that day. A few months later, on December 12, 1962, Khrushchev defended his conduct of the Cuban venture in a major speech to the Supreme Soviet. Khrushchev did not allude to having received an ultimatum; however, he did say that he had been placed under urgent pressure to settle the crisis immediately because of information that an attack on Cuba would soon take place: "We received information from our Cuban comrades and from other sources on the morning of October 27 directly stating that this attack would be carried out in the next two or three days. We interpreted these cables as an extremely alarming warning signal. And the alarm was justified. Immediate action was necessary to prevent the attack on Cuba and to preserve the peace."[28] Soviet and Cuban sources have recently added useful details on some of the reasons for Khrushchev's sense of urgency.[29] And I have already alluded to the role played by the shootdown of the U-2, Scali's statement to Fomin, advanced U.S. military preparations for an invasion of Cuba, the possibility that Cuban air defenses might succeed in their efforts to shoot down U.S. reconnaissance planes, and Robert Kennedy's warning to Dobrynin that time was running out as all heightening Moscow's sense of urgency for ending the crisis.

ANALYTICAL CONCLUSIONS

As we have seen, the strategy of coercive diplomacy was eventually successful in this case. The explanation for its effectiveness touches upon many variables. First, Kennedy adopted a *limited* objective—the removal of the missiles—rather than a more ambitious one of seeking the removal of Castro or the elimination of Soviet influence from Cuba. Restricting his demand on Khrushchev to removal of the missiles was critical in several respects. Either of the more ambitious objectives would have strengthened Khrushchev's motivation not to yield and made it more difficult for Kennedy to impress upon him that the United States was more strongly motivated to achieve its objectives than the Soviet Union should be to resist U.S. efforts to achieve them.

If the target state believes that what is at stake in the crisis creates an *asymmetry of motivation* that favors the coercing state, the likelihood is increased that coercive diplomacy will be successful. The relative strength of motivation in confrontations of this kind reflects the *underlying balance of interests;* it is little influenced by deliberately inflated claims or posturing. For this reason Kennedy could persuasively convey to Khrushchev that the missiles were a greater threat to important U.S. interests (and, indirectly, to his own personal political stakes) than was the damage their voluntary removal would entail to important Soviet interests. The president would have found it much more difficult to achieve a similar asymmetry of motivation in his favor had he embraced as his crisis objective the removal of Castro or of Soviet influence from Cuba. In that event it would have been less certain that the underlying balance of interests and relative motivation favored Kennedy.

In sum, and for these reasons, the demand one side makes on its opponent when employing the strategy of coercive diplomacy shapes the balance of interests at stake. This, in turn, helps to determine the relative degree of motivation of the two sides, which plays so important a role in the crisis bargaining between them.

Limiting the objective to removal of the missiles also gave greater legitimacy to Kennedy's policy than would have been the case had he embraced either of the two more ambitious goals. Kennedy's advantage over Khrushchev with respect to the legitimacy of their competing claims was invaluable, in turn, in gaining for Kennedy the support of the Organization of American States and that of much of the international community. The task of gaining domestic support for a policy that entailed the risk of war was also made easier for Kennedy by his embrace of an objective that seemed more clearly to reflect the fundamental security interests of the United States. Limiting the U.S. objective to removal of the missiles also exacerbated Khrushchev's problem of reconciling the secrecy and deception with which he had carried out the missile deployment with his claim that the deployment constituted a legitimate contribution to the security of his Cuban ally.[30]

If the limited objective Kennedy adopted was a major factor in the success of his strategy, it was by no means a sufficient condition for the outcome. To create in the opponent the perception that the underlying balance of interests and the relative motivation do favor the coercing power, the latter must act in ways that convey determination to protect those important interests. Only by doing so will the coercing power succeed in convincing the opponent that an asymmetry of motivation does exist that operates in its favor. In the missile crisis, the United States enjoyed considerable superiority in conventional military capabilities in the Caribbean area as well as a margin of superiority in the strategic nuclear equation. Kennedy chose to base his coercive diplomacy not on the threat of initiating nuclear war if Khrushchev refused to remove the missiles but rather on the threat of making use of his local conventional superiority. The buildup of U.S. naval, land, and air forces in the theatre, therefore, was a necessary condition (but again not a sufficient one) for the success of coercive diplomacy. Other variables also played a role, and I now turn to these.

Kennedy's success in getting the missiles removed from Cuba was probably facilitated by the concessions he made as part of the quid pro quo that ended the crisis. As I said earlier, Kennedy ultimately employed the carrot-and-stick variant of coercive diplomacy. It is arguable whether the president's effort to coerce Khrushchev would have worked had he not made the concessions he did. He was criticized by some at the time and by others ever since for committing the United States to not attack Cuba in the future.[31]

Other factors that contributed to the peaceful resolution of this crisis have not been present in other war-threatening confrontations. Absent in this crisis was the occurrence of a serious *miscalculation or incident* that might have triggered unwanted escalation. The image of thermonuclear war shared by the two leaders created powerful *incentives* on both sides to manage and terminate the crisis peacefully. *Opportunities* for avoiding escalation were available; these were highly valued by both leaders and were carefully cultivated. The two leaders operated with sufficient understanding of the requirements of crisis management and with adequate *skill* to bring the confrontation to a close without escalation to a shooting war.

However, several serious threats to effective crisis management did occur. Foremost among them were the shootdown of the U-2 and the aggressive antisubmarine activities conducted by the U.S. Navy—activities that might have led, but did not, to serious incidents between the opposing forces. Under different circumstances, either of these developments might have triggered escalation to a shooting war.

Finally, as I have noted, the image Kennedy and Khrushchev held of each other played an important role in the resolution as well as the inception of the crisis. Khrushchev's defective image of Kennedy—as a young, inexperienced leader who could be pushed around and who was too weak or too "rational" to risk war to get the missiles out—influenced his decision to deploy missiles to Cuba. So too did Kennedy's correct image of Khrushchev, as a rational, intelligent man who would retreat if given sufficient time and shown determination, play a critical role in his decision to engage in coercive diplomacy and in his determination to give such diplomacy a chance to succeed. Thus, we cannot adequately understand the missile crisis without taking into account the personalities of the two leaders and the personal aspects of the interaction between them.

Coercive diplomacy was successful in this case because of the special conditions I have identified. As some of the other cases examined indicate, conditions favoring the success of coercive diplomacy are not always present in war-threatening confrontations.

BIBLIOGRAPHICAL NOTE

This chapter draws heavily from George's earlier analysis of the Cuban Missile Crisis in Alexander L. George, David K. Hall, and William E. Simons, *The Limits of Coercive Diplomacy: Laos, Cuba, Vietnam* (Boston: Little, Brown, 1971), and particularly from his update of the case on the basis of new primary source materials and a number of excellent secondary analyses, which appeared in Alexander L. George, ed., *Avoiding War: Problems of Crisis Management* (Boulder: Westview Press, 1991). Particularly useful in updating the case study have been the publications (cited in the Notes) by James Blight, David Welch, and Bruce Allyn; Joseph Bouchard; Scott Sagan; Richard Ned Lebow; Raymond Garthoff; McGeorge Bundy; and Michael Beschloss. All students of the missile crisis remain indebted to the seminal study by Graham Allison, *Essence of Decision* (Boston: Little, Brown, 1971). New information on the role of U.S. overhead aerial reconnaissance is provided by former intelligence officer Dino Brugioni, *Eyeball to Eyeball* (New York: Random House, 1992).

Important new materials on the crisis also emerged during the conference in Havana, January 9–12, 1992, in which former Soviet, Cuban, and U.S. officials and scholars and Fidel Castro participated. At this meeting retired Soviet General Anatoly Gribkov, who had been stationed in Cuba during the crisis, stated that the Soviets did have short-range tactical missiles with nuclear warheads in Cuba and that authority to use them in case of a U.S. invasion had been predelegated to local Soviet commanders by Moscow. Gribkov also stated that forty-three thousand Soviet troops, not ten thousand as previously estimated, had been stationed in Cuba at the time. A lively controversy has developed regarding General Gribkov's statements and their significance. See "Castro's Cuba: An Exchange," letters in response to article by A. M. Schlesinger, "Four Days with Fidel" (March 26, 1992), *New York Review of Books,* May 28, 1992, pp. 54–56; and the authoritative transcript of the Havana meeting, to appear in James G. Blight, David A. Welch, and Bruce J. Allen, *Cuba on the Brink* (New York: Pantheon, forthcoming).

More recently, Allyn and Blight have reported that newly declassified documents in Moscow include an order from Defense Minister Rodion Malinovsky, delivered in late September–early October 1962 to General Issa Pliyev, commander of Soviet forces in Cuba, that supports the statement made by General Gribkov at the Havana meeting concerning predelegation of authority to use the tactical nuclear missiles in case of a U.S. invasion in the event that "there is no possibility to receive directives from the USSR Ministry of Defense" (Bruce J. Allyn and James G. Blight, Letter to the Editor, *New York Times,* November 2, 1992).

Although the Gribkov disclosure does not alter the analysis set forth in the present case study, it would make even more understandable Khrushchev's motivation to end the crisis before it spun out of control, possibly leading to a U.S. invasion of Cuba. In their letter, Allyn and Blight report that Khrushchev's son Sergei "recently doubted that his father was fully informed" of Malinovsky's order, but they also report that "Russian generals insist he approved the order about the tactical nuclear warheads, notwithstanding his fear of nuclear war."

As Allyn and Blight conclude: "The new Russian documentation suggests we were much closer to nuclear war than we knew in October 1962." This new information also lends unexpected weight to the position of the doves among Kennedy's advisers.

I am indebted to Scott Sagan and David Welch for many incisive comments and to Barton Bernstein for many stimulating discussions over the years and for his own publications on the missile crisis that forced me to address relevant issues and to clarify and revise some of my interpretations. I also thank Richard Ned Lebow for allowing me to see portions of an important new study of the missile crisis, to be included in Richard Ned Lebow and Janice Gross Stein, *We All Lost the Cold War* (Princeton: Princeton University Press, 1994).

NOTES

1. Critical accounts of Kennedy's handling of the Cuban crisis on this and other matters include Barton J. Bernstein, "'Courage and Commitment': The Missiles of October," *Foreign Service Journal* (December 1975); and "The Cuban Missile Crisis," in L. H. Miller and R. W. Pruessen, eds., *Reflections on the Cold War* (Philadelphia: Temple University Press, 1974), pp. 108–142; I. F. Stone, "The Brink," a review of Elie Abel's *Missile Crisis* (Philadelphia: J. B. Lippincott, 1966), in *New York Review of Books,* April 13, 1966; Louise FitzSimons, *The Kennedy Doctrine* (New York: Random House, 1972); David Horowitz, *The Free World Colossus* (New York: Hill and Wang, 1965); Thomas M. Mongar, "Personality and Decisionmaking: John F. Kennedy in Four Crisis Decisions," *Canadian Journal of Political Science* 2 (1964): pp. 200–225; Ronald Steel, "Endgame," a review of Robert F. Kennedy's *Thirteen*

Days, in *New York Review of Books,* March 13, 1969; Nancy Gager Clinch, *The Kennedy Neurosis* (New York: Grossett & Dunlop, 1973). For critical assessments of Kennedy's alleged "macho" personality, see Arthur Schlesinger, Jr., *Robert Kennedy and His Times* (New York: Ballantine Books, 1978), pp. 551–554; and Graham Allison, "Cuban Missiles and Kennedy Macho: New Evidence to Dispel the Myth," *Washington Monthly* (October 1972): pp. 14–19.

2. I should note that had U.S. intelligence discovered the movement of missiles into Cuba much earlier, the purely diplomatic option might have appeared more promising to Kennedy and may have seemed worth trying before ordering a blockade and a massive mobilization of U.S. military power. Even in this alternative scenario, the president might have found it necessary to engage in some variant of coercive diplomacy that included the threat of a blockade in order to impress Khrushchev. As for the Soviet leader, with few, if any, missiles in Cuba, his bargaining position would have been much weaker, but it might also have been easier for him to call off the missile deployment at so early a stage.

3. Available materials and interpretations concerning President Kennedy's concern that he was perceived as lacking in resolve and Soviet officials' recollections of Khrushchev's image of Kennedy are summarized in Alexander L. George, "Cuban Missile Crisis," in *Avoiding War: Problems of Crisis Management* (Boulder: Westview Press, 1991). For a recent discussion of this and related issues, see Richard Ned Lebow, "Domestic Politics and the Cuban Missile Crisis," *Diplomatic History* 14, no. 3 (Fall 1990): pp. 484–488.

4. On President Kennedy's basic image of Khrushchev as a rational, intelligent leader who could be persuaded that he had miscalculated and should remove the missiles, see Robert Kennedy, *Thirteen Days* (New York: Norton, 1969), pp. 126–127.

5. See note 1 and Lebow, "Domestic Politics."

6. On President Kennedy's belief that any talk of concession and accommodation should be avoided until he had impressed Khrushchev with his resolve, see Arthur Schlesinger, Jr., *A Thousand Days* (Boston: Houghton Mifflin, 1965), pp. 807–811; Schlesinger, *Robert Kennedy,* pp. 554–560; Theodore C. Sorensen, *Kennedy* (New York: Harper & Row, 1965), p. 699; Kennedy, *Thirteen Days,* pp. 66–67; Michael R. Beschloss, *The Crisis Years: Kennedy and Khrushchev 1960–1963* (New York: Edward Burlingame Books, 1991), pp. 462, 468, 508–509.

7. Legitimate questions can be raised concerning the wisdom of Kennedy's decision to withhold any indication of a willingness to offer concessions until late on Friday, October 26. Such a bargaining strategy risks conveying to the opponent that one is unalterably opposed to any modification of one's demands, and it violates the principle of crisis management that emphasizes the desirability of leaving open to the opponent a face-saving way out of the crisis. Failure to leave such an opening may result in an unwanted, unexpected hardening of the opponent's determination to reject the demands of the coercing state and to consider escalation. (For additional discussion, see George, "Cuban Missile Crisis," in *Avoiding War.*)

8. Thus, on Friday morning, in order to increase the pressure on Khrushchev, the president ordered more low-level flights over Cuba and asked State and Defense officials to prepare to add petroleum and lubricants to the embargo list for enforcement by the blockade. Kennedy also rebuked the State Department press officer for indirectly hinting that an invasion of Cuba might follow if work on the missile sites did

not stop. Cf. Kennedy, *Thirteen Days,* p. 83; Roger Hilsman, *To Move a Nation* (New York: Doubleday, 1967), pp. 213–214; Abel, *The Missile Crisis,* p. 173; Sorensen, *Kennedy,* pp. 711–712.

9. For a detailed discussion of crisis management principles and their relevance for avoiding escalation of diplomatic crises to war, see George, *Avoiding War.*

10. Of the nineteen Soviet freighters en route to Cuba when the blockade was announced, all sixteen suspected by U.S. intelligence of carrying missiles and other military cargoes turned back soon after Kennedy announced the quarantine. Bouchard, drawing on declassified sources, reports that as a result of intensive surveillance, the U.S. Navy already had a complete list of Soviet bloc ships en route to Cuba and had identified all those suspected of carrying military cargo. (Joseph F. Bouchard, "Use of Naval Forces in Crises: A Theory of Stratified Crisis Interaction," Ph.D. diss., Department of Political Science, Stanford University, September 1988, pp. 628–629, 633). A much condensed version of this dissertation, *Command in Crisis: Four Case Studies,* was published by Columbia University Press (New York) in 1991.

11. Early accounts of the missile crisis all contain some information (not always correct) on various aspects of the design and implementation of the blockade and the U.S. Navy's efforts to force Soviet submarines to surface. The most authoritative account relied on for this section is Bouchard, "Use of Naval Forces." Important material based on declassified documents and interviews is also contained in Scott A. Sagan, "Nuclear Alerts and Crisis Management," *International Security* 9 (Spring 1985).

12. On Wednesday, October 24, U.N. Secretary-General U Thant called for a "voluntary suspension of all arms shipments to Cuba" coupled with "the voluntary suspension of the quarantine." Seeing advantages in this proposal, Khrushchev quickly accepted; he had already suspended further shipment of military materials to Cuba, and U Thant's proposal would prevent the United States from stopping any ships en route to Cuba indefinitely. Given its obvious disadvantages for his strategy, Kennedy quickly rejected the proposal. The next day, U Thant offered a more even-handed, time-limited proposal; Kennedy quickly accepted it, and Khrushchev did so on Friday. U Thant's second proposal was accompanied by a request to Castro that Cuba stop work on the missile sites, to which Castro did not agree until Saturday. But by then the crisis had evolved into a new phase, and hence U Thant's initiative was overtaken by events. (The relevant documents are reproduced in David L. Larson, ed., *"The Cuban Crisis" of 1962: Selected Documents and Chronology* [Boston: Houghton Mifflin, 1963]; and in Henry M. Pachter, *Collision Course* [New York: Praeger, 1963].) For additional discussion, see George, *Avoiding War.*

13. Bouchard, "Use of Naval Forces," pp. 659–660.

14. Ibid., pp. 678, 684, 662–663.

15. Ibid., pp. 660–661.

16. Ibid., pp. 664–668; also Sagan, "Nuclear Alerts," p. 117.

17. Sagan, "Nuclear Alerts," pp. 113, 115; Bouchard, "Use of Naval Forces," pp. 669, 657–658. However, the alternative interpretation that the president himself ordered the navy to undertake assertive, vigorous pursuit of the Soviet submarines is suggested by Beschloss (*The Crisis Years,* p. 507), who states that during the height of the crisis in an executive committee meeting on Thursday, October 25, President Kennedy ordered the navy to follow the Soviet submarines and to harass them and

force them to surface in the presence of U.S. warships. Beschloss gives as his sources a "memcon" and McGeorge Bundy, Ex. Comm. Record of Action, 10/25/62, both in the John F. Kennedy Library.

18. In an interview with German correspondent Bernd Greiner on October 13, 1987, Sergei Mikoyan stated that Soviet leaders, after being initially surprised by Kennedy's announcement of the blockade, "wanted to find out how far he would go. See, we knew that despite the blockade some [Soviet] ships had been allowed to pass. ... *When some of our submarines in the Caribbean were forced to surface, we knew: this is a sign that war might be at hand.* Perhaps this was the episode when we understood that the blockade was a very serious thing." Bernd Greiner, "The Soviet View: An Interview with Sergei Mikoyan," *Diplomatic History* 14, no. 2 (Spring 1990) [emphasis added]. I am indebted to Marc Trachtenberg and Barton Bernstein for calling this source to my attention.

19. This section and the next summarize the detailed account of the closing phase of the crisis presented in George, *Avoiding War.* In addition to the standard sources on the crisis, important new material on its interpretation is contained in recent publications: James G. Blight and David A. Welch, *On the Brink* (New York: Hill and Wang, 1989); Bruce J. Allyn, James G. Blight, and David A. Welch, "Essence of Revision," *International Security* 14, no. 3 (Winter 1989–1990): pp. 138–149; McGeorge Bundy, *Danger and Survival* (New York: Random House, 1988); Raymond L. Garthoff, *Reflections on the Cuban Missile Crisis,* revised ed. (Washington, D.C.: Brookings Institution, 1989); Bruce J. Allyn, James G. Blight, and David A. Welch, eds., *Proceedings of the Moscow Conference on the Cuban Missile Crisis, January 27, 28, 1989* (Cambridge: Center for Science and International Affairs, Harvard University, December 1989); James G. Blight, David A. Welch, and Bruce J. Allyn, *Cuba on the Brink: Fidel Castro, the Missile Crisis and the Collapse of Communism* (New York: Farrar, Straus and Giroux, 1992); and Arthur Schlesinger, Jr., "Four Days with Fidel: A Havana Diary," *New York Review of Books,* March 26, 1992.

20. External and subjective pressures contributing to a sense of urgency to resolve the crisis are discussed in Blight and Welch, *On the Brink,* pp. 128–131, 310–312; also James G. Blight, *The Shattered Crystal Ball: Fear and Learning in the Cuban Missile Crisis* (Savage, Md.: Rowman and Littlefield, 1990), and Bundy, *Danger and Survival,* pp. 423–427.

21. The dilemma the shooting down of the U-2 created for Kennedy is clearly identified in earlier accounts of the crisis by his advisers (Hilsman, *To Move A Nation,* p. 220; Kennedy, *Thirteen Days,* p. 98; Sorensen, *Kennedy,* p. 713) and was emphasized in Alexander L. George, David K. Hall, and William E. Simons, *The Limits of Coercive Diplomacy: Laos, Cuba, Vietnam* (Boston: Little, Brown, 1971), pp. 124–125. Important details that depict the gravity with which this policy dilemma was experienced have emerged in the transcript of the meetings of the advisory group on Saturday, October 27, reproduced in McGeorge Bundy and James G. Blight, "October 27, 1962: Transcripts of the Meetings of the ExComm," *International Security* 12, no. 3 (Winter 1987–1988).

22. Kennedy, *Thirteen Days,* p. 169. Supporting the accuracy of this account is the fact that a similar version of what Robert Kennedy told Dobrynin was included in a written account of the meeting he gave Rusk three days later. Cited by Schlesinger, *Robert Kennedy,* p. 561. That Robert Kennedy gave Dobrynin the equivalent of an ul-

timatum is indirectly supported by Bundy (*Danger and Survival*, pp. 432, 438) who was present when the president told his brother what to convey to the Soviet ambassador. On p. 441 of his book, Bundy refers to this as an "ultimatum." As for Sergei Mikoyan, in his interview with Bernd Greiner ("The Soviet View," pp. 27–28), he states that Robert Kennedy "delivered an urgent message, and we got it."

Robert Kennedy's account of his conversation with Dobrynin appears at first glance to have been contradicted by the former Soviet ambassador at the Harvard-sponsored Moscow conference on the Cuban crisis. Dobrynin at first denied that any ultimatum was conveyed or, indeed, that any threats were made. Rather, his recollection was that Robert Kennedy had downplayed the danger of imminent U.S. action and that his own cable to Moscow summarizing his meeting with the president's brother was similarly low-key on this point. Later in the conference, however, Dobrynin acknowledged that Robert Kennedy had indeed conveyed acute time pressure for a response; he "persistently asked, it is true, to convey the president's request that if possible he wanted to receive an answer on Sunday. So I conveyed this to Moscow." Dobrynin added that he himself had experienced time urgency for a reply and made the telling comment that "according to the evidence we had available [in the Soviet embassy], an air strike was considered very likely, perhaps in the coming days. There might have been also an invasion." The former Soviet ambassador to the United States did not disclose or quote from his cable to Moscow, nor did he say that he had recently reread it to refresh his memory. If Dobrynin's cable is declassified, it might help to clarify what Robert Kennedy told him on that occasion. (Allyn, Blight, and Welch, *Proceedings of the Moscow Conference*, pp. 54, 93; Allyn, Blight, and Welch, "Essence of Revision," p. 163.)

23. Allyn, Blight, and Welch, "Essence of Revision," p. 166. The authors add, reinforcing this interpretation of the significance of Scali's threat, that after the Cuban crisis was settled, Fomin communicated to Scali a personal message from Khrushchev, saying that his outburst had been very valuable. See also John Scali, "I Was the Secret Go-Between in the Cuban Crisis," *Family Weekly*, October 25, 1964, p. 14. The possible importance of Scali's "ultimatum" to Fomin was also stressed by Bundy, *Danger and Survival*, pp. 438–439. See also Garthoff, *Reflections*, pp. 80–81, 90, 103, 158.

24. New information supporting this interpretation, gained from Soviet and Cuban sources, reinforces what was known earlier regarding the sense of urgency with which Khrushchev acted to terminate the crisis on Saturday night and early Sunday morning. See Allyn, Blight, and Welch, "Essence of Revision," pp. 166–168. These authors report, without giving a source, that President Kennedy (perhaps in response to an official recommendation by the Joint Chiefs) issued instructions on Saturday morning, October 27, to prepare for a possible attack on Cuba on the morning of October 30, and they suggest that this may have become known to Soviet and Cuban intelligence.

25. Bundy and Blight, "October 27, 1962." The president's willingness to include the Jupiters in the negotiations may have been conveyed by his brother to Dobrynin in a private meeting the preceding evening. This observation is based solely on Dobrynin's recollection at the Moscow conference (cf. Allyn, Blight, and Welch, "Essence of Revision," p. 158).

26. Sorensen's explanation for the change he made in *Thirteen Days* was that the missile swap was still a secret at the time, known only to six members of the presi-

dent's advisory group. Information on the meeting of this smaller group after the executive committee meeting is contained in Bundy, *Danger and Survival,* pp. 432–435. What these other advisers knew as to the exact nature of the quid pro quo regarding the removal of the Jupiters from Turkey, however, remains uncertain. Thus, in his written report to Rusk three days after his meeting with Dobrynin, Robert Kennedy evidently concealed the fact that the Jupiters were part of the formal quid pro quo; instead, he stated that he had told Dobrynin "that there could be no quid pro quo—no deal of this kind could be made. ... It was up to NATO to make the decision." Schlesinger, *Robert Kennedy,* p. 562.

For an account of the abortive effort Khrushchev made several days later to make the quid pro quo part of the formal diplomatic record, see Schlesinger, *Robert Kennedy,* pp. 563–564.

27. Blight and Welch, *On the Brink,* pp. 83–84; also pp. 171–174.

28. *Pravda* and *Izvestia,* December 13, 1962. Translation in *Current Digest of the Soviet Press* and quoted in Ronald R. Pope, *Soviet Views on the Cuban Missile Crisis* (Washington, D.C.: University Press of America, 1982), pp. 87–88.

29. Allyn, Blight, and Welch, "Essence of Revision," pp. 166–168. See also Beschloss, *Crisis Years,* pp. 538–540.

30. For a discussion of the ways in which international law entered into Kennedy's handling of the crisis and its contribution to the legitimacy of his actions, see Abram Chayes, *The Cuban Missile Crisis: International Crises and the Role of Law* (New York: Oxford University Press, 1974).

31. The release in early January 1992 of classified correspondence between Kennedy and Khrushchev documented earlier sources on the crisis that had noted that Kennedy had qualified his noninvasion pledge by refusing to make it part of a formal agreement unless adequate inspection of the removal of the missiles was agreed to by Castro and was carried out and the United States received assurance that Cuba would not engage in "aggression" against other states in the Western hemisphere. The exchange of letters also revealed that Kennedy had asked for an assurance that the Soviets would not establish submarine bases in Cuba, but the letters do not indicate Khrushchev's reply (*New York Times,* January 7, 1992, and *Washington Post,* January 7, 1992). Subsequently, Jack Anderson and Michael Binstein referred to still-classified documents they had seen that indicated that State Department legal experts had expressed the opinion in 1983 that Kennedy's noninvasion of Cuba pledge, even though not embodied in a formal agreement, should not be regarded "as less than legally binding" (*Washington Post,* February 2, 1992).

7

U.S. Coercive Pressure on North Vietnam, Early 1965

WILLIAM E. SIMONS

In early 1965, the Johnson administration implemented a policy of openly exerting various forms of military pressure against the government of North Vietnam. In this chapter I analyze this policy in several key respects. An underlying theme is the fact that President Lyndon B. Johnson was reluctant to engage in a direct military confrontation with the Asian Communist governments supporting the Viet Cong (VC) insurgency, largely because he wished to avoid public pressure for policy changes that could destroy domestic political harmony. The president perceived such an outcome as interfering with governmental progress toward the Great Society. Thus, when the policy of military pressure was put into effect, he declined to authorize the kinds of threatening actions and explicit demands usually associated with a vigorous strategy of coercive diplomacy. When VC actions and the political situation in South Vietnam forced his hand, he resorted to carefully measured actions and damage-limiting expedients more akin to crisis management techniques than to an exercise of coercive pressure.

In analyzing the implementation of this policy, I address questions including the following: Why did the pressures policy take so long in materializing? To what extent did it embrace a coercive objective? What other policy motivations and objectives intruded? Which of these were dominant, and why? What were the key constraints on adopting a stronger variant of coercive diplomacy?

THE ISSUE OF
INCREASING MILITARY PRESSURES

The policy of using direct military operations against the Democratic Republic of Vietnam (DRV) to pressure the DRV to abandon its campaign to take over South Vietnam was seriously debated in Washington for over a year. Just days before President Kennedy's death, officials from his administration and top military advisers met in Honolulu to reassess U.S. strategy following the overthrow of the Diem government in Saigon. Their decisions led to a program of covert operations against North Vietnam, carried out by armed forces of the new government of South Vietnam (GVN), that began on February 1, 1964.[1] Almost as soon as the covert operations began, various U.S. agencies began to advocate more direct measures—principally air strikes—against North Vietnam. Their chief argument was that the potentially coercive effects on Hanoi from strictly covert operations would be limited at best. President Johnson authorized detailed interagency planning for U.S. and GVN air strikes in the event they might be necessary at some future date.[2]

Interagency contingency planning became more elaborate and more focused as the administration dealt with a series of crises in Southeast Asia during 1964. U.S. responses included low-level reconnaissance missions over Communist-occupied territory in Laos, one-time retaliatory air strikes against North Vietnamese torpedo boat bases, and a formal resolution affirming congressional support for administration policies in Southeast Asia. During each of these crises, which included a devastating mortar attack on U.S. aircraft at Bien Hoa air base, heavier air strikes against North Vietnam were proposed by the Joint Chiefs of Staff (JCS) but were rejected by President Johnson's principal advisers.

Early Policy Confirmations

By mid-September 1964, most of the president's advisers were not questioning the desirability of ultimately subjecting North Vietnam to direct attacks. However, at a high-level meeting to review possible courses of action in Southeast Asia, the chairman of the JCS and other principal advisers recommended little more than preparation for reprisal strikes against related DRV targets for any further attacks on U.S. units or in response to special DRV-VC actions against South Vietnam. They supported Ambassador Maxwell Taylor's judgment that the GVN was currently too weak and potentially too unstable to run the risks incurred by taking more drastic action.[3]

This proclivity for caution continued until late November, when the president's top-level advisers met again to consider the recommendations of an interagency study group on Vietnam policy established by the president following the VC attack on Bien Hoa. Before meeting with the president, the principals deliberated several times on the study group's analysis of U.S. stakes and objectives and alternative courses of military action in the region. Significantly, they added the objective of influencing Hanoi to remove its support and direction from the VC insurgency at the head of the list of objectives prepared by the NSC working group. Although several military options were discussed, the hard, fast bombing campaign favored by the JCS received little serious consideration.[4]

By the time the president met formally with his advisers, on December 1 and 3, 1964, the only U.S. military operation against North Vietnam recommended to him was a carefully graduated program of air strikes to take place during Phase II of a specified course of combined U.S.-GVN actions. Once again, Ambassador Taylor had impressed upon his colleagues the facts of the unstable and ineffective nature of the Saigon regime and its resultant present inability to cope with the likely DRV-VC reactions to stronger military pressures. Until these shortcomings in the GVN were seen to improve, the president's principal advisers advocated (for Phase I) only the kinds of military actions already authorized in September plus U.S. armed reconnaissance air operations over Laos.[5]

There is ample reason to doubt that Lyndon Johnson actually bought the entire Phase I–Phase II package. That formulation stands out mainly for the expectations it generated among the president's advisers. The most significant outcome of the two meetings he held with his advisers on December 1 and 3, and the topic that absorbed much of the president's attention, was the message he authorized Ambassador Taylor to deliver to the GVN, which for the first time indicated the U.S. intention ultimately to participate directly in systematic military actions against North Vietnam.[6] Moreover, the message held out the promise of a firm commitment to such actions *provided* the GVN instituted certain specified reforms. As if to add substance to this incentive to effect the desired improvements, the message also instructed Taylor to begin joint planning with the South Vietnamese military leaders for reprisal strikes and for the larger Phase II operations, should these be authorized at some future time.

Another immediate outcome of the December meetings was the beginning of regular U.S. armed reconnaissance air operations over the Laotian infiltration corridors into South Vietnam. U.S. air units were authorized to attack targets of opportunity along the infiltration routes and to plan strike missions against fixed targets along the Communist lines of communication (LOCs). Initially called BARREL ROLL, these unacknowledged operations over Laos began on December 14, 1964, and continued throughout most of the war. During Phase I, Royal Laotian Air Force (RLAF) air operations against North Vietnamese infiltration efforts and assorted GVN maritime operations against the North were added to exert additional military pressure against Hanoi.

Administration Perceptions of Pressure

Before I examine how further pressures were actually applied against the government in Hanoi, it is important to review how the Johnson administration perceived the concept of pressure. Clearly the concept meant different things to different officials and the approach to air strikes in particular changed over time. Although the president's advisers focused on air strikes as the means for increasing pressure on North Vietnam, they regarded air operations as useful for several different purposes as well. These other purposes gained prominence as the advisers became increasingly less confident that bombing would cause Hanoi to alter its policies.

Reducing the DRV's Capability. In addition to attacking Hanoi's will, air strikes were seen by the JCS in particular as a means of reducing North Vietnam's capability to continue its support of the Viet Cong.

Encouraging GVN Resistance and Solidarity. Given the administration's commitment to strengthen GVN capabilities for combating the VC, the president's advisers increasingly anticipated that air strikes against North Vietnam would help to stiffen GVN resistance.[7]

Conveying U.S. Resolve. Most of the president's advisers saw success in combating the insurgency in Vietnam as essential for convincing the rest of the world that the Communist strategy of promoting wars of national liberation could be defeated. At times some of them doubted that the U.S. role in Southeast Asia to date had demonstrated credibly to other nations the U.S. determination to stop Communist expansion in Southeast Asia. Bombing North Vietnamese targets was perceived as a potent way to demonstrate U.S. power and determination to Communist and non-Communist governments alike.

Improving U.S.-GVN Negotiating Position. Administration officials saw direct strikes at the source of support for the insurgency in the South as an important prelude to the negotiations that would eventually be needed for an effective settlement of the Vietnam problem. Many advisers looked toward 1965 as providing an opportunity for a systematic air offensive against the North and were anxious to delay negotiations until after the bombing had made a telling impression on the DRV and its backers.[8]

Although it gained general acceptance by the Johnson administration, the concept of exerting increased military pressure on the government in Hanoi was nevertheless approached with a good deal of caution. Throughout much of 1964, of course, caution with respect to the war in Southeast Asia was an important adjunct of Johnson's campaign for reelection as the candidate of prudence and restraint. But even after the election, the administration continued to see the national interest as best served by avoiding a polarization of public opinion, either in favor of massively punishing North Vietnam or of withdrawing from the struggle.[9] In particular, the president wished to preclude political polarization that might divert support away from the Great Society legislation he would propose to the new Congress. Moreover, the administration wanted to retain policy flexibility regarding Southeast Asia and to assure that it could maintain control over the direction taken by events in the area.

The administration was also wary of taking actions that could compromise the position of the cooperative regime in Laos. The legitimacy of Prince Souvanna Phouma's "Neutralist" government rested on the 1962 Geneva Protocol on Laos. Should more flagrant U.S. air operations or cross-border operations by GVN ground forces—both of which were being advocated by the JCS—result in embarrassment for Souvanna's regime, dire consequences could result: Either Souvanna might terminate the military and other operations already under way in Laos, or the Geneva diplomatic machinery might be called in to tinker with the Laotian political arrangements. So far, the U.S. government had depended upon these arrangements to foil Communist expansion in Laos, and it did not want to see them altered.

The International Political Context, 1965

Administration officials had recognized for some time that the most promising basis for an eventual settlement of the Vietnam conflict was reinstatement of the essential provisions of the 1954 Geneva Accords. If honored by all parties, these provisions would not only preserve the right of self-determination for the people of South Vietnam but would guarantee the security of existing borders for all the states of Indochina. The Geneva formula provided for flexible international participation, including that of the five major powers capable of influencing compliance with the agreement. The United Kingdom and the Soviet Union had agreed to serve as permanent cochairs, and the original conference had established a three-party international commission (ICC) that continued to observe and report on treaty compliance.[10] The Geneva Conference framework had already been used by the United States in 1962 to obtain political stability in Laos, and the Johnson administration took pains in its public actions to preserve the image and the potential of this diplomatic vehicle.

One of the major powers in the Geneva Conference framework was Communist China. Barely a decade after the Korean War, this huge nation loomed ominously in the background of the struggle for control of Vietnam. Moreover, the People's Republic of China (PRC) was now a nuclear power, having successfully tested a nuclear weapon in the Gobi Desert in October 1964. The Johnson administration was acutely concerned over a Chinese military reaction in the event of direct U.S. intervention in the Vietnam War. Although the administration regarded the DRV as the principal actor on "the other side," it saw the PRC's role in the crisis as significant and potentially dominant. It regarded Beijing, not Hanoi, as the major benefactor should U.S. policies and actions in the region be discredited.[11]

The Soviet Union had also reemerged as an active player in Indochina. Following the 1962 Geneva Agreement, the Soviets had been relatively inactive in the politics of Southeast Asia, but Khrushchev's ouster as party secretary in October 1964 marked a change in policy. In November, Moscow pledged to increase its economic and military aid to North Vietnam, and in early January 1965, it made public Soviet Foreign Minister Andrei Gromyko's assurances that the USSR would support the DRV if it were attacked by the United States. Significantly, this followed several private talks between Secretary of State Dean Rusk and Gromyko at the United Nations and in Washington during December, in which U.S. intentions to hold to its course in Indochina were made clear.

Of particular concern to the administration was the potential impact on the rest of Southeast Asia and on U.S. standing globally of a failure by the United States to prevent a Communist takeover in South Vietnam. The president and his principal advisers believed fervently that if South Vietnam were to succumb to the VC insurgency, then the rest of Indochina would quickly fall under the control of Hanoi and Beijing. In these circumstances, Thailand and other free governments in the region would lose confidence in the United States, and the security of all of Southeast Asia would be in jeopardy. Indeed, as 1965 began, the administration was expressing great concern over the threatening emergence of a "Jakarta-Peking Axis" that would put great pro-Communist pressure on the governments of Malaysia and Thailand.[12]

Some of the president's advisers, particularly Secretary Rusk and the chairman of the JCS, General Earle Wheeler, were convinced that the loss of South Vietnam would have repercussions far beyond Asia. The Joint Chiefs felt strongly that the resulting loss of U.S. credibility would lead inevitably to "progressive unraveling" of wider-ranging defense structures that would affect even the North Atlantic Treaty Organization (NATO). Dean Rusk believed U.S. conduct relative to its obligations under the Southeast Asia Treaty Organization (SEATO) agreement would have an impact on other treaties to which the American government was a party worldwide. He told me that "right from the beginning," in his conversations with President Johnson about Vietnam, he encouraged the president to view the issues as global in impact rather than just in terms of Southeast Asia.[13]

DECIDING ON STRONGER U.S. ACTION, JANUARY–FEBRUARY 1965

The Johnson administration approached 1965 in a spirit of anticipation. Johnson's landslide victory the previous November had indicated widespread popular support for his policies. The weeks since the election had seen a flurry of executive activity to prepare the annual budget and an early package of Great Society legislation. Policy decisions regarding Southeast Asia that followed the extensive November policy review had set in train Phase I military and diplomatic actions for the region and encouraged the national security community to look forward to the onset of Phase II operations early in the new year.

Implementing Phase I

Phase I military operations got under way in mid-December and were coupled with new efforts to bolster the GVN and by a series of diplomatic missions to other allied governments, which were asked to contribute assistance to South Vietnam. However, the Phase I scenario was soon altered by political events in Saigon. Buddhist street demonstrations against the current civilian government were seized upon by a group of ambitious generals as an excuse to disband the high civilian council that had been acting as a provisional legislature. Washington instructed the Saigon embassy to inform the GVN and the generals that any future movement toward Phase II would be impossible unless stability and unity were restored to the government. Secretary Rusk warned in a timely press conference that the United States would be forced to cut back on further assistance to South Vietnam if a unified government were not soon reestablished.

The political upheaval in Saigon also impeded the Phase I provision for reprisals in response to VC excesses. On Christmas Eve 1964, at the height of the political crisis, the Brink officers' billet in downtown Saigon was bombed, killing two Americans and injuring thirty-eight. Despite strong recommendations from Ambassador Taylor and the Joint Chiefs for immediate reprisals against North Vietnamese targets, the president decided against such actions. Reprisals were considered too risky at this time in view of the vulnerability of American dependents to an escalation of political violence—particularly given the recent behavior of the U.S. ally the reprisals were designed to benefit.

Pressures on the President

As reflected by his Southeast Asia policy decisions in early December, President Johnson thus far was committed to the middle ground between assuming a greater U.S. military role and leaving the Vietnamese to their own devices. Increasingly, however, as 1965 got under way, he came under pressure from advocates of each of these alternatives. Moreover, he received word that the administration's latest attempt to communicate with Hanoi through the Canadian member of the ICC had been thwarted. As National Security Adviser McGeorge Bundy counseled the president, this apparent hardening of the DRV's position suggested "that the people in Hanoi have a fairly accurate appreciation of our current policy and that they are confident that time is on their side."[14] With his heart and energies focused primarily on the domestic political actions needed to initiate the Great Society programs, Johnson found the situation in Vietnam and the seeming inability of committed U.S. resources to affect that situation a source of heightening frustration.

The Johnson administration's current policy was also being subjected to increasing political heat. By the first week of January 1965, publications such as the *New York Times, New York Journal American, Providence Journal, St. Louis Post Dispatch, Life,* and *Newsweek* had printed major editorials criticizing either U.S. policy objectives in Vietnam or U.S. support for the inept GVN. Within the U.S. Congress, the Senate in particular had become divided over administration policy in Southeast Asia. Although the majority of senators continued to support the existing policy, dissatisfaction was expressed both by conservatives, who urged the use of U.S. forces against North Vietnam, and by liberals, who urged a negotiated withdrawal.[15] The president's middle-of-the-road policy in Southeast Asia was increasingly under attack.

The problem was that both alternatives had drawbacks. Withdrawal was out of the question; it was seen as only confirming to world Communist leaders the wisdom of their policy of fomenting wars of national liberation. And negotiation of a political settlement at this time, without repudiation of this militant doctrine by Hanoi and Beijing, was regarded by the administration as tantamount to withdrawal.[16]

The only marginally acceptable alternative—an air campaign against North Vietnam—was one in which President Johnson had little confidence. It was seen by the president and some of his top advisers as starting down a path with uncertain consequences. Johnson told Ambassador Taylor at the end of December that he had "never felt that this war will be won from the air." At the time, he also had doubts about the effectiveness of bombing for lesser objectives, confiding to his advisers early in January that he never believed reprisal air strikes would help stabilize the GVN or bring the DRV leaders to the conference table.[17]

The president's personal preference was to bolster his middle-of-the-road policy, but this aroused little support from within the national security bureaucracy. In his cable to Taylor on December 30, President Johnson stated his view that "what is much more needed and would be more effective is a larger and stronger use of rangers and special forces and marines ... to stiffen the aggressiveness of Vietnamese military units up and down the line." He also urged the ambassador to encourage more vigorous U.S. participation in joint planning and execution of South Vietnamese military operations in support of the pacification effort.[18] Taylor and the Saigon mission opposed any larger use of U.S. ground forces. Foreseeing an "ever increasing commitment" if American troops were used in combat against the VC, Taylor argued that their "military value would be more than offset by their political liability."[19] In Washington, Taylor's view was supported by Secretary of Defense Robert McNamara. This led the president to urge McNamara to "develop some alternatives" to larger U.S. forces that would nevertheless strengthen the direct U.S. military contact "with the Vietnamese at all levels."[20]

Acknowledgment of Soviet Interests

Administration attempts to inform the new Soviet regime of the growing seriousness of the situation in Indochina led to multiple concerns over the implications of Soviet reentry into Southeast Asian politics. During his talks with Gromyko, Rusk had emphasized that the United States intended to remain in South Vietnam until the threats from Hanoi and Beijing had been removed. Without some change in those policies, Rusk implied, there was a real risk of war. Gromyko countered with a challenge—U.S. participation in a new international conference to discuss both Vietnam and Laos. (In subsequent weeks, the Soviet position shifted publicly to exclude Vietnam.) Much of the conversation apparently dealt with their respective views on provisions of the existing Geneva agreements on Southeast Asia and highlighted conflicting positions as to which side had been guilty of violating those accords.[21] The talks gave little assurance that the Soviets were willing to concede merit to the U.S. and South Vietnamese case or to question Hanoi's actions.

Nevertheless, reflecting an awareness of the deepening Sino-Soviet rift and a belief that the prospect of resultant Chinese gains served to limit Soviet desire for a Viet Cong victory, key figures in the Johnson administration were hopeful of eventual Soviet cooperation.[22] The Soviets were perceived to view increased prospects of a Communist victory in South Vietnam as encouraging even stronger U.S. intervention, thereby heightening the possibility of direct Chinese involvement in the conflict. Therefore, the reasoning went, as the crisis worsened, the Soviets might assist in promoting an acceptable diplomatic solution in Southeast Asia. And the United States, in keeping with the Johnson administration's broader policy of seeking resolution of its disputes with the Soviet Union, should make every effort to keep alive the possibility of a constructive Soviet role.[23]

Accompanying this aspiration for eventual Soviet cooperation, however, was the administration's more immediate expectation of greater Soviet economic and military assistance to North Vietnam. Accordingly, Washington viewed the Kremlin's announcement on January 31, 1965, of Premier Aleksai Kosygin's forthcoming visit to Hanoi as entirely consistent with expected Soviet behavior.

The Decision to Undertake Reprisals

As the Johnson administration prepared for its inauguration, many key officials in the national security bureaucracy urged the president to authorize stronger action in Southeast Asia. Particularly influential in this regard was the Saigon embassy, which began advocating the use of air operations against North Vietnam to encourage a determination to resist within the South. A series of cables from Ambassador Taylor stressed South Vietnam's political and psychological deterioration as well as a growing conviction there that the United States did not really intend to take a stronger hand in the conflict with Hanoi. Taylor cited U.S. unwillingness thus far to act in response to provocations, such as the Brink's attack, to bolster his case for an early transition to Phase II actions against the North and the prompt use of air strikes in reprisal for further VC atrocities.[24]

Although he rejected Taylor's urgings relative to Phase II, on January 7, 1965, the president indicated his "readiness to adopt a policy of prompt and clear reprisal."[25] However, it would be nearly a month before concrete steps were authorized to implement that policy. In the interim, the president concentrated on final preparation of the elementary and secondary education bill and other domestic issues and engaged in an extended dialogue with Ambassador Taylor on pros and cons of removing American dependents from Saigon.

As it turned out, the dependents issue and its relation to reprisals were resolved by the impact of external events. On January 27, South Vietnam's Armed Forces Council withdrew its support from the civilian leadership and, in return for Buddhist cooperation, designated General Nguyen Khanh to again form a government. In Washington, amid reports anticipating that the Khanh-Buddhist union could lead to attempts to negotiate an all-Vietnamese accommodation with Hanoi and the National Liberation Front (NLF),[26] a meeting of the president and his top advisers was hastily arranged to deal with the crisis.

Even before the latest episode of the Saigon political circus, McGeorge Bundy and Secretary McNamara had arranged to apprise the president of their lack of confidence in the administration's current policy. Essentially, they had come to agree with Ambassador Taylor that attainment of U.S. objectives was no longer possible if the administration continued to wait for a stable government in Saigon before acting more forcefully. They were convinced that adherence to that course of action would only lead to eventual defeat and a humiliating invitation to withdraw from South Vietnam. Prior to the larger meeting with all his advisers, they told the president: "We both agree that every effort should still be made to improve our operations on the ground and to prop up the authorities in South Vietnam as best we can. But we are both convinced that none of this is enough, and that the time has come for harder choices."[27]

President Johnson approached the crisis meeting on January 27 with fresh knowledge that only Secretary Rusk, among his top advisers, still preferred to continue with the middle course in Vietnam. His national security adviser, secretary of defense, and ambassador in Saigon clearly favored using military power to force a change in Hanoi's policy. His chairman of the JCS advocated a systematic bombing campaign directed against North Vietnamese targets. The under secretary of state, George Ball, had already advised seeking an early diplomatic solution designed to cut U.S. losses from a Vietnam commitment he considered futile. Still, before any firm decisions for future action could be made, the president saw it as essential first to get U.S. dependents out of South Vietnam.

Meeting notes and subsequent instructions to the field make it evident that no decisions were made at the meeting that included firm commitment to any new actions against North Vietnam.[28] With respect to political features of the current crisis, the president decided promptly to regard General Khanh as the real source of power in the new GVN and to instruct Ambassador Taylor to meet with him and encourage forceful public statements conveying the new government's determination to continue the campaign against Communist aggression. This was regarded as essential to avoid an appearance of evacuating U.S. civilians out of a fear of anti-American demonstrations or terrorist acts. Other initiatives were also ordered to convey the impression of U.S. determination to take forceful action: (1) General William Westmoreland, Commander U.S. Military Assistance Command Vietnam (COMUSMACV), was authorized to employ U.S. jet aircraft for air strikes in critical ground combat situations inside South Vietnam; (2) intelligence-gathering missions by U.S. destroyers (DESOTO patrols) were again authorized in the Tonkin Gulf, to begin on February 3; and (3) deployment of a Marine HAWK antiaircraft missile battalion was authorized for protection of DaNang Air Base, in northern South Vietnam. Finally, the president indicated that once the dependents were out of South Vietnam, he was prepared to "move strongly."[29]

As a consequence of the meeting, most of the preparations for conducting reprisal air strikes were already under way when the VC attacked a U.S. helicopter base and barracks at Pleiku on February 7 (Saigon time). Since the issuance of National Security Action Memorandum 314 the previous September, operational planning for DESOTO patrols had included designating possible reprisal targets south of the 19th parallel in North Vietnam for carrier aircraft prepositioned within striking range of the mainland.[30] Thus, appropriate targets sets and a potential strike force were already provided to carry out the reprisals, and an operation order (FLAMING DART) was issued at the headquarters of the Commander in Chief, Pacific Command (CINCPAC) in Honolulu on January 31. All that was needed was an "execute" order from the president. This was issued after a hastily called meeting of the NSC following the attack on Pleiku.

Operation Flaming Dart

In the days immediately following the January 27 policy meeting, some of the president's principal advisers were briefed on CINCPAC's reprisal plans, and changes were made in the target selection. On February 4, however, the intelligence-gathering patrol of U.S. destroyers was cancelled. President Johnson did not want to undertake what might be regarded as an intrusive action during Premier Kosygin's visit to Hanoi and thereby risk eroding what was perceived as a prospective improvement in U.S.-Soviet relations. Still, the aircraft carriers that had been deployed to the South China Sea in support of the intended destroyer mission continued to maneuver within re-call distance from their preplanned operating areas.

The crisis meeting that initiated preparations to remove U.S. dependents also occasioned the president's decision to send McGeorge Bundy and sev-eral other officials for a fresh look at the situation in South Vietnam.[31] The at-tack on Pleiku came as the Bundy group was finishing its visit and compiling its observations and recommendations for the president. As other National Security Council (NSC) members met in the White House, McGeorge Bundy was called to the telephone at the Saigon embassy several times to re-late what was being learned about the casualties and about VC actions else-where. During these conversations, Bundy recommended that retaliatory air strikes be ordered at once and relayed affirmations of endorsement from Ambassador Taylor and General Westmoreland. Having had similar recom-mendations from NSC members in Washington, the president issued instruc-tions to begin removing all U.S. dependents and to carry out the air strikes. So the reprisal strikes against North Vietnamese military barracks that had been planned as contingency actions along with the aborted DESOTO patrol were now set in motion.

Official comments concerning the reprisals on February 7 and 8 stressed that the U.S. and GVN military actions were essential to make clear their re-spective governments' determination to resist the intensified aggression against South Vietnam. However, Secretary McNamara was quite emphatic in a question-and-answer session at a press conference on February 7 in de-nying that the U.S. actions should be interpreted either as a threat or an ulti-matum. The White House announcement invoked the Tonkin Gulf prece-dent to stress the limited nature of the reprisal action.

Yet, the administration also took pains to make it clear that its actions marked an important change from its earlier reprisal policy. Unlike the Ton-kin Gulf reprisal, the February responses were in answer to hostile acts by the VC forces inside South Vietnam, which the administration explicitly linked to Hanoi. During the February 7 press conference, McNamara specifi-cally cautioned reporters against "characteriz[ing] this as a tit-for-tat raid." He went on to state that "our [future] actions will depend upon the degree to which the North Vietnamese carry out previous international agreements."

When the Viet Cong attacked a U.S. enlisted men's billet at Qui Nhon on February 10, retaliatory strikes were once again directed against facilities on the FLAMING DART target list. The strikes involved almost twice as many U.S.

aircraft as FLAMING DART I, but the targets were quite similar and were still roughly fifty miles north of the border. Moreover, the administration's public statements that accompanied the strikes were only slightly different from before.

TRANSITION TO PHASE II, "TRY AND SEE"

About the only hint that U.S. and GVN actions on February 11, 1965, could have represented something new was an official statement after the reprisal raids linking them with terrorist activities and VC attacks on South Vietnam's railroads that had been occurring continually since February 8.[32] Nevertheless, although not actually implemented until weeks later, a new policy of continual air strikes had been adopted. The intervening ten or twelve weeks saw dramatic changes in the scope and pace of air operations against North Vietnam and in the Johnson administration's accompanying rationale—both declaratory and actual. Despite public claims that U.S. policy had not really changed, this transitional period even included a weak try-and-see attempt at coercive diplomacy. Although it substantially increased military pressure, however, the administration stated its demands on Hanoi rather vaguely and without imparting any sense of urgency for North Vietnamese compliance.

"Graduated Reprisals"
and Other Concepts of Pressure

On Monday morning, February 8, policy deliberations concerning a program of sustained pressures against the North were resumed. The previous afternoon, McGeorge Bundy had returned from Saigon with a personal assessment of the situation in South Vietnam and with a recommendation. He argued that a major reason for South Vietnam's flagging will was the conviction that the United States lacked "the patience and determination to take the necessary actions and stay the course." To correct this misperception, he argued, the United States should embark now on a policy of "sustained reprisal" whereby repeated, deliberately paced attacks would be carried out against infiltration targets in North Vietnam, rather than responding only to specific incidents. These attacks would be "justified by and related to the whole Viet Cong campaign of violence and terror in the South."[33]

Just prior to an NSC meeting scheduled for February 8, to which the president had invited the congressional leadership, Johnson discussed some of the pros and cons of bombing North Vietnam with the chairman of the JCS and his top civilian advisers. During this discussion, he agreed to go forward with something more than individual reprisals.[34] Either then or later, he also decided to limit planning for the air operations against the DRV to military targets south of the 19th parallel. In a follow-up action, the president cabled

Ambassador Taylor with his decision to carry out a plan "for continuing action against North Vietnam with modifications up and down in tempo and scale in the light of your recommendations … and our own continuing review of the situation."[35]

Later, in his autobiography, President Johnson was to write that the advisers' discussions before the NSC meeting had led to "unanimous support" for Bundy's recommendation of "a program of sustained reprisal against the North." However, this support was not as unanimous as Johnson recalled.

In addition to Bundy's proposal, two different concepts for using air power against North Vietnam also contended for presidential approval throughout February 1965: Ambassador Taylor's graduated reprisals and the JCS-proposed eight-week air campaign. Although all three called for U.S. and GVN air and naval action in retaliation for the continuing Viet Cong campaign of violence and terror in South Vietnam, the concepts differed in their objectives and in the rationales governing the tempo and intensity of recommended punitive actions. Bundy's recommended U.S.-GVN actions were regarded as preliminaries to Phase II and were intended primarily to bolster the resistance inside South Vietnam. Taylor envisioned the allies' military actions as constituting Phase II and focused on an immediate objective of altering Hanoi's will to continue its aggressive behavior. The JCS also regarded its proposed actions as elements of Phase II but linked them to a more modest objective of demonstrating to Hanoi the likelihood of "more serious punishment."[36]

Accordingly, whereas Taylor and the JCS both emphasized establishing a steadily increasing pattern of pressure on the DRV, Bundy saw value in a more varied approach. A key feature of the sustained reprisal concept was that the tempo and intensity of the allies' actions would remain "in close correspondence to the level of outrage in the South." In other words, the reprisals should vary both upward and downward in response to the intensity of VC activity—and be "stopped when outrages in the South are … stopped." Taylor and the JCS, however, urged early movement away from explicit association of reprisals with VC provocations and the elimination of a reactive image. They wanted to acquire U.S.-GVN control over the dialogue with Hanoi by keeping the justification for reprisals vague and gradually accelerating the tempo of air and naval operations in the North.

The "continuing action" program authorized by the president was faithful to neither of these concepts, although elements of each were used apart from their original logical contexts. The air strikes were to be justified publicly as responses to continual VC aggressive actions but with the criteria for responding left vague and flexible so as to keep maximum control over their tempo. The intended tempo would be slower than that contemplated in November for Phase II in order to delay the peaking of outside pressures for negotiation and to forestall a sharp Communist response. The principal objective of the air actions would be to help strengthen the political situation in South Vietnam and, in the process, increase U.S. bargaining power for the anticipated negotiating situation.[37]

Whereas the three contending concepts had concentrated on military actions directed against North Vietnam, the president's approved course of continuing action specified "first and foremost" other actions within South Vietnam. In a phrase used repeatedly in cables to convey the policy decision, the administration asserted its intent to "intensify by all available means the program of pacification within South Vietnam, including every possible step to find and attack VC concentrations and headquarters within SVN by all conventional means available to GVN and U.S."[38] Pointedly, the NSC staff activity that was generated to analyze and support possible elements of the administration's new policy included an exploration of potential targets for air strikes and other military missions within South Vietnam.

Neither the internal high-level affirmations nor the public statements that accompanied the formulation of President Johnson's continuing action policy specified the immediate objectives of that policy. Johnson seldom provided a specific rationale at the time of his decisions.[39] Purposeful links between continuing action and a strengthened, stabilized GVN or an improved U.S. bargaining position are identifiable, however, from the accepted position papers of close advisers and from notes of Johnson's comments at high-level meetings.[40]

Self-Imposed Constraints and Problems of Implementation

Although in principle the president made a commitment to continuing action on February 8 and authorized a general concept of operations on February 13, the air strike element of this concept was not actually implemented until March. Meanwhile, other aspects of the continuing action policy were taking shape.

The president was careful during this period to not spell out any change in his existing policy for Southeast Asia. He preferred to cite only the overall objective of the U.S. commitment: to assist the South Vietnamese in defending their freedom against an attack controlled and directed from outside their country. Despite repeated staff suggestions that he clarify publicly the direction and new elements of his policy, Johnson declined to do so. The closest he came during this period was in a few remarks he made at the end of a speech on economic policy to the National Industrial Conference Board on February 17, 1965. After stating once again the U.S. government's overall policy objective in Vietnam, he added: "We have no ambition there for ourselves. We seek no dominion. We seek no conquest. We seek no wider war. But we must all understand that we will persist in the defense of freedom, and our continuing actions there will be those which are justified and those which are made necessary by the continuing aggression of others. These actions will be measured and fitting and adequate."

This reticence to acknowledge publicly that U.S. policy in Southeast Asia had entered a new phase is one of the decisions for which the president offered no explanation, but several factors were likely to have affected his judgment. He was being advised at the time to avoid a public posture that would tend to demand some reciprocal action on the part of the Chinese or the Soviets.[41] Then, too, he was known to be wary of stimulating international or domestic pressure for premature negotiations even though he preferred an eventual diplomatic solution. He also wanted to avoid a public political debate on Vietnam policy, which might polarize and cement differences between conservatives and liberals. Such a domestic political outcome could only complicate the prospects for his Great Society programs, key elements of which were then under consideration in the Congress.

Instructions given to Ambassador Taylor in mid-February suggest that the administration intended to proceed with its continuing actions until the DRV halted its infiltration of manpower and other forms of support for the war in South Vietnam.[42] But the only intended recipient of this message, at least for the present, was the government in South Vietnam, not that in Hanoi or other Communist capitals. The specter of possible Chinese intervention loomed large in the background.

The possibility of Chinese intervention had drawn greater attention with the recent discovery of Chinese MIGs based at the DRV's Phuc Yen airfield. Several advisers expressed their expectations of having to attack those aircraft in the likely event they attempted to intercept U.S. air sorties directed toward targets in northern Vietnam. This concern led directly to the initial decision to limit air operations to the region south of 19° north latitude—at least for several weeks. Officials who believed the Chinese would probably respond to U.S. attacks against the MIGs by operating them from bases in the southern PRC warned the president that he would then be under strong pressure to authorize attacks on those bases as well—and perhaps on Chinese nuclear production facilities. They warned further of the increasing threat of a Chinese introduction of ground combat forces, a contingency noted by intelligence estimates as increasingly likely as damage to North Vietnam became more severe.[43]

Such warnings created a climate of caution with respect to the projected tempo of air operations and the explicitness of declared U.S. intentions. Public statements, such as that given by Secretary Rusk on February 25, 1965, avoided making any explicit demands on Hanoi and made no attempt to link U.S. military actions directly with specified patterns of North Vietnamese behavior. During his prepared remarks, Rusk, who had been designated as the administration's official spokesperson on U.S. policy, would only repeat the phrase President Johnson had stated in public a week earlier: "Our continuing actions will be those … that are made necessary by the continuing aggression of others." That aggression, Rusk asserted earlier, consisted of North Vietnam's actions to direct and supply manpower and arms for the guerrilla campaign to overthrow the lawful government in the south. Even when asked directly in the question period if cessation of the infiltration from the north should be regarded as some kind of precondition and what the administration would regard as evidence that Hanoi was stopping the infiltration, Rusk declined to go beyond general formulations. He repeatedly drew attention only to Hanoi's aggression, calling it "the heart of the problem" and "the meat of the matter," and he painstakingly avoided making an explicit link with U.S. actions.[44]

Even in the administration's private communications with the DRV leadership—through contacts with the Chinese in Warsaw and through Canadian diplomatic contacts in Hanoi—the emphasis was on U.S. restraint and limited objectives and not on a firm demand for a specified change in DRV behavior. On February 24, 1965, the U.S. ambassador to Poland delivered a note to the PRC ambassador reaffirming that the United States had no desire to destroy the Hanoi government or to obtain territorial concessions at its expense. The administration's determination to stay the course was emphasized, as were its purposes in preserving South Vietnam's independence and bringing peace and stability to the region. In early March, Blair Seaborn, the Canadian ICC representative, responded to a State Department request by reading a similar statement to DRV officials in Hanoi. The North Vietnamese confirmed that they had already received the message delivered in Warsaw through the Chinese, and they gave Seaborn the impression that the air strikes were of little concern to them.[45]

Meanwhile, military elements of the president's continuing action policy with a focus on South Vietnam were being set in motion. U.S. Air Force tactical air strikes against VC concentrations in the countryside began in the last half of February. With GVN military manpower approaching critical limits, planners saw the deployment of selected elements of U.S. ground forces to South Vietnam to perform security functions at key U.S. bases as a way of releasing more Vietnamese units for assignment to pacification roles. Accordingly, when General Westmoreland reported on February 25 that the GVN's pacification effort had deteriorated, particularly in the northern half of the country, his earlier request for two U.S. Marine battalions to help protect DaNang Air Base was given quick approval. Also approved was his longstanding request for a battalion of military police and additional air police personnel. Similar efforts to make more GVN forces available for combat were signaled by the arrival in Saigon of six hundred South Korean engineer troops and by confirmation that fourteen hundred more would arrive shortly.

As February drew to a close, the president became increasingly agitated and frustrated with the sorry state of the GVN's pacification effort.[46] A spate of newspaper stories, alleging that the VC had successfully divided South Vietnam in two and questioning the president's strategy there, apparently exacerbated the already discouraging impacts of periodic Central Intelligence Agency and Military Assistance Command Vietnam (MACV) reports. At a strategy breakfast on March 2, the president decided to send General Harold K. Johnson and others to Saigon to review with the U.S. mission and COMUSMACV what more could be done to improve the situation there. General Johnson, the army chief of staff, later reported that the president had personally admonished him to "get things bubbling" in South Vietnam.[47]

However, the administration's intended politico-military scenario for continuing action was running into difficulties. The air strike element, code-named ROLLING THUNDER (RT), was supposed to begin early during the week of February 15; the first actual strike operation did not occur for another two weeks. In the interim, strike missions (RT I through IV) were scheduled and cancelled in deference to the weather, to the fragile political situation in Saigon (twice), or to the increasingly active diplomatic scene. One of these incidents was another coup attempt that ultimately led to the resignation of General Khanh.

The air campaign actually got under way with ROLLING THUNDER V on March 2, 1965. Nearly 130 U.S. and Vietnam Air Force (VNAF) aircraft struck North Vietnam's Quang Khe naval base and an ammunition storage depot at Xom Bang. A similar number were used in RT VI on March 14 and 15, which included a U.S. strike on a key ammunition depot forty miles above the 19th parallel. Although these were the largest raids yet carried out, the official White House announcement stated that they represented "no change" in policy. Press Secretary George Reedy linked them specifically to the president's public statement of February 17.

Through ROLLING THUNDER VI, planning for the air strikes was accomplished under extremely tight White House control. The targets for each of the RT missions were reviewed personally by the president. JCS target recommendations were forwarded to the White House after having already been screened by civilian officials in the Pentagon and the State Department. Moreover, even after the individual missions were approved and communicated to the field, specific permission from Washington was required before alternate targets could be struck—as in the case of RT VI, when unsatisfactory weather prevented an attack on the primary target on the originally specified date.

Brief Attempt to Threaten Major Damage with Bombing

The slow tempo and rigid controls imposed on operation ROLLING THUNDER by the White House brought several expressions of dissatisfaction from the field. Those who favored an air campaign primarily as a means of eroding Hanoi's will saw the current air effort against North Vietnam as likely to have little useful impact. On March 4, the JCS resubmitted its proposal for a pre-determined eight-week program of air strikes. On March 8, a pair of cables from Ambassador Taylor—one with General Westmoreland's explicit con-currence—contained strong complaints about the limited pressure exerted by the air attacks thus far. Stating that "a rate of once or twice a week for attacks involving two or three targets on each [attack] day" was a reasonable tempo, Taylor urged moving the strikes steadily northward. What was needed, he said, was "an agreed program covering several weeks which will combine the factors, frequency, weight, and location of attacks into a rational pattern which will convince the leaders in Hanoi that we are on a dynamic schedule … a moving growing threat which cannot be ignored."[48]

In the days immediately following the receipt of Taylor's critical cables, decisions were made that lifted some of the constraints on U.S. action and led eventually to an expansion of U.S. military roles in Vietnam. Significantly, this was a period when President Johnson was particularly absorbed in civil rights and other domestic political issues.[49] Yet, he took the unusual step of holding three different meetings on as many consecutive days with his princi-pal advisers on Southeast Asia, culminating with a meeting at Camp David on March 10. On March 9, following an oral report by Assistant Defense Secre-tary John McNaughton on his recent observations and discussions in Saigon, the president authorized (1) removing most restrictions on the use of U.S. aircraft in South Vietnam, and (2) moving north of the 19th parallel to strike a key target during RT VI.[50]

At Camp David, the president indicated his readiness to up the ante mili-tarily in order to check the perceived deterioration of the pacification effort in South Vietnam. In a discussion of prospects for moving toward an early settlement, Johnson expressed his judgment that the leaders in Hanoi and Beijing were not ready to even consider backing down because "we've not done anything yet." Then the president made a number of comments that conveyed his readiness to commit U.S. resources directly to combat roles in South Vietnam and to intensify the air war in the North. Indicating that the JCS should pursue its various activities inside South Vietnam on an acceler-ated basis, he said the United States had to be "prepared to pay some price ourselves." And later, "You gotta get some Indians under your scalp"—pre-sumably (from the context) to demonstrate a willingness to fight. He also ap-parently directed preparation of a "consistent-regular" program of air strikes, similar to that recommended by Ambassador Taylor, to make the North Vietnamese "pay" for their continuing support of the war in the South. "Then," he stated, "maybe by May 1 they'd be more responsive."[51]

In characteristic fashion, President Johnson did not authorize concrete measures reflecting these decisions until after the army chief of staff returned from his well-publicized visit to Saigon and submitted his formal report. The president discussed the general's recommendations at a publicized meeting with all the Joint Chiefs on March 15 and approved a number of them on the spot, including General Johnson's recommendations on the air war that were similar to Taylor's and a number of small U.S. force augmentations and reconnaissance operations to strengthen the war effort in South Vietnam.[52]

After the president's approval on March 15, subsequent planning for air strikes against North Vietnam provided for more flexibility in their execution. The strikes were approved by the White House in packages for a week at a time, not individually, and their specific timing within the week was left up to commanders in the field. The approved targets for U.S. forces included both primary targets and alternates, specified in advance. The requirement for simultaneous U.S. and VNAF operations was eliminated. Publicity to be given the U.S. and VNAF ROLLING THUNDER strikes was reduced and no longer contained reference to specific VC atrocities.[53]

But the White House continued to control the selection of targets and, hence, the intensity and movement northward of the bombing campaign. Throughout the spring of 1965, weekly target packages were approved, usually during the president's Tuesday lunch with his principal national security advisers, to be put into effect by Pacific air commanders each Friday. Attempts by the JCS and CINCPAC to obtain approval for a multiweek program of air strikes were consistently denied.[54] As we will see, however, the types of targets and overall targeting rationale recommended by high-level military authorities had some influence on the weekly White House decisions. From the standpoint of closely integrating U.S. military and political actions in pursuit of a common national objective, the targeting arrangements offered many advantages. The key issue, however, was what the bombing was intended to accomplish.

Whatever positive outcomes the president may have sought, the most notable targeting motivations—as described by the ROLLING THUNDER missions—were essentially negative. The weekly mission packages for March and April seemed to indicate a desire to avoid provocations that might widen the conflict and to minimize domestic and international pressures to pursue negotiations prematurely. Even though the U.S. and VNAF strike missions that began with RT VII (March 19–25) were more frequent than the earlier operations, few were flown to within a hundred miles of the Hanoi-Haiphong area. Moreover, with few exceptions, the targets could be justified to potential critics of administration policy as strictly military or related directly to the flow of men and materiel toward South Vietnam. That the ROLLING THUNDER missions would continue for many weeks at this "slowly ascending tempo" and stay clear of the radar-controlled intercept range of the DRV's MIG aircraft was determined in a major Southeast Asia policy review on April 1 and 2 and confirmed in a new national security action memorandum.[55]

Until the first deliberate bombing pause in mid-May, there was only one exception to this pattern of almost daily air strikes against North Vietnamese military targets. The exception came on April 3 and 4 when over a hundred U.S. Air Force and U.S. Navy aircraft struck and restruck bridges above Thanh Hoa, only about sixty-five miles south of Hanoi. On April 4, U.S. Air Force aircraft also bombed a nearby power plant. Apparently, the mission against these targets was approved at the White House policy luncheon on March 30 as part of the RT VIII package. Strikes against these particular bridges had been recommended by the JCS initially as an early element of a deliberate multiweek campaign against North Vietnam's LOCs to the South. According to the initial JCS rationale, dropping these bridges would trap all rolling stock below the bridges and make possible its systematic destruction.

However, the Johnson administration also attempted to exploit the unique geographical and value-laden features of these exceptional targets for coercive purposes. First, the Department of Defense (DOD) announced the strikes with considerably more detail than it had any attack since ROLLING THUNDER began, which was at variance with the March 16 policy decision to reduce the publicity given to individual raids. Emphasizing that it had taken the DRV seven years to restore one of the bridges and that "the present regime has taken great pride in its restoration," the DOD announcement claimed that the raids closed off "vital links in the North Vietnamese transportation system."[56] Second, the president used the immediate aftermath of these dramatic raids on high-value targets near Hanoi to announce U.S. readiness for "unconditional discussions" in pursuit of a peaceful settlement of the conflict. Lest this be read as evidence of some carefully crafted coercive strategy, it should be noted, as I discuss later, that there is ample reason to question the president's readiness to seek a diplomatic solution at this time.

The announcement was made in the president's speech at Johns Hopkins University in Baltimore on April 7. Circumstances surrounding the speech make it appear that Johnson's endorsement of this element of coercive diplomacy was, at best, either hastily arranged or skillfully shielded from premature disclosure. Although the merit of a future presidential statement on Vietnam policy had been discussed with Johnson's advisers on several occasions, available records and personal anecdotal accounts give no indication that a major policy speech was being planned for early April.[57]

Johnson' speech improved the president's position for a time and lent balance to the administration's increasingly tough military actions. Its public posture now contained classic elements of the carrot-and-stick approach to political bargaining. Not only did the president suggest publicly the administration's willingness to participate in negotiations—even in large groups as provided for by the Geneva formula—but he also offered Hanoi an added incentive in the form of benefits from a "greatly expanded cooperative effort for economic development" in Southeast Asia. In characteristic Lyndon Johnson style, he projected an image of a developed Mekong River basin providing "food and water and power on a scale to dwarf even our own TVA [Tennessee Valley Authority]." He also pledged to ask Congress for a $1 billion appropriation to finance the project as soon as the nations of Southeast Asia agreed to support such a venture; and he named former World Bank president Eugene Black to head a team of special appointees "to inaugurate" U.S. participation in the effort. Johnson's anticipation of having strengthened his hand is shown in his remark to an associate right after the speech that "old Ho can't turn that down."[58]

But the Johns Hopkins speech was not all carrot. In a subtle allusion to the recent heavy bombing mission against high-value targets, the president waved the stick rather prominently as well: "We have no desire to see thousands die in battle—Asians or Americans. We have no desire to devastate that which the people of North Vietnam have built with toil and sacrifice. We will use our power with restraint and with all the wisdom that we can command. But we will use it."

Influence of the Ground War

As we see in the next section, a potential increase in coercive pressure on Hanoi was probably not President Johnson's only motivation for publicly combining the carrot with the stick. In any event, a coercive rationale did not long influence the ROLLING THUNDER target selections. Despite strong urgings for heavier bombardment of the North from Ambassador Taylor, CIA Director John McCone, retiring Treasury Secretary Douglas Dillon, State Department Counselor Walt Rostow, and some congressional Republicans, the White House stayed largely with the target selection and geographical limits that prevailed in March. Except for the April 3 and 4 air strikes, RT missions seldom ventured closer than a hundred miles from Hanoi, and only rail and highway bridges were added to the approved targets. Missions were flown almost daily against these targets and radar facilities, supply depots and logistical targets of opportunity along North Vietnam's highways and rail LOCs leading south.

This LOC target set reflected the rationale that accompanied the JCS multiweek program recommendations. Until March 1965, the JCS and the military commands had consistently advocated a harsher, more intensive bombing campaign as offering more potential for bringing Hanoi directly to heel. In late February and early March, however, as the VC showed signs of consolidating their resources for a major offensive in the central highlands, U.S. military advice on targeting began to shift. Both the JCS and Admiral Ulysses Sharpe, CINCPAC, urged an emphasis on air interdiction of North

Vietnam's LOCs with Communist forces in the South. The concept was given strong endorsement by General Westmoreland in Saigon. Moreover, striking targets that could affect the flow of resources to the VC assumed greater significance in Washington as increasingly more U.S. forces were exposed to hostile actions by the Communists.

This chapter is not the place to recount the series of decisions by which deployment of U.S. ground forces to South Vietnam was gradually increased. Larry Berman, Bill Gibbons, Andrew Krepinevich, and others have provided detailed narratives of these decisions and their effects on the Americanization of the war. It will suffice to recall that by the first deliberate bombing pause in mid-May, the numbers of U.S. forces in Vietnam had increased from approximately 23,300 in early January to 51,700; the increase included nine maneuver battalions. This buildup was getting strong impetus from the president himself; a commitment to send at least another 14,300 U.S. ground forces had already been made.

The buildup of U.S. ground forces may help to explain why the administration, following a high-level strategy meeting in Honolulu on April 20, chose to publicize its endorsement of the interdiction approach to the air war in the North. At the meeting's conclusion, Secretary McNamara, who led the Washington contingent, confirmed publicly that plans were discussed to improve the interdiction of infiltration traffic from North Vietnam. A week later, he told a television audience that the air campaign was "designed to impede [the] infiltration of men and materiel" into South Vietnam, which was making it impossible for the GVN to manage the insurgency internally. He assured his listeners that the strikes were being "carefully limited to transit points, to barracks, to supply depots, to ammunition dumps, to routes of communication, all feeding the infiltration lines" into the south.[59] Even though the administration had not yet openly acknowledged its intentions to commit forces to ground combat, it apparently felt it was necessary to assure the public that everything possible was being done to limit the magnitude of the VC threat.

NEGOTIATIONS: ISSUES AND POLICY

To assess fully the Johnson administration's early attempts at exerting military pressure on North Vietnam, we must look closely at the role it defined for negotiations to play in the coercion process. In particular, we must see how the president's public affirmation at Johns Hopkins of readiness for "unconditional discussions" related to his administration's long-term policy aims. The president and his top advisers realized at least as early as November 1964 that issues of Southeast Asian security would eventually have to be resolved through diplomatic negotiation. The problem was to assure that the negotiations took place at a time and under circumstances that would protect the perceived vital interests of the United States and provide reasonable opportunity for the survival of its regional allies.

The President's Concern with Maintaining Control

The basic element in the administration's view of negotiations in the early spring of 1965 was its recognition that, as yet, it could exert very little leverage over the DRV leadership. Increasing VC strength and the faltering GVN pacification program reflected ominous trends inside South Vietnam, and the series of government crises in Saigon only encouraged Hanoi's expectations of success. Envisioning himself in Ho Chi Minh's shoes, President Johnson saw little reason why the DRV leadership should be willing to bargain. As the president observed to his advisers on March 10, the United States had not yet "done anything" to alter the DRV's favorable situation.[60] The continuous action program had just gotten under way with the first ROLLING THUNDER mission and the landing of two Marine battalions at DaNang. Even later, after the magnitude and tempo of the air campaign had been affirmed by high-level politico-military agreement, Johnson's advisers conceded that it would not be sufficient to change Hanoi's policy calculus.[61] Accordingly, the president was determined to control the nature and pace of events so as to avoid a negotiating situation that would threaten U.S. objectives.

The situation was particularly worrisome because of increasing international pressure to begin negotiations. France, under Charles DeGaulle, had long advocated a Geneva-type settlement to neutralize the states of Indochina. In February 1965, DeGaulle again called for a conference to end the war in Vietnam; and on March 11, the French and Soviet governments agreed jointly to seek a reconvening of the 1954 Geneva Conference for this purpose. On April 1, following a two-day summit meeting of nonaligned countries, seventeen heads of state addressed a public appeal to President Johnson to enter into negotiations without preconditions to find a political solution for the Vietnam conflict. The same appeal was made to the heads of state of the principal 1954 conference signatories and to the DRV, the GVN, Canada, and Poland as well as to the U.N. secretary-general.

Even firm U.S. allies were advocating a resort to negotiations. Shortly after the administration's retaliations for VC strikes against U.S. facilities at Pleiku and Qui Nhon, Canadian Prime Minister Lester Pearson called for a resumption of talks at Geneva. He later incurred President Johnson's personal ire by repeating the appeal, along with proposing a pause in U.S. air strikes, during a speaking engagement in the United States.[62] The United Kingdom likewise favored invocation of the Geneva formula, proposing on February 2 that the conference on Laos be resumed to discuss ways of policing the original truce.[63] However, despite strong opposition from the radical wing of its own party, the Labour government publicly maintained solidarity with the United States throughout the early months of 1965. About as far as Westminster would move publicly was to announce in the House of Commons on April 1 its intention unilaterally to canvass Geneva participants on ideas for "a basis for settlement" of the Vietnam conflict.

Apart from the timing issue, the Johnson administration saw inherent problems in several of the negotiating formulas being advocated by others. Both the 1954 Geneva structure and the "5-plus-2" formula advanced in 1965 by U.N. Secretary-General U Thant depended organizationally on what appeared to be a stacked deck. William Bundy frames the essence of this problem quite clearly:

> The "5-plus-2" grouping in effect set 3 (South Vietnam, the U.S. and a support-ing but reserved UK) against 3 (North Vietnam, China, and the Soviet Union), with a critical seventh member, France, not neutral but in fact heavily commit-ted to a solution that tacitly accepted North Vietnamese control of the South and Chinese hegemony in Southeast Asia. A less tough and wary negotiator than the President might have seen in this [arrangement] the possibility of loaded dice.[64]

The administration also came to recognize problems with using the U.N. Security Council as a forum to sponsor negotiations. The president's initial policy position in the immediate aftermath of Pleiku and Qui Nhon had in-cluded public acknowledgment of his desire to negotiate and to pursue this path through the Security Council, as recommended by Acting Secretary of State George Ball, Adlai Stevenson, and others.[65] Even though this position was quickly discarded and was never made public, the concept was openly advocated by Senators Mike Mansfield and Wayne Morse and by Americans for Democratic Action (ADA). However, even U Thant argued against this idea, pointing out that the constant threat of a Soviet veto would make mean-ingful bargaining impossible in that forum.[66]

Signaling Both Resolve and Restraint

The Johnson administration's public position on negotiations, as well as its actions, was shaped by the perceived need to show both firm resolve and pru-dent restraint. With respect to the Communist capitals, it endeavored to pro-ject a firmness regarding the timing and a preferred forum for negotiations that would belie any eagerness to enter into a diplomatic settlement and pro-vide time in which to heighten the pressure on the DRV. It felt compelled to counter the Chinese line, promulgated in *People's Daily,* that Washington feared the consequences of extended war and sought early negotiations in or-der to inhibit the VC and strengthen the comparative U.S. position.[67]

At the same time, the administration wanted to appear willing to consider eventual negotiations and lend credence to its frequently delivered message that the United States had no designs on Vietnamese territory and no desire to conquer the Marxist state in the north. This approach stemmed from a perception that the most influential determinant of the extent of Soviet support to Hanoi was Moscow's view of U.S. war aims and of the degree of risk to DRV survival indicated by U.S. actions.[68]

A similar dilemma was posed by the imperatives of encouraging the correct perceptions on the part of the GVN. The administration was wary of signaling a readiness to talk with its adversaries that would encourage South Vietnamese fears of U.S. abandonment. One unusual aspect of the situation was the reported tendency in South Vietnam to interpret "negotiate" as moving toward a "neutralist (coalition government) solution as opposed to seeing the war through to a satisfactory conclusion."[69] The administration was also wary, however, of signaling a heavy, long-term commitment to South Vietnam—with the risk of either suggesting an American replacement of the French as permanent colonizers or encouraging the belief that the United States would fully shoulder the burden of providing for South Vietnam's security.

The pressures felt by the Johnson administration regarding the views of other U.S. allies on negotiation were less evenly bifurcated. The Thai government and the Laotian coalition, having an immediate stake in the outcome, shared the GVN's sensitivity to any sign of flagging American will. Most other allies, however, wanted an early move toward negotiation. To them, this would offer assurance that the conflict in Indochina would not expand into a larger regional conflagration involving the Chinese—or a worse scenario. For example, even before Prime Minister Pearson's embarrassing public call for a halt to the U.S. bombing, the Canadian government had privately suggested seeking a mutual agreement to a "cessation of provocations" as a prelude to a Geneva-type conference.[70]

The administration's principal sensitivity respecting its non-Vietnamese allies was toward the British. Soon after President Johnson's decision to undertake continuing action against North Vietnam, Prime Minister Harold Wilson told U.S. Ambassador David Bruce that continual air strikes without parallel movement toward negotiations would have "disturbing repercussions" in the United Kingdom. A month later, following the protest resignation of a subcabinet official and repeated outcries from Labour MPs, Westminster sought U.S. sanction for unilateral British efforts to explore the possibility for diplomatic talks. This prompted some of the president's top advisers to urge relaxing somewhat the administration's currently rigid refusal to express a readiness for talks.[71]

Domestic pressures for a more flexible approach to negotiations were also rising. During a Senate debate on Vietnam policy that began on February 17 and ran for approximately two weeks, voices such as Frank Church's and George McGovern's joined Wayne Morse in advocating a U.S. effort to initiate negotiation of a diplomatic settlement. As he had previously done in private, Senator Mansfield spoke out to urge the president to consider the possibility of using negotiations to neutralize all of Southeast Asia. Most of the senators who participated, both Democrats and Republicans, fully supported the president's policy. However, after the bombing in the North intensified in mid-March, more advocates of negotiations spoke out. Both the *New York Times* and the *Washington Post* ran editorials urging the administration to put more effort into the diplomatic track. On March 18, syndicated columnist Walter Lippmann ridiculed the administration's policy as "all stick and no carrot" and provoked a chorus of news analysts and editors into calling for a diplomatic settlement. A week later, the few Senate critics in the president's party were joined by a group of Republicans who urged that U.S. military actions against North Vietnam be accompanied by a clear statement that "honorable negotiations" were a national goal. Meanwhile, university campuses were becoming frequent sites of "teach-in" sessions that provided public forums for increasingly vocal advocates of a negotiated end to the war in Vietnam.[72]

The Geneva Cochair Initiative

One way the administration tried to combine a tough public image with actual attempts at energizing the diplomatic process was to encourage quiet initiatives by the Geneva cochairs. We recall earlier reference to an administration hope that the Soviets might eventually cooperate to help bring greater stability to Southeast Asia. This hope was shared in staff-level discussions with the British in December 1964, and the United Kingdom's Foreign Office remained alert for signs of Soviet interest.

A hopeful sign was given soon after Premier Kosygin's return from his tour of Asian Communist capitals in early February. As U.S. officials later learned, on the same day that the Soviets allegedly proposed a peace conference on all of Indochina to both Hanoi and Beijing, a Soviet foreign ministry official held an encouraging conversation with the British ambassador. The conversation, including the Soviets' apparent interest in resuming their Geneva cochairs' role along with the British, was reported to Secretary Rusk on February 17. Rusk obtained British agreement to suggest to the Soviets that they ask each of the other Geneva participants to express its views on the current situation in Southeast Asia "so that the co-chairmen could then consider what further action they might usefully take." The United States would then use the cochairs' request as an opportunity to fully state its position in response. The administration would make its reply public, including the point that DRV aggression against South Vietnam and Laos was at the root of the problem and therefore must cease. It would also state its willingness to "give consideration to any proposal the Co-Chairmen might make to deal with … cessation of DRV aggression in all respects."[73]

The Johnson administration hoped for a prompt Soviet response so the U.S. statement could be integrated with its scenario for initiating ROLLING THUNDER operations. As events unfolded, however, neither element of the hoped-for scenario materialized as planned. The bombing campaign sputtered into existence, as we have seen, and the Soviet reply did not come for several weeks. Finally, on March 17, the Soviet government responded officially to the British proposal and made its response public. It asked the United Kingdom to sign a joint declaration condemning U.S. violations of the 1954 Geneva Agreement and urging the United States "to stop immediately the aggressive actions against the Democratic Republic of Vietnam, withdraw all forces and arms from South Vietnam, and give the Vietnamese people a chance to decide their destiny themselves."[74]

Elements of the U.S. Bargaining Position

Even though the cochairs' initiative did not evolve as the Johnson administration had hoped, it enabled the administration to maintain a tough public posture toward negotiations and buy valuable time in which to strengthen its bargaining hand. With the Geneva machinery effectively locked up and the Communist states going public with their extreme and apparently intractable demands for preconditions, the administration managed to deflect for a time the clamor for a negotiated solution. In the meantime, it needed new measures to contain the growing pressures because, by its own analysis, the administration could not expect either its action or the potential dynamics of the growing Sino-Soviet tensions to bring about a DRV readiness to bargain on acceptable terms until midsummer at the earliest.[75]

It is from this perspective that President Johnson's brief movement toward a stronger form of coercive diplomacy must be evaluated. Clearly, his decision to announce at Johns Hopkins his administration's readiness for unconditional discussions was motivated by several factors. Not the least of these was his desire to quiet the building storm over negotiations. So sensitive was the president to his critics on this score that he took pains to give private previews of his Johns Hopkins speech to Walter Lippmann and to leaders of the ADA. The latter group, which was in Washington for its national convention, requested a meeting specifically to protest the bombing policy. According to some accounts, Johnson read the group portions of his intended speech, stressing in particular his desire to negotiate and his proposal for regional development along the Mekong River basin.[76] Other principal targets of the new policy statement were the seventeen nonaligned nations, whose appeal had been received a few days before. President Johnson's speech began with a direct reference to their appeal, and, on the day following his Baltimore appearance, a reply in words similar to the text of his speech was sent to each of these governments and to U.N. Secretary-General U Thant.[77]

Administration estimates that it could both indicate readiness to talk unconditionally and hold off actual negotiations for a while longer were proven correct when the DRV rejected the seventeen-nation appeal outright. This was fortunate because the Johnson administration had not yet formulated a firm negotiating strategy. As key elements of what became the president's Johns Hopkins speech were being assembled, his advisers still did not agree on whether to insist merely that Hanoi halt its infiltration of men and materiel into South Vietnam or to further insist on a reduction of VC activity in exchange for stopping the bombing.[78] The closest the administration came to a specific demand was Secretary Rusk's oft-repeated public statement that "the missing piece" for securing arrangements to bring hostilities to an end was Hanoi's willingness "to stop doing what it is doing to its neighbors."

Of course to have developed a firm strategy for negotiations meant working out an agreed-upon approach with the GVN. In March 1965, this kind of initiative risked stirring up corridor talk throughout a government still regarded by American observers as shaky about a quick U.S. exit. Indeed, immediately after the Johns Hopkins speech, unnamed GVN officials told reporters that President Johnson's endorsement of unconditional discussions suggested to some of them that Washington was ready to abandon its demand that North Vietnam indicate its readiness to stop support of the war before negotiations could take place.[79] Administration concern for South Vietnamese sensitivities on the subject of negotiation was reflected in its careful phrasing of the reply to the nonaligned nations. It specified U.S. willingness, in a variety of settings, to pursue "discussion or negotiation with the governments concerned," thereby ruling out talks with the National Liberation Front. Nevertheless, the president recognized that a negotiating strategy was needed and shortly before his speech instructed Ambassador Taylor to explore the different options with Prime Minister Phan Huy Quat.[80]

Efforts by the U.S. mission in Saigon to work out an acceptable negotiating approach with the GVN were soon engulfed in parallel diplomatic efforts to prepare for the arrival of U.S. and "third-country" ground troops. A concept advanced earlier by some officials and held strongly by the president had now become a firm administration conviction: that regardless of the negotiating demands finally determined, the U.S.-GVN bargaining position would be improved by strengthening the U.S. presence on the ground. As McGeorge Bundy wrote in preparation for a Tuesday lunch meeting, "This U.S. ground presence is likely to reinforce both pacification efforts and Southern morale, while discouraging the VC from their current expectation of early victory."[81] Later, following the high-level strategy session in Honolulu, Secretary McNamara informed the president that all of the participants agreed that "a settlement will come as much or more from VC failure in the South as from DRV pain in the North, and that it will take more than six months, perhaps a year or two, to demonstrate VC failure in the South." In consequence, the agreed-upon strategy for a U.S.-GVN victory was "to break the will of the DRV/VC by denying *them* victory."[82]

Real bargaining and a posture to support it were still goals for the future. In the meantime, the administration would strengthen its capabilities to wage war in the South and continue its measured use of air strikes in Laos and the North. At Honolulu, Ambassador Taylor stated the view, apparently shared by the other participants, that "it is important not to 'kill the hostage' by destroying the North Vietnamese assets inside the [Hanoi-Haiphong target area]." A still-available threat to damage such high-value targets was considered an important bargaining counter at such time as real negotiations might begin—at least six months into the future.

CONCLUSIONS

President Johnson's display of a stronger variant of coercive diplomacy was short-lived. He had chosen the moment when the pressures from air strikes in the North had reached a temporary crescendo to offer a substantial economic carrot to the DRV and to make known the U.S. willingness to talk. Of course, the announcement served other presidential purposes as well, as we have seen. For example, it would be easier to build and hold public support for an extended ground force commitment if the administration were on record as seeking a reasonable political settlement. Yet, some of the basic ingredients of a coercive strategy were now in place. Only the situation in the South was clearly incompatible with a coercive objective, and the buildup of ground combat forces was still piecemeal and was a long way from presenting a threat to the Communists. Administration officials fully realized that these circumstances gave Hanoi little reason to alter its aggressive policy toward the GVN.

Surely, under these circumstances, an administration fully intent on eroding Hanoi's will to resist would have increased the intensity of its pressures against the DRV and made more explicit its threats of greater damage yet to come. Yet, as we have seen, the ROLLING THUNDER campaign became less menacing as April unfolded, and the administration's public statements followed suit. The interpretation the administration encouraged reporters to make during background interviews emphasized measured restraint and careful limitation of targets within specified infiltration-related categories. Secretary McNamara and others continued for the most part to follow the earlier policy guidance that cautioned against making statements about the character of future bombing actions except to stress their measured nature and their relatedness to Hanoi's aggression.[83]

The administration avoided stronger statements and more threatening actions in deference to a number of serious constraints. Several of these continued to affect U.S. conduct of the war in Southeast Asia—even well into the

Nixon years.[84] First, the White House was determined to avoid widening the war. This imperative was manifest in the Johnson administration's concerns over possibly drawing Chinese aircraft into the fight and later provoking intervention by Chinese ground forces. A related constraint was its desire to limit alienation of the Soviet government—certainly to avoid provoking the Kremlin into more direct support of the DRV's war effort and, it was hoped, to convince the Soviets to help bring about a negotiated settlement.

However, meaningful negotiation to end the conflict could only occur after the U.S.-GVN bargaining position had been strengthened, so the Johnson administration was also constrained to avoid actions and statements that could provoke greater pressures for premature diplomatic initiatives. In this respect, it was sensitive to both domestic political opinion and the attitudes of foreign governments, particularly those governments whose cooperation was important for the implementation of U.S. policy.

Both the GVN and the United Kingdom represented special cases with respect to this constraint. South Vietnamese performance was essential to successful prosecution of the pacification effort against the VC. GVN confidence and solidarity, which required time to nurture, were essential to the development of an effective joint negotiating stance. By contrast, the United Kingdom was leaning toward a policy of early negotiations; but as cochair of the Geneva Accords, Westminster's diplomatic activity in comfortable conjunction with Washington's timetable was an important element in the Johnson strategy.

Finally, the administration apparently was also constrained by its tacit assumptions concerning the ways the conflict with North Vietnam might be brought to an early end: Once the DRV leaders had been shown that the ground battle inside South Vietnam had no chance of bringing victory, they would become more conscious of the potential costs of continuing the war. At that point, later in the year, the threat of increased damage to high-value targets from continued air attack might prompt serious thoughts in Hanoi about seeking a true negotiation—particularly if encouraged by its Soviet benefactors. Apparently anticipating this kind of scenario, administration officials accepted the view that the United States should avoid early destruction of high-value targets in North Vietnam so as to preserve something with which to threaten Hanoi in subsequent attempts at bargaining.

At best, therefore, the Johnson administration had implemented a weaker variant of coercive strategy. It was content to approach the target system that might have had coercive payoff—the high-value targets in the Hanoi-Haiphong industrial area—at a somewhat leisurely pace.[85] Thus, in neither its public statements nor its actual military operations did the administration explicitly threaten the Communist side with increasing punishment or eventual damage to the DRV's urban-industrial resources if Hanoi did not comply with its demands. Neither did it attempt to convey a sense of urgency by indicating a time period within which Hanoi's compliance was expected. Rather, the administration readily acknowledged, beginning in April 1965, that its objectives probably could not be achieved until after the bombing had continued for a considerable period of time, and other aspects of its public behavior continued to project an image more akin to crisis management than to coercive intent.

BIBLIOGRAPHICAL NOTE

This chapter benefits greatly from the careful research and more general accounts of others that have appeared since the first publication (1971) of Alexander L. George, David Hall, and William E. Simons, *The Limits of Coercive Diplomacy* (Boston: Little, Brown). Among these works are Larry Berman's *Planning a Tragedy: The Americanization of the War in Vietnam* (New York: W. W. Norton and Co., 1982); Leslie Gelb and Richard Betts's *The Irony of Vietnam: The System Worked* (Washington, D.C.: Brookings, 1979); William Gibbons's multivolume *The U.S. Government and the Vietnam War* (Princeton: Princeton University Press, 1989); and of course *The Pentagon Papers, Senator Gravel Edition: The Defense Department History of U.S. Decision-Making on Vietnam, Vol. 3* (Boston: Beacon Press, 1971). The latter work, augmented by the personal recollections of former officials, provides the basic source for the origins of the Johnson administration's concept for increasing military pressures on North Vietnam. Particularly valuable for adding perspective and occasionally correcting the *Pentagon Papers* account is the unpublished manuscript of William Bundy, former assistant secretary of state for Far Eastern affairs, held by the Lyndon B. Johnson (LBJ) Library in Austin, Texas.

My account of President Johnson's decisions to take military action and of the implementation of his policies in early 1965 is based primarily on original source documents in the files of the LBJ Library. Most of these were cables or memoranda that have been declassified for public use. These have been supplemented through research interviews and correspondence with former Johnson administration officials McGeorge Bundy, William Bundy, and Dean Rusk and by a series of oral history transcripts of LBJ Library interviews with other former officials, military commanders, and journalists. Background material was gleaned from contemporary newspaper accounts.

I wish also to acknowledge several individuals whose contributions to this effort deserve special note. Larry Berman, who read an earlier version, urged me to explore the then-recently opened Vietnam holdings of the LBJ Library. David Humphrey, Vietnam archivist at the library, has been immensely helpful in directing me to relevant materials. Fred Greenstein made available his document collection on the Johnson presidency at Princeton University. RAND colleague Steve Hosmer provided valuable insights on the subject in our many conversations on Vietnam policy and the use of force in crises. Finally, I am indebted particularly to Alex George whose generous advice and continuing encouragement largely enabled the underlying research to go forward.

NOTES

1. Details regarding the origins and implementation of these covert operations, designated 34A, are in *The Pentagon Papers, Senator Gravel Edition: The Defense Department History of U.S. Decision-Making on Vietnam, Vol. 3* (Boston: Beacon Press, 1971), pp. 150–151. Uncopyrighted, this edition is hereinafter referred to as *Gravel, Vol. 3.*

2. In National Security Action Memorandum (NSAM) 288, March 17, 1964. NSAM 288 is reproduced in full in ibid., pp. 499–510 (Doc 158).

3. The recommendations of the president's principal advisers, September 8, 1964, are reproduced in both *Gravel, Vol. 3,* pp. 561–562, and William Conrad Gibbons, *The U.S. Government and the Vietnam War, Part 2: 1961–1964* (Princeton: Princeton University Press, 1986), pp. 343–350; the former is apparently an earlier and slightly longer version. Compare these with the text of NSAM 314, September 10, 1964, approved by President Johnson on September 9. NSAM 314 is reproduced in full in *Gravel, Vol. 3,* pp. 565–566 (Doc 195).

4. For a detailed description and reasonably accurate analysis of the interagency study group's efforts, see *Gravel, Vol. 3,* pp. 192–195.

5. See note 3 for the September decisions. The principal advisers' recommended December position paper is reproduced in full in *Gravel, Vol. 3,* pp. 677–683 (Doc 246). Changes made in the draft for presentation to the president are speculated upon in the text, p. 246. In an unpublished manuscript, former Assistant Secretary of State William Bundy confirms several of these changes; see, in particular, "Part I: The Decisions of 1961–65," pp. 18-31, 18-32, and 19-7, Papers of William P. Bundy, Box 1, Lyndon B. Johnson Library (hereinafter LBJL). The basis for Ambassador Taylor's contributions to the policy deliberations is contained in his briefing text, "The Current Situation in South Vietnam—November 1964," November 17, 1964, reproduced in full in *Gravel, Vol. 3,* pp. 666–673 (Doc 242). The importance of this text is highlighted in the Bundy manuscript: "The Taylor memorandum was not inconsistent in any significant respect with the laborious work of the Working Group. In effect, the two reinforced each other, with the Taylor paper more personal and direct, and far more thorough on the immediate political need in Saigon. It went at once to the president in Texas, and perhaps more than any of the Washington papers set the basis for the president's decisions of December 1st and 3rd" (p. 19-5).

6. I am indebted to William Bundy for pointing out the significance of this aspect of the president's decisions of December 1964, particularly compared with the policy decisions of the previous September, in the Bundy manuscript, p. 19-17.

7. *Gravel, Vol. 3,* pp. 242, 246. See also paragraph 5 of William Bundy's "Memorandum of Meeting on Southeast Asia," November 17, 1965, reproduced in full in *Gravel, Vol. 3,* pp. 674–676 (Doc 244). Although it was not presented as a recommendation to the president at the end of November, deliberate use of air strikes against the North as a pulmotor to encourage the GVN to pull itself together was discussed favorably by Ambassador Taylor and the other principal advisers.

8. January 1, 1965, was first proposed as a contingency readiness date for actions against North Vietnam by Ambassador Taylor. See the secretary of state message in

ibid. as Document 175. A summation of the views of different advisers on the issue of negotiations, as of the autumn of 1964, is in ibid., pp. 202–206.

9. Dean Rusk explained to interviewer Paige Mulhollan that "we were trying to do a kind of police job to fend off this aggression against South Vietnam but to do it calmly and, in effect, in cold blood. Our objective was peace. It was not to let the situation go down the chute … into larger war." He said that the reason the administration deliberately avoided stirring up a war psychology in the United States was "because there's too much power in the world to let the American people become too mad. Public opinion could get out of hand." See Dean Rusk Oral History Interview, 7/28/69, by Paige E. Mulhollan, Tape 1, p. 42, LBJL. Secretary Rusk confirmed this administration judgment in an interview with the author on November 16, 1988.

10. The International Commission for Supervision and Control in Laos (ICC) was established by the 1954 Geneva Accords. Neutral India was named chair; Canada and Poland were the other members. None of these countries was among the nine delegations participating in the original Geneva Conference. However, all three ICC members were full participants in the fourteen-nation Geneva Conference on Laos in 1962.

11. See the press conference held by Secretary of State Dean Rusk on December 23, 1964, in Department of State *Bulletin,* January 18, 1965, pp. 38–39; and the speech in Washington, Missouri, by Assistant Secretary of State William Bundy on January 23, 1965, in Department of State *Bulletin,* February 8, 1965, p. 171.

12. See the account by Tad Szulc in the *New York Times,* January 4, 1965. For telling evidence of the consensus among the president's top advisers on likely consequences of the loss of South Vietnam to Communist control, see William Bundy's "Memorandum of Executive Committee Meeting, November 24 1964: Issues Raised by Papers on Southeast Asia," November 25, 1964, Meeting Notes File, Box 1, National Security File (NSF), LBJL. The "draft paper" referred to in the memorandum is found in *Gravel, Vol. 3,* pp. 656–666 (Doc 241). For a comprehensive argument supporting the principal advisers' views, see William Bundy's memo to Secretary Rusk, "Notes on the South Vietnamese Situation and Alternatives," January 6, 1965, *Gravel, Vol. 3,* p. 685 (Doc 248).

13. Author's interview with Dean Rusk, November 16, 1988.

14. Note, McGeorge Bundy to President Johnson, December 23, 1964, "McGeorge Bundy Memoranda to the President, Vol. 7," Memos for the President, Box 2, NSF, LBJL.

15. See Jack Raymond, *New York Times,* December 17, 1964; Tad Szulc, *New York Times,* January 5 and 7, 1965; *Washington Post,* January 4 and 18, 1965. An Associated Press poll of eighty-three senators on January 6, 1965, showed the following split: Ten favored immediate negotiations, and three others urged immediate withdrawal of U.S. advisers and military aid; eight favored greater U.S. military action against North Vietnam; thirty-one suggested negotiating a settlement—but not until the U.S.-GVN bargaining position had been improved; eleven stated that they did not know what should be done beyond helping to strengthen the GVN; and twenty others declined to comment.

16. "A Conversation with Dean Rusk" (transcript of an NBC television interview, January 3, 1965), Department of State *Bulletin* 52, no. 1334, January 18, 1965, pp. 63–65.

17. McGeorge Bundy's handwritten notes of White House meeting, January 6, 1965, Papers of McGeorge Bundy, Box 1, LBJL. President Johnson's comment to Taylor in CAP 64375, December 30, 1964, "Deployment of Major U.S. Forces to Vietnam, Vol. 1, Tabs 1–10," NSC Histories, NSF, LBJL (hereinafter referred to as "Deployment, Vol. no., Tabs no.").

18. President Johnson to Taylor, Department Telegram (DEPTEL) 1419, January 7, 1965, "Vietnam NODIS, 1/65-2/65," Country File, Box 45–46, NSF, LBJL.

19. Taylor to President Johnson, Embassy Telegram (EMBTEL) (Saigon) 2058, January 6, 1965, "Vietnam NODIS-LOR [No Distribution Letter of Response]," Country File, NSF, LBJL.

20. President Johnson memorandum to McNamara, January 7, 1965, "Vietnam Memos, Vol. 25," Country File, NSF, LBJL. In this memorandum, Johnson confided to McNamara, "I expect you and Max are right in opposing larger U.S. forces," but he personally excised a similar concession from an early draft of his January 7 reply to Taylor. He stressed to his ambassador the importance he placed on "use of U.S. military command judgment and energy" to prevent repetition of the errors committed by the South Vietnamese at Binh Gia and to achieve "a few solid military victories" on the ground.

21. Secret memorandum of conversation, dated December 30, 1964, paraphrased in *Gravel, Vol. 3*, p. 266. In his November 1988 interview with the author, Secretary Rusk recalled few details of his December 1964 conversations with Gromyko, but he stated that throughout the period, U.S. representatives consistently urged the Soviet government to exercise its role as Geneva cochair. In particular, the Soviets were urged to help enforce the agreements already in existence.

22. See Douglass Cater's memorandum to President Johnson, "The View from the Kremlin," December 28, 1964, Aides File, LBJL. The memo was prepared as "talking points you may wish to use in any backgrounder comparing your foreign policy problems … with those of the Soviet leadership."

23. William Bundy attributes this way of thinking to Ambassador Foy Kohler (in Moscow) and Ambassador-at-Large Llewellyn Thompson (in Washington), whom he describes as "the two senior men on whom Rusk and the president overwhelmingly relied for knowledge and 'feel' of the Soviet Union." Bundy ms., pp. 21-7, 21-8.

24. See Taylor to Rusk, EMBTEL (Saigon) 2010, December 31, 1964, "Vietnam, Vol. 25," and Taylor to President Johnson, EMBTEL (Saigon) 2052, 2055, 2056, 2057, 2058, January 6, 1965, "Vietnam NODIS 1/65-2/65," all in Country File, NSF, LBJL.

25. In DEPTEL 1419.

26. U. Alexis Johnson to Rusk, EMBTEL (Saigon) 2295, January 26, 1965, "Vietnam, Vol. 26," and Taylor to President Johnson, EMBTEL (Saigon) 2322, January 27, 1965, "Vietnam NODIS-LOR, Vol. 1(A) 1/65-3/65," both in Country File, NSF, LBJL.

27. McGeorge Bundy memorandum to President Johnson, "Re Basic Policy in Vietnam," January 27, 1965, "McGeorge Bundy—Memos to the President, Vol. 8," NSF, LBJL. This memorandum was given to the president before a private discussion scheduled with Bundy and McNamara for 11:30 A.M. that day.

28. McGeorge Bundy's handwritten notes of White House meeting, 4:30 P.M., January 27, 1965, Papers of McGeorge Bundy, Box 1; Rusk to Taylor, DEPTEL 1548, January 27, 1965, "Vietnam NODIS 1/65-2/65," Country File, NSF; OJCS (J-3) to

CINCPAC, JCS 004213, January 27, 1965, "Vietnam Cables, Vol. 26," Country File, NSF; President Johnson to Taylor, DEPTEL 1549, January 27, 1965, "Vietnam NODIS 1/65-2/65," Country File, NSF; McGeorge Bundy to Taylor, DEPTEL 1559, January 28, 1965, "Deployment, Vol. 1, Tabs 11–41," NSC Histories, NSF; Ball to Taylor, DEPTEL 1566, January 29, 1965, "Vietnam-NODIS 1/65-2/65," NSF; all in LBJL.

29. McGeorge Bundy's handwritten notes, January 27, 1965.

30. *Gravel, Vol. 3,* pp. 298–299. The initial DESOTO patrol was at first rescheduled for February 7, 1965, in order not to coincide with TET, the annual Vietnamese holiday. Later, it was cancelled.

31. DEPTEL 1549 (to Saigon), January 27, 1965. For Bundy's specific areas of inquiry during the visit, see McGeorge Bundy to Taylor, DEPTEL 1570, January 30, 1965, "Deployment, Vol. 1, Tabs 11–41," NSC Histories; Taylor to Bundy, EMBTEL (Saigon) 2365, February 1, "NSC Meetings, Vol. 3, Tab 26," NSC Meetings File; Bundy to Taylor, draft of DEPTEL 1581, February 1, 1965, "NSC Meetings, Vol. 3, Tab 26," NSC Meetings File; all from NSF, LBJL.

32. White House press release, February 11, 1965, reproduced in Department of State *Bulletin,* March 1, 1965, p. 290. See also accounts by Charles Mohr, *New York Times;* Murrey Marder, *Washington Post;* John Norris, *Washington Post;* William Beecher, *Wall Street Journal,* all February 12, 1965.

33. McGeorge Bundy memorandum to President Johnson, "The Situation in South Vietnam," February 7, 1965, quoted in part in *Gravel, Vol. 3,* pp. 309–311. Slightly different portions are quoted in Larry Berman, *Planning a Tragedy: The Americanization of the War in Vietnam* (New York: W. W. Norton & Co., 1982), pp. 40–41, 43–44. *Gravel* also contains Annex A to Bundy's memorandum, "A Policy of Sustained Reprisal," written primarily by Assistant Secretary of Defense John McNaughton, who accompanied Bundy and several others to Saigon in early February 1965.

34. "Summary Notes of 547th NSC Meeting, February 8, 1965, 10:30 A.M."; "Partial record of … meeting with the president by a group which met before NSC meeting," February 8, 1965, NSC Meetings File, NSF, LBJL. This decision apparently was made in the earlier meeting because the president conveyed his intent to the congressional leaders *before* discussion in the NSC meeting moved beyond the Pleiku reprisal actions.

35. President Johnson to Taylor, DEPTEL 1653, February 8, 1965, "Vietnam NODIS, Vol. 1(A)," Country File, NSF, LBJL.

36. The "sustained reprisal" concept is in McGeorge Bundy to President Johnson, "Annex A: A Policy of Sustained Reprisal," February 7, 1965, *Gravel, Vol. 3,* pp. 687–691 (Doc 250). "Graduated reprisal" is described in Taylor to secretary of state, EMBTEL (Saigon) 2445, February 9, 1965, "Vietnam Policy (cables)," Country File, and Taylor to secretary of state, EMBTEL (Saigon) 2530, February 12, 1965, "Deployment, Vol. 1, Tabs 42–60," NSC Histories; both in NSF, LBJL. The JCS concept is in "Courses of Action, Southeast Asia—First 8 Weeks," JCSM 100-65, February 11, 1965. This recommended program is quoted in part and described in *Gravel, Vol. 3,* pp. 318–320.

37. Rusk to Taylor, DEPTEL 1718, February 13, 1965, *Gravel, Vol. 3,* pp. 321–322. Ball memorandum to President Johnson, "Vietnam," February 13, 1965, "De-

ployment, Vol. 1, Tabs 42–60," NSC Histories, NSF, LBJL. At the time of his February 13 memo, Ball was acting secretary of state and, in Rusk's absence, served as policy coordinator and occasional spokesperson for the president's principal advisers. This memo was not forwarded as the minority view of a "devil's advocate," as has often been alleged.

38. Rusk to Ambassador Graham Martin, DEPTEL 1268 (to Bangkok) (circular message to nine East Asian embassies), in *Gravel, Vol. 3,* p. 324.

39. Author's interview with McGeorge Bundy, October 11, 1988. President Johnson's former assistant for national security affairs commented that this feature of Johnson's decision-making style and the fact that the president never gave explanations for deciding *not* to do something caused considerable concern among his staff. White House staff members sometimes felt they needed more policy guidance from the president.

40. Contrast these immediate purposes for the early U.S. air effort against North Vietnam with what author Robert Pape alleges erroneously to be a "broad consensus" of coercive intent. From disparate sources, some taken out of context, Pape describes a "strategy" (called "Lenient Schelling") and asserts that it "dominated" the conduct of President Johnson's air war against the North through the spring and summer of 1965. See Robert A. Pape, Jr., "Coercive Air Power in the Vietnam War," *International Security* 15, no. 2 (Fall 1990): 113–118.

41. McGeorge Bundy to President Johnson, "Vietnam Decisions," February 16, 1965, "McGeorge Bundy—Memos to the President, Vol. 8," Memoranda to the President, NSF, LBJL. William Bundy relates that Llewellyn Thompson in the State Department and Ambassador Kohler from Moscow were particularly active during February 1965 in advising against actions or statements about Vietnam that would put the Kremlin on the spot and force its hand; Bundy ms., pp. 22B-21, 22B-27.

42. DEPTEL 1718, February 13, 1965. It is important to note that this cable is basically an instruction as to what Ambassador Taylor was authorized to say confidentially to the South Vietnamese head of state. It was not a statement of U.S. policy for internal guidance or external exploitation.

43. CIA, "Communist Reactions to Possible U.S. Actions," Special National Intelligence Estimates (SNIE) 10-3-65, February 11, 1965, "Vietnam Memos, Vol. 28," Country File; Ball to President Johnson, February 13, 1965; "Partial record of ... meeting with the President," February 8, 1965 (see note 34), all in NSF, LBJL.

44. "Secretary Rusk's News Conference of February 25," Department of State *Bulletin* 52, no. 1342, March 15, 1965, pp. 362–371.

45. Rusk to Taylor, DEPTEL 1845, February 27, 1965, "Vietnam, Vol. 29," Country File, NSF, LBJL. The exchange with the Chinese in Warsaw was confirmed by Secretary Rusk at his press conference on February 25, and the details of that exchange are in *Gravel, Vol. 3,* p. 330. For reports of North Vietnamese reactions to the Seaborn mission, see Taylor to Rusk, DEPTELS 2888 and 2889, March 8, 1965, "Deployment, Vol. 2, Tabs 88–119," NSC Histories, NSF, LBJL.

46. Cooper memo to McGeorge Bundy, "Vietnam," March 1, 1965, "Vietnam Memos, Vol. 30," Country File, NSF, LBJL. Important background is provided in *Gravel, Vol. 3,* pp. 337, 442–443.

47. Reported in William Conrad Gibbons, *The U.S. Government and the Vietnam War, Part 3, January–July 1965* (Princeton: Princeton University Press, 1989), p.

149. See also David Halberstam's account in *The Best and the Brightest* (New York: Fawcett Crest, 1972), pp. 683–684. On the day before his breakfast meeting with General Johnson, the president was particularly incensed by a *New York Times* article that was seemingly based on leaks from authoritative U.S. and GVN sources in Saigon. The article suggested that the White House had decided to rely on a limited air war against North Vietnam as its primary means "to bring about a negotiated settlement ... on honorable terms" to end "the Vietnam problem." See Robert Kleiman, *New York Times*, March 1, 1965.

48. EMBTEL (Saigon) 2888, March 8, 1965.

49. Martin Luther King's large-scale voting rights demonstration in Selma, Alabama, met with violent repression from state and local police on March 7, 1965; President Johnson sent personal representatives to intercede and for several days kept close track of the situation through the attorney general's office. He held important meetings with the congressional leadership on the administration's education bill on March 9 and later that day hosted a reception for many guests who attended the signing of the bill on aid to Appalachia.

50. McGeorge Bundy's handwritten notes of the Tuesday lunch meeting, March 9, 1965, Papers of McGeorge Bundy, LBJL. This meeting marked the first resumption of the president's "regular" Tuesday lunch with his key national security advisers since September 1964. See David C. Humphrey, "Tuesday Lunch at the Johnson White House: A Preliminary Assessment," *Diplomatic History* (Winter 1984): 86.

51. McGeorge Bundy's handwritten notes of the Camp David meeting, March 10, 1965, Papers of McGeorge Bundy, LBJL. See also Bundy's memo to President Johnson, March 12, 1965, "McGeorge Bundy—Memos to the President, Vol. 9," Memoranda to the President, NSF, LBJL.

52. See General Harold K. Johnson memo to McNamara, Wheeler, and the other Joint Chiefs, with enclosure, "Report on Survey of the Military Situation in Vietnam," March 14, 1965, "Vietnam—General Johnson Report," Country File, NSF, LBJL. See also the accounts by John Norris, *Washington Post*, March 16, 1965, and Jack Raymond, *New York Times*, March 17, 1965.

53. Rusk to Taylor, DEPTEL 2000, March 16, 1965, reproduced in full in *Gravel, Vol. 3*, pp. 339–340. The description of the planning for ROLLING THUNDER air strikes in this and the following paragraph differs slightly from that given by Mark Clodfelter in *The Limits of Airpower: The American Bombing of North Vietnam* (New York: Free Press, 1989), pp. 85–87. Although based on excellent sources, Clodfelter's description of the White House role in target selection uses some of these sources without consistent regard for their historical time sequence.

54. "Luncheons with the President," Files of McGeorge Bundy, NSF, LBJL. See also Humphrey, "Tuesday Lunch," p. 86. One of the suggested agenda items for the luncheon held on March 30 was the JCS proposal for a "12-week program" of ROLLING THUNDER missions. However, even the recommendation to implement only three weeks of the program was neither approved nor followed as a multiweek plan. See *Gravel, Vol. 3*, pp. 342–344.

55. NSAM 328, April 6, 1965, para. 9, National Security Action Memorandums, NSF, LBJL. This document is also reproduced in full in *Gravel, Vol. 3*, pp. 702–703 (Doc 254).

56. Reported by Tad Szulc, *New York Times*, April 5, 1965.

57. William Bundy, whose office would normally have given substantial input, writes that he left Washington on April 3 completely unaware that the president had such a speech in mind. Johns Hopkins President Milton Eisenhower told his student audience on the night of April 5 that both he and McGeorge Bundy had just learned, a few minutes before the latter's scheduled address that evening, of President Johnson's agreement to speak there on April 7. See "Bundy Speech Raps Foes of Viet Policy," *Baltimore Sun,* April 6, 1965. See also the William Bundy ms., p. 23-25.

58. Observed by Bill Moyers and reported in John Burke and Fred Greenstein, *How Presidents Test Reality: Decisions on Vietnam, 1954 and 1965* (New York: Russell Sage Foundation, 1989), p. 188. For details of the president's speech, see Lyndon B. Johnson, "Pattern for Peace in Southeast Asia," delivered at Johns Hopkins University, Baltimore, Maryland, April 7, 1965, reprinted in Department of State *Bulletin,* April 16, 1965, pp. 608, 609.

59. "Mr. McNamara's News Conference," April 26, 1965, reprinted in Department of State *Bulletin,* May 17, 1965, pp. 750–751. The secretary's comments following the Honolulu Conference were reported in the *Washington Post,* April 21, 1965.

60. McGeorge Bundy's handwritten notes, March 10, 1965. Dean Rusk told me that President Johnson often tried to place himself in Ho Chi Minh's shoes to speculate on how the DRV leader might react to the combination of current circumstances inside South Vietnam, U.S. actions in the North and in Laos, and the evidence of U.S. intent to sustain its support of South Vietnamese independence.

61. McNamara to President Johnson, April 21, 1965, reproduced in full in *Gravel, Vol. 3,* pp. 705–706 (Doc 256); McNaughton to McNamara et al., "Minutes of April 20, 1965, Honolulu Meeting," April 23, 1965, "John McNaughton Files," Papers of Paul C. Warnke, LBJL.

62. Pearson's remarks were made in Philadelphia just a few days before the president's speech at Johns Hopkins and were reported by William Weart, *New York Times,* April 3, 1965. Johnson delivered his angry reprimand at Camp David, to which Pearson had been invited for lunch on his way back to Ottawa. Also, see Cabell Phillips, *New York Times,* April 4, 1965; Rowland Evans and Robert Novak, *Lyndon B. Johnson: The Exercise of Power* (New York: New American Library, 1966), p. 546.

63. Reported by Anthony Lewis, *New York Times,* April 2, 1965.

64. William Bundy ms., p. 22B-17.

65. DEPTEL 1718 (to Saigon), February 13, 1965; Ball to President Johnson, February 13, 1965; Stevenson's advocacy, on February 11, 1965, is described in Gibbons, *U.S. Government and the Vietnam War, Part 3,* p. 98.

66. Gibbons, *U.S. Government and the Vietnam War, Part 3,* p. 99; William Bundy ms., p. 22B-16.

67. This view from Beijing is reported in a Department of State Intelligence Note, "Tough Chinese Communist Posture on Vietnam," February 19, 1965, p. 2, "Vietnam Memos, Vol. 28," Country File, NSF, LBJL.

68. See Kohler to Rusk, EMBTEL (Moscow) 2569, March 2, 1965, "Vietnam NODIS, Vol. 1(A)," Country File, NSF, LBJL.

69. Taylor to Rusk, EMBTEL (Saigon) 2762, February 26, 1965, "Vietnam Memos, Vol. 29." The dangers of confirming popular suspicions of a U.S. decision to pull out of the conflict were frequently commented on by the U.S. embassies in Southeast Asia. See also EMBTEL (Bangkok) 1129, February 14, 1965, "Vietnam Pol-

icy—Cables," Box 190, and EMBTEL (Saigon) 2588, February 15, 1965, "Vietnam NODIS, Vol. 1(A)," all in Country File, NSF, LBJL.

70. Rusk to American Embassy Seoul, DEPTEL 771 (circular cable to eight other East Asian embassies), February 20, 1965, "Vietnam NODIS/LOR, Vol. 1(B)," Country File, NSF, LBJL.

71. McGeorge Bundy to President Johnson, March 6, 1965, "Deployment, Vol. 2, Tabs 88–119," NSC Histories, NSF, LBJL. For Prime Minister Wilson's comments, see McGeorge Bundy to President Johnson, "Wilson's Talk with Bruce Today," February 17, 1965, "Vietnam Memos, Vol. 28," Country File, NSF, LBJL.

72. Republican senators' criticism was reported in the *Washington Post,* March 26, 1965. Walter Lippmann's policy attacks started in his column in the *New York Herald Tribune* and elsewhere; his influence on other critics and a former ambassador's proposed elements for a successful settlement were discussed in *Newsweek,* March 29, 1965.

73. Rusk to Bruce, DEPTEL 5222 (to London), February 18, 1965, "Vietnam NODIS/LOR, Vol. 1(B)," Country File, NSF, LBJL. A description of the cochairs' initiative is contained in *Gravel, Vol. 3,* pp. 325–330, but the date of Rusk's initial involvement is printed erroneously as February 7.

74. *New York Times,* March 18, 1965.

75. McGeorge Bundy memorandum, "Key Elements for Discussion, Thursday, April 1, at 5:30 PM," April 1, 1965, "McGeorge Bundy—Memos to the President, Vol. 9," Memoranda to the President, NSF, LBJL.

76. See Evans and Novak, *Lyndon B. Johnson,* pp. 541–542; Halberstam, *Best and Brightest,* pp. 694–695. Cryptic handwritten notes of the president's meeting with the ADA leaders indicate some discussion of the problems of initiating negotiations and mention topics such as development and encouraging harvests, but they include no reference to a speech. Papers of McGeorge Bundy, Box 1, LBJL. The president's daily diary for April 1–7, 1965, does not record his meeting with Walter Lippmann.

77. The text of the U.S. reply to the seventeen nonaligned nations is in Department of State *Bulletin,* April 26, 1965, pp. 610–611.

78. Rusk to Taylor, DEPTEL 2067, March 23, 1965; McGeorge Bundy, "Memorandum for Discussion, Tuesday, March 16, 1:00 PM," March 16, 1965, para. d. Both in "Deployment, Vol. 2, Tabs 88–119," NSC Histories, NSF, LBJL. See also the narrative, based on State Department files, in Gibbons, *U.S. Government and the Vietnam War, Part 3,* pp. 181–185.

79. Jack Langguth (reporting from Saigon), *New York Times,* April 9, 1965.

80. McGeorge Bundy's handwritten notes of meeting with Ambassador Taylor on April 1, 1965, Papers of McGeorge Bundy, Box 1, LBJL.

81. "Memorandum for Discussion," March 16, 1965, para. e.

82. McNamara to President Johnson, April 21, 1965 (emphasis added). Participants at the Honolulu conference, April 20, 1965, also included Assistant Secretaries William Bundy (State) and John McNaughton (Defense), Ambassador Taylor, General Wheeler (Chairman, JCS), Admiral Sharpe (CINCPAC), and General Westmoreland (COMUSMACV). Citing Admiral Ulysses S. Grant Sharpe's critical memoirs as his principal source, Mark Clodfelter characterizes McNamara's April 21 memo as "more an expression of [McNamara's] own concern with a deteriorating

military and political situation at the moment than the report of an enduring consensus of conference participants." Clodfelter, *Limits of Airpower,* p. 82.

83. See reports filed by Philip Geyelin, *Wall Street Journal,* April 21, 1965; Murrey Marder, *Washington Post,* April 22, 1965; Tom Wicker, *New York Times,* April 22 and 25, 1965. See also Robert McNamara's press interview in which he laid out the rationale for the interdiction campaign, April 26, 1965. See transcript in the *Washington Post,* April 27, 1965.

84. See Stephen T. Hosmer, *Constraints on U.S. Strategy in Third World Conflicts* (New York: Crane Russak & Co., 1987), Chapters 1–3. Hosmer relates the effects of these and other constraints on the conduct of different U.S. military interventions since World War II. His references to the Vietnam War include not only the period considered in this chapter but also the later air and ground campaigns during both the Johnson and Nixon administrations.

85. In Honolulu, the president's principal military advisers and high civilian officials from both the Defense and State Departments agreed to avoid this potential target area for at least six months; see "Influence of the Ground War." Heavy strikes on these targets during Operation Linebacker II, in December 1972, did have a coercive effect; but this occurred only after the DRV had already suffered prolonged erosion of its war-making potential, had observed significant moves toward a rapprochement between its chief adversary (the United States) and its two sources of material and moral support (the People's Republic of China and the Soviet Union), and had experienced a number of reverses and blunted thrusts in the military contest for dominance in the South. Moreover, as a condition for the settlement that was negotiated in Paris, Hanoi was conceded the right to keep its military forces in South Vietnam and to maintain control of the areas it still occupied pending political negotiations with the GVN through Hanoi's proposed Council on National Reconciliation.

8

The Reagan Administration Versus Nicaragua: The Limits of "Type C" Coercive Diplomacy

BRUCE W. JENTLESON

The main task of coercive diplomacy is to convince an opponent that it is in his best interest to change his behavior. This may involve either stopping short of the goal (Type A coercive diplomacy) or undoing or reversing the action already taken (Type B).[1] As Chapter 2 makes clear, an adversary's inclination to comply is highly dependent on the kind of demand made by the coercer: "Thus, asking relatively little of the opponent should make it easier for him to be coerced. Conversely, demanding a great deal of an opponent will … make the task of coercive persuasion more difficult."[2] Because the Type B variant involves a less limited objective than Type A (undoing an action requires more of an opponent than stopping short of the goal), it can entail greater difficulty in achieving the desired effect.

The case of the Reagan administration's policy toward Nicaragua demonstrates a Type C variant of coercive diplomacy, in which the objective is not just to induce a change in the adversary's policy but *to bring about a change in the composition of its government.* This is an even less limited objective than Type B calls for, requiring not just the reversal of an action but the undoing of the governing regime itself. Thus, I argue, it is an even more difficult objective for coercive diplomacy to achieve.[3]

This article was written before the author joined the Department of State. The views expressed are solely his own and do not imply the approval of the U.S. Government.

I make this argument based on the Nicaragua case but also as a more general proposition. The principal reasons for this are that the nature of the Type C objective makes it difficult to satisfy five key conditions for the success of coercive diplomacy: (1) usable military options, (2) a favorable asymmetry of motivation, (3) a basis for diplomacy, (4) international legitimacy, and (5) adequate domestic support. I first develop this analytic framework and then apply it to the Nicaragua case.

ANALYTICAL FRAMEWORK

There are, of course, ways of overthrowing governments other than by coercive diplomacy, such as through direct military interventions, as in Grenada (1983) and Panama (1989). In both of these cases the military action in and of itself achieved the objective.

But one should not conclude from these cases that military intervention is a foolproof strategy. In many other cases—for example, the United States in Vietnam, the Soviet Union in Afghanistan, and Israel in Lebanon—military interventions were much more protracted and much less successful than anticipated. I address the scope and limits of military intervention in greater detail elsewhere.[4]

The pertinent point here concerns the limits of coercive diplomacy as a strategy for bringing down or otherwise remaking governments. In the 1971 edition of *The Limits of Coercive Diplomacy,* Alexander George lays out a number of conditions that must be present for coercive diplomacy to have a strong likelihood of success.[5] The five I specify are adaptations and extensions of some of these.

Usability of Military Options

The key military requisite of coercive diplomacy is that if force is used, it must be wielded in a "controlled, discriminating manner".[6] Costs are to be inflicted on the adversary, but these should be of a type and magnitude geared more toward influencing his decision than to physically imposing one's will upon him. "The activity of the military units themselves," as Barry Blechman and Stephen Kaplan state in their study of coercion short of war, "does not attain the objective; goals are achieved through the effect of the force on the perceptions of the actor."[7] This is no easy task in any situation; the Cuban Missile Crisis is one exception that proves the general rule. Type C coercive diplomacy, however, has two further disadvantages.

First is the inherent disproportionality between the maximalist objective of remaking a government and the limits on the military means to be used for the task. In the A and B types of coercive diplomacy, the objectives being pursued are more limited and therefore less disproportionate to limited military means. The option of direct military intervention, however, has its own risks, uncertainties, and necessary conditions. The essence of the problem of using limited military force to remake another government is how to translate this type of political objective into operational military terms. This was the problem in the Vietnam War, for example, "When you commit military forces," said Vietnam veteran Gen. H. Norman Schwarzkopf,

> you ought to know what you want that force to do. You can't kind of say, "Go out and pacify the entire countryside." There has got to be a more specific definition of exactly what you want that force to accomplish. ... But when I harken back to Vietnam, I have never been able to find anywhere where we have been able to clearly define in precise terms what the ultimate objectives of our military were.[8]

A second problem in finding usable military options for Type C coercive diplomacy concerns the reliability of the indigenous political and military forces with which the coercer state allies itself. The limited nature of the coercive diplomacy strategy confers a crucial, if not leading, role on a local ally. Ultimately it is the ally's army that must make the military option usable and the local political leadership that must present the populace with a meaningful alternative to the adversary. Yet finding truly reliable local allies has proven to be a problem both in instances when U.S. troops were directly involved (such as Vietnam) and when surrogates were relied upon (as in Nicaragua). The problems have involved everything from command and control to operational military competence to the internal political legitimacy of the indigenous group and its leaders.

Asymmetry of Motivation

George puts great emphasis on the advantage given to the side that is more strongly motivated to achieve its objectives. He raises the possibility that the coercer state may seek to tilt the asymmetry in its own favor, either by increasing its own motivation or decreasing that of the adversary. Yet he also points out that "in some cases the relative motivation of the two sides tends to be fixed by the nature of the conflict and may not be subject to much manipulation."[9] Type C cases are precisely such situations: The motivation of an adversary to resist efforts to overthrow him is fixed—and fixed at a rather high intensity—by the very nature of the conflict.

Thus, although these may have been dubbed "limited wars" or "low-intensity conflicts," such terminology is flawed because it substitutes a description of the anticipated scope of the conflict for an analysis of the nature of that conflict. For the adversary who is to be overthrown, nothing is limited about the conflict; it is total. Thus the adversary is likely to have a heightened willingness to bear the costs of the conflict in the name of survival. Indeed, historically, and not just in the U.S. post–World War II experience, a greater willingness to suffer has been the key to smaller, weaker nations defeating bigger, more powerful ones.[10]

Basis for Diplomacy

Even if military options can be made usable, the essence of coercive diplomacy strategy is that these options must also be paired with effective diplomacy. Again, to return to George's basic definition, coercive diplomacy "is essentially not a military strategy at all but rather a *political-diplomatic* strategy."[11] Clausewitz's oft-quoted dictum should not obscure the fact that all uses of military force are not politics by the same "other means." We can go back to the distinction between the quick, decisive, purely military strategy and coercive diplomacy, which is a political-military strategy. Among other things, the greater role for diplomacy in the effort to resolve the conflict often means that the coercer must offer a carrot as well as brandish a stick. "To employ coercive diplomacy successfully," George states, "one must [often] find a combination of carrot and stick that will suffice to overcome the opponent's disinclination to grant what is being asked of him."[12]

Given its objective, however, Type C coercive diplomacy offers only a limited basis for diplomacy. The opponent's disinclination to concede to such an extreme demand is much greater than is the case when the objective is limited to a change in his policy. It is hard to imagine what kind of carrot could overcome the zero-sum nature of such stakes. Thus, any diplomatic activity is more likely to be geared to providing a cover for coercion than to complementing it.

International Legitimacy

A fourth distinction is in the differing claims to international legitimacy that can be mustered, on the one hand, by coercing a policy change and, on the other, by coercing the overthrow of a government. Principles of nonaggression, national self-determination, and the rights of sovereignty—however abused in practice—are the closest things the international system has to a universal set of rules and norms. A coercive diplomacy strategy aimed at restraining an aggressor nation in defense of these basic principles, therefore, can draw upon historical tradition as well as canons of international law for its justification. The moral authority that comes with international legitimacy is important in its own right, but even more important is the greater coercive potential of a broad-based international coalition that brings to bear the authority and resources of other countries and of international institutions, along with those of the United States.

The Reagan administration, however, had a different viewpoint. The essence of the Reagan Doctrine was that there could be no higher calling than to rid the world of Marxist-Leninist regimes and others it deemed illegiti-mate.[13] Internationally, there were few other subscribers to this view, even among other Western liberal democratic societies. Part of the disaffection was that few other countries so readily subscribed to the blanket criterion of "anything but communism" (the "ABC" of U.S. cold war foreign policy) in determining regime legitimacy. Even more fundamental was the concern, as identified by Robert Johnson, that the Reagan Doctrine tried by definition to equate anti-Communist insurgencies with struggles against foreign domina-tion.[14] This was true in countries that had experienced foreign military inter-vention, such as Afghanistan and Cambodia, but not in those in which the Communist government was indigenous, as in Nicaragua. The Reagan ad-ministration in effect was conferring upon itself a "right of intervention," which, as Robert Tucker objected, risked "subordinat[ing] the traditional bases of international order to a particular vision of legitimacy."[15]

Domestic Political Support

A fifth problem of Type C coercive diplomacy is that of both garnering and then sustaining adequate domestic political support. A strong domestic sup-port base is crucial both for establishing the credibility of threats to use force (or to escalate from levels already being used) and for maintaining the discre-tion necessary to manipulate the signaling and bargaining aspects of the dip-lomatic strategy. Yet at each of the three key levels of domestic politics—public opinion, Congress, and the executive branch—domestic support is more difficult to build for overthrowing governments than for restraining them.

If consensus could always be manufactured through public relations cam-paigns, then it would not matter whether one policy objective was more in-herently disposed to lower domestic constraints than another. As with Harry Truman and Dean Acheson in the selling of the Truman Doctrine, the right words and framing of an issue could evoke support even from a reluctant Congress and an isolationist public. But precisely because of Ronald Rea-gan's well-deserved reputation as the "great communicator," his limited ca-pacity to forge consensus on issues like Nicaragua is all the more significant. The political reality, at least since the Vietnam War, has been that Congress is less automatically deferential, the public much more attentive, and the execu-tive branch less strictly unitary than was the case in the past.[16] Whether this is a positive or negative development for U.S. foreign policy is a separate ques-tion. The relevant point here is that different types of issues carry inherent dispositions toward higher or lower domestic constraints.

I develop this argument with respect to public opinion more extensively elsewhere, showing a significant general trend in the "post-post-Vietnam" period toward higher levels of support for military force when the perceived policy objective has been to coerce foreign policy restraint than when it has sought to overthrow a government or otherwise engineer internal political change in another country.[17] A similar pattern can be seen in congressional behavior, as well as within the executive branch.

The reasons for this are related to the broader distinction made by William Schneider between *valence* and *position* issues.[18] Valence issues involve threats to shared basic values and are likely to evoke consensual reactions, whereas position issues allow for legitimate alternative value preferences and thus tend to encourage a more divisive politics. Efforts to coerce foreign policy restraint by an aggressor state are more likely to be treated as valence issues because the threat is clearer, present, and more dangerous. Compare, for instance, the reactions in the case of Iraq's invasion of Kuwait, with its immediate threats to vital American geopolitical and economic interests, or in a more limited sense the reactions to Libya's support of terrorism in 1985–1986, with reactions to the U.S. effort to depose the government of tiny Nicaragua because of still-hypothetical threats.

THE REAGAN NICARAGUA POLICY

From the very first days of the Reagan presidency, it was clear that Nicaragua and the United States would not easily coexist. The Sandinistas were ardently Marxist-Leninist; the Reagan administration was fervently anti-Communist. The Sandinistas supported their ideological brothers, the leftist Faribundo Martí Liberation Front (FMLN), in the civil war in neighboring El Salvador; the Reagan administration supported the right-wing Salvadoran military government. The Sandinistas counted Fidel Castro as an ally, indeed as a hero; the Reagan administration thought of him as an archenemy. From 1981 on, over the next eight years—through the ups and downs of support for the Nicaraguan contras, the starts and stops of various diplomatic negotiations, and the details of different articulations of U.S. objectives—the basic goal remained the same for the Reagan administration: the overthrow of the Sandinistas.

My analysis of the Reagan administration's Nicaragua policy has three aspects: establishing that it was a Type C case, assessing its effects, and applying the analytic framework previously discussed as the basis for explaining the limits of its success.

Multiple and Shifting Policy Objectives

There was much intra-administration disagreement over what U.S. objectives regarding Nicaragua should be—indeed, often over what they were—at any given point in time. This lack of consensus in part reflected substantive splits within the Reagan administration. However, as we now know, it reflected even more a conscious political strategy of saying one thing but doing another. Officially, at least during the first Reagan term, the rationale for supporting the contras was said to be merely to pressure the Sandinistas to live up to their 1979 pledges to the Organization of American States (OAS) of regional nonaggression and internal democratization. In reality, however, the Reagan policy was never about striking a deal but, as the president himself finally acknowledged in a February 1985 press conference, involved forcing the Nicaraguan government into "saying uncle."[19]

Consider the gap between the objectives as declared and the policy as pursued.

Arms Interdiction. The initial charge of regional aggression was that the Sandinistas were supplying arms to the Salvadoran FMLN guerrillas. Concerning the Sandinista-FMLN arms link during this November 1980–January 1981 period, there was, as *Washington Post* correspondent Christopher Dickey attests, "an avalanche of incriminating evidence." The Carter administration had already suspended foreign aid just before it left office in January, citing such irrefutable intelligence data as aerial photographs showing the conversion of a small, 800-meter airstrip at Pamplonal in northern Nicaragua—previously used mostly for agricultural purposes—"to a 1200-meter graded strip with turnarounds, hard dispersal areas and storage buildings." In addition to conducting the actual arms flows, the Sandinistas were doing everything from providing safe haven for the FMLN's Radio Liberación to using Nicaraguan cities for practice marches for the triumphal parade into San Salvador.[20]

With regard to arms interdiction as the explanation for U.S. support for the contras, however, the evidence is much weaker. U.S. ambassador to Nicaragua (1979–1981) Lawrence Pezzullo has long argued that the leverage gained by the aid suspension was already causing Sandinista restraint and that the termination of aid, let alone the funding of the contras, was unnecessary. "You're throwing away your chips, man," Pezzullo told Secretary of State Alexander Haig. The pressure had to be maintained, Pezzullo readily acknowledged, but why so precipitously abandon a strategy that was at least producing some results on such an ostensibly high-priority objective?[21]

Moreover, if in fact arms interdiction really was such a high priority, and if it was the real mission of the contras, then why was there so little concern about how inept they were in achieving that mission? "Interdiction became a joke," one State Department official recounts, "as the contras grew without interdicting so much as a helmet liner."[22] And why were they not trained for commando operations rather than for insurgency warfare? Why did they blow up bridges and economic targets inside Nicaragua but not the Cessnas in Pamplonal that were waiting to deliver their cargoes to El Salvador? And why were major Nicaraguan ocean harbors mined, but no targeting occurred of the small boats ferrying arms across the Gulf of Fonseca?

Cuban-Soviet Beachhead. National Security Decision Directive (NSDD) 17, signed by President Reagan on November 17, 1981, defined the need to conduct "political and paramilitary operations against the Cuban presence and the Cuban-Sandinista support infrastructure." Under Secretary of Defense Fred Iklé raised the specter that "if we deny arms, ammunition and money to those fighting the Cuban-backed forces ... then the military strength that the Soviets and Cubans have assembled in the region is quite adequate to turn Central America into another Eastern Europe."[23] Even in February 1988, the more general improvement in U.S.-Soviet relations notwithstanding, Defense Secretary Frank Carlucci warned key senators on the eve of a critical vote on contra aid that Nicaragua "provides another base of Soviet intelligence and operational activities directed against the US and greatly enhances the Soviet capability to conduct surveillance along our West Coast. Air bases and port facilities would permit Soviet bombers, ships and submarines rapid access to the Continental US and the Panama Canal."[24] The Joint Chiefs of Staff, Carlucci added, shared his assessment.

Here too, as with the Sandinista aid to the Salvadoran FMLN, the problem cannot be dismissed strictly as a concoction of administration propaganda. The Sandinistas did come to power with a long-standing relationship with Fidel Castro and Cuba. Castro had played a vital role in the victory of their revolution, as both political godfather helping the various factions of the Sandinista Liberation Front (FSLN) forge unity and then as an arms supplier. Cuban military advisers and civilian brigades (medical personnel, teachers, road engineers, and others) arrived within days of the fall of Somoza.[25] Over time the number of Cubans in Nicaragua, both military and civilian, grew. Most important, the ideological bond was a strong one, fed by Marxism-Leninism but rooted especially in the common historiography of "anti-Yanquiism."

Nor was the relationship with the Soviet Union illusory. In early 1980, Soviet and Nicaraguan leaders signed a series of economic and political agreements, including a joint communiqué condemning "the imperialistic policy of interference in the internal affairs of LA [Latin American] peoples" and "the preservation of colonial ownership in the Western hemisphere."[26] Soviet military aid did reach $500 million by 1987. Cause and effect are not altogether clear, since it could be argued that this was defensive aid in response to U.S. aid to the contras. But at some point one has to say that $500 million is $500 million. Economic aid was also substantial; it reached almost $3 billion between 1981 and 1988 and included large volumes of oil at subsidized prices.

However, this hardly amounted to the epochal "test of wills" over the future of the Western hemisphere that administration officials warned against. More to the point, the administration's assumption that any relationship between another country and the Soviet Union had to be a total one was more a

reflection of the Reagan world view than of reality. The threat of Soviet influence in Nicaragua was always grossly exaggerated, even before Gorbachev.[27]
The Kremlin was never willing to write the Sandinistas the kind of blank
check it had given Castro. It granted Nicaragua associate status but not mem-
bership in its economic bloc, the Council on Mutual Economic Assistance
(CMEA). It repeatedly turned down Sandinista requests for MIG fighters
and other sophisticated military equipment that would have significantly escalated the level of conflict. Nor did it ever provide the firm mutual defense
guarantee the Sandinistas repeatedly requested.

   U.S. Credibility. President Reagan proclaimed the stakes:

> If Central America were to fall, what would the consequences be for our posi-
> tion in Asia, Europe and for alliances such as NATO? If the United States can-
> not respond to a threat near our own borders, why should Europeans or Asians
> believe that we are seriously concerned about threats to them? If the Soviets can
> assume that nothing short of an actual attack on the United States will provoke
> an American response, which ally, which friend will trust us then?[28]

The message was that much more than regional security was at stake. It was
not just a matter of revolution being exported or of Sandinista tanks rolling
into neighboring countries or even of Soviet and Cuban bases being located
on the hemisphere's mainland. What was at stake was the global credibility of
U.S. power. The "Vietnam syndrome" had to be purged if a favorable global
balance of power was to be restored. Nicaragua was one of the key places (albeit not the only one) in which to achieve this.

   Yet although we must give appropriate weight to the credibility objective,
it too has flaws and gaps as an explanation for the Reagan policy. Its major
flaw is that, rhetoric aside, considerations of U.S. global credibility cannot be
said to have compelled support for the contras as partners in a surrogate
war.[29] There was a lesson from Vietnam here, but it was not the neo-
conservative belief that the Vietnam syndrome had to be overcome. The real
lesson was the one drawn by those such as Hans Morgenthau, who was
hardly a dove yet was an outspoken critic of the Vietnam War. Morgenthau
would have been the last to deny the importance of credibility in establishing
a nation's power. "What others think of us," he stated in his classic treatise
Politics Among Nations, "is as important as what we actually are."[30] He nevertheless saw the drawing of a necessary link between U.S. global power and
small-country radical revolutions as flawed strategic logic. To the contrary,
he warned against "the error of anti-communist intervention per se" and
"the self-defeating character of anti-revolutionary intervention per se." Even
in Vietnam, and even as late as 1967, he argued that it was still possible "to
prevent ... a communist revolution from turning against the interests of the
United States."[31]

Seen in this light, the elements of a Central American regional security accord could have served U.S. interests quite well. Considerations of global
credibility may have required that the United States demonstrate the will to
take a firm stand against Sandinista provocations, avoid being perceived as an
apologist for Sandinista anti-imperialism rhetoric, and pursue policies that
protected its interests and the interests of its allies. None of these objectives,
however, required the involvement of the contras.

Democratic Reform. Here too it was not that the antidemocratic charge
against the Sandinistas was unfounded. The "72-Hour Document," which
resulted from the First National Assembly of Cadres of the FSLN in September 1979, depicted the initial coalition Government of National Reconstruction as only a temporary ploy to "neutralize" any threat of U.S. intervention
until the FSLN could consolidate its control.[32] Within a year, Alfonso
Robelo and Violeta Chamorro, the two principal non-Sandinista members of
the ruling junta, had been forced to resign. And a few months later, Jorge
Salazar, a popular agrarian leader widely believed to have had a good chance
of being elected president, was assassinated by Sandinista agents.[33] When
elections finally did occur in 1984, the best assessment was that they were
neither as free as the Sandinistas claimed nor as unfree as the Reagan administration claimed.

Numerous other instances and examples can be cited of Sandinista
antidemocratic rule: These include press censorship and repeated closings of
the newspaper *La Prensa,* harassment of the Catholic church, large numbers
of political prisoners, the forced relocations of the Miskito Indians, and the
political hooliganism of street gangs known as *las turbas.* However, two
questions must be raised about the Reagan administration's claim to be promoting democracy in Nicaragua.

The first involves the abundant evidence of the antidemocratic nature and
practices of the contras. This did not simply involve the fact that many of the
contra leaders had been members of the Somocista National Guard, or that
the contras had engaged in brutality toward civilian populations, or that they
were internally corrupt and involved in drug running; it included all of these.
Sam Dillon, a Pulitzer Prize–winning journalist for the *Miami Herald* who
spent over five years covering the contras, tells of their routine torture, rape,
and murder of civilians. He also details the high standard of living of many
contra leaders, who jetted in and out of Miami financed by skimmed-off U.S.
dollars.[34] Contra involvement in drug running was further attested to during
the 1991 trial of Manuel Noriega, with allegations made of $10 million in
payments from the Colombian cocaine cartel and of planes that flew in military equipment for the contras and flew back to the United States loaded
with cocaine.[35] The Reagan glorification of the contras as "freedom fighters"
and "the moral equal of our Founding Fathers" belittled those to whom they
were compared.

A second question about the administration's professed concern for democracy pertains to consistency. From a historical perspective, it is significant that the February 1990 election was the first truly free election in Nicaragua—not just since the Sandinistas came to power in 1979, but ever. The Somoza family did not allow free elections in its forty to fifty years of rule, and the United States aided and abetted them in maintaining this policy. Indeed, American troops have invaded Nicaragua more often than they have any other country in the world. Further, as Thomas Carothers argues, the Reagan administration's posture as a champion of democracy is not particularly strengthened by reference to its companion policies toward other Central American countries. The Reagan policy on Honduras "was if anything a negative force for democratization in that it greatly strengthened the antidemocratic military, reified a formal electoral process that did little to change the antidemocratic structural features of the society, and made a mockery of Honduran sovereignty." And in El Salvador, during the Reagan years, there was no sense of a truly democratic political solution "in which the military was not the dominant actor, the economic elite no longer held the national economy in its hands, the left was incorporated into the political system, and all Salvadorans actually had both the formal and substantive possibility of political participation."[36]

The Superseding Objective of Overthrow. The congressional committees that conducted the principal (but by no means the only) investigation of the Reagan administration's Nicaragua policy stated their conclusion in no uncertain terms: "The contras were not in the field to stop Sandinista arms flowing to El Salvador; they were in the field to overthrow the Sandinistas."[37] Bob Woodward's account of a meeting between Central Intelligence Agency (CIA) Director William Casey and Deputy Director Bobby Inman also speaks to the point:

> They [Casey and Duane Clarridge, the principal CIA operative] were busy building an army, and Inman had some questions: Where are the contras going? Where is the CIA heading? The Administration? ... Do we know who these people are? They are not fighting to save El Salvador. They want power, don't they? This is an operation to overthrow a government, isn't it? ... Casey and Clarridge didn't have the answers, and they didn't like the questions.[38]

Among themselves, Clarridge and other CIA operatives and the contras were more than ready to acknowledge their true purposes. According to one source, "CIA operators told the contras *from the outset* that the U.S. intended them to overthrow the regime." Contra leaders themselves bragged, "The people who are fighting, they are not fighting to stop the weapons ... We are fighting to liberate Nicaragua." As Suicida, a top contra commander, brashly told an American reporter, "We're not going to stop the transport of arms and supplies to the Salvadoran guerrillas until we cut the heads off the Sandinistas."[39]

Only in the context of such revelations can the Reagan policy be understood on its own terms. Only then does it make sense, for example, that the CIA was providing covert assistance to Eden Pastora on the southern front, about three hundred miles from any possible Salvadoran-bound arms supply routes. It also then makes sense (again, on its own terms) that aid was going as well to the Miskito Indians in the Atlantic coast provinces, also far from arms supply routes. And the true Reagan objectives explain why CIA operatives were conspiring with General Gustavo Alvarez in Honduras on launching raids inside Nicaragua rather than working out an operational plan for shutting down the overland arms routes running through its territory.[40]

Similar points can be made about the revelations concerning the "fundraising" from foreign governments and the Iran-contra operation itself. If the administration's objective really was the more limited one of regional security, surely the costs and risks of these (and other) CIA and contra operations were far greater and their impact much more indirect than any of the potential diplomatic opportunities for a modus vivendi (which I discuss under "Disinterest in a Basis for Diplomacy"). The fact that all of those efforts were made to ensure plausible deniability for the president meant that Oliver North, Casey, Robert McFarlane, John Poindexter, and other officials were aware that there were risks. Why take these on when, as far as regional security and internal reform were concerned, much less costly and less risky options were available?

The Fall of the Sandinistas
and the Debate over "Success"

Given the fact that the Sandinistas did fall from power (losing the 1990 elections to the National Opposition Union [UNO] coalition led by Violeta Chamorro), some have argued that the Reagan policy should be considered a success. "Partisan rivalry must not cloud the truth," one analyst asserted. "This was Ronald Reagan's victory."[41] Any such claims, however, must be weighed against a number of other considerations.

First there is the matter of relative causal attribution. As Kenneth Roberts concludes from his analysis, "Political change in Nicaragua was precipitated not by U.S.-supported guerrillas but by an electoral process which the U.S. government had always doubted, and by an extended, tortuous series of regional negotiations which the U.S. had consistently undermined."[42] This brings in two other key actors who deserve credit for the fall of the Sandinistas.

One in particular is Costa Rican President Oscar Arias Sanchez, who along with other Latin American leaders played key roles first in the

Contadora and then in the Esquipulas-Arias Plan diplomatic processes—
diplomatic efforts initiated and led by Latin Americans that, as Roberts observes, amounted to "a form of collective action that was unprecedented in
the Americas both for its level of multilateral cooperation and for its sustained challenge to the 'hegemonic presumption' of the United States."[43]
And, although the military pressure from the contras cannot be totally dismissed, President Arias strongly contends that "the Contras always were the
problem, not the solution … they gave the Sandinistas a ready excuse for not
signing the peace treaty … the [February 1990] elections finally came about
in spite of, not because of, Washington."[44] Moreover, by the time of the election, U.S. military aid to the contras had already been cut off for almost two
years, and U.S. domestic political realities made it highly unlikely that military aid would be resumed except under the most extreme circumstances.

The other strong claimant to credit for the fall of the Sandinistas is the
Nicaraguan people. On February 25, 1990, they did what they might have
done many times in the past had they had the opportunity to vote in a genuinely free election: They threw out a corrupt and repressive regime.[45] The
Sandinistas grossly mismanaged the economy and systematically and often
brutally repressed political opposition. They also engaged in acts of personal
corruption and conspicuous consumption that may have been the most infu-
riating factor for the masses in whose name the revolution had been undertaken.[46] The vote in the 1990 election was anti-Sandinista, not pro-contra.
The loser was Daniel Ortega; the winner was Violeta Chamorro but not top
contra leaders Adolfo Calero or Enrique Bermudez or Comandante Suicida.

Even to the extent that some credit can be attributed to the Reagan policy,
a net assessment must also be made that includes the human costs incurred by
that policy. After all, around thirty thousand Nicaraguans were killed, and
tens of thousands of others were wounded and displaced or had their lives
otherwise disrupted or shattered by nearly a decade of so-called low-intensity war. A realistic accounting must also include the toll taken on the United
States. Here I mean less the budgetary costs than the political ones of bitter
ideological warfare and especially of the constitutional crisis raised by the actions of Oliver North and his colleagues.

Beyond these immediate costs is "the day after" problem. When one de-
stroys a country to save it, when the time actually comes to save it the task is
much harder. Since the UNO–Violeta Chamorro victory, the effects of the
means used in pursuit of the ends that purportedly justified them have lin-
gered and complicated the actual achieving of those ends. The demobilization
of the contras, as Robert Pastor noted at the time, was "the most dangerous
issue during the transition."[47] Yet by mid-1991, there were reports of "re-
contras," by some estimates as many as a thousand contras rearming and reactivating.[48] And the shambles in which the Nicaraguan economy was left—
in part because of Sandinista economic malfeasance but also in part because

of U.S. economic sanctions and the destructiveness of the war—has provided a frail and shaky base for building a stable society. Even Piero Gleijeses, who otherwise lauds the Reagan policy, quotes at length "the anguish of a Central American":

> You, Mr. Yankee, you've won. What are you going to do now? This is your Eastern Europe. You laugh at the Russians—what a mess they've made of Eastern Europe. But what a mess you've made of Central America. What are you going to do? When the history of Central America is written, what's going to be—as you say—the bottom line? That you left Guatemala to an army of assassins? D'Aubuisson in El Salvador? The corrupt officers in Honduras? Nicaragua desolated? You won. What are you going to do?[49]

Thus, whatever contribution the Reagan policy may have made to the fall of the Sandinistas came at a very high immediate and long-term cost. Especially when one considers that other policy options were possible, the U.S. involvement in Nicaragua can hardly be held up as a model of success.

EXPLAINING THE LIMITS OF SUCCESS

Each of the five conditions identified as inherently difficult for Type C coercive diplomacy to meet can be seen in the Nicaragua case.

Limited Usability of Military Options

The objective of forcing the Sandinistas to "say uncle" was disproportionate to the amount of military pressure that could be brought through the indirect means of using the contras as surrogates. Some members of the Reagan administration pushed for greater force—if not direct military intervention by U.S. troops, at least ampler support for the contras. Although the advocates of greater military pressure can be credited with recognizing the disproportionality between their ends and means, their effort to ratchet the means upward rather than adjust the ends downward exacerbated the other problems of international legitimacy and domestic support.

One should not assume, however, that in the absence of such constraints Nicaragua could have been another Grenada or Panama. In Nicaragua there would have been much less popular support for U.S. intervention than was the case in these two countries: Whatever the disillusionment with the Sandinistas, it was much less than that found in Grenada toward Coard or in Panama toward Noriega. U.S. forces would also have encountered much greater military resistance (not just a few battalions of armed Cuban "construction workers"). Moreover, the United States did not have 13,000 troops already prepositioned as it had in Panama. Indeed, according to Professor Richard Brennan of West Point, a study by the U.S. Southern Command (SOUTHCOM) estimated that a U.S. attack on Nicaragua would have required 125,000 soldiers, taken a minimum of four to six weeks, and incurred over 4,000 casualties—and even then a U.S. military occupation of the country would have been necessary.[50]

The effort to make military options usable thus relied heavily on the contras. Yet the contras lacked two qualities essential to being effective military surrogates. First, this force, whose name in Spanish simply means "those against," lacked the internal political legitimacy necessary to build extensive and genuine support among the Nicaraguan people. Reagan's glorification of them as "freedom fighters" was more effective in Miami than in the Nicaraguan countryside. The contras could be "repackaged," in ex-contra Edgar Chamorro's term, for political consumption in the United States through the continued efforts of the Reagan administration and kindred Washington, D.C., public relations firms.[51] But their past links to the Somoza National Guard and the human rights abuses they were inflicting on civilian populations severely limited the support they received from the Nicaraguan populace.

Second, the contras proved to be quite unreliable and ineffective as a fighting force. They were repeatedly torn by factionalism and corruption. After one of his frequent trips to the field, Robert Owen (Oliver North's courier) complained that "there are few of the so-called leaders ... who really care about the boys in the field. This has become a business to them." More aid, Owen told North, would be "like pouring money down a sinkhole."[52]

It was thus exceedingly difficult to meet such operational requisites as ensuring that military force as used had a discriminating character and coordinating military action and political-diplomatic initiatives. The contras could neither be counted on nor controlled. And even though U.S. troops never became directly involved, such incidents as the CIA's 1984 mining of Nicaraguan harbors and the 1986 crash of Eugene Hasenfus's supply plane exposed and implicated the United States ever more directly.

Unfavorable Asymmetry of Motivation

The Nicaraguan case also exemplifies how and why the asymmetry of motivation is more likely to favor the target over the coercer in Type C coercive diplomacy. When what is at stake is not just his policies but his very power, an opponent is likely to be strongly motivated to resist. On the other side the coercer is likely to have some difficulty mobilizing domestic support for what still appears to be something less than a clear and present danger. Indeed, the great frustration of the Reagan administration was its inability to persuade the Congress or even the American people that overthrowing the Sandinistas was vital to national security.

Nevertheless, in the 1990 elections, the internal asymmetry between the Sandinistas and the Nicaraguan people asserted itself. (As with Ferdinand

Marcos in the Philippines, it is revealing that the Sandinistas were so out of touch that they assumed they had popular political support.) The war had inflicted heavy costs on the country, and the Sandinistas had resorted to one policy after another—military conscription, forced resettlement, human rights abuses, rationing, hyperinflation—that disaffected the Nicaraguan people. But the bottom line, as it were, was protecting their own power. For leaders like the Sandinista Directorate, there is no stronger motivation than preservation of personal power and the accompanying perquisites. This is not a motivation easily shaken by coercive diplomacy. In the end, it was not so much that their will to resist faltered; they simply miscalculated the political trends among their own people.

Disinterest in a Basis for Diplomacy

The Reagan administration often presented its strategy as two-track, of bringing force to bear as a means of pressuring the Sandinistas to negotiate more seriously through diplomatic channels. In fact, however, diplomacy was little more than a cover, something that, as stated in a 1984 National Security Council (NSC) document, needed to be "co-opted" rather than pursued seriously. "It is preposterous to think," Assistant Secretary of State Elliot Abrams stated, "that we could sign a deal with the Sandinistas to meet our foreign policy concerns and expect it to be kept."[53]

This is not to imply that the Sandinistas were particularly eager for a diplomatic settlement. Nevertheless, there were at least five key junctures at which the Sandinistas did seem disposed to accept diplomatic compromises on the key regional security issues, but these opportunities were not seriously pursued by the Reagan administration.

One such example has already been mentioned: the Sandinista's willingness in March 1981 to reduce arms shipments to the Salvadoran guerrillas when the Reagan administration first started funding the contras. Ambassador Pezzullo was not alone in believing that diplomatic and economic pressures were producing results. CIA Deputy Director Inman, who was the most widely respected intelligence professional in Washington and was the original choice of Senate Intelligence Committee Chairman Barry Goldwater over William Casey for CIA director, also questioned whether the contras were really necessary. As Bob Woodward recounts it: "Inman tried to find ways to share his skepticism gently around the agency. He asked Casey if DDO John Stein was backstopping him on the operation to make sure there was an experienced professional fully informed of each step. ... But Casey was impatient and left Inman with the clear impression that his views were neither needed nor welcomed. The Director mumbled, 'Yeah, yeah.'"[54]

A second example came in the wake of the October 1983 U.S. invasion of Grenada, when there was what former State Department official Francis

McNeil assessed to be a "magnificent opportunity for a durable peace in Central America."[55] The Sandinistas were afraid they were next. Over the next month they expelled the Salvadoran FMLN leaders from their safe haven in Nicaragua, stopped supplying the FMLN with arms, dismantled their support structure, and announced that a thousand Cuban advisers were being sent home. They also took a much more constructive approach to the Contadora negotiations and submitted their own draft treaty, which included agreed-upon language on free elections, a prohibition on foreign military advisers, and a regional arms freeze. They also indicated for the first time a willingness to discuss reducing the size of their army.[56]

These were the core issues of regional security. But the dominant position within the Reagan administration, despite some internal splits, was to ignore even these offers of concessions. Finally, in June 1984, Secretary of State George Shultz made a surprise trip to Managua and met with Ortega. The trip was kept secret mainly because of Shultz's fear of being undermined by what Roy Gutman calls "the war party" within the administration (which consisted of Casey, U.N. Ambassador Jeane Kirkpatrick, National Security Adviser William Clark, NSC staffer Constantine Menges, and White House Co-Chief of Staff Edwin Meese). The meeting with Ortega actually went reasonably well, and Shultz cabled back, "We are proceeding on the premise that a negotiated settlement is possible and that practical reasons exist on all sides to reach agreement." But as Gutman describes it, "Hardly had the secretary of state left Managua when he came under sniper fire from White House staff." By the time the bilateral talks began in late June (at Manzanillo, Mexico), the prospects for any real progress had been severely constrained by this intra-administration opposition. Although the talks formally stayed in session, U.S. envoy Harry Shlaudeman was said to have been given "strict instructions not to explore with the Sandinistas how differences in the two positions could be narrowed." According to one State Department official, "No one will tell Shlaudeman what the end game is, what the road map to a final agreement is. The reason is that the Administration doesn't really want a settlement with the Sandinistas."[57]

A third example involved the Contadora negotiations. This effort at a diplomatic settlement had been initiated by Mexico, Venezuela, Colombia, and Panama in January 1983. The Reagan administration opposed Contadora virtually from the start and notably at key junctures, such as in September 1984 when the Sandinistas (who also up to that point had largely opposed Contadora) unexpectedly agreed to sign a draft treaty. The draft included provisions prohibiting support for insurgent movements, imposing regional arms control, requiring the withdrawal of all foreign military advisers and banning foreign military bases, and commiting all nations to democratic political reforms and to promoting national reconciliation among warring factions. The Reagan administration, however, denounced the Sandinistas' agreement to the treaty as a "publicity stunt" and increased pressure on El Salvador, Honduras, and Costa Rica to reverse their initial acceptance. An NSC background paper boasted of having "trumped" the draft treaty.[58]

In an effort to revive the Contadora process, the following year four South American countries (Brazil, Uruguay, Argentina, and Peru) formed the Contadora Support Group. Talks resumed, and new proposals were drafted. Nicaragua conditioned its willingness to sign on a formal U.S. nonaggression pledge, including ending aid to the contras. This effort came to a head in April 1986 when Ambassador Philip Habib, the newly appointed special envoy to Central America, stated that the administration would end aid to the contras "from the date of signature" of a Contadora treaty. However, Habib, despite his personal prestige and past accomplishments in other sensitive diplomatic postings, was accused by conservatives in Congress of "selling out" the contras and was repudiated by other Reagan administration officials.[59]

Another juncture involved the Arias Plan. One of the ironies of the Arias Plan is that when Costa Rican President Arias first made his proposal in early 1987, the Sandinistas opposed it as "an American plot."[60] They only decided to sign the accords on August 5, 1987, when the bipartisan plan jointly announced the previous day by President Reagan and House Speaker Jim Wright raised the fear of separate U.S. action. And although they balked at various points and their compliance was uneven, the Sandinistas largely complied with the peace process established by the Arias Plan.

The Reagan administration, however, worked against the plan, calling it "fundamentally flawed." President Arias's status did necessitate paying him some lip service, but according to a former NSC official, "privately they [Reagan administration officials] have a low opinion of him that borders on despising him." And far from rewarding Arias's efforts, they held up foreign aid payments, exerted pressure for the removal of the Costa Rican ambassador, provided information that led to the arrest of an Arias political supporter on drug money laundering charges, and accused the Arias government of mismanagement of foreign aid funds on the basis of an audit that contained so many inaccuracies that the U.S. ambassador had to disown it.[61]

On March 23, 1988, at the small border town of Sapoa and to the surprise of many, the Sandinistas and the contras signed accords establishing a sixty-day cease-fire and creating a framework for a political settlement. Both sides made concessions, and both sides pledged to negotiate in good faith toward a more permanent settlement. Curiously, however, at the time, even as contra leaders spoke of sharing a feeling of "special nationalism" with the Sandinistas, there were reports of Reagan administration efforts to block the accords from being signed.[62] Over the next two months the negotiations did fall apart; the truce held for over eighteen months, but no final agreement was reached. By all accounts there was enough blame to go around. The extremists on both Nicaraguan sides, notably Sandinista Interior Minister Tomas

Borge and contra commander and former Somoza National Guard Colonel Enrique Bermudez, pushed for maximalist demands certain to drive wedges into a negotiating process and pull the respective positions apart. The Reagan administration, for its part, threw its support to Bermudez in the power struggles that ensued within contra ranks, continued to push Congress for more contra aid, and availed itself of every opportunity to ensure that the process failed.

Lack of International Legitimacy

The Nicaragua case also shows the difficulties inherent in gaining international support for efforts to overthrow a foreign government. Again, it was not so much that other nations supported the Sandinistas (although some did) as the fact that they would not endorse the U.S. effort to overthrow them. This can be seen in the three principal political arenas within which international legitimacy comes into play for the United States: multilateral organizations such as the United Nations, the OAS as the principal regional multilateral organization, and the Western alliance as the principal global U.S. alliance.

The U.N. General Assembly passed numerous resolutions condemning U.S. policy. Given that the General Assembly was also passing resolution after resolution condemning Soviet policy in Afghanistan, its actions could not be written off as simply constituting anti-Americanism. Quite the contrary, there was a consistency between the two sets of actions.[63] And although the United States had its veto in the Security Council, it still lost face when, in 1984, thirteen of the fifteen members (Britain abstained) voted to condemn the U.S. mining of Nicaraguan harbors. The World Court also ruled against the United States in a suit brought by the Sandinista government over the harbor mining.

Within Latin America, beyond the specifics of the respective peace plans, the broader consensus was to reject the traditional U.S. hegemonic role. "We Central American leaders," President Arias stated, "have to begin to solve our own problems." Of a meeting between Arias and Reagan, a senior Costa Rican government official recounted, "I don't think anyone had ever told Ronald Reagan to his face that no respectable country publicly supports the contras ... and that the United States is alone on the issue." Most Latin American leaders, including Arias, had no illusions about or love lost for the Sandinistas, but they would not confer legitimacy upon U.S. efforts to overthrow them.[64]

As for the Western allies, they were so unsupportive of the Reagan Nicaragua policy that there were widespread concerns about, as the title of one book on the subject described it, *Central America as a European-American Issue.*[65] The European Community issued its own communiqué in 1983 stating that "the problems of Central America cannot be resolved by military means, but only by a political solution springing from the region itself and respecting the principles of non-interference and inviolability of frontiers."[66] A number of Western European countries also provided economic aid to the Sandinistas. Even more refused to go along with the U.S.-imposed economic sanctions.

Weak Domestic Political Support

Nicaragua stands, along with the Vietnam War and the signing of the Treaty of Versailles, as one of the most bitter cases of Congressional-presidential conflict over foreign policy in U.S. history. The intermittent pattern of contra aid tells part of the story: Aid was approved initially by the congressional intelligence committees in 1981 and 1982, approved by the full Congress for the first time in 1983, defeated in 1984, passed again but with restrictions in 1985, increased and derestricted in 1986, cut back and rerestricted in 1987, and cut back and restricted further in 1988.

Even more disturbing was the often vitriolic tone and tenor of the debate. Former contra leader Edgar Chamorro later told of how the CIA trained him to lobby both in Washington and in the home districts of targeted representatives so as to "place them in a position of looking soft on communism." White House Communications Director Patrick Buchanan, on the op-ed page of the *Washington Post,* labeled the Democrats "with Moscow, co-guarantor of the Brezhnev doctrine in Central America." He portrayed the upcoming vote on contra aid as the test of whether the Democrats stood "with Ronald Reagan ... or Daniel Ortega."[67] Assistant Secretary of State Abrams not only lied directly to Congress in prepared committee testimony (he was later convicted of withholding information from Congress) but in his public statements repeatedly cast the debate in similar terms of "whose side are you on?" And the essence of the Iran-contra affair was an executive branch driven by a belief in the correctness and even righteousness of its objectives to intentionally deceive the legislative branch, even to the point of breaking the law of the land.

The administration itself was also ridden with conflict. The battles were fought not only between but also within departments (especially the State Department). The fate of Philip Habib, who ultimately resigned out of frustration with both the political obstruction and personal condemnation he encountered, was but one example. Then, of course, the operations of Oliver North and his colleagues were intended to circumvent not only Congress but also normal channels within the State Department and the CIA.

In addition, public opinion polls rather consistently showed very low levels of support for the Reagan policy.[68] The mean score of support for contra aid in forty-three polls conducted between May 1983 and March 1988 was 27.3 percent. The "Ollie North effect" did increase support for contra aid to

44 percent in July 1987, but this did not last long; within a month public support was back down to 29 percent.

Moreover, when the polls are disaggregated to isolate those that specifically mention the objective of overthrowing the Sandinistas from more general contra aid questions (which could be interpreted as also, or instead, involving Type A or B objectives), the pattern is even stronger. Elsewhere I have separated the forty-three polls on contra aid into those that explicitly mention "overthrowing" the Sandinistas as the purpose of the aid and those that simply ask for general approval or opposition to contra aid. When the question proposed an invasion by U.S. troops to overthrow the Sandinistas, support was only 19.7 percent, support for contra aid to overthrow the Sandinistas was 23.7 percent, and support for just contra aid without specification of the objective was 29.8 percent. To these are added eight polls that measured support for U.S. military maneuvers and training exercises in the region. Although these measures all involved a more direct use of force than contra aid, they had the least to do with overthrowing the Sandinistas and came the closest to being geared to a Type A or Type B foreign policy restraint objective. Public support in these eight polls averaged 35.2 percent. Although still not particularly high in absolute terms, this figure was relatively higher than the percentages in polls reflecting opinion on the Type C overthrow objective.

This point is further strengthened by additional data from the 1986 survey of the Chicago Council on Foreign Relations (CCFR). One question asked about support for sending U.S. troops "if Nicaragua invades Honduras to destroy contra bases." Only 24 percent of respondents expressed support, and 60 percent were opposed. But when asked about support "if Nicaragua allows the Soviets to set up a missile base," 45 percent expressed support, and only 42 percent were opposed.[69] This ranked the establishment of a Soviet missile base third on the CCFR list of eleven possible scenarios for using U.S. troops, behind only Soviet invasions of Western Europe or Japan, and ahead of such other scenarios as defending an endangered government of El Salvador or overthrowing Noriega. In the missile base scenario, the issue was not the pro-Soviet coloration of the Nicaraguan government. The prospect of Soviet missile bases on the North-Central American mainland dealt very directly with foreign policy restraint. And when the question was cast in those terms, the American public was far more supportive of the use of force than it was for any other objective related to Nicaragua.

CONCLUSIONS: THE LIMITS
OF TYPE C COERCIVE DIPLOMACY

There are always two possible explanations for policy failure (whether partial or total). It may be a case of flawed policy implementation—that is, the policy could have worked, but those in charge made key errors in how they pursued their objectives. Or it may be a case of flawed policy conceptualization—in other words, the flaws were inherent in the logic of the policy itself, in the basic calculation that the objectives in question could be achieved through this particular policy.[70] My argument has been that the problem with Type C coercive diplomacy is of the second type, that the limits that were evident in the case of Nicaragua are inherent to the pursuit of this objective (overthrowing a government) through these means (coercive diplomacy). This is not to claim that it is absolutely impossible to overthrow a government through coercive diplomacy. An effort to do so, however, is highly unlikely to succeed, carries substantial costs, and can crowd out better policy alternatives.

Nor do the effects and consequent problems stop there. Especially when an issue so dominates the agenda, as did Nicaragua for the Reagan administration, one also has to look at the externalities the single-minded pursuit of this policy produced. For virtually the entire decade of the 1980s, other problems in the region such as debt, drugs, and development received very little high-level official U.S. attention. Neglect of such pressing problems rarely is benign, and in the post–cold war world, it is likely to be precisely these problems that most threaten political stability and economic prosperity in Latin America. Thus the full costs of the Reagan effort to overthrow the Sandinista regime may well remain to be seen.

NOTES

Kerry Chase, Sid Childers, and Maria Courtis provided able research assistance. Thanks also to Melody Johnson for her assistance and to Alexander George, Richard Brennan, and Robert Pastor for their helpful comments and criticisms.

1. See Chapter 1, pp. 8, 9.

2. See Chapter 2, p. 15.

3. For an initial development and broader application of this argument, see Bruce W. Jentleson, "The Reagan Administration and Coercive Diplomacy: Restraining More Than Remaking Governments," *Political Science Quarterly* 106 (Spring 1991): 57–87.

4. Ariel Levite, Bruce W. Jentleson, and Larry Berman, eds., *Foreign Military Intervention: The Dynamics of Protracted Conflict* (New York: Columbia University Press, 1992).

5. Alexander L. George, *The Limits of Coercive Diplomacy* (Boston: Little, Brown, 1971), pp. 215–228.

6. Ibid., p. 18.

7. Barry M. Blechman and Stephen S. Kaplan, *Force Without War: U.S. Armed Forces as a Political Instrument* (Washington, D.C.: Brookings Institution, 1978), p. 13.

8. C.D.B. Bryan, "Operation Desert Norm," *The New Republic*, March 11, 1991, p. 26.

9. George, *Limits of Coercive Diplomacy,* p. 219.

10. Andrew J.R. Mack, "Why Big Nations Lose Small Wars: The Politics of Asymmetric Conflict," in Klaus Knorr, ed., *Power, Strategy and Security: A World Politics Reader* (Princeton: Princeton University Press, 1983), pp. 126–151; Steven Rosen, "War, Power and the Willingness to Suffer," in Bruce Russett, ed., *Peace, War and Numbers* (Beverly Hills: Sage, 1972), pp. 167–184.

11. George, *Limits of Coercive Diplomacy,* p. 18 [emphasis added].

12. Ibid., p. 243.

13. Charles Krauthammer, "The Poverty of Realism," *The New Republic,* February 12, 1986; Joshua Muravchik, *Exporting Democracy: Fulfilling America's Destiny* (Washington, D.C.: AEI Press, 1991), pp. 144–146.

14. Robert H. Johnson, "Misguided Morality: Ethics and the Reagan Doctrine," *Political Science Quarterly* 103 (March 1988): 512.

15. Robert W. Tucker, *Intervention and the Reagan Doctrine* (New York: Council on Religion and International Affairs, 1985), p. 13.

16. Thomas E. Mann, ed., *A Question of Balance: The President, Congress and Foreign Policy* (Washington, D.C.: Brookings Institution, 1990); John H. Aldrich, John L. Sullivan, and Eugene Borgida, "Foreign Affairs and Issue Voting: Do Presidential Candidates 'Waltz Before a Blind Audience?'" *American Political Science Review* 83 (March 1989): 123–142; David C. Kozak and James M. Keagle, *Bureaucratic Politics and National Security: Theory and Practice* (Boulder, Colo.: Lynne Rienner Publishers, 1988).

17. Bruce W. Jentleson, "The Pretty Prudent Public: Post Post-Vietnam American Opinion on the Use of Force," *International Studies Quarterly* 36 (March 1992): 49–74.

18. William Schneider, "Conservatism, Not Interventionism: Trends in Foreign Policy Opinion, 1974–82," in Kenneth A. Oye, Donald Rothchild, and Robert J. Lieber, eds., *Eagle Defiant: United States: Foreign Policy in the 1980s* (Boston: Little, Brown, 1983), pp. 39–40.

19. Hedrick Smith, "President Asserts Goal Is to Remove Sandinista Regime," *New York Times,* February 22, 1985, p. A1.

20. Christopher Dickey, *With the Contras* (New York: Simon & Schuster, 1985), p. 105; Frank McNeil, *War and Peace in Central America* (New York: Charles Scribner's Sons, 1988), pp. 225, 150–151, 223–228.

21. Dickey, *With the Contras,* p. 106; Robert A. Pastor, *Condemned to Repetition: The United States and Nicaragua* (Princeton: Princeton University Press, 1989), pp. 232–233; Bob Woodward, *Veil: The Secret Wars of the CIA, 1981–1987* (New York: Simon & Schuster, 1987), pp. 115–116, 119–122.

22. McNeil, *War and Peace in Central America,* p. 153.

23. Roy Gutman, *Banana Diplomacy: The Making of American Policy in Nicaragua, 1981–1987* (New York: Simon & Schuster, 1988), p. 84.

24. Letter from secretary of defense to a United States senator (name withheld), February 2, 1988.

25. Shirley Christian, *Nicaragua: Revolution in the Family* (New York: Vintage Books, 1988), pp. 159–161, 299–300.

26. Joint Nicaraguan-Soviet Communiqué (March 1980), included in Robert S. Leiken and Barry Rubin, eds., *The Central American Crisis Reader* (New York: Summit Books, 1987), p. 675.

27. Nicola Miller, *Soviet Relations with Latin America, 1959–1987* (Cambridge: Cambridge University Press, 1989); "Leonid Brezhnev: Reply to Ortega at Kremlin Dinner" (May 1982) and "Yuri Andropov: On Nicaragua and Afghanistan" (April 1983), in Leiken and Rubin, *Central American Crisis Reader,* pp. 687–689.

28. "President Reagan's Address," *New York Times,* April 28, 1983, p. A12.

29. Bruce W. Jentleson, "American Commitments in the Third World: Theory vs. Practice," *International Organization* 41 (Autumn 1987): 667–704.

30. Hans J. Morgenthau, *Politics Among Nations* (New York: Alfred A. Knopf, 1969), p. 73.

31. Hans J. Morgenthau, "To Intervene or Not to Intervene," *Foreign Affairs* 45 (April 1967): 434.

32. "FSLN '72 Hours' Document" (September 1979), in Leiken and Rubin, *Central American Crisis Reader,* pp. 218–227.

33. Christian, *Revolution in the Family,* pp. 197–215.

34. Sam Dillon, *Comandos: The CIA and Nicaragua's Contra Rebels* (New York: Henry Holt and Company, 1991).

35. Michael Isikoff, "Drug Cartel Gave Contras $10 Million, Court Told," *Washington Post,* November 26, 1991, pp. A1, A8.

36. Thomas Carothers, "The Reagan Years: The 1980s," in Abraham F. Lowenthal, ed., *Exporting Democracy: The United States and Latin America* (Baltimore: Johns Hopkins University Press, 1991), pp. 97, 99; and Thomas Carothers, *In the Name of Democracy: U.S. Policy Toward Latin America in the Reagan Years* (Berkeley: University of California Press, 1991).

37. U.S. Congress, *Report of the Congressional Committees Investigating the Iran-Contra Affair* (November 1987), p. 31.

38. Woodward, *Veil,* p. 207.

39. McNeil, *War and Peace in Central America,* p. 152 (emphasis added); Dickey, *With the Contras,* p. 205.

40. Gutman, *Banana Diplomacy,* p. 55.

41. Piero Gleijeses, "Reflections on Victory: The United States and Central America," *SAIS Review* 10 (Summer-Fall 1990): 168. See also Arturo Cruz, Jr., and Mark Falcoff, "Who Won Nicaragua?" *Commentary* (May 1990): 31–38; Jeane Kirkpatrick, "Nicaragua: The Credit," *Washington Post,* March 5, 1990; International Security Council, "Nicaragua's Opportunity—and Ours," *New York Times,* March 14, 1990; John Felton, "In Washington, The Spin Patrol," *Congressional Quarterly Weekly Report,* March 3, 1990, p. 678.

42. Kenneth Roberts, "Bullying and Bargaining: The United States, Nicaragua and Conflict Resolution in Central America," *International Security* 15 (Fall 1990): 68.

43. Ibid., p. 69. The term *hegemonic presumption* is from Abraham Lowenthal, "The United States and Latin America: Ending the Hegemonic Presumption," *Foreign Affairs* 55 (October 1976): 199–213.

44. Statements by President Oscar Arias Sanchez at a seminar at the University of California, Davis, October 23, 1991.

45. The 1928 and 1932 elections have been viewed by some as fair elections, but as Robert Pastor observes, "since both were supervised by the U.S. Marines, they were not exactly ideal examples of self-determination. ... If the criterion for a free election

is that the losers accept the results as fair, then Nicaragua had never had a free election—until 1990." Robert A. Pastor, "Nicaragua's Choice: The Making of a Free Election," *Journal of Democracy* 1 (Summer 1990): 13–14.

46. William Branigan, "House Hunting Is High Politics in Managua," *Washington Post,* April 16, 1990, pp. A1, A20; "IN THE VIEW OF ONE DIPLOMAT, 'CORRUPTION WAS THE BIG UNSPOKEN ISSUE' OF THE RECENT ELECTION CAMPAIGN ... THEY [SANDINISTA LEADERS] HARDLY BOTHERED TO HIDE IT."

47. Pastor, "Nicaragua's Choice," p. 24.

48. Edward Cody, "Disenchanted Contras Take Up Arms Again," *Washington Post,* April 9, 1991, p. A15; Shirley Christian, "If Contras Are Rearming, Can War Be Far Behind?" *New York Times,* September 12, 1991, p. A4.

49. Gleijeses, "Reflections on Victory," p. 176.

50. Richard R. Brennan, "Force and Diplomacy: U.S. Policy Toward Nicaragua During the Reagan Administration," paper presented to the Annual Meeting of the American Political Science Association, Washington, D.C., September 1, 1991, p. 36 (note 58).

51. Chamorro, with Jefferson Morley, "How the CIA Masterminds the Nicaraguan Insurgency: Confessions of a 'Contra,'" *New Republic,* August 5, 1985, p. 21.

52. Dickey, *With the Contras;* Gutman, *Banana Diplomacy;* James Chace, "The End of the Affair?" *New York Review of Books,* October 8, 1987, p. 30; William LeoGrande, "Rollback or Containment: The United States, Nicaragua and the Search for Peace in Central America," *International Security,* 11 (Fall 1986), pp. 89–120.

53. *New York Times,* August 18, 1985, p. 6.

54. Woodward, *Veil,* pp. 175–176.

55. McNeil, *War and Peace in Central America,* pp. 137–138, 170–171; Woodward, *Veil,* pp. 234–235.

56. McNeil, *War and Peace in Central America,* p. 175; Gutman, *Banana Diplomacy,* pp. 170–172; LeoGrande, "Rollback or Containment," pp. 102–103.

57. Gutman, *Banana Diplomacy,* p. 211; LeoGrande, "Rollback or Containment," p. 109; see also Clifford Krauss, *Inside Central America: Its People, Politics and History* (New York: Summit Books, 1991).

58. Chace, "The End of the Affair," p. 24; McNeil, *War and Peace in Central America,* pp. 18, 31, 89, 204.

59. Rowland Evans and Robert Novak, "A Box Called Contadora," *Washington Post,* May 13, 1986; Joanne Omang, "Habib Called Wrong, Imprecise, in Letter on U.S. Latin Policy," *Washington Post,* May 24, 1986.

60. McNeil, *War and Peace in Central America,* pp. 31, 189.

61. Ibid., pp. 18, 189, 204.

62. *Washington Post,* March 26, 1988, pp. A17, A21.

63. Jentleson, "The Reagan Administration and Coercive Diplomacy," pp. 73–75.

64. James Le Moyne, "Arias: Whom Can He Trust?" *New York Times Magazine,* January 10, 1988, p. 69; McNeil, *War and Peace in Central America,* pp. 118–139.

65. Andrew J. Pierre, ed., *Third World Instability: Central America as a European-American Issue* (New York: Council on Foreign Relations, 1985).

66. "European Community: Joint Communiqué at Stuttgart" (June 1983), in Leiken and Rubin, *Central American Crisis Reader,* p. 661.

67. Chamorro, "Confessions of a 'Contra,'" p. 21; Patrick J. Buchanan, "The Contras Need Our Help," *Washington Post,* March 5, 1986, p. A19.

68. Jentleson, "Pretty Prudent Public."

69. John Rielly, ed., *American Public Opinions and U.S. Foreign Policy, 1987* (Chicago: Chicago Council on Foreign Relations, 1987), p. 32.

70. George Kennan poses the question as follows: "To the extent that it was the fault of American diplomacy, what went wrong—the concepts or the execution?" George F. Kennan, *American Diplomacy, 1900–1950* (Chicago: University of Chicago Press, 1951), p. vii.

9

Coercive Diplomacy and Libya

TIM ZIMMERMANN

During the eight years of the Reagan presidency, Libya's Col. Muammar Qaddafi was one of the administration's most persistent antagonists. The frequency and publicity with which Qaddafi and his policies piqued the Reagan administration, together with the Reagan administration's desire from the outset to make an example of Qaddafi, ensured a consistently adversarial and combustible relationship between Libya and the United States.

For the first five years of the administration's tenure, that relationship was generally characterized by derogatory rhetoric, occasional clashes, economic and political pressures, and desultory covert U.S. attempts to thwart Qaddafi's ambitions and undermine his leadership.[1] However, in 1985, the growing problem of international terrorism (much of it directed at U.S. interests), and Qaddafi's persistent and public involvement with that terrorism, moved the Reagan administration to sharply focus its policies with regard to Libya. In January 1986, the administration took the first formal step in a comprehensive and intensive strategy of coercive diplomacy. The stated aim of that policy was to persuade Qaddafi—through the use of diplomatic, economic, and military means—to end his sponsorship of terrorism.

Taking a firm line against terrorism was an important touchstone of the Reagan presidency. And from 1983 to 1985, as the incidence of terrorism continued to climb,[2] the administration's rhetoric increasingly reflected its concern regarding terrorism and reaffirmed its determination to respond decisively. In a 1984 speech, Secretary of State George Shultz asserted that although passive measures were necessary and could do much to help prevent terrorism, it was time to "think long, hard, and seriously about more active means of defense—about defense through appropriate preventive or preemptive actions against terrorist groups before they strike."[3] One year later, following the hijacking and seventeen-day hostage drama of TWA 847 (which prompted a "never again" resolve among many within the administration) and the murder of four Marines and two American businessmen in El Salvador, President Reagan himself raised the administration's rhetoric to a fever pitch. In a speech to the American Bar Association, he argued that by sponsoring international terrorism, Iran, Libya, North Korea, Cuba, and Nicaragua were committing "acts of war against the government and people of the United States. ... And under international law, any state which is the victim of acts of war has the right to defend itself."[4] After the president's speech, one official commented that in administration discussions of terrorism, "the difference now is that everyone recognizes that we're going to have to hit back at the terrorists."[5]

As Washington's frustration and resolve regarding terrorism mounted over the course of 1985, Qaddafi further riveted the administration's attention through involvement in a succession of terrorist incidents. In addition to being linked with plans to assassinate the American ambassador in Rome and bomb the American embassy in Cairo,[6] Qaddafi's government was connected with the bloody November hijacking of an EgyptAir flight by three men affiliated with the terrorist group led by Abu Nidal —which was considered by the State Department to be one of the most dangerous and effective radical Palestinian terrorist groups.[7]

On December 27, the Abu Nidal gang struck again, this time at the Rome and Vienna airports. In simultaneous attacks, which Qaddafi called "heroic actions," gunmen attacked the ticket halls with gunfire and grenades, killing twenty people (five of them American). One of the Americans killed was an eleven-year old girl named Natasha Simpson, and once again evidence of Libyan complicity emerged.[8] The random brutality of the Rome and Vienna attacks, and particularly the fate of Natasha Simpson, galvanized Reagan into action against Libya. American lives and the Reagan administration's credibility, as well as the credibility of the United States as a superpower and world leader, were seen to be at stake. As George Shultz put it in January 1986: "The worst thing we could do to our moderate friends in the region is to demonstrate that extremist policies succeed and that the United States is impotent to deal with such challenges. If we are to be a factor in the region— if we want countries to take risks for peace relying on our support—then we had better show that power is an effective counterweight to extremism."[9]

Thus, moving from a rather sporadic policy of responding to provocation,[10] at the beginning of 1986 the Reagan administration set in motion an active policy that would utilize coherent and escalating political, economic, and military pressures in an attempt to achieve the declared objective of ending Qaddafi's sponsorship of international terrorism. In announcing a package of U.S. economic sanctions against Libya in January, Reagan argued that "by providing material support to terrorist groups which attack U.S. citizens, Libya has engaged in armed aggression against the United States under established principles of international law, just as if it had used its own armed forces." Referring to the sanctions, Reagan added, "If these steps do not end Qaddafi's terrorism, I promise you that further steps will be taken."[11]

THE NATURE OF THE COERCIVE POLICY

The Nature of the Objective

As noted in Chapter 1, the objective of coercive diplomacy can be to induce an adversary either to stop an action (the easier variant) or to stop and undo an action (the more difficult variant). With respect to Qaddafi, the Reagan administration's objective constituted the easier variant of coercive diplomacy in that the administration wanted Qaddafi simply to stop his sponsorship of terrorism—he could not really undo the effects of his previous support of terrorism. Nevertheless, the notion that Qaddafi could be induced under pressure to change his behavior, the essence of coercive diplomacy, was itself problematic. Any change in behavior in response to U.S. pressure would invariably entail some loss of prestige for Qaddafi, and he was evidently more jealous of his prestige than are most leaders. Moreover, such a change would also be especially conspicuous given Qaddafi's previous vocal and enthusiastic support of terrorism.

Predicting the response of any individual to coercive pressure is a highly subjective exercise at best because it turns on estimating the balance of incentive between the coercer and the target. Certainly the Reagan administration, with the support of the American people, was determined to act decisively. But as a self-styled revolutionary, who compared himself to figures such as Che Guevara and Garibaldi, Qaddafi had a lot at stake in defying the United States.[12] The funding of subversive and terrorist groups was the principal basis on which he staked his claim to being a world revolutionary. According to Libya analyst Lisa Anderson, writing just before the April 14, 1986, bombing raid by the United States, Qaddafi considered subversion of the status quo an article of faith.[13] If his commitment to his revolution and to his chosen means of instigating it was as absolute as some of his rhetoric, then he would be very difficult to coerce.

Given these considerations, there was some ambivalence within the Reagan administration over the question of whether Qaddafi could be coerced into moderate behavior or whether he would resist U.S. pressure at almost any cost. The Central Intelligence Agency's (CIA) national intelligence officer for the Near East concluded in a June 1984 Interagency Intelligence Memorandum that "no course of action short of stimulating Qaddafi's fall will bring any significant and enduring change in Libyan policies." Seven months later, a National Security Council (NSC) paper offered two alterna-

tive courses of action for dealing with Libya. The first, a "broad" approach
that would simply escalate pressure on Qaddafi, implied a belief that Qaddafi
might respond to such pressure. The second, a "bold" approach that consisted of a "number of visible and covert actions designed to bring significant
pressure to bear upon Qaddafi and possibly cause his removal from power,"
implied some doubt that anything short of his ouster would work.[14] This
ambivalence was also later seen in clear indications that the administration
would have been satisfied to kill Qaddafi in the April 14 bombing raid. Although its basic purpose clearly was not to assassinate Qaddafi, the raid was
consciously structured in a way that made Qaddafi's death possible.[15]

Thus, although the administration eventually embarked on a coercive
strategy of escalating pressures in an effort to persuade Qaddafi to change his
behavior, it seems clear that, at the outset, there were few illusions as to how
easy this would be and some question as to whether he could be coerced at
all. And given the nature of the U.S.-Libyan relationship, the sensitivity
within the administration to "credibility," and the professed policy of not
negotiating with terrorists, there was no consideration, as in fact there never
had been, of trying to change the balance of incentives by offering Qaddafi a
positive inducement—a carrot to complement the imminent stick—to secure
his compliance.

In addition to the potential difficulty of coercing Qaddafi, the nature of
the administration's objective—a reversal of Qaddafi's support for terrorism—also posed difficulties because it did not lend itself to a definitive resolution. Because there could only be clear evidence of noncompliance (that is,
a terrorist act that could irrefutably be traced to support from Qaddafi), the
policy was bound to be open-ended. A pledge from Qaddafi was unlikely to
be trustworthy, and a sufficient verification arrangement was improbable;
thus, there could be no adequate positive indicators of compliance, and it
could only be inferred from the absence of noncompliance. This contrasts
with a coercive policy that demands a change in behavior but has a finite resolution, such as the withdrawal of an invading force. As Thomas Schelling
noted in *Arms and Influence,* "If the opponent's compliance necessarily takes
time—if it is sustained good behavior—the compellent threat requires some
commitment, pledge, or guarantee, or some hostage, or else must be susceptible of being resumed or repeated itself."[16] This contextual factor added another element of unpredictability to the coercive equation. By the end of
1985, the prevailing conditions, particularly solid domestic political support,
were highly propitious for a serious attempt at coercing Qaddafi. Over a long
period of time, however, there was no guarantee that those conditions would
not change to the detriment of the policy.

Such considerations, then, were the theoretical factors that at the outset
contributed to the element of risk in the coercive policy initiative against
Libya. These factors were by no means prohibitive; they do illustrate the

highly subjective and uncertain nature of coercive diplomacy, even when it is being conducted against a seemingly vulnerable Third World poseur. But given the fact that to a large degree foreign policy constitutes the management of risk, how did the Reagan administration set about pursuing its objective?

The Operational Strategy: "Tacit Ultimatum" Versus "Try and See"

At the end of 1985, having resolved to respond decisively to Qaddafi's public support and advocacy of terrorism, many members of the administration—particularly Shultz and the NSC staff—were in favor of retaliating immediately against Qaddafi for the December airport attacks. U.S. Air Force officers at Lakenheath Royal Air Force Base in England began working on strike plans almost immediately following the incidents. Such a response would have escalated the administration's strategy at once to the strong end of the operational continuum by using military force as an instrument of reprisal. But despite the pressures in support of this response, a number of factors weighed in favor of a more considered response, one that would leave the option of military reprisal for future use if necessary. The result was an operational strategy that started at the "try and see" end of the operational continuum.

The first factor that weighed in favor of try and see was opposition from Secretary of Defense Caspar Weinberger and the Pentagon to any quick resort to military action. Aside from a concern regarding the political fallout of a military strike, Weinberger and the Joint Chiefs of Staff (JCS) asserted that it was very difficult to find targets in Libya that were directly related to Abu Nidal's terrorism. This point spoke directly to the president's preference for using force as an instrument of counterterrorism only if it could target people or facilities directly related to the terrorism and if the use of force was proportional to the terrorist act itself.[17]

More important, Weinberger argued that immediate military action would put American lives in danger. Although in December 1981 President Reagan had asked Americans in Libya to leave, approximately fifteen hundred had returned to Libya by the end of 1985—each one of whom represented a potential hostage. The administration could implement measures stronger than the 1981 edict to force Americans to leave Libya, but to do so would require allowing a reasonable amount of time for Americans in Libya to comply. Once all those who elected to obey the administration's order to leave had been given a chance to do so, the administration's responsibility to any remaining Americans, as well as the risk of a debilitating hostage crisis, would be minimized.

In addition, Weinberger argued that all other political and economic sanctions had not yet been exhausted and that force should be used only as a last resort, a principle with which President Reagan was sympathetic. When the administration finally did use military force against Libya, Reagan emphasized that "we Americans are slow to anger. We always seek peaceful avenues before resorting to the use of force. And we did. We tried quiet diplomacy, public condemnations, economic sanctions, and demonstrations of military force. None succeeded."[18]

Finally, one of the themes most fundamental to Weinberger's view was that if force were to be used, it should be used under conditions of overwhelming U.S. military superiority.[19] Planning of military options proceeded immediately following the December 27 attacks, and on January 3 a naval task force, led by the carrier *Coral Sea*, got under way from Naples. But preparing the most appropriate plans and assembling adequate forces required time. The planning exercise did not start from scratch because some plans had been developed for retaliating against Libya in the wake of the 1981 furor over alleged Libyan hit squads in the United States.[20] But planning in earnest, down to the last detail, did not begin until after December 27. In any case, at the time of the December 27 attacks, the *Coral Sea* was the only U.S. carrier operating in the Mediterranean. If a strike were to be conducted, Weinberger wanted three carriers.[21]

One final factor that weighed in favor of a try-and-see approach was the fact that if the Reagan administration hoped to cultivate any unity among its allies, more time was again needed. The administration had long maintained that terrorism was a problem not just for the United States but for all members of the "civilized world community." The fact that much of Libyan-supported terrorism had taken place in Europe justified this position. If the administration could muster a unified policy toward Libya, this point would be underscored. More important, any antiterrorism policy, particularly one geared to coerce Qaddafi, would be more effective if he felt isolated from his most important trading partners.[22] A unified approach would also minimize the degree to which the United States would become a lightning rod for any political or terrorist backlash that might be catalyzed by a campaign against terrorism.

For all these reasons administration planners developed a graduated try-and-see strategy rather than one that quickly resorted to strong measures. Meeting with his principal defense and foreign policy advisers on January 6, Reagan formally opted for economic retaliation in the short term. At the same time, he authorized increased resources for covert efforts to undermine Qaddafi and shortly thereafter authorized expanded contingency planning to include possible U.S. support for a preemptive Egyptian attack on Libya. During this period of decision, the president also encouraged an emphasis on public and private diplomacy and the continuation of naval movements in the Mediterranean calculated to intimidate Qaddafi.[23]

THE TRY-AND-SEE STRATEGY:
FROM SANCTIONS TO BOMBS

Phase I: Peaceful Pressure

The Reagan administration's try-and-see strategy of this period can be roughly divided into three phases. In the first phase, which lasted from December 27, 1985, until January 23, 1986 (when President Reagan ordered the U.S. Navy to begin a week of extensive naval flight operations in the vicinity of Libya), the administration focused on applying additional political and economic pressures on Qaddafi by expanding restrictions implemented in March 1982 and encouraging U.S. European allies to participate in the campaign against Qaddafi.

On January 7, President Reagan, noting that the 1982 economic sanctions had apparently been insufficient to influence Qaddafi, imposed a total ban on direct import and export trade with Libya (except for humanitarian purposes). Whereas the 1982 measures allowed some restricted trade with Libya, the January 7 executive order was designed to preclude any direct U.S. contribution to the Libyan economy. Concerned about the number of Americans still residing in Libya, Reagan also asked all Americans to leave by February 1 or face "appropriate penalties" upon their return home. In addition, he warned Qaddafi that his government was fully responsible for the "welfare of those Americans still in Libya, and that Libya [would] be held accountable for any attempt to harm them or restrict their freedom to depart."[24]

The January 7 sanctions had the effect of maximizing the political-economic pressure the United States could exert on Libya, although the success of the March 1982 measures in imposing some costs on Libya tended to dilute the impact of the new sanctions. The severing of diplomatic relations, usually a powerful political signal, had already been carried out. The March 1982 trade restrictions had also diminished U.S. exports to Libya from $860 million in 1979 to under $200 million, and Libyan exports to the United States had similarly declined from more than $5 billion in 1979 to approximately $9 million.

Consequently, although the January 7 measures could honestly be said to have virtually exhausted the U.S. political and economic options vis-à-vis Libya, if there were any chance that political and economic sanctions were to have a meaningful impact on Qaddafi it was imperative that the Reagan administration's European allies join the effort.[25] Voluntary European support of the January 7 measures would be critical to putting real economic and political pressure on Libya, in addition to having the psychological value of a unified front. Recognizing this fact, the president in his January 7 announcement made a strong plea for cooperation. And as a warning that implied some pessimism regarding the expected response, Reagan added that: "Americans will not understand other nations moving into Libya to take commercial advantage of our departure. We will consult with all our key allies to pursue the goal of broader cooperation."[26] Despite this skepticism, which was somewhat prevalent within the administration due to previous European resistance to its efforts to pressure Qaddafi, Reagan dispatched Deputy Secretary of State John Whitehead to Europe.

Whitehead's mission was intended to convey U.S. concern over terrorism, explain President Reagan's January 7 executive order, and encourage Europeans to reinforce the American action with punitive measures of their own. In addition, the Reagan administration wanted to send its allies another message: In the absence of sufficient allied support, the United States would consider further, more persuasive action. As State Department spokesperson Bernard Kalb said on January 8, it would be a "very serious mistake to misread our determination to confront international terrorism." With or without allied help, the United States would "press forward regardless, with a graduated course of retaliation."[27]

Despite these warnings, individual allied responses to the Reagan administration's efforts amounted to a rejection of the U.S. policy of pressuring Qaddafi (although most countries explicitly stated their intention not to undercut the American measures).[28] In the end, the collective response of the U.S. European allies was embodied in the declaration that followed a January 27 meeting of European Community (EC) foreign ministers. The declaration implemented a ban on arms sales that "were clearly implicated in supporting terrorism" but did not mention Libya by name. With this statement the EC strengthened its policy to a point just short of a January 1980 U.S. ban on any exports that contributed to Libya's military or terrorist potential. Whitehead publicly welcomed the January 27 EC decision, but the overall allied response to the Reagan administration's sanctions initiative—although perhaps not surprising—was not the one the administration had hoped for.

Although there was disappointment with the lack of allied cooperation and the manifest weakness of the sanctions applied,[29] to some the lack of European cooperation had a positive side. Donald Fortier, the NSC's new deputy national security adviser, for example, saw the implementation and failure of the sanctions as a necessary prelude to rallying the more restrained members of the administration behind more forceful measures. Qaddafi also assisted in this regard. Instead of moderating his policies in response to the January 7 measures, on January 15 he declared a "receding threat of American military action," condoned once again the Rome and Vienna attacks, and, referring to the various Arab groups under his authority, vowed that "we shall train them for terrorist and suicide missions and allocate ... all the weapons needed."[30] This rhetoric was reinforced by increased signs of Libyan terrorist planning. Clearly, unless President Reagan was willing to increase the pressure on Qaddafi, the policy would stall.

Phase II: The Show of Force

On January 23, President Reagan, with two U.S. aircraft carriers now at his disposal in the Mediterranean, ordered that a week of naval flight operations begin off the coast of Libya. This order marked the beginning of the second phase of the try-and-see approach and is distinguished from the first phase by the show of military force. This phase was characterized by a frequent and deliberately conspicuous U.S. naval presence off the coast of Libya, which was achieved through two "freedom of navigation" exercises. It ended on March 14, when President Reagan decided to send three ships over the 32′30″N latitude line that bounded the Gulf of Sidra, in a deliberate attempt to provoke Qaddafi into combat.[31]

The naval operations off Libya—which State Department spokesperson Bernard Kalb called "part of the war of nerves"—had been planned two weeks earlier as the next step in the administration's try-and-see strategy if it became apparent that the Whitehead mission was not going to achieve satisfactory results. Although the January and February "operations in the vicinity of Libya" would not cross over 32′30″N Reagan administration officials made it clear that U.S. Navy planes would be clearly and frequently visible on Libyan radar screens.

The ostensible rationale for the January operation was, in the words of Kalb, "to demonstrate, once again, American resolve to continue to operate in international waters and airspace throughout the world."[32] The Reagan administration had consistently carried out such exercises around the world, particularly off the coast of Libya, so on the face of it the administration could argue that it was conducting business as usual. But sources from the White House, Pentagon, and State Department made it clear that the naval operations had four other, more important purposes. The first was to demonstrate that Qaddafi's warnings and the presence of Soviet warships would not inhibit the United States from making a show of force off the coast of Libya. The second was to warn U.S. allies that unless they applied more effective sanctions against Libya, the United States might initiate military operations of a more punitive nature. The third was to convince both radical and moderate states in the region that Washington was losing patience with state-sponsored terrorism and was prepared to back up rhetoric with action if necessary. And the fourth was to wear down and test the effectiveness of Qaddafi's antiaircraft and command and control defenses.[33]

The first set of operations began on January 26. The day before, Qaddafi rode a patrol boat out into the Gulf of Sidra and declared that the 32′30″N latitude that ran across the top of the gulf was henceforth a "line of death" for anyone who dared cross it. Although the administration did not plan to send ships over the line during the first two exercises, Qaddafi's gambit provided a useful indication of a way in which the administration could provoke combat if it wished to do so. During the January operations, only fourteen Libyan air force jets even approached the fleet, where they were routinely intercepted.

The January exercises were followed by similar operations in mid-February. In the meantime Qaddafi hosted the second "terrorist convention" of the Pan-Arab Command and urged more attacks on the United States, conducted his own naval maneuvers, and initiated another attack on Chad. In the February exercises U.S. planes and ships again did not cross into the Gulf of Sidra, but this time the Libyan reaction was much more confrontational. In contrast to the January operation, over the four-day period of the February exercise the United States recorded approximately 160 encounters with the Libyan air force.[34]

Taken together, the January and February operations in the vicinity of Libya represented an incremental escalation in the administration's try-and-see approach. Although President Reagan had verbally asserted the U.S. right to undertake unilateral military action throughout the first phase, he had not underscored this right with a show of force. Against this backdrop, the naval demonstrations marked a shift from the administration's initial emphasis on economic and political measures to an emphasis on military pressures. The administration had not given up on political and economic measures—these naval operations, and the subsequent uses of military force, were for European as well as Libyan consumption—but it seemed clear that peaceful measures needed to be supplemented by more direct action. If the Reagan administration were to sustain any sort of pressure on Qaddafi and Libya, which was critical to convey the determination (and hence, credibility) of the coercive policy, it had to move beyond political and economic sanctions.

The January and February naval exercises added a new dimension to the Reagan administration's coercive diplomacy but had little impact other than communicating the intent to keep worrying at Qaddafi until something happened. Despite the increasingly military aspect of the administration's diplomacy, allied governments did not modify their policies with regard to Libya. And Qaddafi, although he could have thwarted the U.S. policy simply by not responding to the provocations, did not choose to do so. Instead of moderating his rhetoric and behavior, Qaddafi attempted to broaden the division between the United States and Europe over the question of Libya by engaging in a bit of coercion himself—ominously threatening that "Libya may sometime be compelled to wage war in the Mediterranean zone to divert and deter the American threat. ... It's not a matter of days, or weeks, or months, but when the provocation becomes too much."[35] In addition, Libya continued to conduct surveillance on American diplomats in preparation for possible terrorist attacks. Not surprisingly, President Reagan concluded that Qaddafi "was not getting the message" and raised the stakes again. On March 14, as a third U.S. aircraft carrier was about to arrive in the Mediterranean, Reagan personally approved a plan to have U.S. naval forces cross the "line of death" into the Gulf of Sidra.[36]

Phase III: The Use of Force

On March 19, the aircraft carrier *America* joined the *Saratoga* and *Coral Sea* off the coast of Libya. The addition of the *America* created a military capability and flexibility that reassured those within the Reagan administration, namely Weinberger, who were reluctant to commit military forces unless a safe margin of superiority existed. Armed with this third carrier, the administration initiated the third phase of its try-and-see strategy. This phase, which lasted from the March 14 decision until the April 14 bombing raid, was distinguished from the previous two by the actual use of force against Libya.

The decision to send U.S. forces into the Gulf of Sidra was made with the expectation that it might provoke a military clash with Qaddafi. Again, the action was described as a "freedom of navigation" exercise. But Qaddafi's rhetoric about the "line of death" and a previous clash between Libyan and U.S. planes over the Gulf of Sidra in 1981 indicated that combat was possible, perhaps even probable. To protect U.S. air personnel in this volatile situation, the Rules of Engagement (ROE) were adjusted to allow U.S. forces greater flexibility in returning fire.[37]

Although the administration was thus making efforts to protect its personnel, hardliners within it who wanted to force the issue with Qaddafi seized upon the possibility that an American might be killed as a trigger for full military reprisal against Qaddafi. There still was not absolute unity within the administration as to how far, and under what conditions, the United States should go in its use of force as an instrument of counterterrorism against Qaddafi, but the guidelines for the exercises were set up so that the U.S. fleet, after confirming authorization with the president, would respond to any loss of American life by bombing five coastal targets. If Qaddafi responded with a full-scale counterattack, U.S. planes would initiate (again, only after presidential approval) a powerful bombing raid on Libyan oil assets and terrorist training camps.[38] On March 19, CBS News quoted an anonymous U.S. official who said that the Reagan administration hoped Qaddafi would attack the Sixth Fleet forces because "if and when that happens, we'll clobber him."

On March 24, the administration's expectation that Qaddafi would respond to U.S. activity below 32'30''N was realized. At 1 p.m., three U.S. ships crossed the "line of death" (for the eighth time since 1981). Within two hours, the Libyan air defense installation at Sirte fired two SA-5 missiles at two U.S. F-14s that were approximately sixty miles off the Libyan coast and closing. Both missed. Of all the Libyan sites, Sirte was considered to be most directly under Qaddafi's authority, so the missile firings were taken to be a deliberate response on his part.[39] Despite pressure from the White House Situation Room to respond immediately, Sixth Fleet commander Frank Kelso waited until dark, when it was safer, to attack the missile site. In the meantime, a U.S. Navy A-6 sank a Libyan patrol boat making a high-speed run at the guided missile cruiser *Ticonderoga,* which was still operating below the "line of death." The action continued into the next morning, with the navy sinking or damaging two more Libyan patrol boats and twice attacking the launch site at Sirte.

Despite the clash, no Americans were killed; consequently, the plan for a full attack on Libyan targets was not implemented. On March 27, following a call from members of Congress and foreign leaders for the withdrawal of U.S. forces on the grounds that America's freedom of navigation had been established, the U.S. Navy withdrew north of the "line of death." This withdrawal, which terminated the exercises three days ahead of schedule, caused some complaints among administration hardliners, who charged that Weinberger had made the decision unilaterally.[40] According to then-Secretary of the Navy John Lehman, Kelso's plan had been that the U.S. forces would continue to approach the internationally recognized twelve-mile limit in the hope that Qaddafi would be forced to launch his air force, which would then be decimated.[41] Nevertheless, Qaddafi had suffered some losses. Two weeks after the action, Brigadier Abu-Bakr Younis, commander in chief of Libya's armed forces, said that fifty-six Libyans had been killed.

Because the nature of the exercise—a test of freedom of navigation—did not directly relate to the administration's try-and-see campaign against Qaddafi's support of terrorism, officials quickly confirmed that the exercise was planned in anticipation of a military confrontation and as a chance to underscore President Reagan's determination to deal firmly with terrorism.[42] In addition, there was always the hope—which had been expressed in the earlier administration analyses of the possibilities of undermining Qaddafi—that a military defeat, even if only a small one, might prompt the Libyan armed forces to overthrow or constrain Qaddafi.[43] Even if the armed forces did not cooperate in such an effort, the possibility that they might do so was something else for Qaddafi to worry about and thus represented a source of additional pressure. As it happened, following the conflict there were unconfirmed reports of a revolt by the Libyan navy and an assassination attempt on Qaddafi.[44]

Despite the deaths and the ominous course events were taking, Qaddafi again refused to cease and desist, and again his response to the pressure quickly became apparent. On March 25, U.S. intelligence intercepted directives from the Libyan intelligence service to the Libyan People's Bureaus in East Berlin, Paris, Rome, Madrid, and other capitals, exhorting them to plan terrorist attacks against Americans.[45] Most of the directives were phrased in general terms; however, some had specific suggestions, including a plan to attack people waiting for visas outside the American consulate in Paris. Once again Qaddafi had decided to resist U.S. pressure and raise the stakes. He publicly confirmed this decision himself the following morning, when he declared: "It is time for confrontation, for war. If they [the United States] want to expand the struggle, we will carry it all over the world."[46]

With this declaration, it seemed obvious that only a major blow would give Qaddafi pause. The administration had been prepared to deliver that blow if the March 24 exercises had resulted in an American death, but they had not done so. With that opportunity missed, Washington was forced to wait for another provocation, which, predictably, was not long in coming. On April 5, three days after the bombing of a TWA flight killed four Americans and put the issue of terrorism back in the public eye,[47] the Qaddafi government was involved in the bombing of the *La Belle* discotheque in West Berlin that killed three people (two Americans) and injured more than a hundred (around seventy of whom were U.S. service personnel). Evidence implicating Libya in the *La Belle* bombing consisted of communications between Tripoli and the Libyan People's Bureau in East Berlin that contained instructions to proceed on April 4 and a confirmation of success on April 5.[48]

The *La Belle* incident provided all the provocation the president needed to decide to launch a full-scale bombing raid. Americans had been killed in yet another terrorist attack, and there was convincing evidence that Qaddafi's government was involved. Reagan authorized an air strike on Libya the day after the disco bombing, after receiving the incriminating intercepts. Planners immediately began to finalize the plans that would guide the strongest measure the Reagan administration would adopt in its coercive policy. The only debate within the administration at this point was over what targets to hit to maximize the coercive impact of the raid while minimizing political fallout.

Although no military option other than an air strike was seriously considered, thirty-six targets, ranging from oil refineries to military bases, were examined. In the end, five targets were chosen. Three were in Tripoli: Qaddafi's command compound, the Azziziyah barracks; a frogman training school; and the military portion of the Tripoli International Airfield. Two were in Benghazi: the Benina Airfield, which was the base for much of the Libyan air defense force; and the Benghazi barracks, which housed many of Qaddafi's elite troops. The common denominator in the target choice (except for Benina, which was important to Libyan air defense) was that the chosen targets could all be linked to Qaddafi's involvement with terrorism. This would send the appropriate message, as well as provide some grounds for a legal defense of the attack based on Article 51 of the U.N. Charter, which recognizes an inherent right of self-defense. In addition, there was hope that the largely military nature of the targets would provoke a Libyan military backlash against Qaddafi. Finally, all of the targets were near the coast, which would lower the risk to the U.S. air personnel. Minimizing the probability of American casualties or prisoners was a high priority.

There had been debate over these choices, however. In the meetings of a special targeting committee that had been set up in the aftermath of the December 27 attacks, the NSC had argued that hitting the terrorism-related targets, particularly the frogman training facility (which essentially consisted of a swimming pool), made a nice statement but was virtually meaningless in terms of its cost to Qaddafi. Instead, the NSC staff preferred high-value economic targets such as oil facilities. The destruction of such targets, although perhaps inflicting greater costs on Qaddafi's regime, would also have guaranteed a higher number of civilian deaths. Although this was a trade-off the NSC was evidently willing to accept, the JCS was uncomfortable with it.[49] Since Reagan himself was highly sensitive to the chance of civilian casualties, in the end the added impact of hitting Libyan economic assets was sacrificed in favor of preserving civilian life and helping to justify the raid through a focus on terrorist-related targets.

One target, however, that was not avoided due to concerns about "collateral damage" was the Azziziyah barracks, which housed Qaddafi's command center and family residence. Of all the targets considered, Azziziyah had been deemed the most problematic because it was situated in downtown Tripoli, where it was surrounded by apartment buildings and air defenses. Because of this location, the air force planners had not even drawn up a detailed strike plan, as they had for the other thirty-six targets.

Nevertheless, according to JCS Chairman Adm. William Crowe, after the decision had been made to stage the raid, "there was strong sentiment for psychological purposes that we should do something in his personal compound and get his communications center and his headquarters."[50] Although bombing Azziziyah posed greater risks than striking other targets because it increased the likelihood of innocent deaths and was well defended, at the same time it offered the greatest coercive rewards, including the possibility that Qaddafi himself might be injured or even killed. Ultimately, the decision went to the president, who personally ordered that Azziziyah be made a target. To achieve a strong probability of successfully hitting Azziziyah, the commander of U.S. Air Forces (Europe) increased the number of F-111s to be sent to attack it despite the increased probability that one would be shot down.

Although the president did relax his standard regarding civilian casualties in ordering a strike at Azziziyah, some limits remained. To minimize possible civilian casualties, all F-111 pilots, before they dropped their bombs, had to have all their equipment operating normally and be locked onto their targets with both radar and the infrared targeting device that would sight the laser that guided the bombs. Applying this strict "double-lock" standard increased the chances that a plane would not drop its bombs, but it was considered the best way to restrict collateral damage. As it turned out, the strict ROE prevented at least four of the nine F-111s sent against Azziziyah from dropping their bombs.

In addition to refining its target plans, the administration undertook one other initiative in an attempt to maximize the coercive impact of its plan. On April 12, American Ambassador to the United Nations Vernon Walters was sent to Europe to solicit support from London, Bonn, Paris, and Rome. The administration was still determined that Qaddafi not be allowed to portray the situation as a strictly Libyan-American confrontation. But of the four governments consulted, only Margaret Thatcher's provided support—the use of airbases in Britain, where U.S. Air Force F-111s were stationed.

The Reagan administration's emphasis on minimizing civilian casualties and targeting terrorist-related facilities turned out to be important in receiving British support. Thatcher had publicly stated that "retaliatory strikes" would be "against international law." But she relented in the use of the England-based U.S. F-111s, in part because Reagan insisted that these were the best aircraft for minimizing civilian and U.S. casualties and, more important, because each proposed target had a specific connection to Qaddafi's support of terrorism (which she demanded be explained to her). In her view, as in the view of the administration, terrorist-related targets were legally justifiable.

Undeterred by the lack of allied support, and in part as a result of it, the U.S. Air Force and the U.S. Navy combined forces to bomb the five targets in Tripoli and Benghazi in the early hours of April 15 (Libya time). As a result of some equipment and timing problems and the strict ROE, many planes—six of seventeen F-111s and three of fifteen A-6s—did not release their bomb loads. Nevertheless, all five targets were hit, with evident damage. One F-111 crashed into the sea, probably as a result of antiaircraft fire. The most disappointing aspect of the raid was that despite the care taken, a number of bombs went astray. The most damaging were those that landed in the residential Bin Ashur district of Tripoli, destroying the back of the French embassy and killing many civilians. The total number of Libyan civilians killed in the entire raid, in contrast to some exaggerated reports, was probably between twenty-five and thirty.[51]

The April 14 bombing raid constituted the strongest measure of the Reagan administration's try-and-see approach. Once a commitment had been made to bring about some change in Qaddafi's policies, the bombing raid was a logical escalation from previous failed measures—as President Reagan emphasized in his announcement of the raid. In this context, the raid culminated an incremental progression from the weak end of the operational continuum of the try-and-see coercive strategy—marked by the relatively benign (and therefore mostly symbolic) January 7 executive order—to the stronger end of the continuum. The strongest measure, an urgent classic ultimatum, was never adopted, although by April 14, the Reagan administration's coercive strategy had progressed to a point just short of that measure. And although in his announcement of the raid President Reagan acknowledged the limitations of U.S. power when he said he had "no illusions that [the] action will ring down the curtain on Qaddafi's reign of terror," he hoped it would curb the Libyan ruler's terrorist attacks and "bring closer a safer and more secure world." If it did not, Reagan warned, "if necessary, we shall do it again."[52]

Despite the amount of ordnance delivered, the key to the mission from the standpoint of the administration's coercive diplomacy was its psychological impact on Qaddafi. When added to the previous measures, would it convince him that the price of his support for terrorism was too high, or would he resume his terrorist provocations? The Reagan administration had made good on its threats to impose heavy costs on Qaddafi for his support of terrorism and in doing so gave credibility to the president's statement that, if necessary, he would punish Qaddafi again. But only time would tell whether the power to inflict punishment, once established, was sufficient to compel a change in Qaddafi's behavior.

AFTERMATH AND EVALUATION

The April 14 air raid, which was supported overwhelmingly by the American public, had numerous positive results. In addition to the physical costs it imposed on Libya, there was evidence that it caused considerable unrest and dissent within the Libyan military.[53] Qaddafi's general popular support also seemed to decline in the months following the raid.[54] And Libyan relations with the Soviet Union appeared compromised, with Mikhail Gorbachev privately expressing "general displeasure" with Qaddafi and hinting that Qaddafi should avoid provoking any further U.S. action.[55] For his part, after remaining hidden for two days, Qaddafi emerged to condemn the United States and Britain, declare April 15 to have been a great victory for Libya, and retreat to his desert quarters and away from publicity.

Perhaps most important for the fight against terrorism, the administration's use of military force, and the threat to use it again if necessary, galvanized the U.S. European allies into adopting the sorts of political and economic sanctions vis-à-vis Libya that the administration had been calling for all along. Despite widespread popular condemnation of the April 14 raid, Libyan representation in EEC countries was reduced, and restrictions were placed on remaining Libyan diplomats. West Germany withdrew its ambassador from Tripoli and expelled more than half of the Libyan diplomatic representation in Bonn. Libyan student programs were terminated in Spain, Ireland, and Great Britain. In all, more than a hundred Libyan diplomats and around four hundred Libyan citizens were expelled from Europe during the summer of 1986. In addition, oil imports from Libya as well as general economic ties were reduced, and European law enforcement agencies initiated much greater counterterrorism cooperation among themselves and with the United States. In its May 4–6 meeting in Tokyo, the Group of Seven pledged to take strong steps against state sponsors of terrorism and identified Libya as a particular example.

Yet despite these substantial (and mostly indirect) benefits, on the core issue of Qaddafi's sponsorship of terrorism, the April 14 raid had more mixed results. In the two weeks following the raid, gunmen who were suspected of acting on behalf of Qaddafi's government shot and wounded two U.S. State Department officers in Sudan and Yemen. Two British hostages and one U.S. hostage (who was believed to have been purchased from his captors by Libyan intelligence) were fatally shot in Beirut, and another Briton was hanged, allegedly in reprisal for the raid. And Turkish police thwarted an attempt, which was traced directly to Libya, to launch grenades at a U.S. Air Force officers' club in Ankara.

Following this immediate rash of terrorist counterattacks, Qaddafi did appear to be quiescent for a few months. However, toward the end of the summer there was increasing evidence that he was resuming his terrorist activities. On July 23, authorities in Togo arrested nine Libyan-sponsored terrorists for planning to bomb a marketplace and the American embassy in Benin. Also during the summer, a senior Libyan diplomat associated with terrorism reappeared in East Berlin (after the Reagan administration informed the Soviet and East German authorities, he was quietly removed). On August 3, terrorists whom the British believed had been sent by Libya attacked the British base at Akrotiri on Cyprus and a nearby crowded beach. And American diplomats in Sudan reported that they were again under surveillance.

This trend continued into 1987 and beyond. In its report *Patterns in Global Terrorism: 1987,* the U.S. State Department noted that "although detectable Libyan involvement in terrorist activity dropped significantly in 1986 and 1987 after the US air raids in April 1986, Qaddafi shows no signs of forsaking terrorism."[56] In both 1987 and 1988, Libya (after Afghanistan and Iran) was the third-most-active state sponsor of terrorism. In April 1988, on the second anniversary of the U.S. air raid, circumstantial evidence linked Libya to four attacks on U.S. Information Agency buildings and the bombing of a U.S. Officers' club in Naples that killed a U.S. servicewoman and four Italians. Although administration officials debated the degree to which Qaddafi was directly involved in the attacks, there was agreement that Qaddafi was doing more to support terrorist groups.[57] In sum, Qaddafi remained a significant—although a slightly less active and certainly more covert—sponsor of international terrorism.

Thus, although there was an apparent moderation of Libyan terrorist activity from the levels experienced in 1985, it became clear soon after the April

14 raid that the administration's objective of ending Qaddafi's sponsorship of terrorism had not yet been achieved. As Reagan had implied in his announcement of the raid, there was an expectation that the United States would have to continue to pressure Qaddafi and perhaps even bomb Libya again. Almost immediately after the April 14 raid, planning for a second strike was initiated in case another compelling terrorist incident occurred. Suspecting that there was a limit to public and congressional tolerance of repeated uses of military force, and wanting to avoid a tit-for-tat scenario, the administration made plans for a more decisive strike—this time probably including the valuable Libyan oil facilities.[58] But despite evidence of continued Libyan sponsorship of terrorism against Americans, no second raid was ever conducted.

Instead, the Reagan administration continued its efforts to pressure Qaddafi through a psychological campaign that was designed to unnerve him and exploit the possibility of internal opposition. On April 27, Shultz noted that "covert action is something that we need to be using. It is certainly intended to be disruptive."[59] According to reports, from May through October navy Seal teams made landings in Libya and disrupted telephone communications with Soviet-made and Israeli-made explosives while leaving behind detritus, such as Israeli and Syrian cigarette butts and American Kleenex, to confuse and alarm Qaddafi.[60] Toward the end of the summer, as the evidence of possible renewed Libyan sponsorship of terrorism emerged and was being evaluated, the psychological campaign was escalated. However, it all fell apart in October when, as a result of a leaked memo, the administration was charged with having deliberately misled American newspapers in August in an effort to create the impression that U.S. military reprisals against Libya were imminent.[61]

The resulting embarrassment and public furor over this incident seemingly marked the end of the Reagan administration's coercive campaign against Libya. One month later, revelations about the administration's arms for hostages deals with Iran, and the diversion of profits to the Nicaraguan contras, became public. All attention inside and outside the administration was sharply diverted from any terrorism Qaddafi might still be sponsoring. According to one report, in a series of high-level meetings to review policy for the Middle East in February 1987, the Reagan administration decided to strongly diminish the visible involvement of President Reagan and other cabinet members in responding to terrorism.[62] Whether such a decision was in fact made, a serious coercive policy vis-à-vis Libya was no longer in evidence after 1986; Libya had simply ceased to be a priority. Thus, despite the evidence that Qaddafi's government was continuing to sponsor terrorism, the administration's coercive campaign against him was never brought to a decisive conclusion.

Even with the advantages of hindsight, it is difficult to accurately assess the degree to which the Reagan administration's policy was directly responsible for the apparent moderation of Qaddafi's terrorist involvement. There is no doubt that the policy, and in particular the April 14 raid, had an impact on Qaddafi's balance of calculation. But other factors were involved, and these blur the picture somewhat. For example, the apparent moderation in Qaddafi's sponsorship of terrorism might have been due in part to his efforts to disguise his involvement.[63] In addition, after April 14, Europe adopted stricter counterterrorism measures that made it possible to preempt a number of terrorist plots.[64] The Europeans' stricter treatment of Libyan nationals and the reduction in economic ties might also have helped to discourage Qaddafi's support of terrorism. Finally, other political developments, such as Libya's dramatic defeat in Chad at the end of 1986 and in 1987 (in which perhaps three thousand Libyans were killed) may also have cooled Qaddafi's ardor for adventurism.

In short, although it is fair to say that the Reagan administration's coercive diplomacy played a direct role in affecting Qaddafi's behavior, without an explanation from Qaddafi himself it is impossible to determine precisely how significant that role was in relation to the indirect effects of the raid, such as European cooperation in counterterrorism and other potential factors. What can definitely be said is that Qaddafi continued to sponsor terrorism, albeit with reduced enthusiasm, in defiance of the Reagan administration's demands.

CONCLUSIONS

Although it is difficult to draw definitive conclusions about the success of the Reagan administration's coercive diplomacy vis-à-vis Libya, some conclusions can be drawn that are relevant to coercive diplomacy in general. The first point that stands out in this case is the difficulty of fashioning a successful coercive policy if allied cooperation is at all important. Allies frequently have different interests at stake and make different assessments of common threats. So any coercive policy that seeks to achieve pressure on an adversary through political and economic sanctions is likely to suffer from the difficulty of achieving multilateral unity on all but the most pressing issues. There are situations in which the United States so dominates the foreign and trade relations of a country or region that unilateral sanctions can result in substantial pressure. However, this was not the case with Libya. As a result, the most ready instrument at the administration's disposal to pressure Qaddafi was almost totally ineffective. Universally applied, the economic and diplomatic sanctions levied on Libya by the Reagan administration would have given Qaddafi enormous inducement to alter his behavior.

Similarly, even though the United States is essentially a self-sufficient military power, allied dissent had a negative effect on the coercive impact of the April 14 raid. French denial of overflight rights, for example, doubled the F-

111 flying times, reduced the bomb loads each plane could carry, and reduced to six (from eighteen) the number of F-111s that could hit each target selected. Furthermore, although the Reagan administration had other options if necessary, Margaret Thatcher's determination not to allow another raid to be staged from British airbases, as well as general European popular sentiment, no doubt affected administration thinking regarding a second strike. It is easy to imagine situations—particularly if targets are not easily accessible from the sea, as they were in Libya—in which denial of staging rights could undermine U.S. military options in a coercive policy. Conversely, allied support for, if not participation in, the military reprisals would have greatly increased Qaddafi's sense of isolation.

The Libya case also demonstrates the difficulty of carrying out coercive diplomacy that relies heavily on military force to create pressure for compliance. The United States, by objective standards, possesses great military power. However, this case, as well as numerous other U.S. experiences with the use of force, demonstrates that there are significant indigenous structural limitations on that power. For a multitude of reasons, it is often difficult to unite the U.S. government behind any significant use of force. The facility with which an administration resorts to force can vary according to the individuals who occupy key positions in the government—Weinberger, for example, was a particularly cautious secretary of defense when it came to the use of force. However, there are structural impediments that will survive any personnel transitions. For example, throughout the postwar era, the U.S. military establishment has been consistently wary of policies that require easy or frequent resort to force, particularly if the use of force must be very specific and limited according to "political" criteria. In the case of Libya, the views of Weinberger and the Pentagon in general exerted a constraining influence on both policy deliberations and the use of force.

Similarly, political criteria also often serve as a structural limitation on the use of U.S. military power. As noted in the case of Libya, emergence of the issues of proportionality and culpability had a significant influence on whether force was seen as an available option and on the choice of targets. Not only did the highly legalistic approach the administration adopted tend to inhibit its resort to force, but Qaddafi also learned to exploit U.S. attacks. As the State Department's reports on terrorism acknowledged, after the April 14 raid Qaddafi made efforts to mask his involvement with terrorism.[65] But despite the clear evidence of Qaddafi's continued sponsorship of terrorism, the administration claimed never to have found another "smoking gun." This may have been because the administration found it politically expedient not to find any more smoking guns. But if Washington was sincerely looking for incriminating evidence to justify further action against Qaddafi, his measures to shield his involvement could only have made the task more difficult. Furthermore, as the case also demonstrated, there was a sense in the administration that even though Qaddafi and terrorism were sources of great public frustration and animosity, there were limits to public support for reprisal raids.

One final point about the limitations of force is that the administration's reliance on force to bring pressure to bear on Qaddafi compelled it to surrender much of the initiative to Qaddafi. Economic and political sanctions can be unilaterally levied against an adversary any time a country chooses to do so, with little question of illegality. Military force cannot be justifiably applied, however, unless there is a legitimate provocation. As a result, because military force was essentially the only instrument by which the Reagan administration could impose severe costs on Qaddafi, it was in the position of having to either provoke Qaddafi, as it did with the March naval exercises in Sidra, or wait for Qaddafi to commit some atrocity, such as the bombing of the *La Belle* discotheque. Had Qaddafi refused to be provoked or refrained from committing any blatant provocations, the administration's coercive policy might have stalled.

Moreover, the limitations on force as an instrument of coercion against Libya were particularly profound given the weakness of the sanctions and the fact that offering Qaddafi any kind of positive inducement was apparently not an option. The effectiveness of the coercive policy thus depended heavily on the effectiveness with which the difficult instrument of force could be used to pressure Qaddafi.

The deficiencies of force as a coercive instrument are perhaps not so onerous if a tangible, finite settlement is possible—such as withdrawal from an invasion. As the Libya case demonstrates, however, these deficiencies are magnified by coercive policies that admit of no finite resolution—such as when sustained good behavior is the objective. As Thomas Schelling pointed out, such policies are open-ended in that the application of coercive pressure is susceptible to being required again and again.[66] Since the use of U.S. military force, particularly against terrorism, requires such specific circumstances (for example, a smoking gun or any number of political prerequisites), it is not an instrument that is easily used again and again. In 1985, the American public became intensely frustrated by terrorism (one poll indicated that 78 percent of all Americans considered terrorism to be one of the most serious problems facing the U.S. government[67]), as well as offended by Qaddafi's bloodthirsty public cheerleading; hence, there was widespread support for the use of force. By the end of 1986, however, the domestic political context, from which any coercive policy ultimately must draw its strength, had altered drastically. The American public's fervent desire to strike back at terrorism had been relieved to some extent by the April 14 raid, and the Reagan administration was poised on the brink of the Iran-contra scandal—the worst political crisis of its tenure. For the policy toward Qaddafi to have been credible, and ultimately successful in terms of its defined objective, the Reagan admin-

istration had to be ready and able to apply the stick of military power whenever concrete evidence of Libyan involvement in terrorism again surfaced.

The coercive campaign against Qaddafi may have withered away because
the administration was truly satisfied with the above-noted benefits, which
the policy had reaped, and would have opted to end it no matter how favorable the political circumstances were for a drawn-out battle of wills with the
Libyan leader. But if the Reagan administration had not been satisfied simply
with a moderation of terrorist activity on Qaddafi's part, it would have been
difficult to relentlessly use U.S. military power to punish and deter Qaddafi
in the face of dubious public support and certain European outrage. Even
Secretary of State Shultz, who had said privately after the April 14 raid that
the United States would go back again and again until Qaddafi relented, felt
obliged to offer public assurance that "we're not going to get into a kind of
automatic pilot on this."[68] Thus, when a Libyan-trained group bombed the
United Services Organization in Naples on the two-year anniversary of the
April 14 raid—which was an act highly analogous to the *La Belle* discotheque bombing and came among numerous other signs of resurgent Libyan
involvement with terrorism—there was not even a pretense that the Reagan
administration might respond with military reprisals.

In the final analysis, then, in terms of ending Qaddafi's support for terrorism the Reagan administration's coercive policy had significant weaknesses.
It benefited greatly from the initial determination to confront Qaddafi decisively, the mobilization of powerful public support for doing so, and a sufficient array of controllable military options. But its effectiveness over time
was ultimately undermined by the difficulty of bringing the conflict to a durable settlement, the almost total reliance on a coercive instrument—military
force—which was subject to significant constraints (particularly over time),
and Qaddafi's strong motivation and ability to continue his sponsorship of
terrorism while minimizing the risks of repeated military reprisal. Libya is
still designated by the U.S. State Department as a state that supports terrorism and is currently under U.N.-imposed sanctions until it extradites two intelligence agents indicted in the December 1988 bombing of Pan Am 103
(which killed 270 people), sends four other Libyans to France for questioning in connection with the 1989 downing of a French airliner over West Africa (which killed 177), and takes "concrete actions" to show it has re-
nounced terrorism.

BIBLIOGRAPHICAL NOTE

This chapter updates an original effort, "The American Bombing of Libya: A Success
for Coercive Diplomacy?" that appeared in *Survival* (May/June 1987), pp. 195–214.
Although the essential elements of the Libya policy were evident by the end of 1986,
much of the behind-the-scenes policy debate was not. Two books, on which this ver-

sion draws heavily, provided that background: David C. Martin and John Walcott, *Best Laid Plans: The Inside Story of America's War Against Terrorism* (New York: Harper & Row, 1988), which benefits from numerous interviews with those involved in the formulation and implementation of the policy; and Brian L. Davis, *Qaddafi, Terrorism, and the Origins of the U.S. Attack on Libya* (New York: Praeger 1990), which provides a comprehensive look at Qaddafi's involvement with terrorism as well as the U.S. response. Other books about the Reagan administration, which contain information about the Libya policy but are not nearly so useful, are Bob Woodward, *Veil: The Secret Wars of the CIA 1981–1987* (New York: Simon and Schuster, 1987); Caspar Weinberger, *Fighting For Peace* (New York: Warner Books, 1990), and John F. Lehman, Jr., *Command of the Seas* (New York: Scribner's, 1988).

In addition to profiting from the new information provided by these books, this chapter benefited greatly from insights into the administration's thinking provided by Dr. Elaine Morton, Dr. Peter Rodman (both of whom were involved with the policy at the State Department and then at the NSC), and Howard Teicher. Dr. Morton and Dr. Rodman also read carefully a lengthy draft of this study, for which I am grateful. I would especially like to thank Dr. Morton for taking all the time she did in an effort to help me avoid errors and misinterpretations. Any that remain are my own responsibility.

NOTES

1. For information on the Reagan administration's relationship and policies regarding Libya for the period 1981–1985, see Brian L. Davis, *Qaddafi, Terrorism, and the Origins of the U.S. Attack on Libya* (New York: Praeger, 1990); Bob Woodward, *Veil: The Secret Wars of the CIA 1981–1987* (New York: Simon and Schuster, 1987); and David C. Martin and John Walcott, *Best Laid Plans: The Inside Story of America's War Against Terrorism* (New York: Harper & Row, 1988).

2. Between 1979 and 1983, the number of international terrorist incidents averaged five hundred per year. In 1984, the number increased to approximately six hundred and resulted in 1,279 casualties (312 dead). In 1985, the number jumped to more than eight hundred, with 2,177 casualties (877 dead).

3. Secretary of State George Shultz, "Terrorism: The Challenge to the Democracies," address before the Jonathan Institute's second Conference on International Terrorism, June 24, 1984. Department of State *Bulletin,* August 1984, p. 33.

4. "Remarks at the Annual Convention of the American Bar Association," July 8, 1985, *Public Papers of the Presidents: Ronald Reagan, 1985* (Washington, D.C.: U.S. Government Printing Office, 1988), p. 897.

5. Lou Cannon, "U.S. Mulls Reprisal for Terrorism," *Washington Post,* July 12, 1985, p. 1.

6. For a good account of the Qaddafi government's terrorist and other provocations between 1981 and 1985 and the Reagan administration's responses, see Davis, *Qaddafi, Terrorism,* pp. 38–69.

7. During and after the hijacking, evidence mounted that the Libyan government was a sponsor. The CIA picked up one report that Qaddafi had paid up to $5 million for the operation, and intercepts of communications between Tripoli and the Libyan People's Bureau in Malta, where the plane had been forced to land, indicated that the

Libyan government was probably aware that the hijacking was going to occur and passed instructions to the hijackers once the plane had landed in Malta. The grenades used in the operation were also later definitely traced to Libya (Martin and Walcott, *Best Laid Plans,* p. 267; and Davis, *Qaddafi, Terrorism,* p. 77).

8. The terrorists who survived the attack admitted to being members of Abu Nidal's gang. Some carried Tunisian passports, which the Tunisian government identified as passports confiscated from Tunisian workers who had been expelled from Libya (Martin and Walcott, *Best Laid Plans,* pp. 267–268; and Davis, *Qaddafi, Terrorism,* pp. 78–80).

9. Secretary of State George Shultz, "Low-Intensity Warfare: The Challenge of Ambiguity," speech to the National Defense University's Low-Intensity Warfare Conference, January 15, 1986. Department of State *Bulletin,* March 1986, p. 16.

10. Prior to 1986, the Reagan administration had closed Libya's diplomatic mission in Washington (May 1981); authorized covert activities to undermine Qaddafi (June 1981); asked all Americans to leave Libya and invalidated American passports for travel to Libya (December 1981); and banned all U.S. purchases of Libyan oil, as well as U.S. exports to Libya of all commodities already banned in trade with the Communist bloc (implemented March 1982).

11. "The President's News Conference," January 7, 1986, *Public Papers of the Presidents: Ronald Reagan, 1986* (Washington, D.C.: U.S. Government Printing Office, 1988), pp. 17–18.

12. For background on Qaddafi and his revolution, see David Blundy and Andrew Lycett, *Qaddafi and the Libyan Revolution* (Boston: Little, Brown, 1987); John H. Colley, *Libyan Sandstorm* (New York: Holt, Rinehart and Winston, 1982); Lisa Anderson, "Qaddafi's Islam," in John L. Esposito, ed., *Voices of Resurgent Islam* (New York: Oxford University Press, 1983); and John Wright, *Libya: A Modern History* (Baltimore: Johns Hopkins University Press, 1982).

13. *International Herald Tribune,* April 14, 1986.

14. Martin and Walcott, *Best Laid Plans,* pp. 262–264.

15. The efforts to bomb Qaddafi's headquarters, where he spent much of his time, led to allegations that the administration had made an assassination attempt in violation of its own executive order. Although no conclusive evidence has emerged that a major objective of the bombing raid was to kill Qaddafi, the most determined effort to prove that this was the case is Seymour Hersh, "Target Qaddafi," *New York Times Magazine,* February 22, 1987, p. 17. Hersh's article has been widely criticized by administration officials and analysts alike as containing many inaccuracies.

16. Thomas Schelling, *Arms and Influence* (New Haven: Yale University Press, 1966), p. 76.

17. These two criteria had emerged from the debate over the use of force against terrorism, principally between Weinberger and Shultz, that had been ongoing since the 1983 bombing of the Marine barracks in Lebanon. In publicizing his views on the appropriate role of force, Shultz argued for rather permissive standards, advocating the use of preemptive or retaliatory strikes—against cities if necessary—on the basis of evidence that would not necessarily stand up in a U.S. court of law. But according to Weinberger, President Reagan was uncomfortable with this "unfocused" approach and strongly opposed any option that might indiscriminately kill or wound innocent people. Instead, Reagan was more sympathetic to Weinberger's approach, which was

to make a "focused" response whenever the identities and locations of terrorists could be ascertained—that is, the response would target only terrorists or their facilities and be appropriate to the terrorist action (Caspar Weinberger, *Fighting For Peace* [New York: Warner Books, 1990], p. 188).

18. "Address to the Nation on the United States Air Strike Against Libya," April 14, 1986, *Public Papers of the Presidents: Ronald Reagan, 1986*, p. 469.

19. For Weinberger's views on the proper role of force in U.S. foreign policy, see his "The Uses of Military Power," speech before the National Press Club, November 28, 1984 (a text can be found in the appendix of Weinberger, *Fighting For Peace,* pp. 433–445); "What Is Our Defense Strategy?" speech before the National Press Club, October 9, 1985; and "U.S. Defense Strategy," *Foreign Affairs* 64, no. 4 (Spring 1986): 675–697.

20. Targets selected were Qaddafi's terrorist training camps and piles of uncrated Soviet military equipment at Libyan bases.

21. Martin and Walcott, *Best Laid Plans,* p. 277.

22. Ninety percent of Libya's export earnings derived from the sale of oil, and by 1985 more than 80 percent of the oil Libya exported went to Europe (with Italy and Germany purchasing the bulk share). Much of Libya's oil-lifting equipment also came from Western Europe.

23. Davis, *Qaddafi, Terrorism,* pp. 82–83.

24. For a complete list of specific measures, see "Factsheet: Executive Order on Libya," U.S. Information Service, January 8, 1986. The administration had, in fact, seriously considered applying this full range of sanctions in March 1982. But the package had been watered down in response to complaints from agencies such as the Treasury Department.

During an interview, Reagan characterized the measure requiring the departure from Libya of U.S. citizens as a step to remove "potential hostages … to untie our hands with regard to whatever action might be necessary in the future" ("Reagan Lists Terms for Lifting Libyan Sanctions,"*New York Times,* January 12, 1986) p 12.

25. This was particularly the case since the only step the administration did not take in its January 7 package was the application of the restrictions to U.S. foreign subsidiaries. These restrictions were not instituted because Secretary of State Shultz wanted to avoid a reprise of the uncomfortable imbroglio that had occurred in 1982 over the Reagan administration's attempt, in response to the declaration of martial law in Poland, to embargo the flow of Western technology to the Soviet natural gas pipeline to Western Europe that was then under construction.

26. "The President's News Conference," January 7, 1986, *Public Papers of the Presidents: Ronald Reagan, 1986,* pp. 17–18.

27. Michael White and Alex Brummer, "Reagan Steps Up Pressure on Allies," *Guardian,* January 9, 1986.

28. Reasons ranged from skepticism about the effectiveness of sanctions to professed inability to restrict crude oil purchases by private oil companies (some of which were primarily owned by U.S. companies) to the belief that isolating Qaddafi would only give him political strength and make him more reckless. In addition, the European allies unanimously expressed opposition to the use of military force against Libya.

29. The administration froze $1 billion in Libyan assets, only to have a British bank return $320 million following a British court's ruling that the sanctions did not apply to British branches of U.S. banks. In addition, Qaddafi raised $3.2 billion through the sale of Libya's share in Fiat and demonstrated that the technology restrictions were porous by importing two Airbus jets with U.S. engines through Jordan by the use of a dummy corporation in Hong Kong (Martin and Walcott, *Best Laid Plans*, p. 276).

30. Bernard Gwertzman, "U.S. Navy Exercise Starts Off Libya," *New York Times*, January 15, 1986, p. 1.

31. Qaddafi claimed 32'30''N latitude as the boundary of his territorial waters, although it is more than a hundred miles from the Libyan coast. International law recognizes a twelve-mile territorial limit.

32. *New York Times*, January 24, 1986.

33. Radio Free Europe, January 25, 1986; interviews with administration officials.

34. See Lt. Cmdr. Robert E. Stumpf, "Air War with Libya," *Proceedings* 112, no. 8 (August 1986): 42–48.

35. Judith Miller, "Qaddafi Says He has Called 'Full Alert,'" *New York Times*, January 25, 1986, p. 4.

36. *New York Times*, March 26, 1986. In the view of at least one Reagan administration policy analyst, this decision was prompted more by the imminent arrival of a third aircraft carrier than by Qaddafi's continuing resistance. According to this interpretation of events, the administration had already determined (in late January or February) that it would use force against Qaddafi, and the January and February operations—rather than being a phase of try and see—were simply a means to maintain pressure while Americans were given a chance to leave and sufficient forces were being marshaled.

Although Shultz and National Security Advisor John Poindexter had been in favor of a foray below 32'30''N since January, the evidence seems to indicate that Reagan did not decide to implement actions until February, following the signs that Qaddafi was continuing to contemplate terrorist attacks (see *New York Times*, March 26, 1986; and Davis, *Qaddafi, Terrorism*, pp. 101–102).

37. Whereas in the January and February exercises U.S. forces could only retaliate against the particular Libyan that committed a hostile act, in the March exercises the U.S. forces were given leave, once the first shot had been fired, to attack any Libyans deemed to be in a hostile position (Martin and Walcott, *Best Laid Plans*, p. 281).

38. Hersh, "Target Qaddafi," p. 74; Martin and Walcott, *Best Laid Plans*, p. 281; Davis, *Qaddafi, Terrorism*, pp. 103–104; Woodward, *Veil*, p. 441; and interviews with administration officials.

39. Martin and Walcott, *Best Laid Plans*, p. 281.

40. Davis, *Qaddafi, Terrorism*, p. 105.

41. John F. Lehman, Jr., *Command of the Seas* (New York: Scribner's, 1988), pp. 370–371.

42. *New York Times*, March 26, 27, 1986.

43. R. W. Apple, "U.S. Said to Hope Clashes Prompt Moves in Libya to Oust Qaddafi," *New York Times*, April 3, 1986, p. 1. There were at least four possible coup attempts in 1985.

44. Davis, *Qaddafi, Terrorism*, p. 108.

45. Martin and Walcott, *Best Laid Plans,* p. 284.

46. John Kifner, "Qaddafi Threatens a Wider Struggle," *New York Times,* March 26, 1986, p. 1.

47. The bombing was carried out by the Arab Revolutionary Cells in retaliation for the Gulf of Sidra operation, but no connections to Libya were apparent. Intelligence officials later concluded that the operation was conducted by an associate of Yasir Arafat.

48. Almost concurrent with the discotheque bombing, other Libyan terrorist plots came to light. On the same day, the French government expelled two Libyan diplomats who were planning the suggested attack on the American visa office. On April 6, Libyan agents attempted to fire a rocket-propelled grenade at the American embassy in Beirut. Three Libyans were caught trying to kidnap the American ambassador to Rwanda, and there were some reports that Qaddafi was trying to buy U.S. hostages in Beirut (Martin and Walcott, *Best Laid Plans,* p. 289).

49. Ibid., pp. 272–273.

50. Ibid., p. 287.

51. Davis, *Qaddafi, Terrorism,* p. 142.

52. "Address to the Nation on the United States Air Strike Against Libya," April 14, 1986, *Public Papers of the Presidents: Ronald Reagan, 1986,* p. 469. The administration had at least some hope that the raid would end Qaddafi's life. On the chance that he was killed, a statement about his death—which called it "fortuitous"—had been prepared for the president's news conference.

53. The morning following the raid, there were reports that the Libyan air force was forced to bomb a rebel convoy of the Libyan army at the Uqba bin Nafi military base, as well as dissident troops attempting to march to Tripoli from a base southeast of the city. In addition, Qaddafi's German advisers allegedly were forced to squelch a minor rebellion at Azziziyah two days after the raid. The administration encouraged just this sort of rebellious activity through Voice of America broadcasts that all but called for Qaddafi's overthrow (Davis, *Qaddafi, Terrorism,* pp. 143–144).

54. During a summer soccer riot in Tripoli the crowd yelled opposition to Qaddafi and defaced posters of him. Opposition from Islamic fundamentalists increased over the course of the summer, and following the assassination of three government officials in the fall, Qaddafi was forced to close forty-eight Islamic institutes in an effort to quell opposition (Davis, *Qaddafi, Terrorism,* pp. 144–145).

55. Ibid., p. 147.

56. *Patterns of Global Terrorism:* 1987 (Washington, D.C.: Department of State, August 1988), p. 36. For more evidence, see *Patterns of Global Terrorism* for 1986, 1988, and 1989.

57. *Washington Post,* June 3, 1988; and *New York Times,* June 3, 1988.

58. For a second strike, U.S. planners also had to do without the F-111s based in Britain. Thatcher had made it clear that she did not want to be asked again. Consideration was given to using cruise missiles (Davis, *Qaddafi, Terrorism,* pp. 159–160; Martin and Walcott, *Best Laid Plans,* p. 315; interviews with administration officials).

59. Bernard Gwertzman, "Shultz Advocates U.S. Covert Action Programs to Depose Qaddafi," *New York Times,* April 28, 1986, p. 7.

60. Davis, *Qaddafi, Terrorism,* pp. 161–162.

61. Martin and Walcott, *Best Laid Plans,* pp. 317–321; Davis, *Qaddafi, Terrorism,* p. 164.

62. David K. Shipler, "One Year After U.S. Raid, a Lower Libyan Profile," *New York Times,* April 12, 1987, p. 14.

63. According to *Patterns of Global Terrorism: 1987:* "We have little doubt that the US air raids on Libya in 1986 contributed heavily to Qadhafi's subsequent caution. At the same time, however, we are equally sure that he continued planning for anti-US attacks involving the use of surrogate groups to disguise Libyan responsibility" (p. 37). The 1988 assessment notes that "most regimes that sponsor or otherwise support terrorism have become less active or have hidden their activities more successfully since 1986" (p. 44).

64. These improvements in counterterrorist operations were a welcome development, one the State Department consistently emphasized as a factor in any apparent reductions in terrorism. See introductory "Year in Review" in *Patterns of Global Terrorism,* 1987, 1988, and 1989.

65. See note 63.

66. Schelling, *Arms and Influence.*

67. *Public Report of the Vice-President's Task Force on Combatting Terrorism* (Washington, D.C.: U.S. Government Printing Office, February 1986), pp. 5, 17.

68. Martin and Walcott, *Best Laid Plans,* p. 312.

10

Coercive Diplomacy and the Crisis over Kuwait, 1990–1991

RICHARD HERRMANN

Why did the U.S. coercive diplomacy fail in the Gulf crisis of 1990–1991? Washington was successful in constructing a multilateral sanctions regime endorsed by the United Nations and moved a massive number of troops to make its threat to use force credible, and yet Saddam Hussein refused to comply and instead took the risks of war. Why? And why did the Bush administration give up on coercive diplomacy and resort to war after only five months, before the sanctions regime took its full toll? These are difficult questions to answer given that we do not have any definitive information about the thinking in Baghdad and can only speculate on Saddam's perceptions and calculations. We cannot be entirely sure what the calculations in Washington were, either.

Explanations for the failure of coercive diplomacy can differ depending on which variables are emphasized. For instance, one answer might propose that the U.S. threat was not seen as credible by the Iraqis despite the Bush administration's efforts. Perhaps Secretary of State James Baker's mission to Geneva in early January 1991 to convey Washington's resolve personally to Iraqi Foreign Minister Tariq Aziz backfired and only convinced Baghdad that President George Bush was reluctant to go to war. The legacy of Washington's "tilt" toward Iraq during much of the Iran-Iraq War may have left residual beliefs in Baghdad that worked to undermine the effective communication of U.S. threats.

Perhaps, however, Saddam Hussein did not see the opportunities for expansion the previous paragraph implies but instead saw immutable threats emanating from the United States. In early 1990, he began to advertise his fear that, emboldened by the collapse of Soviet power, Israel and Washington were tempted to attack Iraq. Soviet envoy Yevgeniy Primakov has argued that coercive diplomacy failed because of Saddam's "masada" complex. In his view, the Iraqi president convinced himself that an Israeli-American assault was inevitable and that honor required suicide before surrender. He regrets that Washington did not do more to reassure Iraq that there was a way out of the crisis that would preserve Iraq's capability base and Saddam's "face." According to this analysis, the Iraqi perception of noncontingent threats more than perceptions of lack of U.S. resolve explained the failure of coercive diplomacy.

It is also possible that the answer will vary across different moments during the crisis. Perhaps it was ineffective reassurance early in the crisis that made Iraq dig in and then later, in December and January, it was a failure to convince Saddam that the U.N. coalition would really go to war. Or ineffective deterrence before the invasion and a policy of only sanctions after the aggression may have signaled insufficient U.S. credibility, whereas Washington's later determination to humiliate Saddam Hussein convinced the Iraqi dictator that the risks to his personal power from surrender without dignity were greater than the risks of defeat in war. This latter theory points to yet another variable that might explain the failure—that is, Washington's interest by early January 1991 in preventive war.

For many Arabs who were sympathetic to Iraq's arguments during the crisis, it was George Bush, not Saddam Hussein, who was moving beyond coercive diplomacy and pushing the situation toward war. In their view, coercive diplomacy failed because Washington did not give it enough time to work and did not really want it to work. They believed the Bush administration had primary objectives that went well beyond liberating Kuwait, which was the putative purpose of the coercive diplomacy. The United States, according to this perspective, was determined to destroy Iraq's capability base, overthrow Saddam Hussein if possible, and guarantee Israel's regional supremacy. These objectives could not be achieved with coercive diplomacy alone but required large-scale offensive military action against Iraq.

We are still too close to the experience and have too little reliable evidence about the prevailing views and calculations to draw definitive conclusions about the possible answers to the question of why coercive diplomacy failed in the Gulf crisis. We can, however, set out the basic arguments and consider the evidence that is available with regard to the competing interpretations. That is the purpose of this chapter.

The Gulf conflict can be divided into four periods: (1) a pre-crisis period before the Iraqi invasion of Kuwait on August 2, 1990; (2) a reactive crisis phase between August 2 and early October in which the U.S. deployed a deterrent force to protect Saudi Arabia and employed an economic sanctions strategy against Iraq; (3) a transition phase beginning in late October and running through December in which U.S. coercive diplomacy moved beyond an economic strategy and threatened the direct use of force to eject Iraq from Kuwait; and (4) a period of air war in January 1991 followed in February by a ground defeat of Iraqi forces and their expulsion from Kuwait. This chapter concentrates mainly on the second and third phases, the periods in which coercive diplomacy was practiced. The balance is organized into three parts, with one part devoted to each phase and a third assessing the failure of coercive diplomacy to resolve the crisis.

The chapter does not detail the day-by-day exchange of notes, threats, and maneuvers in a tit-for-tat type of sequence but focuses instead on the key interpretative arguments about U.S. and Iraqi perceptions, calculations, and policy moves. Each time period opens with a discussion of prevailing U.S. views and the decision process leading to the implementation of coercive diplomacy. Following this is a discussion of Iraq's reaction to the U.S. efforts, which involves interpreting Saddam Hussein's perceptions of the situation and trying to understand his calculations. In each time period, a subsection is devoted to the various attempts to find a negotiated solution that either Iraq or the United States might have pursued. Organizing the discussion of the second and third phases of the crisis around sections on U.S. and then Iraqi perceptions has the disadvantage of partially disrupting the chronological sequence of events. It has the great advantage, however, of focusing directly on the key questions of why President Bush decided to move from the sanctions regime to the threat of using force and finally to war, and why Saddam Hussein refused to comply.

Iraqi and U.S. perceptions are not simple data points waiting to be discovered. They must be inferred from a complex set of evidence and will inevitably be based on auxiliary arguments and interpretations. Instead of jumping back and forth between judgments about U.S. and Iraqi views as day-to-day events unfolded, I concentrate on inferring American views in the first section of each time period. I then tackle Iraqi views. This requires organizing the evidence from each phase as it pertains to the propositions about U.S. and Iraqi calculations rather than presenting them in a straight chronological fashion. My purpose is not to retell the story in a sequential time line but to examine the key variables that relate to coercive diplomacy and explain why diplomacy failed.

PHASE TWO: DETERRENCE AND SANCTIONS-BASED COERCIVE DIPLOMACY, AUGUST–OCTOBER 1990

U.S. Calculations and Policy

Only five days after the Iraqi invasion of Kuwait, President Bush addressed the nation and spelled out four principles that would guide U.S. policy: (1)

Iraq's unconditional and complete withdrawal from Kuwait, (2) the restoration of Kuwait's legitimate government, (3) a commitment to security and stability in the Persian Gulf, and (4) the protection of American citizens abroad.[1] A week later, the president defined these four principles as "our objectives" and described the methods of deterrence and compulsion that would be used to achieve them.[2] The United States would send military forces to Saudi Arabia to deter an Iraqi attack on the kingdom or any other target in the Gulf beyond Kuwait. It would also attempt to isolate Iraq and rely on the embargo of Iraq's exports and imports to compel an Iraqi retreat.

Hours after Iraqi troops crossed into Kuwait, the United States began to freeze Iraqi and Kuwaiti assets and moved in the United Nations to mobilize the international condemnation of Iraq.[3] Almost immediately, on August 2, the United Nations passed Resolution 660 condemning Iraq's aggression and on August 6 passed U.N. Resolution 661 calling on all states to prevent the commercial trade of all commodities with Iraq and occupied Kuwait. By August 16, the United States had begun to enforce U.N. 661 with a naval blockade. Near the end of the month, on August 25, the United Nations passed Resolution 665 outlawing trade with Iraq. Throughout September the United Nations continued to tighten the economic squeeze; on September 13 it passed U.N. 666 limiting humanitarian supplies to Iraq and empowering the U.N. Security Council (including the United States, with its veto power) to decide when and if these shipments were necessary. At this point, the variant of coercive diplomacy Washington was applying was that of the "gradual turning of the screw."

In explaining and justifying his decisions, in a series of statements President Bush identified a number of U.S. interests at stake.[4] Oil was an important factor. The president also stressed the "truly significant" importance of proving that America will stand by its friends. "The mission of our troops," he said, was "wholly defensive. ... They will not initiate hostilities, but they will defend themselves, the Kingdom of Saudi Arabia, and other friends."[5] In addition to preserving credibility, the president emphasized "the lesson of history" and the protection of principle. Drawing a direct analogy to the 1930s, he argued that "we must resist aggression ... appeasement does not work."[6] In September, Secretary Baker picked up on this theme and said that at this "defining moment" in the new era, the United States had to stop aggression; not doing so would invite an explosion of violence. He said that from "a strategic standpoint, we must show that intimidation and force are not successful ways of doing business in the volatile Middle East—or anywhere else."[7]

Although the secretary of state, along with Secretary of Defense Richard Cheney, identified the economic importance of the Gulf as the most obvious U.S. interest at stake, it would be a mistake to minimize the importance of the "strategic" issue.[8] In 1990, the Arab world was divided. Both Iraq and Egypt were reclaiming their traditional importance in intra-Arab politics. President Hosni Mubarak was being accepted back into the Arab fold despite Egypt's peace agreement with Israel. President Saddam Hussein, free from the constraints of the Iran-Iraq War, was again interested in leading the eastern Arabs. Mubarak was ready to work closely with the United States on regional matters and to pursue a strategy of compromise on Arab-Israeli issues. Saddam, however, in 1990 revived the old symbols of Arab nationalism, playing heavily on anti-American, anti-Israeli, and anti-imperial Arab and Islamic populist sentiments and promoting an "Arab peace through strength" strategy. Baker argued that Saddam's aggression could not be allowed to reap benefits that Mubarak's efforts at reconciliation and accommodation had not.

The U.S. strategic interest in discrediting Saddam Hussein's resort to power politics required going beyond the deterrent mission. The United States also had to compel Iraq to leave Kuwait and to do so without giving Iraq any auxiliary concessions on the issues of Gulf security or Israeli-Palestinian relations. Even in early August, politicians in Washington wondered whether coercive diplomacy backed only by economic sanctions would be sufficient to compel Iraq's retreat.[9] Moreover, some policy makers wondered whether a strategy geared only to the objective of returning to the status quo ante would be sufficient to achieve President Bush's third objective pertaining to security in the Gulf. If Iraq retreated with all of its military assets intact, then it could still intimidate the other Gulf states. Given Saddam's interest in nuclear, chemical, and missile technologies, such an outcome would also contribute to Israel's insecurity.

Although scenarios for a preventive war to deflate Iraq's offensive military potential were circulating in Washington, in the early period of the crisis these were mostly theoretical exercises.[10] In mid-September, Gen. Colin Powell described the deployed U.S. forces as not yet at a level that could with confidence defend against further Iraqi aggression, much less eject Iraq from Kuwait or pursue preventive war against Baghdad.[11] Secretary Cheney described the military mission as "clear-cut" and as limited to deterring attack and preparing to defend.[12] U.S. forces would enforce the U.N. sanctions, but the compellent power would have to come from effecting Iraq's isolation, not from a preventive war.

For the sanctions regime to work, international compliance with the U.N. resolutions was vital. This meant that Turkey and Saudi Arabia had to close the pipelines carrying Iraqi oil across their territories and that Syria had to keep the pipelines across its territory closed. Turkey agreed to comply on August 7, evidently confident that its military might would deter any Iraqi military retaliation.[13] In Riyadh the calculations were more complicated. There was uncertainty both about Saddam's original intentions and about what Iraq would do if Saudi Arabia cut off its economic lifeline. Saudi forces were no match for the Iraqi army moving into Kuwait, and a call for international protection would involve allowing large numbers of foreign forces into the kingdom. In the first few days of the crisis, the king appeared unsure of what to do.

President Bush made it clear that Saudi compliance with U.N. 661 was essential and that Washington was prepared to send forces to defend Saudi Arabia. He dispatched Secretary Cheney to Riyadh on August 5, 1990. Although sources presently available do not detail precisely how Cheney's conversation with the king unfolded, there is little doubt that the American delegation went to Saudi Arabia to convince the king that the United States was prepared to send forces to defend the kingdom and that the Bush administration felt it would be good if the Saudis accepted the offer.[14] The secretary of defense may have drawn a rather alarming picture of the possible Iraqi threat and may have explained to the king that the United States would be reluctant to take on the mission unless it could do so with a substantial force and be able to protect itself while minimizing U.S. casualties.[15] Regardless of how the U.S. offer was packaged, however, the purpose of the military move in August was to enforce the sanctions regime and deter further Iraqi action.

No one expected economic sanctions to compel Iraq's retreat within two months, and the fact that Iraq had not retreated by late September was not seen as a failure. To the contrary, Washington's success in isolating Iraq and in obtaining financial and military support for its strategy was impressive.[16] Informal estimates predicted that the sanctions would produce a sharp crisis in spare parts and reduced industrial capacity in Iraq, taking a drastic toll in the second quarter of 1991.[17] At this point, however, Iraq still had stockpiled capacity and could buy time. Even if Saddam Hussein had concluded that Iraq would eventually have to retreat, it was too early to begin to haggle. He could wait to see whether politics in the Arab world would swing to his side and could employ coercive pressures of his own to see whether the international consensus against him could be shaken.

Why Iraq Did Not Comply

A number of motives may have caused Saddam Hussein to order the invasion of Kuwait. Financial pressures, anger over Kuwait's oil policy, desire for better access to the sea, ambition to lead the eastern Arab world, and fear of U.S. hegemony in the area may all have figured into his calculation. The images and arguments Saddam Hussein promoted before the invasion were contradictory. He warned of an impending Israeli attack and a U.S. conspiracy to assert its hegemony in the wake of the collapse of Soviet power, but he also described fantastic opportunities for the Arab world in the post–cold war setting. As Soviet and U.S. influence waned, an Arab great power could emerge in the Middle East.[18] If this Arab power united the population, oil resources, and financial assets of the Arab world, it could aspire to major power status, joining Japan and Germany as critical players in a new multi-polar world. The mix of images that described terrible threats in an almost paranoid fashion with images that promised grandiose opportunities is diffi-cult to decipher. Saddam may have seen great threats and have moved against Kuwait as a preemption against what he believed was an inevitable U.S.-Israeli attack. I find another interpretation, however, far more convincing.[19]

Saddam's desire to lead the eastern Arabs had deep roots. He had invaded Iran in 1980 partly to eclipse Hafez al-Asad of Syria and establish Iraqi he-gemony in the eastern Arab world.[20] In 1990, his demands against Kuwait had economic, territorial, and political dimensions. Whether he would have ordered the invasion of the country if the emir, Jaber al-Sabah, had agreed to restrict oil production, forgive loans, make cash payments to Iraq, and sur-render control of the two northern islands is impossible to know. Under these circumstances Saddam may have felt that Iraq's progress toward Gulf hegemony was sufficient for the time being. His long-term vision, however, left little room for Arab Gulf actors to avoid decisive Iraqi influence.

Saddam Hussein's propaganda in 1990 seemed designed, in preemptory fashion, to anticipate negative reactions from others. It framed any resistance to his ambitions as threats against Iraq.[21] If this were the case, he knew his and Washington's foreign policy agendas would clash, but he may not have been certain how determined and capable of stopping him the United States would be. Washington had tilted toward Iraq during the Iran-Iraq War and, without the Soviet threat, might have less incentive to actively intervene. If Saddam saw an Arab world rife with populist anti-American sentiment, he may have concluded that the weaker Gulf states were trapped. They could not turn to the "imperialists" for protection without endangering their do-mestic legitimacy. Thus the Bush administration's efforts to deter Iraq before the invasion, which were fairly meager anyway, would seem particularly lacking in credibility.[22]

Whatever Saddam Hussein's initial calculations were, once in Kuwait his army moved quickly to consolidate control. He employed the quick fait ac-compli strategy for changing the status quo. On August 8, Iraq annexed Ku-wait, declaring that its previous independence was simply a legacy of British colonialism.[23] The U.N. Security Council, on August 9, voted 15 to 0 to de-clare the annexation null and void through Resolution 662. In response, Iraq intensified its propaganda campaign and announced that Americans and other foreigners in Kuwait and Iraq would not be allowed to leave.[24] On Au-gust 18, the United Nations passed Resolution 664 condemning this Iraqi move as well and reinforced its message, on September 16, with U.N. Resolu-tion 667. As time passed, Iraq used the hostages as human shields and bar-gaining chips.[25] On August 19, Saddam offered to release ten thousand hos-tages if President Bush would withdraw U.S. forces from the area.[26] Meanwhile, by early September, U.S. intelligence estimated that Iraq had eleven divisions deployed in Kuwait, with 173,680 troops and over 1,500 tanks, and another eleven divisions in southern Iraq.[27]

Saddam Hussein responded to the U.N. insistence on Iraq's withdrawal by proposing a peace initiative. Saddam's August 12 initiative (to which he was to return repeatedly during the crisis) contained three parts. First, it linked Baghdad's retreat from Kuwait to "the immediate and unconditional withdrawal of Israel from the occupied Arab territories in Palestine, Syria, and Lebanon, Syria's withdrawal from Lebanon, and a mutual withdrawal of Iraqi and Iranian troops along their disputed frontier."[28] Second, Saddam insisted that U.S. forces leave Saudi Arabia and be replaced by Arab forces under U.N. authority. Third, he demanded that all boycott decisions and sanctions against Iraq be lifted upon its withdrawal from Kuwait. Saddam's initiative seemed designed to mobilize Arab nationalist support by playing on the Palestinian issue and the presence of U.S. forces in the area. It was coupled to an explicit appeal to the Arab masses on August 11 to rise up against President Mubarak in Egypt and King Fahd in Saudi Arabia.[29]

Reactions in the Islamic World. The Gulf Cooperation Council (GCC), composed of the weaker Arab Gulf states, quickly condemned Iraq's aggression in a statement issued August 3. The Organization of the Islamic Conference (ICO), an institution heavily influenced by Saudi Arabia, did likewise on August 5. These verbal reactions could not have surprised Saddam, but he may have expected the other Gulf Arabs to be so intimidated by Iraq's display of power that they would desert their counterparts in the al-Sabah family and eventually appease Iraq. According to Soviet envoy Yevgeniy Primakov, who saw him several times during the crisis, Saddam "did not expect that Saudi Arabia would invite the Americans in."[30] He had to be disappointed when twelve of the twenty-one Arab League members voted at an emergency summit in Cairo on August 10 to support U.N. Resolutions 660, 661, and 662 and to agree, according to Article 2 of the Arab League Charter and Article 51 of the U.N. Charter, to send troops to Saudi Arabia and other Gulf states to participate in the allied defense Washington had announced only three days earlier.[31]

During the first phase of the crisis, Iraq was losing in the United Nations, but the trends in regional politics were mixed. The GCC and Egypt were opposed to the Iraqi occupation, but other Arab governments assumed more complicated postures. The government of Morocco criticized the Iraqi attack and promised to send troops to Saudi Arabia but, facing mounting domestic support for Hussein, sought a middle position based on an "Arab solution." Tunisia and Algeria also faced major Islamic and Arab nationalist sentiments. Abassi Madani, the popular Islamic leader in Algeria, identified the presence of foreign forces in Saudi Arabia as the greatest aggression against Islamic sovereignty, whereas in Tunisia, thousands marched in support of Iraq.[32] The newly unified Yemen also put a heavy emphasis on equating a U.S. withdrawal from Saudi Arabia and Iraq's withdrawal from Kuwait as proposed in the second plank of Saddam's August 12 initiative.[33]

Iraq may also have taken heart from the increasing support Saddam Hussein enjoyed from Jordan. King Hussein agreed to abide by the U.N. decisions at the August 10 Arab League Summit but expressed his great sorrow that the Arab world had not been able to find its own solution.[34] He traveled to Washington three days later and on August 14 tried to persuade President Bush to give the Arab states a chance to find a mediated solution before large numbers of U.S. forces arrived in the region.[35] The king was unsuccessful, but as the crisis evolved in August and September, it became clear that domestic sentiment in Amman was pro-Saddam. Watching the enthusiastic reaction of Sunni Arabs in North Africa and Jordan constrain their respective governments, Saddam may have concluded that similar sentiments would erupt among the Sunni majority in Syria.

Although Syria joined Egypt and the United States in defending Saudi Arabia, President Asad made it clear that foreign forces must leave the Gulf.[36] Saddam may have concluded that Syria would agree to two of the three key linkages he proposed in his August 12 initiative. Asad would reject the linkage between Iraq's withdrawal from Kuwait and Syria's withdrawal from Lebanon, but because of his domestic scene, he might not be able to object to the demand for Israel's withdrawal from the Occupied Territories and the linkage between Iraq's retreat and Washington's military exit from the region.

In Iran, Saddam could also see ambivalent trends. President Ali Akbar Hashemi-Rafsanjani had strongly criticized the Iraqi invasion on August 17 but at the same time had welcomed the Iraqi concessions regarding bilateral Iranian-Iraqi issues and condemned the deployment of U.S. forces to the Persian Gulf.[37] Although Rafsanjani agreed to abide by the U.N. resolutions, Ayatollah Sayyev Ali Khamene'i put increasing emphasis on the U.S. threat.[38] Khamene'i called the U.S. presence itself an aggression and said that confronting the aggressive schemes of the United States was the duty of Islamic forces in jihad.[39]

Avenues Toward a Negotiated Solution—Linkage. Once the contest was joined, Saddam Hussein may have seen no way to escape with his dignity and personal power intact. It seems much more likely, however, that in this phase of the crisis, the many trends toward mediation sustained his determination to hold out for the August 12 terms. As the U.N. General Assembly began to meet in October, the multinational interest in a negotiated settlement increased. The king of Jordan had joined forces with King Hassan II of Morocco and Algerian President Chadli Bendjedid to propose a seven-point settlement compromise.[40] In this plan, Iraq would withdraw from Kuwait, but it would maintain a "special arrangement" with the country, something like that Syria enjoyed with Lebanon. Kuwait would cede the islands of Bubiyan and Warbah to Iraq, along with the al-Rumaylah oil fields, and would agree to exercise self-determination without a return of the al-Sabah monarchy. Additionally, the Iraqi withdrawal would be tightly linked to a fixed date for the withdrawal of all foreign forces from Saudi Arabia and the opening of a broader discussion of the Palestinian problem.

It was not only the Arab world that was moving toward a compromise outcome. On September 24, French President François Mitterrand addressed the U.N. General Assembly and proposed a four-stage process of settlement.[41] In the first stage, Iraq would affirm its intention to leave Kuwait. In a second stage, Kuwait would regain its sovereignty, and the Kuwaiti people could exercise their "democratic will." The third stage would involve an international conference on the Lebanese and Arab-Israeli conflicts. A fourth stage would promote arms control agreements in the Near East. This French proposal did not link the Iraq withdrawal to any preconditions, but it did involve what might be called "sequential linkage." The international community would promise to move forward on other Middle East issues in linked stages in return for Iraq's exit from Kuwait.

When Iraq invaded Kuwait, Secretary Baker was in the Soviet Union, and on August 3 he issued a joint statement with Soviet Foreign Minister Edward Shevardnadze.[42] The statement was a clear condemnation of Iraq's move and a call to the United Nations and the international community for punitive sanctions. Throughout the rest of August, Saddam heard little from the top officials in Moscow that could have encouraged him. In early September, however, Shevardnadze slightly modified his arguments, and other Soviet officials such as Yevgeniy Primakov became actively involved. On September 4, the Soviet foreign minister reiterated his insistence on the restoration of the sovereignty, territorial integrity, and legitimate government of Kuwait but also spoke of a "complex set of interlocking problems" in the Middle East, mentioning specifically the Arab-Israeli and Palestinian conflicts and the civil war in Lebanon.[43] He revived Moscow's long-standing commitment to the idea of an international conference on the Middle East and said that Israel's acceptance of such a mechanism would help to defuse the crisis in the Persian Gulf.

A few days later, on September 9, presidents Mikhail Gorbachev and Bush met in Helsinki and issued a joint statement that reaffirmed their common commitment to the unconditional return to the pre–August 2 status in Kuwait.[44] The statement included a vague notion of sequential linkage, saying that after the U.N. objective had been met, it would be important to work for the resolution of all the conflicts in the Middle East, but it promised nothing in particular. When pressed on the linkage point during the subsequent press conference, Gorbachev said that he did see a link between the Gulf crisis and the Arab-Israeli conflict, but he did not say that the solution of both crises required a common process.[45] A few weeks later, on September 25, Shevardnadze addressed the U.N. General Assembly and strongly denounced the Iraqi move and reinforced Soviet support for the sanctions.[46]

At roughly the same time, however, Yevgeniy Primakov was preparing to depart for Baghdad, reportedly to persuade Saddam that he was leading Iraq into a disaster.[47] After seeing the Iraqi president, Primakov flew to Washington where he met with Secretary Baker, National Security Advisor Brent Scowcroft, and President Bush.[48] He explained that a peaceful settlement was possible if Iraq had a "face-saving" way out.[49] Primakov's plan involved sequentially connecting Iraq's withdrawal from Kuwait with Israel's agreement to attend an international conference on the Palestinian problem.

According to Primakov, Saddam showed little flexibility in his policy toward Kuwait during the October meetings. Given the trends in the Arab world and growing international interest in a negotiated solution, it is not hard to imagine why. Iraq was suffering economically but was far from destitute. There was no compelling military threat to Iraq; to the contrary, the Allied coalition was not scheduled to complete even its defensive deployments until December 1. Although Iraq had not been able to evade the U.N. sanctions, there were signs that the idea of linkage was gaining ground in the regional and international communities.[50] Moreover, Saddam may have felt that Soviet policy would change, especially if the United States tried to use force to compel Iraq's retreat. If Soviet military advisers in Iraq were telling Saddam about the growing admiration for him in Russian nationalist circles, his optimistic calculations may have been reinforced. In any case, Iraq remained steadfast throughout September. In the next phase of the crisis, the Bush administration would increase the coercive pressure by preparing for war.

PHASE THREE:
TRANSITION TO MILITARY COERCION

U.S. Calculations and the Decision
to Issue an Ultimatum

On October 1, 1990, President Bush addressed the U.N. General Assembly: "All of us here at the U.N. hope that military force will never be used. We seek a peaceful outcome, a diplomatic outcome. And one more thing: in the aftermath of Iraq's unconditional departure from Kuwait, I truly believe there may be opportunities for Iraq and Kuwait to settle their differences permanently, for the states of the Gulf themselves to build new arrangements for stability, and for all the states and peoples of the region to settle the conflicts that divide the Arabs from Israel."[51] In this important address, the president did not close the door on a weak version of sequential linkage and gave no indication that he was considering increasing the pressure on Iraq by adding the threat of military action.

A month later, however, on November 8, President Bush ordered an additional 150,000 U.S. ground, sea, and air forces to the Persian Gulf to prepare an "adequate offensive military option." Two days later, Secretary Cheney announced that the Pentagon did not plan to rotate troops through Saudi Arabia and that U.S. forces already in the Gulf would remain there for the duration of the crisis.[52] When forced by contentious congressional hearings to explain these decisions, top administration officials expressed concern that time was on Iraq's side and that the strategy of relying on sanctions would not work because of the authoritarian nature of Saddam Hussein's rule.[53] Evidently, prevailing perspectives within the administration changed substantially during the month of October, and by early November, after congressional elections were over, the president was willing to publicly signal the possibilities of war.

At a tactical level, October was a month of decision because of the military deployment schedule. The defensive forces ordered to the Gulf would be in place by December 1, and given the lead time necessary to prepare more forces for deployment and rotation, the president had to decide in October what to do after December 1.[54] Many factors were part of the decision process, but four major considerations seemed to promote a new sense of urgency. The first was the rape of Kuwait itself and the economic consequences of the crisis. The second was heightened concern that the coalition could not be held together but might become divided over efforts to establish linkage between settlement of the crisis and the Arab-Israeli conflict. The third had to do with the growing popularity of the argument for a preventive war at relatively low cost. Finally, a perception of Saddam Hussein as a survivalist contributed to the decision to threaten war. Each of these factors deserves elaboration.

Kuwait. President Bush met with the emir of Kuwait on September 28, and by all accounts—including the president's own—he was deeply upset by the reports of torture and looting.[55] The fate of Kuwait and the al-Sabah alone may not have been enough to move the U.S. decision process, but Washington saw the implications of Iraq's occupation of Kuwait for the regime in Saudi Arabia as important.[56] In Riyadh, the timing of the liberation could set a disquieting precedent if it came too late to save the al-Sabah rule. With oil prices soaring to over $40 a barrel in early October 1990, President Bush also had to consider the effect continuing uncertainty would have on the international economy.[57]

Linkage. On October 8, 1990, an important event took place in Jerusalem that complicated the ability of the United States to hold the coalition to a "no compromise" policy. Israeli soldiers clashed with Palestinians, killing at least twenty-one Palestinians and wounding one hundred more outside the Al-

Aksa mosque.[58] In response, twelve countries of the European Community (EC) condemned Israel and called for a U.N. conference to settle the Arab-Israeli conflict.[59] The Palestine Liberation Organization (PLO) pushed for a U.N. resolution that would condemn Israel and commission a U.N. team to investigate conditions in the Occupied Territories and report to the Security Council.[60] The Bush administration vigorously opposed the efforts to deepen the U.N. role in the "peace process" and, after a week of intense lobbying, successfully engineered an alternative U.N. resolution, which passed on October 12, 1990. This resolution, U.N. 672, condemned "especially" Israel's violence but implied that Palestinian violence was also to blame.[61] It asked the secretary-general to send a mission to the region and to report back, but it did not involve the United Nations in the situation in any lasting capacity. Israel rejected the resolution immediately and refused to cooperate with the secretary-general's commission.[62]

The incident at Al-Aksa mosque did not undermine the Allied coalition's supporting U.N. sanctions against Iraq. It did, however, highlight the potential for division on the issue of linkage. Saddam Hussein played heavily on the idea that Washington used a "double standard"—condemning Iraq's occupation of Kuwait while defending Israel's occupation of Arab territories.[63] If Washington refused to join with the EC and the rest of the United Nations in condemning Israel's use of force in this case, then President Mubarak and King Fahd would have a more difficult time explaining their close cooperation with the United States. To hold the international coalition together, the Bush administration had to condemn Israel and deal with the broad international support for a U.N.-sponsored conference on Arab-Israeli conflicts. Over time, one would have to expect that similar incidents would strain the relationship between Washington and the Arab participants in the U.N. coalition. This prospect only increased the pressure on Washington to shift its policy on Arab-Israeli issues.

On October 12, 1990, the speaker of Egypt's parliament—the second ranking official in the country—was assassinated.[64] It was not clear who killed Rifaat al-Mahgoub, but Islamic fundamentalists, Palestinians, and Iraqi agents were popular suspects in the rumor mills of Cairo.[65] The murder did not affect Egyptian policy, but it raised concerns about the effects of a drawn-out Gulf crisis on Egypt's internal scene. With time, Mubarak might not be able to resist the domestic pressure for linkage. Moreover, on October 22, Saudi Minister of Defense Prince Sultan suggested that Kuwait could cede the islands of Warbah and Bubiyan to Baghdad in order to settle the crisis.[66] Riyadh quickly reassured the Bush administration that Prince Sultan's ideas did not represent official Saudi policy, but doubts about the chances of internal change in Egypt and Saudi Arabia, and the staying power of those countries, were not put to rest in Washington.[67]

Although depending on the United Nations to legitimate its policy in the Persian Gulf, the Bush administration did not want to allow the organization to play an important role in the Arab-Israeli conflict, at least not now. In 1990, the Bush administration, along with President Mubarak, had worked hard to organize Israeli-Palestinian talks in Cairo, but had failed to do so. To accept a move toward a multilateral forum, in the face of Iraq's threats and occupation, might be seen in the region as evidence that the Sadat-Mubarak strategy of compromise was fruitless and that Saddam Hussein's strategy of force achieved results. Even if the Bush administration had wanted to open the process to a larger international forum, it was determined not to do so under these circumstances.

When U.N. Secretary-General Javier Perez de Cuellar proposed that the Security Council involve itself in the protection of Palestinians in the Occupied Territories, the problem for Washington was again clear.[68] The Bush administration strongly opposed the council's role, but it did so at the risk of damaging the U.N. coalition and weakening Egypt and Saudi Arabia in Arab nationalist eyes because involving the United Nations was the long-standing policy preference of the EC states, the Soviet Union, and most Arab states. The Bush administration, however, felt it could not agree to a new U.N. policy without alienating Israel and Israel's friends in the United States and possibly leaving Israel in a position from which it felt compelled to attack Iraq.

From the outset of the crisis, the Israeli government knew Saddam Hussein would try to transform the situation into an Arab-Israeli conflict and complicate Washington's effort to keep Arab states within the U.N. coalition.[69] Israelis did not disguise their hopes that the United States would deal decisively with Saddam Hussein and reduce the threat Iraqi military power posed for Israel. In mid-September, Israeli Prime Minister Yitzhak Shamir argued that if the Gulf crisis ended with Saddam's regime still in power, then the Gulf states would "fall like a house of cards."[70] He said that containment of Iraq could only be a "temporary strategy" until a more definitive approach produced "radical change" in the situation. The prime minister worried that "a situation may come to pass in which we [Israel] are the only ones confronting Saddam Hussein, and then we will have to come up with an answer as to how to defeat this evil giant."[71]

After the incident at Al-Aksa in October, Israeli fears that international interest in linkage might lead to new pressures for Israeli concessions escalated sharply, as did their concerns that the U.N. coalition might provide a face-saving way for Iraq to withdraw from the crisis with all of its military assets in place. Israel and the Gulf Arabs would then find themselves facing a more powerful and dangerous Arab foe, one that might even be able to issue nuclear threats by the mid-1990s. In this situation, Israel would not enjoy international support for a preemptive attack on Iraq, but it might feel compelled to deliver such a blow. In U.S. calculations, the Israeli concerns were a real constraint. If Washington compromised on the issue of linkage, or even if it did not and forced Iraq out of Kuwait unconditionally with sanctions but did not weaken Baghdad's military potential, then Israel and Iraq might soon go to war. Such a war could escalate in dangerous directions and threaten Washington's relationships with Arab countries such as Egypt and Saudi Arabia. A diplomatic outcome that would constrain Iraq was still seen as possible in the Bush administration, but this possibility was complicated and much less certain in its effectiveness than was a preventive war against Iraq.

Preventive War. The Bush administration was determined that the Gulf crisis would not be another Vietnam.[72] The initial deployment in August was deliberately a large force, in keeping with the Joint Chiefs of Staff's (JCS) post-Vietnam doctrine that if the United States did intervene, it should do so with ample force right from the beginning. According to this strategic doctrine, if it came to war, Washington should not escalate incrementally and should not practice "graduated compellence." The administration promised that if force had to be used, it would be used suddenly, massively, and decisively.[73] There would be no murky outcomes, the president promised.[74] As the military deployments continued into October, the president, along with Secretary Cheney and National Security Adviser Scowcroft, were reportedly increasingly convinced that the Allied coalition could eject Iraq from Kuwait and decisively weaken Iraq's offensive capabilities with minimal U.S. casualties.[75]

In explaining the decision to deploy an offensive option, Cheney put special emphasis on the issue of certainty.[76] He did not argue that sanctions would not work, although he expressed skepticism, but argued that military force certainly would work. The long-term consequences of allowing Iraq to retain its military power also bothered Cheney. He said, "My own personal view is that it is far better for us to deal with him [Saddam Hussein] while the coalition is intact, while we have the United Nations behind us ... than it will be to deal with him 5–10 years from now ... when Saddam Hussein has become an even better armed and more threatening regional superpower than he is at present."[77]

Saddam as Survivalist. The strength of the preventive war argument may have gained ground in Washington by October, but Secretary Baker still relied essentially on political bargaining arguments when explaining the decision to shift to the threat of war as the basis for the coercive strategy. He said, "There is a peaceful solution" if Saddam leaves Kuwait;[78] "he [Saddam] will not make that peaceful choice, however, in our opinion, unless he understands that the alternative to peaceful compliance is that he will be forced to comply. That is the message that we are trying, in every way we know how, to send him."[79] Baker described Saddam Hussein as "very dangerous," a "capricious dictator whose lust for power is as unlimited as his brutality in the pursuit of it." He concluded that Saddam "has an inflated sense of Iraq's leverage" and a "very high pain threshold."[80] As for the president, he compared Saddam Hussein to Hitler and concluded that Saddam had not felt the depth of Washington's will and resolve with regard to Kuwait.[81]

Top administration officials described Saddam Hussein as a risk-taking dictator who pursued opportunities and exploited perceived weakness but who would also abruptly change course and retreat when faced with threats to his survival in power. Once he was convinced that his power base was at risk, Saddam was expected to search seriously for a way out that would preserve his personal position.[82] In the past, according to this perspective, Saddam had shown a remarkable ability to find face-saving justifications for sudden reversals in policy.[83] As long as the United States did not back him into a corner entirely, he could pursue any one of the several options for negotiations being offered by the United Nations, various Arab delegations, or the Soviet Union. To avoid war, consequently, the United States had to move toward war; paradoxically, the closer Washington got to war, the less likely it was that war would actually be necessary, or so the "survivalist" arguments went.

Building Political Support for the Decision to Escalate

President Bush's November 8 announcement that the United States would develop an offensive military option set off immediate reactions in the international community and in the U.S. Congress.[84] The administration dealt with the international scene first. Secretary Baker was already in Moscow when the president made the public announcement, and he met with President Gorbachev on November 8.[85] At this meeting Soviet Foreign Minister Shevardnadze agreed that force could not be ruled out if diplomatic means failed, but along with President Gorbachev, he insisted that force could only be used if the United Nations endorsed such use, and he disagreed with Baker concerning the timing of the U.N. authorization.[86] Reportedly, Gorbachev favored first seeking a resolution to set a deadline for compliance and then, in a second resolution, dealing with the issue of using force.[87] A few weeks later, however, on November 29, the Soviet Union voted with the United States to pass U.N. Resolution 678, which called on Iraq to comply with U.N. Resolution 660 and all subsequent U.N. resolutions pertaining to the Kuwait crisis by January 15, 1991, and authorized member states to "use all necessary means" at some point—although not necessarily immediately after that date—to implement U.N. 660.[88] The evolution of Soviet policy in November is interesting in that it reflects the growing tension between Moscow and Baghdad, as well as Saddam Hussein's refusal to cooperate with Soviet efforts to defuse the crisis.

From August 2, the Bush administration had worked to take the "Soviet card" away from Saddam. It had coordinated its moves with the Soviet

Union in the first phase of the crisis, inviting Moscow to play a role in the Gulf that Washington had opposed for decades and dispatching Secretary Cheney to Moscow in mid-October to further the cooperation.[89] Cheney's visit added to the growing debate in Moscow over the wisdom of supporting Washington's policies against Iraq, and it also convinced Saddam Hussein to make a public issue of not releasing the 5,000 Soviet citizens in Iraq.[90] When Yevgeniy Primakov returned to Baghdad on October 28, the issue of the Soviet hostages was high on the agenda.[91] Primakov announced that Saddam had personally agreed to allow 2,500 Soviet citizens to leave Iraq by the end of November. When presidents Gorbachev and Bush met in Paris on November 19 for the Conference on Security and Cooperation in Europe (CSCE), however, Iraq was still detaining Soviet citizens and was not complying with its agreement to expedite the exit of 2,500 of them. While in Paris, President Gorbachev agreed to the idea of a single U.N. resolution that would both set the deadline for Iraqi compliance and authorize the use of force.[92] Gorbachev insisted that the phrase "all necessary means" be used rather than the word "force" and preferred January 15 to January 1 as a deadline if a date had to be given in the resolution. Nevertheless, he was moving toward the compellent posture.

President Gorbachev did not agree, however, to the U.S. formulation for U.N. Resolution 678. Instead, he left the summit and invited Tariq Aziz to Moscow for one last try at persuasion. When Aziz arrived in Moscow on November 26, 3,315 Soviet citizens were still left in Iraq, with only 350 of the last 1,000 who tried to exit allowed to leave the country.[93] The reception in Moscow was chilly to say the least. Gorbachev's press secretary Vitaliy Ignatenko described the talks as "tough" and reported that the "interlocutors parted coldly."[94] Gorbachev said that the Iraqi foreign minister offered nothing new and that despite Primakov's effort, there was no serious Iraqi movement toward compliance.[95] Gorbachev now endorsed U.N. 678. Soviet reporters covering Gorbachev's decision said that top Soviet officials hoped the U.N. action would be a "cold shower" that would awaken Saddam to the realities of what Iraq faced.[96]

On November 28, 1990, the day before Moscow voted with the United States on U.N. Resolution 678, two former U.S. military chiefs of staff testified before the Senate Armed Services Committee against the Bush administration's policy of shifting to the threat of war. Adm. William Crowe and Gen. David Jones joined former Secretary of Defense James Schlesinger in arguing that the sanctions were working, that Iraq's economy and its military machine would be weakened over time, that threatening to escalate to war was premature, and that war might be politically counterproductive.[97] They all felt the Allied coalition was sound and showed no signs of cracking on the essential issues of sanctions and Iraqi withdrawal. Although rejecting the idea of linkage, both Crowe and Jones suggested that the current crisis reflected

deeper problems in the Middle East and that the United States needed to address these basic conflicts in the area, including the Arab-Israeli issue, with
new ideas and determination.[98]

The congressional hearings that were sparked by the president's November 8 announcement revealed broad-based national support for coercion
through sanctions and a serious uneasiness over the idea of threatening war
to induce Iraqi compliance. Important policy makers in the administration
were concerned that a divisive congressional debate could persuade Saddam
that Washington did not have the political staying power to use force effectively. On November 30, the president moved to defuse the domestic debate
by publicly inviting Iraqi Foreign Minister Aziz to Washington and asking
Secretary Baker to visit Saddam Hussein in Baghdad sometime before January 15, 1991.[99] The offer to talk might have helped to solidify domestic support for the president's policy but also signaled to Saddam Hussein U.S. indecision and a fear of war. The president attempted to contain the risk in the
diplomatic realm by further constricting the time frame for talks, insisting
they must occur in Baghdad before January 3.[100] The talks between Baker
and Aziz that eventually took place on January 7, 1990, did not produce any
compromise, but they did help the Bush administration win the domestic debate. On January 12, 1991, a narrow majority in the Senate granted President
Bush the authority to wage war against Iraq.[101] Four days later the Allied coalition attacked.

The Bush administration had refused to negotiate with Iraq and had opposed any form of linkage or change in regional policy that could be considered a "reward" for Saddam. Secretary Baker told the NATO allies on December 17 that he expected Saddam Hussein to take a dramatic step, such as
initiating a partial withdrawal from Kuwait, just before January 15, and he
urged the alliance to stand united against such an Iraqi maneuver.[102] Unnamed "top administration officials" described the haggle Saddam could initiate as a "nightmare scenario."[103] Although the Bush administration had no
interest in negotiations, it did not and could not prevent Saddam Hussein
from seeking a mediated solution.

Saddam's Calculations and Policy

If preventive war was the U.S. objective from the outset, then this case of
failed coercive diplomacy has an obvious explanation. The evidence suggests,
however, that even though the Bush administration refused to help Saddam
Hussein "save face," it did not trap him into war. Saddam Hussein did not
need the United States to show him a credible way out; the various Arab, Islamic, and Soviet mediators I have discussed had done that.

President Bush made no secret of his desire to see Saddam Hussein overthrown. Even the strategy of economic sanctions had that objective in the

long run. In punishing Iraq for Saddam's aggression, Washington hoped the progressively damaging economic squeeze would induce political change in Baghdad. Unnamed senior officials in the Bush administration also made no secret of their desire to see Iraq's offensive military potential reduced and the economic sanctions extended, even if Iraq did leave Kuwait.[104] All of this may have contributed to Saddam's sense that he would suffer whether or not he went to war, but none of it explains why he chose to let the United States go to war with the full backing of the United Nations and why he did so little to shake Washington's coalition by making serious moves with regard to Kuwait.

Preempting Foreign Plots? Soviet diplomat Yevgeniy Primakov reports that Saddam Hussein was convinced that the United States and Israel were conspiring against him.[105] He attributes Iraq's aggressive behavior to Saddam's feeing that the country was under siege. Saddam, Primakov argues, could not accept the proposition that his own aggressive stance was creating a self-fulfilling prophecy. Convinced that the United States was determined to weaken Baghdad because Iraq had emerged from the war with Iran as such a powerful force, Saddam saw himself as taking the necessary geostrategic countermeasures to protect Iraqi and Arab strength.[106] Primakov contends that Saddam wanted a peaceful solution to the crisis but could not see a safe way out. If he retreated, the conspiracy against Iraq would be emboldened and would only find new ways to destroy his strength. If he stood and fought, he might lose, but the magnitude of the battle might also evoke Arab, Islamic, and perhaps even broader international support. According to Primakov, Saddam was ready to risk defeat in the short run rather than face the longer-term risks involved with a retreat from Kuwait and a diplomatic haggle.

Iraq faced tough economic choices before its invasion of Kuwait, and Saddam Hussein may have perceived threats from the United States and Israel. His speeches, however, also emphasized the attractive opportunities for an Arab great power in the post–cold war Middle East.[107] The move into Kuwait may have been a desperate maneuver by a leader who felt he was preempting a forthcoming attack on Iraq, but if so, it is hard to understand why Iraq did not continue south into Saudi Arabia when it had the chance in early August 1990. This would have required more extensive logistical planning, but if Saddam wanted to bargain from a position of strength, he needed to control northern Saudi Arabia.

If Saddam thought he was preempting a likely attack, it is also hard to understand why, on December 7, he decided to release the foreign nationals Iraq had been holding hostage.[108] From the outset, he had made no pretense about the purpose of the hostages. They were human shields who he hoped would deter the use of force by the United States.[109] If Saddam Hussein thought an attack on Iraq was likely at this point, just after the United Nations had

passed Resolution 678, it is not clear why he would throw away his self-iden-
tified shield. During the war, Saddam told Cable News Network reporter
Peter Arnett that Western diplomats convinced him that releasing the hostages would prevent the outbreak of fighting.[110] Evidently he thought that if
he eliminated the casus belli represented by the hostages, the occupation of
Kuwait alone would be insufficient grounds to cause the U.S.-led coalition
attack. Rather than seeing an American or Israeli attack as inevitable, either
before August 2 or after up until mid-January, Saddam Hussein appeared to
be confident that he could take Kuwait without suffering lasting punishment.

Assumptions About the West and the Middle East. Saddam Hussein operated in the Kuwait crisis, from August until late January, as if he had made
three key assumptions. First, he seemed to think the United States and the
rest of the international community would not fight a war to liberate Kuwait.
They might complain and move to defend Saudi Arabia but over time would
acquiesce to the Iraqi annexation. The second assumption was that the Saudis
and other Gulf Arabs would not be able to align with the United States and
survive the domestic consequences. If Asad and Mubarak stayed with the
United States and the crisis developed into war, they would be rocked by internal revolt, especially if Iraq attacked Israel and evoked a pan-Arab and
pan-Islamic cause. Third, he seemed to think that the United States, if it did
fight, would not have sufficient domestic support to sustain casualties and
therefore would soon look for a negotiated settlement.

Saddam may have been surprised by the Saudi decision to allow U.S.
forces into Saudi Arabia, but he did not adjust to his miscalculation with concessionary moves. Instead he made new efforts to bolster Iraq's leverage. His
August 12 initiative had linked Iraq's action to Palestinian issues and the
presence of "imperialist" forces in the Arab and Islamic world. Saddam used
the Al-Aksa mosque incident to reinforce the message that Iraq was the real
agent of Arab nationalism, whereas King Fahd and President Mubarak were
simply traitorous collaborators of the imperialists.[111] Iraqi officials gave the
impression that they felt most Moslems would support Iraq, that Mubarak
and Asad were "totally exposed," and that regimes backing the U.S.-led coalition would be overthrown from within.[112] Despite the seemingly paranoid
aspects of Saddam's conspiracy theories, the Iraqi leader behaved as if he was
confident that Iraq could bargain from political strength, possibly hold Kuwait, and, if forced to deal Kuwait away during a diplomatic haggle, do so in
return for concessions that would strengthen his leverage in the regional context.

After President Bush announced his decision to move toward war in early
November, Saddam responded by calling up an additional 250,000 Iraqi
troops.[113] He continued to stress the themes that were effective in the Arab
streets. "The Imperialist-Zionist conspiracy against Iraq" led off Saddam's
propaganda and was followed by descriptions of "haves and have nots" in

the Arab world. On November 11, 1990, Saddam Hussein argued that the world was not united against Iraq.[114] Only the industrialized countries were following the United States, he maintained, and even there, public opinion was beginning to change in favor of Iraq's August 12 position on linkage. Saddam described the U.S. decision to escalate the crisis as evidence that it was losing the battle for public opinion and that eventually the world would negotiate on the August 12 terms.[115] As the United Nations moved on Resolution 678, Saddam rejected its compellent purpose, saying that it was impermissible for anyone who is right and is part of a great people and nation to be defeated in the face of threats.[116] He said that God and the Arab nation would protect Iraq as it fought for the honor of all Arabs. On November 30, the Revolutionary Command Council (RCC) rejected U.N. Resolution 678 as illegal and invalid and expressed its confidence in God and the Arab nation.[117]

Saddam Hussein did not reject the Baker talks proposed by President Bush on November 30. On the contrary, he accepted the idea and announced that he would release the Western hostages if President Bush agreed not to attack Iraq before March 25, 1991.[118] He then proposed meeting dates close to the January 15 U.N. deadline and argued that the talks should be genuine negotiations about possible outcomes and not simply a forum for insisting on the implementation of the U.N. resolutions pertaining to the Gulf crisis. A few days later, the Iraqi Ba'ath Party National Command reiterated Iraq's call to the Arab streets and repeated its tough rhetorical stand, insisting that the linkages proposed in the August 12 initiative were the only bases for talks.[119] On December 17, the RCC reaffirmed Iraq's unbending position on the August 12 linkages and Kuwait's annexation, describing the struggle as a "symbol of honor and virtue" in a major battle that had become "the mother of battles."[120] Saddam expressed the same themes throughout December and on Christmas Day argued that the escalation to war threatened by the United States would be terrible for the West—igniting a pan-Arab and pan-Islamic reaction that would sweep away the evil imperialist and Zionist conspiracies along with their illegitimate Arab agents.[121]

In January, as Aziz headed into talks with Secretary Baker, Saddam Hussein called the Iraqi people to war.[122] Taha Yasin Ramadan, Iraq's deputy prime minister, delivered the same message to the Iraqi people on January 9, predicting that all Arabs would eventually fight for Iraq against the U.S. puppets in Najd and Hijaz.[123] On January 11, Saddam again said there was no reason for fear, claiming that victory was near, God willing.[124] Iraqis would cast their fate with the Arab nation and God, said Saddam, as he predicted that eventually the United States would have to meet the Iraqi soldiers in the trenches. Iraqis were not people schooled about war from books, he threatened, but were people who knew what fighting was about. He did not doubt the technical superiority of the Allied coalition but questioned its ability to

sustain the battle once it started to suffer casualties. He seemed to believe domestic pressures would constrain the options of individual governments and
that different regional priorities would fracture the international consensus
once the battle was joined and Iraq moved to involve the Israelis.

After the air assault, Saddam Hussein sent an open letter to President Bush
threatening to spill large amounts of U.S. blood in a long war.[125] He said that
all of the Arab peoples, despite their rulers, would back Iraq. The next day,
January 17, the Ba'ath Party National Command appealed directly to all Arabs and Muslims to join in a jihad against U.S. imperialism.[126] That same day,
Iraq attacked Israel with Scud missiles and tried dramatically to shift the context of the struggle into the Arab-Israeli arena.[127] Throughout the crisis, Saddam apparently believed his greatest lever lay in the public attitudes on the
Arab streets. The more he resisted and the more defiant he looked, the stronger he would be. Taking the contest all the way to war would, in this perspective, strengthen his political leverage for the bargaining situation that would
follow the fighting, assuming he could move the contest into the diplomatic
realm while enough of Iraq's power base was still intact. If these were his calculations it is easy to see why coercive diplomacy failed. It is still difficult to
understand, however, why Saddam Hussein did not pursue the mediation
options to terminate the war before the air war had destroyed Iraq's capability base and the ground war routed and humiliated its army unless, even after
the devastating punishment of the air war, Saddam still clung to his predictions that Iraq's ability to fight a ground war would enable him to recover a
bargaining base from which to negotiate a compromise settlement.

Ignored Avenues for a Negotiated Outcome

Yevgeniy Primakov spent most of October 1990 shuttling among Middle
East capitals, Europe, and the United States. He saw Saddam Hussein twice,
on October 5 and October 28, and talked somewhat optimistically about the
prospects for a political solution. Although Primakov had some sympathy
for the three essential conditions of Saddam's August 12 initiative, he made it
clear that before it could begin a process that could achieve any of these objectives, Iraq had to agree to leave Kuwait.[128] He was unable to persuade Saddam of this, and on his second visit in late October he had to spend considerable time negotiating the release of Soviet citizens from Iraq.[129]

In mid-November, just after President Bush announced that he had decided to prepare an offensive military option, King Hassan II of Morocco
called for a special Arab summit.[130] King Hassan's proposal gave Iraq a
chance to start an Arab negotiation over possible compromise outcomes and
to complicate Washington's efforts to build support for passing U.N. 678,
which authorized the use of force. Iraq took Hassan's proposal seriously
enough to send a high-level envoy to Morocco, but it attached three condi-

tions to the summit idea: First, the talks could not be convened while U.S. forces threatened Iraq; second, the meeting had to take place at a location where Saddam's safety could be assured; and third, the Arab-Israeli conflict had to be part of the agenda.[131] Both presidents Mubarak and Asad rejected the summit proposal after Saddam Hussein attached these conditions and reiterated his commitment to hold Kuwait.[132]

Following the passage of U.N. Resolution 678 in late November, King Hussein of Jordan again tried to find an Arab solution. On December 4, Hussein, the PLO's Yasir Arafat, and the vice chairman of the Yemeni Presidential Council, Ali Salim al-Bid, met with Saddam Hussein in Baghdad. Jordan, the PLO, and Yemen were the closest thing Iraq had to allies, but these leaders also feared Iraq would be destroyed in a war. They supported the three conditions in Saddam's August 12 initiative, but they also agreed to abide by U.N. 660 and recognized Kuwait's sovereignty. They were not credible mediators with the Gulf Arabs, Egypt, Syria, or the United States (if Saddam had wanted to reach any of these parties, he could have done so through King Hassan II) but were able to provide political cover in the Arab nationalist world if Saddam decided to compromise on Kuwait and haggle over the future of the Gulf. Three days after this meeting the Iraqi National Assembly announced that all "foreign guests" could leave Iraq. Saddam Hussein, however, offered no concessions on Kuwait and reiterated his call for jihad.[133]

In mid-December, the president of Algeria, Chadli Bendjedid, decided to search for a peaceful solution. He visited Italy, France, and Spain, and then went to Jordan, Iraq, Iran, Oman, Syria, and Egypt. Bendjedid said that Iraq rightfully insisted on progress related to Arab-Israeli disputes and called on the international community to resolve the Palestinian problem.[134] He also agreed with both Ayatollah Khamene'i and President Rafsanjani of Iran that regional security had to be the responsibility of regional states.[135] He was ready to work with Iraq to find Arab and international support for a negotiated solution, but Saddam Hussein needed to make the necessary moves with regard to Kuwait before the regional process could begin.

Algerian Foreign Minister Sid Ahmed Ghazali expressed his fear that war was nearing after Saudi Arabia declined to receive the Algerian mission.[136] He said, "In all good faith, I say that truly there are some Arabs, whom I do not wish to name, who are convinced or are under the impression that their future depends on the destruction of Iraq."[137] Of course, even if some Arabs were committed to a preventive war, and even if Washington and Israel wanted one too, Iraq, by beginning to withdraw from Kuwait, could have changed the regional and international situations. With a credible negotiation process under way and Iraqi troops in retreat, Mubarak and Asad could not have supported the war option without looking like traitorous stooges, and many Europeans would also have opposed any early use of force under those circumstances, as would the Soviet Union. Saddam, however, made no serious moves to withdraw. Instead, he continued to posture with pan-Arab and pan-Islamic symbols, to reinforce Iraq's preparations for war, and to deal with Fahd and Mubarak by calling for their violent overthrow.[138]

In January, after the U.S. Congress gave President Bush the authority to use force in the Gulf, President Asad made a final appeal to Saddam Hussein.[139] Asad promised the Iraqi leader that if he began the process of withdrawal from Kuwait, there would be no war. Furthermore, Asad reassured Saddam that Syrian troops would fight alongside the Iraqis if the "imperialists" or the "zionists" tried to pursue the war against Iraq despite its compliance. The next day, January 13, 1991, U.N. Secretary-General Perez de Cuellar met with Saddam and tried to obtain an Iraqi agreement to comply with the U.N. resolutions concerning Kuwait.[140] Saddam reiterated his August 12 position, rejected both the Syrian and U.N. efforts, reaffirmed his faith in God and victory, and called on his people to prepare for war.[141] On January 14, Iraq's National Assembly was convened in an "emergency session" to endorse Saddam Hussein's policy of no concessions on Kuwait and to support the country's preparations for jihad.[142]

Shortly after the fighting began, President Gorbachev sent a letter to Saddam Hussein urging him to comply with the United Nations and stop the fighting.[143] Iraq had proved its mettle, and it still was not too late to save the country's capability base and regional interests with a negotiated settlement. Saddam's response was an open letter to Mikhail Gorbachev.[144] In it he said his anger over the Soviet message had abated because he knew Moscow was now intimidated, living "under the mercy of the U.S. law of hegemony." He reiterated his commitment to the August 12 initiative and said, "Bush has committed aggression and must pay the price." He then told Gorbachev that Moscow should have addressed its pleas to the "tyrant Bush and not to Saddam Hussein and his aggrieved people." In his news conference on January 22, Gorbachev concluded that military operations had begun "due to the Iraqi leadership's foolish and reckless policy."[145] Saddam Hussein was apparently ready to test his fate in war rather than agree to a retreat in Kuwait that could steer the conflict toward negotiations.

Saddam's Intransigence

Once the war began on January 16, many of the objectives identified by advocates of a preventive war were pursued by the Allied coalition. Within days the alliance achieved air superiority and within ten days gained total air supremacy. Iraq's military facilities, its missile launchers, its troops in Kuwait and southern Iraq, its industrial base for weapons production, and its communication and transportation infrastructure were high-priority targets.[146]

On February 15, the Revolutionary Command Council issued a statement in which it spelled out Iraq's terms for peace.[147] It announced Iraq's "readiness to deal" with U.N. 660, but only under conditions that were even less forthcoming than Saddam Hussein's August 12 proposal. The RCC linked withdrawal from Kuwait to (1) a total and complete cease-fire; (2) a Security Council agreement to abolish all of the U.N. resolutions pertaining to the crisis and all of their effects, along with an agreement to lift the embargo and a promise that Iraq would not suffer any negative effects; (3) a withdrawal of all U.S. and other Allied forces, weapons, and equipment brought to the Middle East and the Arabian Gulf before and after August 2, 1990; (4) an Israeli withdrawal from Palestine and Arab territories in the Golan and southern Lebanon and, if Israel refused, U.N. Security Council enforcement against Israel of the same resolutions it had passed against Iraq; (5) a promise to guarantee Iraq's historical rights on land and sea; (6) an arrangement in Kuwait that would be based on the will of the nationalist and Islamic forces and not on that of the al-Sabah family; (7) an agreement that all countries in the U.N. coalition would pay the full costs to reconstruct Iraq and forgive all outstanding Iraqi debts; (8) a declaration making the Arabian Gulf a zone free from foreign military bases and any form of foreign military presence.

The Bush administration did not treat this Iraqi proposal as a serious basis for a cease-fire. On February 16, President Bush openly called on the Iraqi people to take matters into their own hands and overthrow Saddam Hussein.[148] Soviet leaders, however, treated the RCC statement as an indication that Iraq was now prepared to retreat and to open the diplomatic haggle Primakov had tried to persuade Saddam to explore since early October.[149] President Gorbachev rejected the Iraqi conditions, but he met with Tariq Aziz in Moscow and on February 19 sent a six-point plan back to Baghdad.[150] These points included (1) an Iraqi agreement to implement U.N. 660 without delay and without conditions; (2) Iraqi troop withdrawal beginning one day after a complete cease-fire; (3) Iraqi withdrawal to be completed in twenty-one days and withdrawal from Kuwait City within the first four days; (4) immediate lifting of sanctions and invalidation of all U.N. resolutions when the withdrawal was complete; (5) release and repatriation of all POWs within three days; and (6) control and supervision of the cease-fire and troop withdrawal by observers or peacekeeping forces determined by the U.N. Security Council.

On February 21, Moscow announced that Iraq was positively inclined toward the Soviet plan, and President Gorbachev reportedly spent ninety minutes on the telephone with President Bush on February 22 relating the Iraqi position.[151] No new statements were issued by Iraq, however, that showed any signs of change. On the contrary, on February 21 Saddam spoke to the Iraqi nation, saying that "something must be done to place the enemies in an embarrassing situation—something that will drive them to behavior and positions that will make those who have been anesthetized by hostile media wake up to new facts. ... Thus came the 15 February initiative. ... This may divide the enemy ranks."[152] He attacked the "tyrannical Arab rulers" such as

King Fahd and President Mubarak for committing "treason" and again appealed to the people in Egypt, Syria, and Saudi Arabia to overthrow them.[153] He then reiterated his faith in the ground war. "O brothers, O people," he proclaimed, "note how those who feared a ground battle have now avoided the showdown for over a month." He said the coalition continued with the war "to cover up their inability to confront our land forces in southern Iraq."[154] Iraq would reverse the tide in the trenches, or so Saddam claimed.

Gorbachev's six points did not link Iraqi withdrawal to any of the objectives the RCC proposal demanded but did give Saddam another chance to avoid total defeat. The plan gave Iraq twenty-one days to leave and provided for the creation of a peacekeeping force that could have moved into Kuwait to protect Iraq's withdrawal. On February 23, President Bush said that Saddam Hussein had twenty-four hours to announce Iraq's decision to withdraw immediately and unconditionally from Kuwait.[155] The U.S. president said a cease-fire could only be considered after Iraq made such a declaration of intention and warned Iraq that if it failed to demonstrate an intent to comply with U.N. 660, a ground war would commence.

At this point, Saddam faced a tough choice. He could announce his retreat and hope that in the ensuing negotiations he could recover from the humiliation of the air war defeat, or he could go for broke with the ground war, clinging to the view that an effective fight on the ground would improve Iraq's bargaining position. To take the first option, Saddam had to publicly declare his decision to leave Kuwait and announce that some units would start to head north on certain routes flying white flags. He could ask for Soviet guarantees that specified routes of retreat would be safe and that as the process of withdrawal continued, the cease-fire would widen. This would initiate the first steps in the Soviet plan and make it more difficult for the Americans to initiate a ground war. If Iraq had taken these steps, the international community would have constrained Washington's options even if the Bush administration had wanted to move on the ground, which it is not clear it did. At the time, U.S. military planners still expected to suffer casualties in a ground war that could perhaps be avoided. Much of the preventive war mission had already been accomplished by air strikes, and still more damage could be inflicted by this method without running the uncertain, even if manageable, risks of a ground engagement.[156] Saddam Hussein, however, made no concessionary announcements following the February 23 U.S. ultimatum, and Iraq's army was routed in the hundred-hour ground war from February 24 to February 27, 1991.[157]

THE FAILURE OF COERCIVE DIPLOMACY

Discussions of the conduct and termination of the Gulf War is beyond the scope of this chapter, but Saddam Hussein's refusal to pursue negotiating avenues even on the verge of defeat suggests that he seriously miscalculated the power relationships Iraq faced. At various moments in the prewar crisis, Saddam could find the evidence he needed to support his belief that trends were moving in his direction. In October 1990, the issue of linkage seemed to gain ground in the multinational environment. In November, as the United States "turned the screw," regional players accelerated their search for a compromise outcome. Even though the United Nations passed Resolution 678, Saddam seemed to believe that Arab and Islamic politics were strengthening his hand. He could look beyond the clear actions of Presidents Mubarak and Asad, who, along with King Fahd, were strongly signaling their opposition with troop deployments and statements, and see support in the "Arab street." His expectations seemed to be so deeply ingrained that disconfirming evidence could not crack his general perspective. Instead, he searched for and found bits of evidence that reaffirmed his initial calculation.

Saddam Hussein behaved as if he believed Iraq could emerge as the dominant regional power in the Persian Gulf in the post–cold war era. The annexation of Kuwait was an important step in this process of consolidating an Arab great power, but it had unforeseen consequences. It appears that fairly early in the crisis, Saddam realized that he had miscalculated on the degree of international resistance annexing Kuwait would generate. His August 12 initiative set the terms for a withdrawal from Kuwait that would nevertheless advance his broader strategic agenda in the region. Although the diplomatic competition was focused on Kuwait, both the United States and Iraq were calculating payoffs and costs on a much broader scale. Saddam adjusted his tactical calculations about Kuwait but not his strategic perceptions of the regional situation. Rather than pull back from Kuwait in the face of U.S. resistance, he decided to up the ante and threaten both war and internal revolt in the Arab world. He seemed convinced that even if Washington went to war, it would not be able to sustain domestic support in the face of heavy casualties. The U.S. Congress authorized the president to use force on January 12, only four days before the war began. Saddam may have thought he had more time, given Iraq's release of the hostages and the congressional debate. If the basis of his miscalculation was simply timing, however, it is hard to understand why he did not pursue negotiating avenues in late January instead of remaining intransigent.

Saddam Hussein seemed to believe that in a war, especially one that involved Arabs fighting Israel and the United States, all of the other Arabs and Moslems would come to Iraq's defense. The fact that Mubarak and Fahd clearly sided with the United States seemed in Saddam's mind only to secure their fate when the great Arab uprising came. He seemed convinced that in the crunch, they would be overthrown, and the peoples of Egypt, Syria, and Saudi Arabia would stand with their Arab brethren. Popular reactions to his rhetoric in the Arab streets only reinforced his confidence and sustained his misplaced expectations. He also seemed to be encouraged by the reaction in Iran. Iraq's bitter enemy in Tehran condemned the invasion of Kuwait but, as the crisis continued, identified the U.S. threat as the primary problem in the region.[158] Saddam could not count on Iranian support in war but may have read Iran's reaction as indicative of the sentiments in populist Islamic circles.

Americans who held a "survivalist" view of Saddam Hussein believed that the closer Washington came to war, the less likely it was that war would actually occur. Saddam, however, seemed to believe that Iraq's best chance for political success would come through war. He may have thought in late July and early August that Iraq could move quickly to achieve regional hegemony through intimidation. Once the U.N. alliance formed, however, he seemed to conclude that Iraq would realize its greatest political leverage, and thus be in a position to drive its best deal, only if it took the crisis all the way to war. His primary card was the Arab and Islamic masses, which he assumed would be mobilized in the critical regional countries such as Egypt and Syria only after the war had started and Iraq had expanded it to include Israel. Rather than make peace with his Arab rivals, he would increase the stakes and try to overthrow them. When Arabs in Syria and Egypt did not respond as Saddam had anticipated, even after the war was well under way, he partially admitted to the magnitude of his miscalculation but, like a gambler determined to reverse huge losses with yet another double-or-nothing wager, decided to test his optimistic propositions about ground war in the trenches of southern Iraq.[159]

Iraq was not trapped into a preventive war by the United States. Even if the Bush administration had decided by early January that a preventive war might be its preferred course, Baghdad still had a number of options for a negotiated outcome. Saddam Hussein, however, was not willing to pursue these as long as he felt Iraq retained sufficient power and bargaining leverage as war neared. He was not calculating power in traditional terms of troops and votes in the United Nations but seemed to be counting on emotional support for Iraq in the Arab and Islamic world. Once the war began, it was hard for him to accept that his basic propositions about the vulnerability of the regimes in Syria, Egypt, and Saudi Arabia were wrong. Saddam also seemed slow to realize that he was not going to be able to inflict heavy casualties on Allied troops. U.S. technical superiority and firepower were so overwhelming that the Iraqi armed forces were not able to test seriously Saddam's propositions about American staying power.

I cannot conclude that war was inevitable or that coercive diplomacy and diplomatic containment would not have worked if given more time. I do suggest that Saddam Hussein would not have pulled back until Iraq's actual power base had been weakened. With the end of the Iran-Iraq War, Iraq had more available military capability than any other Gulf country and had impressive economic potential as well. Iraq's material strength gave Saddam

Hussein substantial leverage in Gulf affairs and, more broadly, in intra-Arab affairs. He could court, intimidate, and, if necessary, coerce other regional actors in order to expand his influence. He would not forgo various perceived opportunities on the basis of U.S. threats alone; he would make new calculations only when there was a change in the material base that underpinned his leverage and gave rise to his perceptions of opportunity. Whether this change could have been accomplished by economic sanctions and the consequent destruction of Iraq's economy is a counterfactual question observers can debate forever.

In the Gulf crisis studied here, the initial variant of coercive diplomacy through the use of sanctions was not in place long enough to test its full effect on Iraq's internal situation, whereas the stronger variant of coercive diplomacy through threatening war failed to undermine Saddam Hussein's perception of his political strength in the Arab and Islamic world. The result was a failure of coercive diplomacy and a resort to war to eject Iraq from Kuwait and weaken Iraq's military capability. The war succeeded in liberating Kuwait and accomplished the four objectives President Bush had outlined in August. It did not end the rule of Saddam Hussein, a more ambitious objective that, although implicit, had never been stated as a priority goal of the war. After the war, the United States returned to the sanctions variant of coercive diplomacy to pursue this additional objective.

NOTES

1. President George Bush, "The Arabian Peninsula: US Principles," August 8, 1990, Current Policy no. 1292, U.S. Department of State, Bureau of Public Affairs, Washington, D.C.

2. President Bush, "Against Aggression in the Persian Gulf," August 15, 1990, Current Policy no. 1293, U.S. Department of State, Bureau of Public Affairs, Washington, D.C.

3. President Bush, "The Arabian Peninsula: US Principles."

4. President Bush, "A Collective Effort to Reverse Iraqi Aggression," August 22 and 30, 1990, Current Policy no. 1296, U.S. Department of State, Bureau of Public Affairs, Washington, D.C.

5. President Bush, "The Arabian Peninsula: US Principles,"p. 2.

6. Ibid.

7. Secretary of State James Baker, "America's Stake in the Persian Gulf Crisis," September 4, 1990, Current Policy no. 1297, U.S. Department of State, Bureau of Public Affairs, Washington, D.C., p. 1.

8. On oil interests, see testimony by Secretary of Defense Richard Cheney before the Senate Armed Services Committee, U.S. Congress, Senate, Committee on Armed Services, *Crisis in the Persian Gulf Region: U.S. Policy Options and Implications,* September 11, 1990, 101st Cong., 2nd sess., 1990, pp. 8–22.

9. See, for example, Senator Albert Gore in ibid., pp. 55–58.

10. Bob Woodward, *The Commanders* (New York: Simon and Schuster, 1991), pp. 290–296; Senator Alfonse D'Amato, *New York Times,* August 24, 1990, p. 29; and Bernard Trainor, *New York Times,* August 12, 1990, p. IV 21.

11. Gen. Colin Powell in U.S. Congress, Senate, Committee on Armed Services, *Crisis in the Persian Gulf Region,* p. 25.

12. Richard Cheney, ibid.

13. *New York Times,* August 8, 1990, pp. 1, 10.

14. See Bob Woodward, *The Commanders,* pp. 254–262.

15. The U.S. deployment would involve forces on land, sea, and air. Early publicized figures of around seventy thousand, outlining the initial ground component, were fairly quickly increased to well over two hundred thousand to reflect the total number of U.S. forces that would be deployed to the Persian Gulf area. The deployment began with a tactical air command, the 82nd airborne troops, fighter aircraft, and the carrier-based naval aircraft nearby. These were quickly reinforced with heavier ground attack forces from the 24th infantry and the 197th infantry and with F-16, A-10, and F-117 aircraft and attack helicopters. Powell in U.S. Congress, Senate, Committee on Armed Services, *Crisis in the Persian Gulf Region,* pp. 23–24.

16. Powell in U.S. Congress, Senate, Committee on Armed Services, *Crisis in the Persian Gulf Region: U.S. Policy Options and Implications,* December 3, 1990, 101st Cong., 2nd sess., 1990, p. 672. For figures concerning the financial commitments made by the Gulf states, Japan, Germany, and Korea during the early phase of the crisis, see Cheney, U.S. Congress, Senate, Committee on Armed Services, *Crisis in the Persian Gulf Region,* September 11, 1990, pp. 94–95.

17. See the testimony of former Deputy Assistant Secretary of State James Placke, in U.S. Congress, House Committee on Foreign Affairs, Hearings before the Subcommittee on Europe and the Middle East, *Persian Gulf Crisis,* October 17, 1990 (Washington, D.C.: U.S. Government Printing Office, 1991), pp. 269–317.

18. Saddam Hussein, "Speech to ACC Summit," Amman Television, February 24, 1990, *FBIS-NES-90-039* (Foreign Broadcast Information Service), pp. 1–5; and Saddam Hussein, "Speech to Arab Summit in Baghdad," Baghdad Domestic Service, May 28, 1990, *FBIS-NES-90-103,* pp. 2–7.

19. See Richard K. Herrmann, "The Middle East and the New World Order: Rethinking U.S. Political Strategy After the Gulf War," *International Security* 16, no. 2 (Fall 1991): 42–75.

20. Stephen Grummon, *The Iran-Iraq War: Islam Embattled* (New York: Praeger, 1982), pp. 1–38.

21. Saddam Hussein, "Address to Arab Cooperation Council Representatives," Baghdad INA, February 19, 1990, *FBIS-NES-90-034,* pp. 1–6; and Saddam Hussein, "Speech to Popular Islamic Conference," Baghdad Domestic Service, June 18, 1990, *FBIS-NES-90-118,* pp. 19–22.

22. On U.S. deterrent efforts, see Don Oberdorfer, "Missed Signals in the Middle East," *Washington Post Magazine,* March 17, 1991, pp. 19–41.

23. *New York Times,* August 9, 1990, p. 1.

24. Ibid., August 10, 1990, p. 1.

25. Saddam Hussein, "Open Letter to Families of Foreigners in Iraq," Baghdad Domestic Service, August 19, 1990, *FBIS-NES-90-161,* pp. 12–14; Saddam Hussein,

"Open Letter to George Bush," Baghdad Domestic Service, August 21, 1990, *FBIS-NES-90-163*, pp. 26–27.

26. *New York Times*, August 20, 1990, p. 1.

27. See Cheney, U.S. Congress, Senate, Committee on Armed Service, *Crisis in the Persian Gulf Region*, September 11, 1990, p. 18.

28. Saddam Hussein, "Initiative on Developments in the Region," Baghdad Domestic Service, August 12, 1990, *FBIS-NES-90-156*, pp. 48–49.

29. See Baghdad Voice of Egypt, *FBIS-NES-90-157*, pp. 33–34.

30. See "Interview with Yevgeniy Primakov," Paris Europe Number One, April 28, 1991, *FBIS-SOV-90-083*, p. 11.

31. For text of Arab League Resolution, see "MENA [Middle East News Agency] Reports Arab Summit Resolution 10 Aug.," Cairo MENA, August 10, 1990, in *FBIS-NES-90-156*, pp. 1–2; and *New York Times*, August 11, 1990, p. 1.

32. For Madani, see "FIS Leader Madani on Saddam's Call, Gulf Forces," Paris Domestic Service, August 11, 1990, in *FBIS-NES-90-156*, p. 20. For reports from Tunisia, see "Imam Calls for Edict Against King Fahd," Baghdad Domestic Service, August 12, 1990, in *FBIS-NES-90-156*, p. 34–35; and "Thousands March in Support of Iraq," Tunis Domestic Service, August 14, 1990, in *FBIS-NES-90-158*, p. 15.

33. 'Ali 'Abdallah Salih, "President Salih Interviewed on Gulf Crisis," Sanaa Domestic Service, August 16, 1990, in *FBIS-NES-90-160*, pp. 17–18.

34. King Hussein, "'Text' of King Husayn's Arab Summit Speech," Amman Domestic Service, August 12, 1990, in *FBIS-NES-90-157*, pp. 1–2.

35. *New York Times*, August 14, 1990, pp. 1, 9, and August 15, 1990, p. 1.

36. See, for example, Hafez al-Asad, "Speech," Damascus Syrian Arab Television, September 12, 1990, in *FBIS-NES-90-178*, pp. 44–49.

37. On August 15, Saddam announced that Iraqi troops would start leaving Iran in two days, followed quickly by an accelerated program for the return of POWs. Saddam Hussein, "Text of Letter to President Ali Akbar Hashemi-Rafsanjani," Baghdad Domestic Service, August 15, 1990, in *FBIS-NES-90-158*, p. 22. Rafsanjani, "Friday Sermon," Tehran Domestic Service, August 24, 1990 in *FBIS-NES-90-166*, pp. 57–63.

38. Rafsanjani, "Friday Sermon"; Khamene'i, "Address to Released POWs," Tehran Domestic Service, August 29, 1990 in *FBIS-NES-90-169*, pp. 51–53.

39. Ayatollah Khamene'i, "Address to Students," Tehran Domestic Service, September 12, 1990, in *FBIS-NES-90-178*, pp. 52–55.

40. "Arab Initiative Outlined," *Al-Dustur*, September 20, 1990, in *FBIS-NES-90-183*, pp. 1–2.

41. See *New York Times*, September 25, 1990, p. 1; and *Washington Post*, September 25, 1990, p. 1.

42. *New York Times*, August 4, 1990, p. 6.

43. Ibid., September 5, 1990, p. A17.

44. For text of joint statement, see *New York Times*, September 10, 1990, p. 7.

45. For transcript of news conference, see ibid., p. A8; and *Pravda*, September 11, 1990, pp. 1, 4, in *FBIS-SOV-90-177*, pp. 10–16.

46. See *New York Times*, September 26, 1990, p. 10.

47. Yevgeniy Primakov, "The Inside Story of Moscow's Quest for a Deal," *Time*, March 4, 1991, pp. 40–48.

48. *New York Times,* October 19, 1990, p. 16, and October 21, 1991, p. 12.

49. See Primakov, "The Inside Story of Moscow's Quest for a Deal," pp. 40–48; and "Interview with Yevgeniy Primakov," *Paris Europe Number One,* April 28, 1991, in *FBIS-SOV-90-083,* p. 11.

50. On Saddam's interest in the French proposals, see *New York Times,* October 1, 1990, p. A9; and *Washington Post,* October 1, 1990, p. 1.

51. *New York Times,* October 2, 1990, p. A12.

52. Ibid., November 10, 1990, p. 1.

53. See Cheney in U.S. Congress, Senate, Committee on Armed Services, *Crisis in the Persian Gulf Region,* December 3, 1990, pp. 638–658; and Baker in U.S. Congress, Senate, Committee on Foreign Relations, *U.S. Policy in the Persian Gulf,* December 5, 1990, 101st Cong., 2nd sess., 1990, pp. 107–110, and prepared statement, pp. 112–114.

54. Woodward, *The Commanders.*

55. See "Excerpts from the Bush News Conference," *New York Times,* October 10, 1990, p. A18; and Woodward, ibid., p. 298.

56. Secretary Cheney emphasized the Saudi issue very strongly. See U.S. Congress, Senate, Committee on Armed Services, *Crisis in the Persian Gulf Region,* December 3, 1990, p. 649.

57. *New York Times,* October 10, 1990, p. A1. See President Bush's press conference, in *Washington Post,* December 1, 1990, p. A26.

58. *New York Times,* October 9, 1990, p. A1.

59. Ibid., October 10, 1990, p. A10.

60. Ibid., October 12, 1990, p. A1.

61. Ibid., October 13, 1990, pp. 1, 5.

62. See Yitzhak Shamir, "Statement to Knesset," Jerusalem Domestic Service, October 15, 1990, in *FBIS-NES-90-200,* pp. 36–39.

63. Saddam Hussein, "Address on Al-Aqsa Incident," Baghdad Domestic Service, October 9, 1990, in *FBIS-NES-90-196,* pp. 22–23.

64. Cairo MENA, October 12, 1990, in *FBIS-NES-90-198,* pp. 10–11.

65. On Egyptian reaction, see the selection of comments from various commentators in *FBIS-NES-90-199,* pp. 10–13; and *FBIS-NES-90-200,* pp. 9–12.

66. See Prince Sultan Bin Abd-al Aziz, "Interview," Riyadh Saudi Press Agency (SPA), October 22, 1990, in *FBIS-NES-90-206,* pp. 23–24.

67. See King Fahd Bin Abd-al Aziz, "Statement," Riyadh Domestic Service, October 24, 1990, in *FBIS-NES-90-206,* pp. 22–23.

68. *New York Times,* November 2, 1990, p. A1.

69. Yitzhak Shamir, "Interview on Gulf Crisis," Jerusalem Israel Television Network, August 22, 1990, in *FBIS-NES-90-164,* pp. 23–26.

70. See Yitzhak Shamir, "Interviews on Foreign, Domestic Issues," *Jerusalem Post* and *Yedi'ot Aharonot,* September 14, 1990, in *FBIS-NES-90-182,* p. 34.

71. Ibid.

72. See President Bush's statement and press conference in *Washington Post,* December 1, 1990, p. A26.

73. See Baker in U.S. Congress, Senate, Committee on Foreign Relations, *U.S. Policy in the Persian Gulf,* December 5, 1990, p. 107. Also Powell in U.S. Congress, Senate, Committee on Armed Services, *Crisis in the Persian Gulf Region,* December 3, 1990, p. 663.

74. See Bush's statement and press conference in *Washington Post,* December 1, 1990, p. A26.

75. Woodward, *The Commanders,* pp. 303–307, 345.

76. See Cheney's testimony in U.S. Congress, Senate, Committee on Armed Services, *Crisis in the Persian Gulf Region,* December 3, 1990, pp. 649, 655, 657.

77. Ibid., p. 650.

78. See Baker in U.S. Congress, Senate, Committee on Foreign Relations, *U.S. Policy in the Persian Gulf,* December 5, 1990, pp. 107–108.

79. Ibid., p. 112 (prepared statement).

80. Ibid., pp. 108–109.

81. "Text of President Bush's Statement and Transcript of News Conference on Persian Gulf," *Washington Post,* December 1, 1990, p. A26.

82. On the importance of assumptions such as these in the senior echelons of the State Department, see David Hoffman's profile of Dennis Ross in the *Washington Post,* October 28, 1991, p. 1.

83. For an example of this argument, see Jerrold Post, "Saddam Hussein of Iraq: A Political Psychology Profile," *Political Psychology* 12, no. 2 (1991): 279–289.

84. Senator Sam Nunn, chairman of the Armed Services Committee, criticized the administration's decision and called for hearings; *New York Times,* November 12, 1990, p. 15. Senator Claiborne Pell also scheduled hearings for the Foreign Relations Committee; *New York Times,* November 14, 1990, p. 1. The hearings were held in the last week of November and early December.

85. David Hoffman, "Six Weeks of Intense Consultations Led to the U.N. Resolution," *Washington Post,* December 2, 1990, p. 1; and Woodward, *The Commanders,* pp. 318–321.

86. *New York Times,* November 9, 1990, p. A13.

87. See Hoffmann, "Six Weeks of Intense Consultations Led to U.N. Resolution," p. 1.

88. See *New York Times,* November 30, 1990, p. 1.

89. *Washington Post,* October 17, 1990, p. 21.

90. Moscow World Service, October 15, 1990, in *FBIS-SOV-90-200,* pp. 8–9.

91. See Moscow Domestic Service, October 29, 1990, in *FBIS-SOV-90-210,* pp. 9–10. Also, "Interview with Yevgeniy Primakov," *Literaturnaya Gazeta,* no. 45, November 7, 1990, p. 1, in *FBIS-SOV-90-220,* pp. 12–16; and "Interview with Yevgeniy Primakov," *Al-Sharq al-Awsat,* November 7, 1990, p. 4, in *FBIS-SOV-90-218,* pp. 10–13.

92. Hoffman, "Six Weeks of Intense Consultations Led to U.N. Resolution," p. 1.

93. TASS, November 26, 1990, in *FBIS-SOV-90-227,* pp. 13–14; *New York Times,* November 27, 1990, p. 1; and *Pravda,* November 27, 1990, p. 1, in *FBIS-SOV-90-228,* p. 15.

94. TASS, November 27, 1990, in *FBIS-SOV-90-229,* pp. 16–17.

95. "Interview with Mikhail Gorbachev," Moscow International Service, November 27, 1990, in *FBIS-SOV-90-229,* pp. 16–17.

96. M. Yusin, "The Persian Gulf: Soviet Diplomacy's Unprecedented Activeness," *Izvestiya,* November 28, 1990, p. 4, in *FBIS-SOV-90-229,* pp. 18–19.

97. See Dr. James R. Schlesinger, Gen. David C. Jones, and Adm. William J. Crowe, Jr., in U.S. Congress, Senate, Committee on Armed Services, *Crisis in the Persian Gulf Region,* November 27 and 28, 1990, pp. 113–257.

98. Ibid., pp. 187–191, 198–208.

99. "President Bush: Statement and News Conference," *Washington Post*, December 1, 1990, p. A26.

100. "Excerpts from Bush's Remarks on Gulf Meetings," *New York Times*, December 15, 1990, p. 8.

101. *Washington Post*, January 13, 1991, p. 1.

102. *New York Times*, December 18, 1990, p. 1.

103. Ibid., December 19, 1990, p. 16.

104. Ibid., December 14, 1990, p. 14.

105. Primakov, "The Inside Story of Moscow's Quest for a Deal," pp. 40–48.

106. Milton Viorst reports that Tariq Aziz developed a similar interpretation. See "Report from Baghdad," *New Yorker*, June 24, 1991, pp. 55–73.

107. Saddam Hussein, "Address to Arab Cooperation Council Representatives," pp. 1–6; Saddam Hussein, "Speech to ACC Summit," pp. 1–5; Saddam Hussein, "Speech to Arab Summit in Baghdad," pp. 2–7; and Saddam Hussein, "Speech to Popular Islamic Conference," pp. 19–22.

108. Baghdad INA, December 7, 1990, *FBIS-NES-90-236*, p. 21.

109. Saddam Hussein, "Open Letter to Families of Foreigners in Iraq," pp. 12–14; Saddam Hussein, "Open Letter to George Bush," pp. 26–27.

110. "Interview with Saddam Husayn," Baghdad Domestic Service, January 30, 1991, *FBIS-NES-90-021*, pp. 20–24.

111. Saddam Hussein, "Address on Al-Aqsa Incident," Baghdad Domestic Service, October 9, 1990, *FBIS-NES-90-196*, pp. 22–23.

112. See "Interview with Taha Yasin Ramadan, First Deputy Prime Minister," *Al-Tadamun*, October 29, 1990, pp. 20–24, *FBIS-NES-90-210*, pp. 23–30; Saddam Hussein, "Speech to Confederations of Arab Trade Unions," Baghdad INA, November 3, 1990, *FBIS-NES-90-214*, pp. 14–18.

113. Baghdad Domestic Service, November 19, 1990, *FBIS-NES-90-223*, p. 9.

114. "Interview with Saddam Husayn," London ITV TV, November 11, 1990, *FBIS-NES-90-219*, pp. 26–31.

115. Ibid.

116. Saddam Hussein, "Speech to Arab Youth Seminar," Baghdad Domestic Service, November 29, 1990, *FBIS-NES-90-231*, pp. 18–20.

117. Revolutionary Command Council, "Statement," Baghdad Domestic Service, November 30, 1990, *FBIS-NES-90-231*, pp. 17–18.

118. "Interview with President Saddam Husayn," Paris Antenne 2, December 2, 1990, *FBIS-NES-90-232*, pp. 16–20.

119. Ba'ath Party National Command, "Statement," Baghdad Domestic Service, December 10, 1990, *FBIS-NES-90-238*, pp. 17–20.

120. Revolutionary Command Council, "Statement," Baghdad Domestic Service, December 17, 1990, *FBIS-NES-90-243*, pp. 24–26.

121. Saddam Hussein, "Address to Islamic Delegation," Baghdad INA, December 15, 1990, *FBIS-NES-90-242*, pp. 14–18; "Interview with Saddam Husayn," Ankara TRT TV, December 19, 1990, *FBIS-NES-90-245*, pp. 14–18; and Saddam Hussein, "Address to Jordanian National Democratic Alliance," Baghdad Domestic Service, December 25, 1990, *FBIS-NES-90-249*, pp. 24–30.

122. Saddam Hussein, "Speech on 79th Anniversary of Iraqi Army," Baghdad Domestic Service, January 6, 1991, *FBIS-NES-91-004*, pp. 23–26.

123. Taha Ramadan, "Speech to Popular Islamic Conference," Baghdad Domestic Service, January 9, 1991, *FBIS-NES-91-007*, pp. 1–4.

124. Saddam Hussein, "Speech to Islamic Conference," Baghdad Voice of the Masses, January 11, 1991, *FBIS-NES-91-009*, pp. 2–4.

125. "Letter from Saddam Husayn to 'Bush,'" Baghdad Domestic Service, January 17, 1991, *FBIS-NES-91-012*, pp. 17–19.

126. Arab Socialist Ba'ath Party National Command, "Call to Arab Strugglers and Mujahidin Everywhere," Baghdad Domestic Service, January 18, 1991, *FBIS-NES-91-014*, pp. 39–40.

127. *Washington Post,* January 18, 1991, p. 1.

128. Yevgeniy Primakov, "The Inside Story of Moscow's Quest for a Deal," and "Interview with Yevgeniy Primakov," pp. 9–15.

129. "Interview with Y. Primakov," *Literaturnaya Gazeta* 45, November 7, 1990, p. 1, in *FBIS-SOV-90-220*, pp. 12–16.

130. "Speech by King Hassan II to Moroccan Parliament," Rabat RTM TV, October 12, 1990, *FBIS-NES-90-200*, pp. 12–15; and "Speech by King Hassan II," Rabat RTM TV, November 11, 1990, *FBIS-NES-90-219*, pp. 17–18.

131. *Washington Post,* November 13, 1990, p. 1; Rabat Moroccan Press Agency (MAP), November 12, 1990, *FBIS-NES-90-220*, p. 2; and Baghdad INA, November 13, 1990, in *FBIS-NES-90-220*, p. 28.

132. Presidents Mubarak and al-Asad, "Joint Statement," Cairo MENA, November 15, 1990, *FBIS-NES-90-222*, p. 46.

133. Baghdad INA, December 7, 1990, *FBIS-NES-90-236*, pp. 21–22; and *New York Times,* December 7, 1990, p. 20.

134. President Chadli Bendjedid, "Press Statement," Amman Domestic Service, December 12, 1990, *FBIS-NES-90-240*, pp. 32–33.

135. Tehran Iran News Agency (IRNA), December 13, 1990, *FBIS-NES-90-241*, pp. 40–41.

136. On the Saudi refusal to receive the Algerian mission, see *New York Times,* December 14, 1990, p. 14.

137. See "Interview with Sid Ahmed Ghazali," Algiers Domestic Service, December 24, 1990, *FBIS-NES-90-249*, pp. 9–12.

138. Saddam Hussein, "Address to Islamic Delegation," pp. 14–17; and RCC "Statement," December 17, 1990, pp. 24–26.

139. "Message from Hafiz al-Asad to Saddam Husayn," Damascus Domestic Service, January 12, 1991, *FBIS-NES-91-009*, pp. 92–93.

140. See "Minutes of Meetings Between Javier Perez de Cuellar and Saddam Husayn, on Jan. 13," *Al Dustur,* February 9, 1991, in *FBIS-NES-91-028*, pp. 1, 14–15.

141. "Message from Saddam Husayn to Hafiz al-Asad," Baghdad Domestic Service, January 13, 1991, *FBIS-NES-91-009*, pp. 39–40; and Saddam Hussein, "Statement to Iraqi Journalists," Baghdad INA, January 13, 1991, *FBIS-NES-91-009*, pp. 41–46.

142. National Assembly Speaker Sa'di Mahdi Salih, "Address," January 14, 1991, *FBIS-NES-91-009*, pp. 37–38.

143. TASS, January 18, 1991, *FBIS-SOV-91-013*, p. 5.

144. "Letter from Saddam Husayn to Mikhail Gorbachev," Baghdad INA, January 21, 1991, *FBIS-SOV-91-014*, p. 37.

145. Mikhail Gorbachev, "News Conference," Moscow Domestic Service, January 22, 1991, *FBIS-SOV-91-015*, pp. 3–4.

146. See Philip Meilinger, "The Air Campaign Against Iraq," U.S. Department of the Air Force, March 1991.

147. Revolutionary Command Council, "Statement," Baghdad Domestic Service, February 15, 1991, *FBIS-NES-91-032*, pp. 17–19.

148. *Washington Post*, February 16, 1991, p. 20.

149. Ibid., p. 11.

150. For text of the six points, see ibid., February 23, 1991, p. 14. Also see TASS, February 22, 1991, *FBIS-SOV-91-037*, p. 10.

151. *Washington Post*, February 22, 1991, pp. 1, 25; and TASS, February 22, 1991, *FBIS-SOV-91-037*, p. 11.

152. Saddam Hussein, "Address to Iraqi Nation," Baghdad Domestic Service, February 21, 1991, *FBIS-NES-91-035*, pp. 21–24.

153. Ibid., p. 22.

154. Ibid., p. 24.

155. *Washington Post*, February 23, 1991, p. 1.

156. See *New York Times,* January 23, 1991, p. A26.

157. "The 100-Hour War," *Army Times,* March 11, 1991, pp. 4–38.

158. Rafsanjani, "Friday Sermon," Tehran International Service, October 12, 1990, *FBIS-NES-90-199*, pp. 63–67; Ayatollah Khamene'i, "Speech," Tehran Domestic Service, November 28, 1990, *FBIS-NES-90-230,* pp. 49–51; Rafsanjani, "Friday Sermon," Tehran Domestic Service, November 30, 1990, *FBIS-NES-90-232,* pp. 63–65; and Ayatollah Khamene'i, "Speech," Tehran Domestic Service, January 9, 1991, *FBIS-NES-91-007*, pp. 53–54.

159. See, for example, Saddam Hussein, "Address to Iraqi Nation," p. 21.

PART THREE

Findings and Conclusions

ALEXANDER L. GEORGE
AND WILLIAM E. SIMONS

We now turn to a comparison of the seven cases presented in Part Two in order to identify contextual factors and conditions that influence the outcome of a government's efforts to employ the strategy of coercive diplomacy. By doing so, we formulate essential generic knowledge about the strategy to supplement the general abstract model described earlier.

It is striking, of course, how different the seven cases are from one another. Impressed with this fact, the reader may well wonder how any useful generalizations can be drawn from the study. Is it not true, as historians are quick to remind us, that each case is unique in important respects? If so, then how can one draw lessons from any past case that can confidently be applied to a new one? Is there not a danger that even if scholars can agree on the correct lessons of a particular case, those lessons are likely to be misapplied to a new case that is bound to be different in some crucially important way?

SCOPE OF THE ANALYSIS

Admittedly, historical analogies can be dangerously misleading. And yet, there is ample evidence that when confronted with an international crisis, policy makers rely on the presumed analogy to an earlier case to diagnose and deal with the crisis. If the present study does no more than discourage this practice by calling attention to the important differences among cases of coercive diplomacy, it will have made a contribution. In addition, the seven case studies enable us to better understand the tasks policy makers face when they try to adapt the general conceptual model of coercive diplomacy to a particular situation. The complex, unique configuration of each case has to be diagnosed by policy specialists, as outlined in Chapter 2, before some variant of coercive diplomacy can be designed and implemented well enough to achieve useful results.

In similar fashion, the study of past experiences also provides an opportunity for decision makers to sharpen their ability to make the essential determinations for new cases that arise. In other words, the accounts of our seven cases provide material for vicarious experience and for the learning of essential diagnostic and policy skills before a policy maker is immersed in the urgent pressures of an actual crisis.

But more than such minimal contributions is possible. The starting point for drawing more ambitious findings from the cases is the recognition that although they are different and in some sense each is unique, the seven cases are all instances of the same class of events. That is, they all share an effort to employ the strategy of coercive diplomacy rather than some other strategy such as appeasement, deterrence, or war. Viewed from this standpoint, the fact that each case seems unique or different in important respects is *not* a reason for pessimism regarding the possibility of developing useful knowledge about coercive diplomacy. Actually, if the cases are compared in a systematic manner, then each case can contribute something useful for an overall understanding of the conditions that contribute to the success or failure of the strategy.

Clearly, the systematic comparison we undertake is *not* intended to formulate a set of sweeping generalizations that purport to explain in a simple way why coercive diplomacy sometimes succeeds and at other times fails. The phenomenon of coercive diplomacy is too complex, and the conditions and variables at play are too numerous, to permit formulation of such generalizations. Rather, we will try to articulate the case findings in ways that will reflect the complexity and variance of these experiences with coercive diplomacy. This will call not for sweeping, unqualified generalizations but rather for *conditional* generalizations that identify those factors and variables noted in our case studies that, if present, favor the success of the strategy. Such generalizations will also identify those factors that are likely to lead to its failure.

We focus on the following question: When is it reasonable for the policy maker to choose a strategy of coercive diplomacy or give it serious consideration? In addressing this question, we maintain the distinction—standard in the study of public policy—between the policy maker's choice of a strategy and the policy outcome. Thus, although the issue of policy success in each of these cases informs our analysis, we recognize that ultimate success may be determined by several factors outside the policy maker's direct influence—or even that of his or her opponent.

In the discussion that follows, major emphasis is given to illuminating the generic knowledge needed to augment the abstract theory of coercive diplomacy and to enable policy makers, when faced with a specific case, to carry out two functions essential to formulation of an effective strategy. The first is to diagnose the current situation; the second is to analyze and choose among the available policy options. These functions depend on the following questions: What variable factors in the international political context can affect the likelihood of success? What kinds of risks may be incurred in threatening punitive action? What potential roles might the opponent's allies play in the unfolding crisis? In what ways can the process of bargaining assist or hinder the achievement of an acceptable resolution? What conditions in the relationship between the coercing power and its adversary tend to favor or obstruct the process of coercive diplomacy?

Another area of emphasis is the kinds of insights policy makers need regarding their opponent's decision-making tendencies. How does this particular opponent tend to react to threats? What are the opponent's high-priority stakes in the anticipated bargaining process? How firm are the political underpinnings of the opponent's leadership, and what factors are crucial to its future stability?

In dealing with such questions, our analysis occasionally makes comparisons between those cases in which coercive diplomacy was successful and those in which the results were ambiguous or clearly negative. Most of these comparisons are made with reference to the single factor then under scrutiny, although success or failure in the employment of coercive diplomacy in any specific case is the product of many factors operating together. Few, if any, factors may be said to be absolutely necessary to the attainment of a particular outcome.

As noted in Chapter 1, three types of coercive diplomacy can be distinguished with reference to the nature of the objective pursued. In Type A, the coercing state attempts to persuade the opponent merely to stop the aggressive action short of its goal. In Type B, the coercing state goes further, demanding that the opponent undo its action. Even more extreme is Type C coercive diplomacy, in which an attempt is made to stop the opponent's unacceptable policies and behavior by demanding that it make changes in its government. Our cases indicate that different results—success and failure—were achieved by both Type A and Type B efforts. The two cases of clear success using coercive diplomacy were the Laos (Type A) and Cuba (Type B) crises. The three cases of clear failure of the strategy were Pearl Harbor (Type B), Vietnam (Type A), and the Persian Gulf (Type B).

Ambiguous results were achieved from attempts at coercive diplomacy in the Libya (Type A) and Nicaragua (Type C) cases. These results are illustrated in Table 2. It is obvious from this comparison of the results that success or failure has little causal relation to the type of strategy attempted, although Bruce Jentleson argues convincingly that Type C coercive diplomacy in particular carries little prospect of success. The factors that contribute to an explanation of these results are discussed in the subsections that follow.

TABLE 2   Outcomes of the Use of Coercive Diplomacy

	Successful	Unsuccessful	Ambiguous
A			
Laos	x		
Vietnam		x	
Libya			x[a]
B			
pre–Pearl Harbor		x	
Cuba	x		
Kuwait		x	
C			
Nicaragua			x[b]

[a] The extent of Libya's influence on the variety of terrorist groups in operation, hence the extent of the impact of a strategy to diminish that influence, is very difficult to ascertain. There is also some question as to how long the positive effects of coercive diplomacy continued to influence Qaddafi in 1986.

[b] Although U.S. policy clearly had some positive impacts on the situation in Nicaragua, many other influences outside of U.S. control also had strong effects. It is difficult, therefore, to assess with confidence the extent of responsibility for the outcome that was achieved by the U.S. contra policy.

VARIABLE ASPECTS OF COERCIVE DIPLOMACY

The seven case studies make clear that coercive diplomacy is a highly flexible strategy that can be implemented according to several variants. The cases also indicate that the policy maker's choice of variants is often constrained by characteristics of the particular situation, which vary strikingly from one case to another. Moreover, as the particular crisis evolves, these situational factors can change, thereby encouraging modifications in policy, including shifts from one variant of coercive diplomacy to another. Of course, strategy shifts may also occur because of an opponent's lack of response to milder variants of coercive diplomacy. In several of the cases, for example, early implementation of coercive diplomacy took the form of the try-and-see variant, only to shift to a gradual turning of the screw or some variant of ultimatum.

Contextual Variables

It is essential to note that coercive diplomacy is highly context-dependent. Many different variables can affect the variant of the strategy the policy maker selects, its implementation, and its outcome. Because these contextual factors vary from one case to another, the fact that the strategy worked in one case does not mean it will be successful in other cases as well. Therefore, each of these seven cases offered a fresh challenge to the ability of policy makers, in effect, to adapt the abstract model of coercive diplomacy to the crisis at hand. The impact of many different contextual variables is such that coercive diplomacy must be tailored in a rather exacting fashion to fit each new situation. Some of these contextual variables, identifiable in the case studies, are examined below.

Global Strategic Environment. The seven cases illustrate that the approach taken by decision makers to a particular regional crisis is affected significantly by the global strategic environment. Other crises or conflicts may be accorded a higher priority. Demands made on the opponent may be subordinated to larger, overarching strategic interests when these interests are also at stake. Proposed terms of settlement may take into account other issues affecting the postcrisis state of relations with the opponent or his third-party benefactors.

In the pre–Pearl Harbor period, for example, White House attention was diverted repeatedly by the war already in progress in Europe and the intense struggle to control the Atlantic sea lanes. Particularly during the autumn of 1941, U.S. diplomatic interaction with Japan and military force deployments to the Pacific were shaped in part by the U.S. strategic interest in assuring Winston Churchill that our embattled British ally's interests in the Pacific were given due consideration.

During the cold war, most regional crises in which coercive diplomacy was applied were strongly influenced by the U.S. competition with the Soviet Union. This tended to make the Soviets significant players even though, except in the Cuban Missile Crisis, it was not their aggressive actions that precipitated a U.S. response. In the Laos crisis, a major portion of the Kennedy administration's diplomatic initiatives were conducted with Soviet officials and directed toward Soviet strategic concerns. Interactions between John Kennedy and Nikita Khrushchev during both of these crises were affected by their mutual hope for movement toward improved U.S.-Soviet relations in the postcrisis period. In the Vietnam case, the fundamental U.S. interest was perceived by the Johnson administration as preserving the credibility of America's global commitments to stem Communist encroachment. Moreover, as its predecessors had done regarding Laos, it attempted to achieve an early halt to North Vietnamese aggression by combining deployments and limited applications of force with diplomatic initiatives directed principally at the Soviet Union. Years later, in Nicaragua, the Reagan administration also perceived the key issues in global cold war terms, and it failed to appreciate the limits of Soviet interest in perpetuating Sandinista influence in Central America.

With the Soviet Union increasingly in disarray and the winding down of the cold war, regional crises could be approached from different strategic perspectives. For example, despite the Soviet Union's early encouragement of nationalist resistance movements in areas still affected by the residual influences of Western colonialism, including extensive training of terrorist organizers, it quietly removed itself from an association with the bombastic and unpredictable Muammar Qaddafi. As a result, Libya's support of terrorism could be dealt with largely as an isolated offense against which an attempt could be made to mobilize the moral outrage of the entire Western community of nations. In the case of Saddam Hussein's seizure of Kuwait, the process of disintegration within the Soviet Union removed both Soviet aspirations in the Gulf and historic Soviet support for Iraq as serious strategic factors. Ultimately, in the evolving crisis, the Soviet government joined the U.S.-led diplomatic coalition and supported the U.N. resolutions condemning, and applying coercive pressure against, Iraq. Accordingly, the Bush administration could focus its attention and energies more fully on the problems of coalition cohesion and on preservation of the fragile separation of the Gulf crisis from the deep-seated Arab-Israeli tensions.

Type of Provocation. Crises in which coercive diplomacy is attempted vary greatly in the challenge they pose depending on the type of provocation that triggered the confrontation. Some types of provocation are easier for the perpetrator to stop or undo, if coerced by the defender, than are others. A successful fait accompli action that quickly overruns and occupies a neighboring country (as in the case of Iraq's seizure of Kuwait) is extremely difficult to reverse. An effort to alter a status quo situation that is only just under way and is highly dependent on outside support (as in the case of the Pathet Lao's attempt to overrun key locations held by the Royal Laotian government) is more susceptible to carrot-and-stick amelioration.

Covert sponsorship or encouragement of internal upheaval and irregular forms of aggression by others (as in Libya's support of international terrorist groups) makes it difficult for the defenders to clearly define the aggressive behavior and assign political responsibility for that behavior. However, clear-cut attempts to alter the status quo through violation of recognized boundaries or other examples of flagrant disregard of international norms tend to give the defending party a kind of strategic high ground. In such cases, the wielder of coercive diplomacy, applying the strategy in obvious defense against another party's aggression, enjoys the kind of legitimacy that norms of international law bestow on the defender. This legitimacy can be extremely helpful in obtaining international as well as domestic support and in denying the opponent the benefits of international backing. Being able to invoke legitimacy on behalf of one's demands in coercive diplomacy can also be helpful (as in the Cuban Missile Crisis) in persuading the opponent that its behavior is indefensible and must be altered.

Image of War. The more horrible the image of war the crisis triggers, the more strongly motivated one or both sides will be (as in the Cuban Missile Crisis) to exercise restraint and to cooperate to avoid such a war. In Vietnam in 1965, neither side regarded the immediate prospect of war as a reason to soften its position and work out an acceptable bargain. As William Simons indicates in his study, the U.S. leadership exuded confidence that if it were necessary to bring American military power directly to bear on North Vietnam, the leaders in Hanoi would surely be forced to back down. For their part, the leaders in Hanoi regarded escalation of the fighting in South Vietnam to a contest between their forces and those of the United States as a battle they could ultimately win. At the same time, President Johnson's image of the escalation that might follow from an immediately expanded conflict inhibited his selection of coercive actions in his brief attempt to move beyond the try-and-see variant of coercive diplomacy.

The respective images of war are only one of several instances of the prominence of perception in the conduct of coercive diplomacy, but surely it is one of the most important of the contextual variables. Had Saddam Hussein perceived "the mother of all battles" in images even approaching the destruction levied on Iraq's forces and infrastructure, he might have more seriously considered the negotiating initiatives advanced by others in the international coalition arrayed against him.

Unilateral or Coalitional Coercive Diplomacy. Coercive diplomacy is likely to be more difficult to carry out when it is employed by a coalition of states rather than by a single government. Although a coalition brings international pressure to bear on the target of diplomacy and can devote greater resources to the task, the unity and sense of purpose of a coalition may be fragile. In the Laos crisis, for example, resistance from France and the United Kingdom to the use of threatened military intervention made the Southeast Asia Treaty Organization (SEATO) less than useful as a base for coercive diplomacy. A partial exception to the rule was the strength and stability of the U.N. coalition President Bush succeeded in building on behalf of coercive diplomacy against Iraq. However, it should be noted that concern over the vulnerability and lack of staying power of this coalition was among the considerations that led President Bush to substitute the threat of war for economic sanctions as the main coercive lever in the coalition's strategy.

By contrast, as Tim Zimmermann shows, President Reagan was unable in early 1986 to build an effective coalition to exert meaningful coercive pressure on Libya's Col. Qaddafi. Despite a commonly asserted objective of seeking an end to international terrorism, European allies declined to join the United States even in a common policy of economic sanctions directed at Libya's encouragement and support of terrorist activities. As in the later Persian Gulf case, U.S. concern over the lack of a firm commitment to sanctions from its allies was one of the factors contributing to Reagan's decision to increase unilateral military pressure on Qaddafi.

Isolation of the Adversary. The task of coercive diplomacy is likely to be more complex and sometimes more difficult when the adversary (as in the Laos crisis of 1961–1962 and in the 1965 Vietnam case) is not an isolated state but is supported diplomatically and militarily by allies. In both of these cases, it was not only the government of North Vietnam that had to be influenced to back away from its original design; Beijing and Moscow also played significant roles in shaping the opponent's reactions to U.S. pressure. Happily, as the Laos crisis progressed, Moscow became convinced of the desirability of a compromise settlement and was able to exercise enough leverage with Laotian and Vietnamese Communist leaders to help bring it about. By 1965, the dominant leverage was being exerted by the Chinese, who strongly encouraged the North Vietnamese proclivity to resist any bargain that compromised their basic national goal.

By contrast, the virtual diplomatic isolation of Iraq in the recent Gulf crisis made it easier for the United States to intervene and to organize the coalition that demanded that Iraq get out of Kuwait. In particular, the fact that Saddam no longer had the support of the Soviet Union meant that the international authority of the U.N. Security Council could be called into play without fear of a Soviet veto. As a result, that authority could be harnessed to attract multinational support for the economic sanctions imposed on Iraq and, later, for the international military force assembled as a coercive threat.

The Risks of Ultimata

The starkest variant of coercive diplomacy, as was noted in Part One, is the ultimatum. It has three components: (1) a demand on the opponent, (2) a time limit or sense of urgency for compliance with the demand, and (3) a threat of punishment for noncompliance that is credible and sufficiently potent to impress upon the opponent that compliance is preferable. An ultimatum, or tacit ultimatum, was employed by the United States in four of the seven cases examined in Part Two: the Pearl Harbor case, the Laos crisis, the Cuban missile case, and the Persian Gulf case.

For various reasons, however, policy makers may consider it necessary to forgo resorting to an ultimatum—for example, in situations in which strong domestic or international opposition to such a course of action could result in a severe political-diplomatic backlash. In the Nicaragua case, as Bruce Jentleson argues, the Reagan administration's ability to engage in stronger coercive diplomacy against the Sandinista regime was severely constrained by domestic political resistance to further U.S. involvement, as well as by strong international opposition. In the Vietnam case, Simons's account indicates that President Johnson felt severely constrained from coupling an ultimatum with the modest air attacks against North Vietnam in early 1965 by his perception of shaky domestic political support and international pressure for premature negotiations. It is also possible that Johnson—knowing that if an ultimatum were rejected, he would not want to order all-out air attacks because of the risk of Chinese and Soviet intervention—chose not to issue an ultimatum and risk having it exposed as a bluff.

Even in cases in which an ultimatum variant of coercive diplomacy was tried, policy makers had to confront certain risks presented by the specific situation. Something approximating the ultimatum was employed successfully in the Laos and Cuban missile cases, and we later review the conditions that made this possible. For the moment, however, we consider two cases in which an ultimatum variant was tried despite the risks but failed.

In the Pearl Harbor case, Scott Sagan indicates that U.S. leaders had held off imposing an embargo on oil to Japan for some time. Aware of Japan's acute dependence on oil imported from the United States, the Roosevelt administration knew that taking this step to back its demand that Japan get out of China would be a serious provocation. In effect, imposing an embargo would be the equivalent of a tacit ultimatum; cutting off access to the oil Japan needed to fuel its military machine would create a sense of urgency to comply with U.S. demands. What is more, President Roosevelt and his advisers realized that to impose an embargo, versus merely threatening to do so, would be a harsh move to which Japan might respond by attacking the Dutch East Indies in order to gain new sources of oil. For this reason, Washington held off imposing an oil embargo until, under the highly unusual circumstances described by Sagan, the embargo was initiated in late July 1941 by Dean Acheson in his capacity as chairperson of the interdepartmental Foreign Funds Committee.

The oil embargo indeed proved to be provocative. Tokyo decided it would have no alternative but to initiate war by early December, not only against the Dutch East Indies but also against U.S. bases in the Philippines and Pearl Harbor, unless the United States softened its demands that Japan get out of China and give up its aspirations for regional hegemony. When the Japanese negotiators were unable to reach an acceptable accommodation with Washington, war was launched. The Pearl Harbor case, therefore, fully exemplifies the fact that under certain circumstances, the strong tacit ultimatum variant of coercive diplomacy can boomerang. The critical variable in the case was the extreme magnitude of the U.S. demand, which strengthened the opponent's motivation to resist. Backed into a corner and given no acceptable diplomatic way out, and confronted by the humiliating demand that they give up their imperialistic achievements and aspirations, Japan's desperate leaders felt they were left with no acceptable alternative but to initiate what they knew to be a highly risky war against a militarily and economically stronger opponent.

The ultimatum variant of coercive diplomacy also failed in the Persian Gulf crisis. As noted by Richard Herrmann, coercive diplomacy in the Gulf war began with U.N. resolutions that approximated the gradual turning of the screw variant of the strategy. The U.N. Security Council made use of increasingly severe economic sanctions. In late November 1990, the approach was replaced by an ultimatum to Iraq, backed by the threat of war. Well before the United States persuaded the Security Council to take this step, the Deputies Committee of the National Security Council in Washington carefully considered the utility and risks of subjecting Saddam Hussein to an ultimatum. Drawing upon knowledge of historical experience with ultimata, the Deputies Committee identified several possible risks of an ultimatum and undertook the difficult task of estimating whether any of these risks were likely to materialize and how they might be minimized, if not avoided altogether. The full results of the group's risk analysis are not yet available, but the following observations appear to be correct.[1]

Initially, the major concern of members of the working group and higher officials appears to have been that of making the threat of punishment credible enough to make it extremely unlikely that Saddam Hussein would dismiss it as a bluff. The original ultimatum left open just when the U.N. coalition might begin military operations. The date attached to the ultimatum—January 15, 1991—was not a deadline after which war would follow immediately but rather was the point at which something approximating the game of chicken would begin. Later, however, as January 15 approached, it took on the character of a deadline for compliance as yet another risk became a significant concern for the Bush administration. It was feared that Saddam might announce partial, conditional, or qualified withdrawal from Kuwait in an effort to erode the coercive pressure to which he was being subjected and to salvage some of his gains. This possibility was referred to by well-informed journalists as the administration's "nightmare scenario," and detailed contingency plans were made to deal with such a development.

We need not review the possible reasons why Saddam did not accede to the ultimatum or at least resort to the strategy of announcing a partial withdrawal. A conclusive answer is not possible given the lack of data on Saddam's thinking. But it seems likely that he rejected the ultimatum at least in part because he regarded acceptance as humiliating, as incompatible with honor, and as too damaging politically.

From these cases, we can see that policy makers in several different crisis situations have wrestled with a number of risks inherent in confronting an opponent with an ultimatum. Paul Lauren summarizes a great deal of additional historical experience on which we can also draw to highlight the constraints and risks encountered with this starkest variant of coercive diplomacy. At least four such risks can be identified:

1. The opponent may reject the ultimatum, thinking it is a bluff, and thus place the burden of deciding whether to carry out the threatened punishment on the shoulder of the coercing party.
2. The opponent may reject the ultimatum because he regards acceptance of it as humiliating, as incompatible with honor, as too damaging politically, with the same consequence as in no. 1.

3. The opponent may take the ultimatum seriously but decide to initiate war himself rather than accept the demand.
4. The opponent may neither accept nor reject the ultimatum outright but may attempt to defuse its coercive impact by partial, qualified, or equivocal acceptance of the demands, hoping thereby to force the coercing power to settle for less.

Components of Crisis Bargaining

One of the most important areas of generic knowledge relevant to the strategy of coercive diplomacy is that of crisis bargaining; that is, the policy maker's timely application of appropriate combinations of threat and accommodation to attain an acceptable change in the opponent's behavior. The two cases in which some variant of coercive diplomacy proved to be clearly effective—the Laos crisis of 1961–1962 and the Cuban Missile Crisis—are also examples of the use of some version of the ultimatum. These cases bear close examination lest an incorrect lesson be drawn; namely, that resort to a strong variant of coercive diplomacy was the sole or primary factor contributing to its success in these two cases. Coercive diplomacy is a form of crisis bargaining, and it is instructive to view President Kennedy's policy decisions in these two crises from this standpoint.

In any crisis, the policy maker must decide *what combination* of persuasion, coercion, and accommodation to employ *and in what sequence.* It is noteworthy that Kennedy employed all three of these components of crisis bargaining in both the Laos and Cuban crises. However, the mixture of the three and the sequence in which he brought them into play differed. The use of threat was significantly greater in the missile crisis, but one should not overlook the fact that his coercive threats were initially coupled with considerable emphasis on persuasion and, toward the end of the crisis, with accommodation. As Alexander George points out, Kennedy believed it was essential to employ coercive threats and actions at the outset of the crisis to demonstrate his resolution and to gain credibility for his warning that he would resort to force if necessary. He gave priority to this objective, deliberately deferring any discussions of concessions until he had first impressed Khrushchev with his resolve.

In his study of the Laos crisis, however, David Hall shows that Kennedy began with an emphasis on the possibility of accommodation, signaling a readiness to reduce the U.S. objective in Laos in return for that country's neutralization. Later, he resorted to occasional threats of intervention in order to discourage the adversary from exploiting his battlefield advantage too far and to motivate the Soviet Union to pressure its Communist allies to be more receptive to the U.S. demands. In fact, Kennedy's earliest attempts to signal a reduced objective, including a statement to the press, at first encouraged reactions from the Communists that illustrate the delicacy of crisis bargaining. Seemingly emboldened by the U.S. inclination to step back from its original posture, the Communist governments rejected outright the U.S.-sponsored diplomatic proposal, and the Pathet Lao–Vietminh embarked on a major new offensive. One must speculate on the degree to which that experience, surmounted by the Kennedy administration only through increased commitment and carefully coordinated diplomacy, convinced the president of the need first to convince Khrushchev of his resolve when the Cuban crisis developed eighteen months later.

Since the major target of Kennedy's strategy in the Laos crisis was likewise engaged globally and also had many reasons to avoid too deep an involvement in a dangerous regional struggle, the threatening nature of these events made an impression in Moscow as well. The Soviets' awareness that these new developments carried a clear potential for rendering mutual control of the crisis more difficult lent greater credibility and coercive impact to Kennedy's new bargaining posture.

Kennedy made considerable use of persuasion in both crises. He employed a variety of diplomatic and open channels to clarify, explain, and justify to his adversary, as well as to others, why the demand he was making was truly important to the United States and why he was strongly resolved to achieve it. And, cognizant of the principles of crisis management, Kennedy deliberately slowed the momentum of events, particularly during the Cuban Missile Crisis, in order to give diplomatic processes and communication an opportunity to help achieve a peaceful resolution.

Coercive diplomacy could work in these two cases because neither Kennedy nor Khrushchev viewed the particular conflict of interests in the dispute or their overall relationship as approximating a zero-sum conflict. The objectives Kennedy pursued in both crises, even in the missile crisis, were limited ones. They did not threaten vital Soviet interests. And, as we noted, Kennedy offered substantial carrots as well as making threats in order to secure compliance with his demands. When the conflict with an adversary is viewed in zero-sum terms—as in the case of U.S. policy toward Japan in 1941, the Reagan administration's view of the Sandinista regime in Nicaragua, and possibly also in the Persian Gulf case—it is much more difficult to employ the carrot-and-stick variant. In extreme cases of this kind, the strategy of coercive diplomacy tends to become all stick and no carrot, and little scope is left for diplomatic efforts to reach a mutually acceptable peaceful resolution of the crisis.

Of course, the process of crisis bargaining requires a perceived freedom to bargain. President Kennedy had this in Laos, in part because of the tradition of bipartisanship that tends to grace the first few months of a newly inaugurated administration. He had it in the Cuban Missile Crisis, principally because of the high priority all Americans attached to peacefully eliminating a nuclear missile threat in our own hemisphere. President Reagan probably had such freedom to bargain with Nicaragua, but because of his administration's strongly held views regarding a Communist hemispheric threat, he chose not to use it.

For analytical clarity, perhaps a better term than freedom is *political capital.* In this sense, the perceived availability of bargaining room may better be thought of as a somewhat finite resource rather than some generally present condition. Moreover, it may more usefully be thought of as a resource the policy maker can choose to use or not rather than some advantageous condition that should be seized upon. For example, in 1965 President Johnson was not willing to risk the political cost of scaling back the U.S. objective in Vietnam to entice North Vietnam into early bargaining sessions. He genuinely feared the political reaction to an abandonment of the policy goal inherited from President Kennedy and the likely impact of this reaction on his domestic strategy for the Great Society.

In each case in which a strategy of coercive diplomacy is contemplated, before entering into a bargaining posture the policy maker would be wise to assess the likely political costs and risks of this step. He or she should (1) calculate the likely nature and strength of domestic political opposition to the particular bargaining position under consideration; (2) contemplate the importance of other future policy objectives for which the support of that opposition might be needed; and (3) assess the opportunities likely to be available for enlisting that support should the imperatives of the immediate crisis seem to describe an urgent need for a bargaining initiative.

Conditions that Favor Coercive Diplomacy

Because coercive diplomacy is not always successful, it is important to identify conditions that, if present, favor its success or, if absent, reduce the likelihood of its being effective. We use the term *favor* advisedly here because our analysis of historical experience suggests that no single condition can be regarded as sufficient for the success of the strategy. Moreover, with very few exceptions, we avoid suggesting even that a particular condition is necessary for successful use of coercive diplomacy. In some cases, the presence of a necessary condition may contribute little to a causal explanation of the outcome; other conditions may be more directly relevant.

In fact, many variables can influence the outcome of efforts to employ coercive diplomacy. Some have to do with the content of the particular version of the strategy that is employed—that is, what is demanded, whether a sense of urgency is created for compliance, whether a credible and sufficiently potent threat of punishment for noncompliance is conveyed, and whether the threat is coupled with positive incentives and assurances that make it easier for the adversary to accept the demands. Other relevant variables have to do with situational and contextual aspects that were illustrated in the case studies and discussed earlier in this chapter.

However, although the seven cases make it clear that no variable suffices in itself as a causal explanation of successful coercive diplomacy, certain conditions in the interaction between a coercing government and its opponent will, if present, favor the strategy. In the sections that follow, we discuss each of these conditions and cite selected cases to illustrate how their presence or absence contributed to the case outcomes. Not all cases are evaluated with regard to each condition; Table 3 (p. 288) summarizes a fuller reporting of our judgments in this respect.

The reader will note some variance from the list of conditions developed for the 1971 edition. In particular we do not include "usable military options" in the current set. This omission does not downgrade the importance of selecting military options that are politically and strategically appropriate when operationalizing a variant of coercive diplomacy. It merely reflects our later recognition, illustrated in some of the newer cases and in Paul Lauren's historical survey, that coercive pressure can sometimes be applied through nonmilitary means. The current list of conditions is meant to be relevant for any situation in which coercive diplomacy might be contemplated.

Clarity of the Objective. Clarity with respect to what is to be achieved through coercive diplomacy is important in two respects. First, it assists policy makers in selecting from among several available response options. Second, clarity and consistency in what is demanded help persuade the opponent of the coercing power's strength of purpose. In both the Laos and Cuban crises, this condition was satisfied and contributed to the success of coercive diplomacy. The condition was also present in the Pearl Harbor and Persian Gulf cases, but coercive diplomacy failed because other factors were also at work.

In the Vietnam and Nicaragua cases, Washington's objectives and demands were not clear, which contributed to the difficulties encountered by U.S. strategy in those confrontations. To the extent that coercion of North Vietnam was attempted in early 1965, Simons demonstrates that other conflicting objectives constantly tended to obscure the demands directed toward Hanoi and to limit the impact of the other components of coercive diplomacy. Attempting through its actions to send messages to different target audiences, the Johnson administration left its demands on Hanoi somewhat opaque. And in the Nicaraguan case, as Jentleson shows, President Reagan's failure to set and enforce a clear policy line led to an intense struggle within his administration over the objectives and modalities of its coercive policy. In both cases, the lack of clear and consistent objectives severely constrained the possibilities for productive bargaining with the opponent.

Strength of Motivation. Obviously, the coercing power must be sufficiently motivated by what it perceives to be at stake in a crisis to act at all. Yet that motivation must be strong enough to encourage national decision makers to accept the costs and risks inherent in steadfastly pursuing a coercive strategy. At root is their perception of the depth of national interest involved when the key decisions must be made.

For example, in the Laos case, until April 1962 President Kennedy exhibited only a questionable commitment to preventing the impending defeat of the Royal Lao forces. Then, as David Hall points out, the added motivation of showing strong national resolve following the embarrassing Bay of Pigs fiasco prompted Kennedy to risk the stronger commitment of placing U.S. military advisers in harm's way and later actually deploying back-up forces to Thailand. Kennedy's behavior until that point was such as to raise questions about what he would have done had the Communist opponents not accepted his demand for a cease-fire. In the Cuban Missile Crisis, however, the Kennedy administration's strong motivation to get rid of the missile threat was obvious from the beginning.

Events quite removed from the crisis may also have affected the coercing power's motivation in the Libyan case—although in a different direction. From late 1985 through the punitive U.S. air strikes against selected Libyan targets, the Reagan administration was determined to maintain a strong public posture against state-supported terrorism. Then, despite a clear warning by the president that Libya would be struck again if it continued its hated policy, the administration declined to follow through. Apparently, the onset of the Iran-contra affair, among other factors, encouraged the administration to assume a less assertive posture toward Qaddafi's links with terrorist activities.

Asymmetry of Motivation. As important as the coercing power's perceptions of its stakes and interests may be, it is essential to recognize that motivation is a two-sided matter. As the theoretical discussion in Part One and the case studies have stressed, the relative motivation of the two sides plays an important role in determining the outcome of coercive diplomacy. The strategy is more likely to be successful if the side employing it is more highly motivated than its opponent by what is at stake in the crisis. What is critical in this respect, however, is that the adversary *believe* the coercing power is more highly motivated than the adversary to achieve its crisis objective.

In some cases, the relative motivation of the two sides tends to be fixed by the nature of the conflict. In other cases, however, the side that engages in coercive diplomacy may be able to create an asymmetry of motivation in its favor in two ways: (1) by demanding of the opponent only what is essential to protect its own vital interests and not making demands that engage the vital interests of its adversary, and (2) by offering a carrot that reduces the adversary's motivation to resist the demands. In the Laos and Cuban crises, as we have seen, Kennedy used both of these levers to create an asymmetry of motivation in his favor. The success of his coercive threats in these two cases cannot be properly understood without taking this leverage into account.

The critical nature of the *opponent's* perception that an asymmetry of motivation favors the coercing power is perhaps best illustrated by the Persian Gulf and Vietnam cases. The air assault that began in January 1991 proved that the Bush administration was strongly motivated to pressure Iraq into reversing its seizure of Kuwait. As Richard Herrmann's case study shows, however, Saddam Hussein apparently believed that Arab politics and Islamic fervor would ultimately disrupt the international coalition aligned against him. Further, he was convinced that the "imperialists" who continued the struggle would have to negotiate a settlement that would permit Iraq to fulfill its destiny as the dominant power in a region consumed by Arab nationalism. He apparently perceived the baser motivations of the Western governments as unable to withstand the righteous power of Islam and the Arab people.

The North Vietnam leaders' belief in the correctness of their mission to drive Western influences from South Vietnam likewise was not shaken by their perceptions of U.S. intent. In 1965 at least, prodded by their Chinese benefactors, they apparently were persuaded that the bombing campaign was intended primarily to improve the U.S. posture for negotiations. In the view from Hanoi and Beijing, the Johnson administration was not projecting a commitment to persevere but was merely maneuvering toward an attempt to win at the bargaining table what it and its allies were not winning in the countryside of South Vietnam. We regard the inability of Washington to create in its opponent a perception of an asymmetry of motivation favoring the United States as important in explaining coercive diplomacy's failure in these and other cases.

Sense of Urgency. Once again, it is the opponent's perception of the condition that is critical. If the state employing coercive diplomacy genuinely experiences a sense of urgency to achieve its objective—as Kennedy did particularly in the last stage of the Cuban crisis—it is more likely to be able to generate a sense of urgency for compliance on the part of the opponent. Otherwise, the coercing power must find other ways to convey a credible sense of urgency for compliance.

Hall's study of the Laos case shows that the Kennedy administration's highly coordinated diplomatic maneuvering was largely responsible for conveying a sense of urgency to the Communist opponents. Bilateral talks with Prime Minister Jawaharlal Nehru, Foreign Secretary Harold MacMillan, and Foreign Minister Andrei Gromyko, SEATO meetings, and bilateral Soviet–United Kingdom talks were all used for this purpose. These initiatives apparently reinforced, at least for Soviet leaders, the urgency of the situation and helped persuade the Chinese to accept a cease-fire and engage in resultant negotiations.

By definition, employment of the lesser variants of coercive diplomacy—try-and-see and gradual turning of the screw—avoids imparting a sense of urgency for compliance. Hence, this condition was inoperative in the cases involving Libya, Nicaragua, and Vietnam. Only in cases in which classic or tacit ultimata are invoked can it be communicated with coercive effect. In the Persian Gulf case, Herrmann relates how the Bush administration tried to create a sense of urgency by getting the U.N. coalition to treat January 15 as a deadline for compliance. It is not clear, however, whether Saddam Hussein perceived this date in urgent terms. On the other hand, as we saw in the Pearl Harbor case, creating a sense of urgency for compliance with one's demand may boomerang and encourage a desperate or committed opponent to initiate war in preference to acceding to the coercing power's terms.

Strong Leadership. The choice, implementation, and outcome of coercive diplomacy depends to some extent on the presence of strong and effective top-level political leadership. Such leadership was provided by President Kennedy in the Cuban Missile Crisis and undoubtedly contributed to the success of the strategy in that case. George shows how Kennedy's decision to opt for the limited objective of withdrawal of the missiles rather than removal of Castro or of Soviet influence in Cuba and his firm control over the deployment and use of military forces were critical to the outcome. Similarly, in the Persian Gulf crisis, although coercive diplomacy did not succeed, President Bush's leadership made it possible to gain coalition support for the ultimatum to Saddam and for the war that followed when the Iraqi leader refused to accept the demands made on him.

By contrast, in the critical months of August and September preceding Pearl Harbor, President Roosevelt apparently allowed a mid-level bureaucrat to convert his administration's potentially most effective carrot into a harsh stick. Skillful control over Japan's access to U.S. oil might have proven a useful bargaining lever had Assistant Secretary Dean Acheson's self-righteous refusal to grant the Japanese request for petroleum licenses, in contradiction of the president's loosely communicated decision, not been allowed to stand as the de facto policy. Had Roosevelt demanded strict supervision over the implementation of his policy or, like President Truman regarding Korea a decade later, insisted on policy loyalty from his subordinates, the use of coercive diplomacy might have led to a negotiated settlement that avoided war.[2]

In a special way, strong leadership in the opponent's government also facilitates the implementation of coercive diplomacy. Because the prospect for success in coercive diplomacy depends so heavily on correct readings of the opponent's political and military reactions to the coercing government's actions and demands, an adversary's control over its military forces and diplomats can become a critical element in the process. In the autumn of 1962, Khrushchev exercised effective control over the Soviet diplomatic corps and over the ship commanders who were bringing the missiles to Cuba. Conversely, the 1941 Japanese government had only limited control over Japan's military leaders, particularly those commanding its occupation forces in China.

Adequate Domestic and International Support. A certain level of political support at home is needed for any serious use of coercive diplomacy by U.S. leaders. It is difficult to go beyond this simple generalization, however, because the extent to which the strategy depends on domestic political support can vary substantially depending on the specifics of the case. In the Laos crisis during his first few months in office, President Kennedy's domestic support rested mainly with Congress, both within his own party and from many Republican members who had supported Dwight Eisenhower's policies in Southeast Asia. It is doubtful that a significant number of Americans had much interest in the situation. However, Kennedy had strong support from both Congress and the American public throughout the Cuban Missile Crisis. Similarly, there was considerable public backing of President Reagan's effort to coerce Qaddafi into giving up his support of international terrorism.

These situations contrast sharply with the Vietnam and Nicaragua cases. At the time of President Johnson's brief attempt at coercive diplomacy in the spring of 1965, U.S. public opinion had not yet turned against the administration's Southeast Asia policy, but increasing numbers of members of Congress were beginning to question it openly. Johnson knew that a substantial increase in the U.S. military commitment in Vietnam would provoke more widespread opposition. In the mid-1980s, support from both the public and Congress for the Reagan policies toward Nicaragua was extremely weak. Opposition to these policies was particularly persistent regarding the possibility of U.S. military intervention of any kind and encouragement of the contras to take guerrilla actions designed to weaken the Sandinistas' hold on the country.

International support (or lack thereof) is also an important factor in some cases of coercive diplomacy. The support of the Organization of American States and the United Nations was helpful to Kennedy in the Cuban Missile Crisis. Unusually strong international and domestic support in the Persian Gulf crisis allowed the Bush administration to adopt an ultimatum strategy. In contrast, concern about international reactions contributed to Johnson's cautious use of air power against North Vietnam. However, the relationship of international support to the rationality of attempting coercive diplomacy is more complex than is indicated by these cases.

This complexity is illustrated by the two cases from the Reagan administration, both of which resulted in ambiguous outcomes. As Jentleson shows, President Reagan's policy of using the contras to apply coercive pressure against the Sandinista regime in Nicaragua received almost universal condemnation abroad. Yet, although probably unintended, this unilateral U.S. policy played some part in motivating Central American leaders to undertake independent efforts to mediate Nicaragua's internal political dispute. Later, despite extremely limited international support for its attempt to coerce Qaddafi's Libya with meaningful economic sanctions, the Reagan administration unilaterally applied graduated military pressures. In this case, as Zimmermann points out, these military operations were intended for European as well as Libyan observation. Ironically, after the military operations culminated in punitive air strikes, some launched from British bases, several of Washington's European allies adopted the kinds of political and economic sanctions against Libya that the Reagan administration had requested of them earlier.

Unacceptability of Threatened Escalation. The impact of coercive diplomacy is enhanced if the initial actions and communications directed against the adversary arouse his fear of an escalation to circumstances less acceptable than those promised by accession to the coercing power's demands. (In some cases [as in Laos] this perception would depend in part on the inducements being offered as well.) This condition occurred in the Cuban Missile Crisis because the accelerating buildup of U.S. combat forces in the southern states and the shooting down of the U-2 aircraft evidently convinced Khrushchev that stronger American military action might be imminent, thereby heightening the prospects for war. This possibility must have been particularly alarming to the Soviet leader because, as we now know, Khrushchev had predelegated to Soviet commanders in Cuba authority to use their tactical nuclear weapons in the event of an attempted U.S. invasion. In the Libyan case, the U.S. air strike appears to have had a similar intimidating effect for a time. Retreating to his desert quarters, Qaddafi remained quiescent for several months, and considerable dissent was provoked among units of Libya's military forces and Islamic fundamentalist groups.

In the Pearl Harbor case, the threat of an oil embargo from the United States, which Japanese leaders feared most, became a reality in July 1941. Sagan explains how the embargo constituted an escalation of the crisis that was unacceptable to the Japanese. They then regarded their options as being limited either to securing an alleviation of the oil embargo through diplomacy or going to war. Though fraught with risk, early war against the United States and other Western powers in Asia was more acceptable than the certain ultimate frustration of regional ambitions stemming from an inadequate supply of petroleum.

Other cases give little evidence that opponents feared U.S. escalation. In early 1965, North Vietnamese leaders showed little concern over any portent suggested by the limited U.S. air attacks or conveyed by Washington's cautious diplomatic signals. In the case of Nicaragua, the Sandinista leadership may have been concerned over the possibility of direct U.S. military intervention in the months following the Grenada invasion, and this condition might have helped shape a settlement had the United States pursued less extreme objectives at that time. However, fear of escalated U.S. military action played only a minor role at best in motivating the Sandinistas to accept the formula for ending the crisis developed later by the Central American leaders. In the Persian Gulf crisis, Saddam Hussein apparently underestimated either the capability of the U.S.-led coalition to wage a decisive ground campaign or the cohesiveness of the multinational alliance arrayed against him, or both.

Clarity Concerning the Precise Terms of Settlement of the Crisis. Clarity of objectives and demands (the first condition listed above) may not suffice. In some cases it may also be necessary for the coercing power to formulate specific terms regarding the termination of the crisis that the two sides can agree on and to establish procedures for carrying out these terms and verifying their implementation. Obviously, this would not be helpful in cases with extreme demands, such as the Reagan administration's Type C strategy against Nicaragua, where the desired terms are more threatening to the opponent's interests than the punishment being inflicted. In other situations, a coercive strategy may be enhanced by this condition.

For example, in the Laos crisis, the Kennedy administration realistically had few resources available with which to effect a settlement that satisfied the objectives endorsed by its predecessors in office. It forestalled a Communist takeover of Laos by achieving a cease-fire in place through a combination of veiled military threats and some political concessions. Kennedy enhanced the persuasiveness of his carrot-and-stick approach by agreeing in advance to some implementing features of a neutralized Laos and later to U.S. participation in an international conference within the Geneva framework to work out the arrangements—*provided that* the cease-fire had already taken effect. Accompanying the elaborate pattern of bilateral talks and third-party entreaties leading to acceptance of the proposals were the administration's assurances to the Soviets that it would withdraw the U.S. military mission in Laos and channel all aid through an international body if the Communist governments would reciprocate.

As with Laos, specifying terms of settlement in advance of formal agreement can also be of major importance to the adversary's side. It may want precise settlement terms to safeguard against the possibility that the coercing power has in mind a broader, more sweeping interpretation of the formula for ending the crisis or will be tempted to renew pressure and push for even greater concessions after the initial agreement for terminating the crisis is concluded. The adversary who contemplates succumbing to coercive diplomacy may need specific and reliable assurances that the coercive power will carry out its part of the termination agreement. Accordingly, suitable U.S. assurances to Nicaragua in 1984 might have led to a negotiated agreement providing for most of Washington's regional security objectives short of the Sandinista collapse the Reagan administration hoped for had the administration recognized the merit of the other conditions for policy success that then existed.

For purposes of better understanding coercive diplomacy, it is also intriguing to speculate as to how Japan's civilian leaders might have reacted in late November 1941 if the Roosevelt administration had given such assurances along the lines of the once-opted-for modus vivendi position rather than choosing an inflexible reiteration of its "fundamental principles of peace." Of course, such a decision would have met with strong opposition from the British and Chinese governments.

✻   ✻   ✻

Elsewhere in this study, we have stressed that coercive diplomacy requires skill on the part of policy makers in tailoring the strategy to the special circumstances of a particular crisis. Our major finding, however, is that strategic skill can contribute to successful application of coercive diplomacy only if the eight conditions that favor the strategy, as described in this section, are present in that crisis situation in some combination or if the coercing state is able by some of its actions to help create favorable conditions. But generally, skill can only capitalize on favorable conditions latent in the situation; it cannot compensate for their absence. Therefore, the failure of coercive diplomacy in a particular case should not necessarily be taken as evidence of an administration's ineptness in implementing the strategy. Rather, it is more likely an indication of that administration's failure to recognize that the situation was intrinsically wrong for the strategy.

Not all of these eight conditions appear to be equally important in determining whether coercive diplomacy is a reasonable strategy to pursue. Three that seem particularly significant for influencing the outcome have to do with the *opponent's perception.* Thus, coercive diplomacy is facilitated if the *opponent* believes that an asymmetry of motivation operates in favor of the coercing power, that it is time urgent to respond to the coercing power's demands, and that the coercing power will engage in escalation that would impose unacceptable costs. Another condition that seems particularly significant is the clarity of settlement terms. Table 3 shows that only the cases in which coercive diplomacy was a clear-cut success—the Laos and Cuban crises—are characterized by all four of these conditions. No other case clearly reflects more than one of them.

However, the condition of time urgency poses a special problem; by definition, it applies only to cases in which some variant of an ultimatum is employed. Should we infer that only the ultimata variants can produce successful outcomes of coercive diplomacy? Unfortunately, the two other cases that might have helped us to answer this question do not provide compelling evidence. Both the Libya and Nicaragua cases, neither of which exemplifies ultimata, displayed some elements of success—however ambiguously. Had these cases had clearer, more positive outcomes or been imbedded in less complex

TABLE 3   Conditions That Favor Coercive Diplomacy

	Pearl Harbor	Laos	Cuba	Vietnam	Libya	Nicaragua	Persian Gulf
Clarity of objective	+	+	+		?		+
Strong motivation	+	+	+	+	+	+	+
Asymmetry of motivation[a]		+	+		?		
Sense of urgency[a]	+	+	+				?
Strong leadership		+	+	+	+	+	+
Domestic support	+	?	+		+		+
International support	+	+	+				
Fear of unacceptable escalation[a]		+	+		?	?	+
Clarity of terms	?	+	+				

Note: A "+" indicates the presence of the conditions; a "?" means that it is not clear whether the condition is present.

[a] Opponent's perception

circumstances, they might have enabled us to answer with a firm "no." As our evidence stands, we can only express doubts that ultimata are required and leave it to other case work to present a more compelling argument.

In addition, these non-ultimatum cases do not offer enough evidence to bolster a strong argument concerning the relative influence of the other three significant conditions, which are not reflected clearly in any of the non-ultimatum cases. We can only point to their coexistence in the two successful cases and to the details of their respective roles in these cases while calling attention to their importance.

As three of these conditions involve perceptions held by the leaders of the state that is being subjected to coercive diplomacy, it should be apparent that whether this strategy will work in any particular situation rests heavily on the correctness of the policy maker's assessment of the opponent's perceptions and strategic reasoning. Thus, even when the three most significant conditions are believed to exist, ensuring success in the use of coercive diplomacy still involves considerable uncertainty; their presence or absence is not always self-evident. The policy maker employing coercive diplomacy often cannot reliably judge as to whether these conditions are sufficiently present or can be created in the case at hand.

The Image of the Opponent

Whether leaders of the coercing power have a correct image of their opponent is a significant determinant of the reasonableness of their choice of a variant of coercive diplomacy for use in a specific crisis. This can also have a major impact on the success or failure of that strategy. The prospects for success in the choice and implementation of coercive diplomacy are greatly enhanced if a policy maker can view the crisis events and his own crisis behavior from the perspective of the opponent.

In the Cuban Missile Crisis, for example, President Kennedy's correct image of Khrushchev as a seasoned Communist leader who was capable of making a tactical retreat if made aware of the risks of not doing so played a major part in the successful U.S. resolution of the crisis. After discovering the Soviet missiles in Cuba, administration policy makers had to choose between removing them by direct military action or by applying coercive diplomatic pressure. Critical for this policy choice was the question of whether Khrushchev and his advisers were capable of withdrawing the missiles once the potential costs of not doing so were made clear. Fortunately, the familiarity of some of Kennedy's advisers with old Bolshevik doctrine—advocating readiness to retreat in order to extricate oneself from overwhelming danger—which was derived from studies of past Soviet behavior, enabled the president to assess his opponent correctly. His choice of coercive diplomacy to persuade Khrushchev to remove the missiles peacefully was a direct result of this correct assessment.

Faulty images of the opponent, however, can lead to ineffective policy choices and other miscalculations. In the absence of adequate information, one side often arrives at such images through attributing to the opponent a value system and reasoning process similar to its own. This tendency toward mirror imaging can distort policy makers' estimates of likely opponent motivation and reactions when initially assessing a crisis situation and implementing a chosen strategy.

For example, in the Vietnam case, President Johnson and several of his advisers miscalculated the tenacity of North Vietnam's leaders in pursuit of their objectives in the South. Although Johnson made an effort to visualize himself in his opponent's shoes for bargaining purposes and apparently recognized the relative advantage experienced by Ho Chi Minh in early March 1965, he did not fully appreciate Ho's strength of motivation and moral conviction. This was demonstrated by Johnson's private assertion, barely a month later, that Ho could not resist the carrot offered openly in the Johns Hopkins speech. Did he really believe such an offer would not be seen in Hanoi as a public bribe for abandoning the Viet Cong to their fate? This misjudgment was also evident in the confidence expressed by his top advisers—which Johnson apparently accepted—that once the leaders in Hanoi realized they could not win in South Vietnam, *then* the threat of destruction to the industries and economic infrastructure around Haiphong and Hanoi would have a truly coercive effect. In addition, the Johnson administration may have failed to appreciate that Hanoi had far more at stake in 1965 than had been the case in Laos four years earlier. Whereas Ho and his advisers could afford to accommodate the modest U.S. negotiating objectives in 1961 in order to preserve a favorable position relative to their high-priority goals in

South Vietnam, those goals were clearly at stake in 1965. The leaders in Hanoi saw Washington's bargaining aims then as taking away what they were close to finally achieving—their long-standing national goal of unifying the two parts of their country. The leaders of North Vietnam were much more strongly motivated to resist the U.S. demand that they give up this objective than they had been to oppose Kennedy's 1961 demand for a neutralized Laos.

Administration officials similarly misjudged their opponents in the Pearl Harbor and Persian Gulf cases. For most of 1941, Roosevelt's advisers were divided in their estimates of whether the Japanese would react to an oil embargo by attacking the Dutch East Indies. When Dean Acheson in effect imposed the embargo, his mistaken judgment on this issue was shared by at least three members of the Roosevelt cabinet. Why the president and his secretary of state allowed the policy to stand after they became aware of it is another question; Roosevelt clearly had been among those who earlier believed an embargo would provoke Japan into more aggressive actions. It seems evident that at the time, none of these officials seriously contemplated the possibility that these more aggressive actions might include a simultaneous attack on U.S. forces in the Pacific.

Those officials in the Bush administration, principally in the Department of State, who expected Saddam Hussein to seek a compromise solution once he was confronted with a credible threat of war clearly misjudged the Iraqi leader. To the extent that the view of Saddam Hussein as a "survivalist" actually prevailed in Washington in the autumn of 1990 and was at the root of the administration's campaign to shift the U.N. strategy to the ultimatum variant, this misjudgment contributed to the failure of coercive diplomacy in this case. Of course, given more time to demonstrate its impact on Iraq, the gradual turning of the screw variant, represented by the progressive economic sanctions, may have proven equally unsuccessful. Saddam's motivations and his faith in an ultimately favorable Arab solution may have been unshakable in any event.

More important for our purposes is the observation that, as in this and other cited cases, many possibilities exist for misjudging an opponent in crisis situations. The policy makers' inner circle often contains influential advisers with quite different images of the opponent. This can result in different perceptions of the opponent's motives, varying assessments of his ultimate objectives, and conflicting estimates of his calculus and probable reactions. As a result, the decision maker may be presented with quite different estimates of the overall situation and competing recommendations for an appropriate response.

Effective coercive diplomacy avoids this kind of problem by meeting certain complex and difficult informational requirements. These include particularly accurate knowledge concerning the opposing leaders, their mind-sets, and the domestic and international political contexts in which they operate.

Using this knowledge, policy making can then draw accurate estimates of these leaders' motivations and develop cost-benefit calculations. Often, however, as we have seen, such estimates must be made on the basis of fragmentary and equivocal information. Providing for the gathering of accurate knowledge on potential opponents and establishing a policy-making climate wherein such information can be considered objectively, relatively free from passions and prejudices, are perhaps the most useful preparations an administration can make for the potential use of coercive diplomacy.

CONCLUSIONS

Our analysis of seven attempts to employ coercive diplomacy highlights several important characteristics of the strategy. Coercive diplomacy is a *flexible* strategy that is highly *context-dependent;* its success depends heavily on *adapting* the abstract model (outlined in Part One) to the specific configuration and dynamics of a particular situation and on *skill in implementation.*

The general strategy of coercive diplomacy is strikingly flexible in three basic respects. The demand made of the opponent is a variable that significantly influences the prospects for success. The demand may be modest—as in President Kennedy's effort in the Laos crisis to get the other side to cooperate with his effort to reduce the U.S. commitment to the anti-Communist Laotian government and to obtain neutralization of the entire country. Or, as in the Pearl Harbor and Nicaragua cases, the demand may require that the opponent give up a great deal that affects its vital interests.

The strategy is also flexible in regard to how much of a concession or side payment, if any, the opponent is offered to induce compliance with the demand. As we have seen, along with a threatened use of the stick, little or no carrot was offered Saddam Hussein in the Gulf crisis, Qaddafi in the Libyan case, or the Sandinistas in the Nicaragua case; only a modest one was conveyed to the Japanese in the negotiations preceding the attack on Pearl Harbor. In contrast, quite substantial carrots were offered in the Laos and Cuban crises.

A third aspect of the flexibility of coercive diplomacy is that it has four significantly different variants: the ultimatum, the tacit ultimatum, the gradual turning of the screw, and the try-and-see approach. These forms vary in coercive impact and in the risks they may entail. Their capacity to influence the adversary varies as well and is affected heavily by the circumstances in each case. However, the state that chooses to employ coercive diplomacy seldom has an unencumbered choice as to which variant of the strategy to employ because there may be significant constraints on its actions. As experience has demonstrated, the lesser variants are not likely to be effective when what is demanded is of major importance to the opponent. Yet policy makers may decide not to resort to an ultimatum because they are unwilling to accept the associated risks.

In judging whether coercive diplomacy is likely to be a viable strategy in any particular situation, policy makers should weigh carefully whether the demand they plan to make, the coercive threat they can convey, the carrot they may offer, and the resolution they can display are likely to create three beliefs in the adversary's mind: (1) that an asymmetry of interest and motivation exists that favors the coercer; (2) that the threatened punishment is credible and potent enough to necessitate compliance with the demand; and (3) in cases where variants of ultimata are used, that a sense of urgency exists for compliance with the coercer's demand. Although our research does not enable us to state that these three perceptual variables are strictly necessary or sufficient conditions for the success of coercive diplomacy, the case studies indicate that the presence of these beliefs in the mind of the target of coercive diplomacy strongly favors successful implementation of the strategy.

All this means that policy makers must tailor the abstract mode of coercive diplomacy in a rather exacting manner to fit the special configuration and context of each situation. This is a challenging task because the relevant characteristics of a situation are not always clearly visible or easily appraised. And, as has been noted, several contextual variables influence the workings of the different components of coercive diplomacy. For example, the nature of the provocation affects both the demands made of the opponent and the inducements offered in the bargaining process. The prevailing image of war influences the creation of a sense of urgency, the threatened punishment for noncompliance, and the inducements offered.

It is important to note, as we have suggested in several earlier observations, that not all situations in which a government determines that an adversary's policy must be changed are appropriate for the employment of coercive diplomacy. Recognition of this fact seems particularly important in light of the variety of regional crisis situations the United States appears likely to face in the future. For example, because of political and diplomatic constraints or perceived risks, other defensive nonmilitary strategies may be preferable (See Chapter 1). Some situations may require dealing with aggressive regimes whose goals are not clear or with regimes that calculate costs and risks according to criteria that are different from the recognized norms of international behavior (see Task 3 under "Converting the Abstract Model into a Strategy" in Chapter 2 and "The Image of the Opponent" earlier in this chapter). Others may contain circumstances wherein the adversary receives external support and encouragement from allies whose disparate objectives make bargaining difficult or impossible (see "Isolation of the Adversary" and "Conditions That Favor Coercive Diplomacy" in this chapter). Each situation must be examined carefully to determine whether its circumstances favor the strategy.

Once policy makers determine that coercive diplomacy is appropriate for the situation, their efforts to use the strategy effectively rest heavily on skill in improvisation. The government that adopts this strategy assumes responsibility for pacing the key events—including actions by supportive third parties—for determining the appropriate interactions between the demands made and the inducements offered, and for clear and timely communications. The government must weigh carefully how the opponent is responding to developments in considering what to do next. Reliable insight into the mindset of the opponent is necessary to orchestrate the strategy skillfully; without such insight the actions taken to influence him can easily backfire, triggering critical misperceptions and misjudgments. Indeed, the state that engages in coercive diplomacy can seldom have full or reliable control over the outcome because so much depends on the adversary's assessment of the situation. Moreover, as we have stressed, skillful use of the strategy can only capitalize on favorable conditions latent in the situation; it cannot substitute for their absence.

For all these reasons, coercive diplomacy will constitute a high-confidence strategy in few crises. If it can be made to work, it is a less costly way of achieving one's objectives than exclusive reliance on military force. Coercive diplomacy is a sharp tool—useful at times but difficult to employ successfully against a recalcitrant or unpredictable opponent. Although the strategy sometimes assumes an attraction that may be difficult to resist, its apparent advantages should not distort judgment of its feasibility in any particular situation. The authors hope the analyses presented in this study—of the variants of coercive diplomacy, the constraints that may come into play in designing and implementing the strategy in different situations, and the conditions that influence its effectiveness—will help policy makers to judge the uses and limitations of the strategy in the challenging crises of the future.

NOTES

1. This analysis draws upon research and interviews conducted by Alexander George for an earlier study, *Bridging the Gap: Theory and Practice of Foreign Policy* (Washington, D.C.: United States Institute of Peace, 1992), pp. 80–82.

2. However, from a broader historical and strategic standpoint, one may question the desirability of a negotiated settlement. Given the nature of Japanese imperialistic ambitions and the emerging U.S. conception of its expanding global and strategic interests one might conclude that a war between the two countries was inevitable and that developments leading to Pearl Harbor merely determined the timing and circumstances of such a war. Some would even argue that however costly the war with Japan proved to be, it was necessary in order to eliminate Japan as a militaristic, imperialistic power. We need not debate the proposition here in order to call attention to the narrower set of lessons this case provides regarding the problems the strategy of coer-

cive diplomacy can encounter and the conditions under which, instead of providing a peaceful alternative, the strong ultimatum variant of the strategy can boomerang and provoke war. We should also note that at the beginning of their prolonged diplomatic crisis and for some time thereafter, neither Japanese nor U.S. leaders believed their disagreement would or should lead to war.

Acronyms

ADA	Americans for Democratic Action
ASW	antisubmarine warfare
CCFR	Chicago Council on Foreign Relations
CIA	Central Intelligence Agency
CINCPAC	Commander in Chief, Pacific Command
CMEA	Council on Mutual Economic Assistance
COMUSMACV	Commander U.S. Military Assistance Command Vietnam
CSCE	Conference on Security and Cooperation in Europe
DESOTO	U.S. destroyer patrols
DOD	Department of Defense
DRV	Democratic Republic of Vietnam
EC	European Community
EEC	European Economic Community
FCC	Foreign Funds Committee
FMLN	Faribundo Marti Liberation Front
FSLN	Sandinista Liberation Front
GCC	Gulf Cooperation Council
GVN	government of South Vietnam
ICC	International Commission for Supervision and Control in Indochina
ICO	Organization of the Islamic Conference
JCS	Joint Chiefs of Staff
LOCs	lines of communication
MACV	Military Assistance Command Vietnam
NATO	North Atlantic Treaty Organization
NLF	National Liberation Front
NSAM	National Security Action Memorandum
NSC	National Security Council
NSDD	National Security Decision Directive
OAS	Organization of American States
PLO	Palestine Liberation Organization
POWs	prisoners of war

PRC	People's Republic of China
RCC	Revolutionary Command Council
RLAF	Royal Laotian Air Force
ROE	Rules of Engagement
RT	ROLLING THUNDER
SAM	surface-to-air missile
SEATO	Southeast Asia Treaty Organization
SOUTHCOM	U.S. Southern Command
U.N., U.S.	United Nations, United States
UNO	National Opposition Union
USSR	Union of Soviet Socialist Republic
VC	Viet Cong
VNAF	South Vietnamese Air Force

About the Book

In an updated and expanded edition of this classic text, Alexander George sets out a framework for examining the effects of what he has labeled *coercive diplomacy*. The three original case studies of U.S. efforts to employ coercive diplomacy (on Laos, the Cuban Missile Crisis, and Vietnam) have been revised in light of new findings, and four new studies (on Pearl Harbor, Nicaragua, Libya, and the Persian Gulf crisis) have been added to provide breadth and dimension to the analysis. Of particular interest is the analysis of the differential effects of coercive diplomacy—revealed by comparisons of events and strategies, such as U.S. handling of the Cuban Missile Crisis versus the U.S. approach to Saddam Hussein after his 1990 invasion of Kuwait. In addition to the new and updated case studies, the book offers a historical review of European statesmanship from the nineteenth century to World War II that places the postwar cases of U.S. coercive diplomacy in a broader perspective.

About the Editors
and Contributors

Alexander L. George is professor emeritus of international relations at Stanford University. His publications include *Woodrow Wilson and Colonel House: A Personality Study,* coauthored with Juliette L. George; *Deterrence in American Foreign Policy,* coauthored with Richard Smoke; *Presidential Decisionmaking in Foreign Policy;* and *Avoiding War: Problems of Crisis Management.* His most recent publication, for the United States Institute of Peace, is *Bridging the Gap: Theory and Practice of Foreign Policy.* He is preparing a book on the use of case studies for theory development.

David K. Hall is vice-president of Hitchcock Automotive Resources. He was formerly Forrest Sherman Professor of Management at the U.S. Naval War College, where he also created and coordinated the Policymaking and Implementation Program. He has served as consultant to the secretary of the navy, the chief of naval operations, and the National Security Council staff on national security organizational issues. He taught at Brown University and the U.S. Air Force Academy and served as consultant to the Brookings Institution and the RAND Corporation. Dr. Hall is the author of *The Past and Future of the NSC Staff, The DOD Reorganization Act of 1986,* and various articles on national security organization. He contributed to the 1971 edition of *The Limits of Coercive Diplomacy, Force Without War,* and *The Soviet Use of Military Power.* He received his Ph.D. in political science from Stanford University.

Richard Herrmann is an associate professor of political science and director of the Program on Foreign Policy Analysis at the Mershon Center for National Security Research at Ohio State University. In 1989 and 1990, he served as a Council on Foreign Relations International Affairs fellow on the secretary's Policy Planning Staff at the U.S. Department of State. He is the author of *Perceptions and Behavior in Foreign Policy* and has published articles on Soviet and Middle Eastern affairs in such journals as *International Security, World Politics, Political Science Quarterly,* and *International Studies Quarterly.*

299

Bruce W. Jentleson is associate professor of political science and director of the Washington Center of the University of California, Davis. He is currently on leave and serving as special assistant to the director of the Policy Planning Staff of the U.S. Department of State. He is the author of *Pipeline Politics: The Complex Political Economy of East-West Energy Trade* and *With Friends Like These: Reagan, Bush, and Saddam, 1982–1990* (forthcoming) and coeditor of *Foreign Military Intervention: The Dynamics of Protracted Conflict.* He has contributed to numerous books and to such journals as *International Organization, International Studies Quarterly,* and *Political Science Quarterly.*

Paul Gordon Lauren is the Regents Professor at the University of Montana. He served as the founding director of the Maureen and Mike Mansfield Center and as the Mansfield Professor of Ethics and Public Affairs and is a former Rockefeller Foundation Humanities fellow. He is the author of *Power and Prejudice; Destinies Shared; The China Hands' Legacy; Diplomacy: New Approaches in History, Theory, and Policy;* and *Diplomats and Bureaucrats.*

Scott D. Sagan is assistant professor of political science at Stanford University. He is the author of *Moving Targets: Nuclear Strategy and National Security;* coauthor of *Living with Nuclear Weapons;* and author of *The Limits of Safety: Organizations, Accidents, and Nuclear Weapons (1993)*; as well as author of numerous articles on crisis management and nuclear strategy. The chapter on the Pearl Harbor case in this book draws upon his Harvard Ph.D. dissertation, "Deterrence and Decision: A Historical Critique of Modern Deterrence Theory," which received the American Political Science Association's 1983 Helen Dwight Reid prize for the best doctoral dissertation in international relations, law, and politics. In 1984–1985, he served as a Council on Foreign Relations International Affairs fellow and special assistant to the director of the Joint Chiefs of Staff.

William E. Simons, a coauthor of the first edition of this book, is consultant on international security policy, the RAND Corporation, Washington, D.C. Formerly Colonel, U.S. Air Force, assigned to the Office of Assistant Secretary of Defense, International Security Affairs, he is one of the authors of the original *Pentagon Papers* and author of *Liberal Education in the Service Academies.*

Tim Zimmermann is a diplomatic correspondent for *U.S. News & World Report.* He received his B.A. in history from Yale University and is a Ph.D. candidate in the War Studies Department at King's College, London. His dissertation is on the role of force in the foreign policy of the Reagan administration.

Index

Abrams, Elliot, 190, 194
Abu Nidal, 202, 205, 224(n8)
Acheson, Dean, 69–70, 179, 275, 283, 290
ADA. *See* Americans for Democratic Action
Adversaries, 57, 269
    behavioral models of, 19–20
    beliefs of, 19, 292, 293
    control over their own military forces by, 283–284
    future relations with, 9
    government of, 8. *See also* Governments, overthrowing/changing composition of
    isolation of, 273–274
    perceptions of, 287, 288, 292. *See also* Misperceptions/miscalculations
    rationality of, 13, 14, 19–20, 70, 83, 113, 126
    resistance of, 15, 275
Afghanistan, 179, 193, 217
Aid programs, 91–92, 93, 181, 182, 192, 194
Air power. *See under* Military force
Al-Aksa mosque (Jerusalem), 240–241, 248
Algeria, 236, 237, 251
Allen, Bruce J., 127
Alliances, 57, 177. *See also* Coalitions; Coercive diplomacy, and coalitions; United States, allies of
Allied powers (World War I), 28, 34
Americans for Democratic Action (ADA), 157, 160, 172(n76)
Appeasement, 42, 74, 81, 232
Arabian Gulf, 253
Arab-Israeli conflict, 238, 239, 240, 241, 242, 246, 250, 272
Arab League, 236, 237
Arab world, 233, 234–235, 242, 248, 250, 251, 255, 256, 257

Sunni Arabs, 237
    See also Arab-Israeli conflict; Palestinians
Arafat, Yasir, 251
Argentina, 55(n), 192
Arias Sanchez, Oscar, 186–187, 192, 193
Arms and Influence (Schelling), 204
Arms control, 96, 191, 238. *See also* Disarmament
Arms interdiction, 181
Arms sales, 208
Asad, Hafez al-, 235, 237, 248, 251, 252, 255
Assets, freezing of, 68–69, 85, 232
ASW. *See* Military force, antisubmarine warfare
Asymmetry of interests/motivation, 15, 105, 124, 125, 176, 177–178, 189–190, 281–282, 287, 292. *See also* Incentives/inducements, balance of incentives
Australia, 81
Austria, 26, 28, 30, 31, 39, 41, 95
Aziz, Tariq, 245, 246, 253

Baker, James, 229, 232, 233, 238, 243, 244, 246, 249
Balance of power, 2, 24, 29
Ball, George, 143, 157, 169(n37)
Baltic States, 41
Bargaining issues, 112, 113–115, 117, 124, 153, 269, 277–279. *See also* Negotiations
Bay of Pigs, 99, 112, 281
Belgium, 26, 35, 40
Bendjedid, Chadli, 237, 251
Berlin, 28, 38–39, 112, 113, 213
    Berlin Blockade (1948), 9, 54, 55(n)
    East Berlin, 217
Blight, James G., 127